The Public Intellectual

The Public Intellectual

Between Philosophy and Politics

Edited by
Arthur M. Melzer, Jerry Weinberger,
and M. Richard Zinman

ROWMAN & LITTLEFIELD PUBLISHERS, INC.
Lanham • Boulder • New York • Oxford

ROWMAN & LITTLEFIELD PUBLISHERS, INC.

Published in the United States of America
by Rowman & Littlefield Publishers, Inc.
A Member of the Rowman & Littlefield Publishing Group
4501 Forbes Boulevard, Suite 200, Lanham, Maryland 20706
www.rowmanlittlefield.com

PO Box 317
Oxford
OX2 9RU, UK

British Library Cataloguing in Publication Information Available

Library of Congress Cataloging-in-Publication Data

The public intellectual : between philosophy and politics / edited by
Arthur M. Melzer, Jerry Weinberger, M. Richard Zinman.
p. cm.
Includes bibliographical references and index.
ISBN 0-7425-0814-5 (Cloth : alk. paper) — ISBN 0-7425-0815-3
(Paperback : alk. paper)
1. Intellectuals. 2. Intellectual life. 3. Progress. I. Melzer,
Arthur M. II. Weinberger, J. III. Zinman, M. Richard.
HM728 .P833 2003
305.2'52—dc21

2002009701

Printed in the United States of America

∞™ The paper used in this publication meets the minimum requirements of American National Standard for Information Sciences—Permanence of Paper for Printed Library Materials, ANSI/NISO Z39.48-1992.

Symposium on Science, Reason, and Modern Democracy
Michigan State University

Contents

Acknowledgments

This is the sixth volume of essays to be published by the Symposium on Science, Reason, and Modern Democracy. Established in 1989 in the Department of Political Science at Michigan State University, the symposium is a center for research and debate on the pressing political and intellectual issues of our time. It sponsors lectures, conferences, publications, and teaching, as well as graduate, postdoctoral, and senior fellowships. Its specific mission is to explore the intersection of public policy and philosophy: to study the problems of America's political culture in their vital connection to America's intellectual culture.

This volume grew from the symposium's eighth annual program, "The Idea of Public Intellectual," a lecture series and a conference held at Michigan State during the 1996–1997 academic year. The conference was organized by the symposium and the Center for Theoretical Study, an institute of advanced studies jointly administered by Charles University and the Academy of Sciences of the Czech Republic. It was designed to celebrate the twentieth anniversary of Charter 77, the human rights movement founded by dissident Czech and Slovak intellectuals that prepared the way for the Velvet Revolution.

In planning the conference, we worked closely with Martin Palouš, then senior research fellow at the Center for Theoretical Study and now ambassador of the Czech Republic to the United States. We thank Ambassador Palouš for his essential contribution to our joint enterprise. We also thank Ivan M. Havel, director, and Ivan Chvatík, codirector, of the center, and their colleagues, especially Josef Moural, for their valuable support.

Most of the essays collected in this volume were originally written for the symposium's 1996–1997 program. Eight are published here for the first time. Versions of five others have appeared elsewhere. A different version of Thomas Pangle's essay appeared in *Canadian Political Philosophy at the*

Turn of the Century: Exemplary Essays, ed. R. Beiner and W. Norman (New York: Oxford University Press, 2000). A much earlier version of Gordon Wood's chapter was published in *Leadership in the American Revolution* (Washington: Library of Congress, 1974). Tony Judt's essay appeared in his book *The Burden of Responsibility: Blum, Camus, Aron, and the French Twentieth Century* (Chicago: University of Chicago Press, 1998). Various versions of Adam Michnik's chapter have appeared in print. Martha Nussbaum's chapter was published in *Ethics* 108, no. 4 (July 1998): 762–96. We thank these contributors and their publishers for permission to reprint.

The symposium's 1996–1997 program and all its activities were made possible by grants from the Lynde and Harry Bradley Foundation of Milwaukee, Wisconsin; the Carthage Foundation of Pittsburgh, Pennsylvania; the Earhart Foundation of Ann Arbor, Michigan; and the John M. Olin Foundation of New York City. Once again, we are grateful for their support.

Michigan State's Department of Political Science has been home to the symposium since its founding. Michigan State's College of Social Science and James Madison College have also aided us in many ways. We thank our colleagues in each of these institutions. In particular, we thank Phil Smith, former acting dean of the College of Social Science; Brian Silver, former chair of the Department of Political Science; William Allen, former dean of James Madison College; Werner Dannhauser, the symposium's senior research fellow; and Larry Cooper, the symposium's postdoctoral fellow for 1996–1997 for their special contributions during our eighth year. We also thank John Hudzik, dean of Michigan State's International Studies and Programs, and Norman Graham, director of Michigan State's Center for European and Russian Studies, for their support of the conference in East Lansing. As always, we are especially grateful to Karen Battin, the symposium's administrative coordinator, for her fine work.

In addition to the authors whose essays are included in this volume, the following individuals took part in the symposium's 1996–1997 program: Stanley Crouch, John Gray, Miklós Haraszti, Ivan Havel, Krysztof Jasiewicz, Martin Palouš, G. M. Tamás, Vladimir Tismaneanu, and Ivan Vejvoda. We thank them for their important contributions.

Introduction

Arthur M. Melzer, Jerry Weinberger, and M. Richard Zinman

There is a growing realization today that the character of intellectual life in the West, especially in its relation to society, is undergoing a fundamental shift. A variety of factors—the rise of postmodernism, rapid changes in the world of computers and the media, the growth of the information economy—contribute to this perception. It would be very difficult at this point, however, to formulate a clear conception of where this change is leading us. But this vague, nagging impression also brings powerfully to the fore the converse question: *From what* are we changing? Exactly what *is* and *has been* the character and social role of intellectual life in the modern West? At or near the core of this issue is the uniquely modern phenomenon of the "intellectual" or "public intellectual" (we use the terms interchangeably). On the principle that the outlines of a phenomenon become clearest when it has begun to change or disappear, the time may be particularly ripe to undertake an examination of the modern intellectual.

According to Aristotle, man is the rational animal—but also the political animal. It is, therefore, a permanent question for human beings: What is or should be the relation between the two, between the life of the mind and social life, between ideas and events, between thought and action, reason and history? Is it possible or even desirable for theoretical speculation to guide political practice or shape history? And through what means? How should the two realms of theory and practice be connected? One possible response to these questions—the one uniquely characteristic of our times—is the "public intellectual": a class of hybrid beings standing with one foot in the contemplative world and the other in the political.

Historically, however, this is a most unusual response. Most cultures do not produce intellectuals. They are a rather late arising Western phenomenon—and one that now seems to be changing and perhaps disappearing (or so it has been reported for the past fifty years). Certainly, societies that produce intellectuals spend a lot of time questioning the meaning and value of what they have produced. Consider only two of the more extreme views heard today.

The first holds that intellectuals are basically perverse and "detached" in an unhealthy way. Theory is for the most part merely an escape from practice ("those who can, do"); so these intellectualizers are out of touch with life and almost always deformed in one way or another—egg-headed, pointy-headed. Specifically, intellectuals are essentially moved by resentment because the mainstream culture does not understand or respect them. Thus they endeavor to pay society back for its neglect by taking a countercultural stance: antipatriotic, antireligious, antibourgeois, anticapitalist, and anti-American. When they teach, they inevitably corrupt the young, as Socrates was said to have done in Athens and as the professorate surely does in the modern university. They've taken a public stand on all the great issues of the day—and almost always wound up on the wrong side: they were wrong about communism, wrong about socialism, wrong about the 1960s.

The opposite view holds that intellectuals are actually secular prophets who would lead us to the promised land if only we had the maturity and good sense to listen to them. They do indeed stand outside and against their cultures, but this very alienation gives them the salutary detachment and the purity that enable them to function as the conscience of society and as the vanguard of enlightenment and social progress.

The thirteen chapters in this book—all by close observers and, in some cases, practitioners of the phenomenon at issue—primarily address, in different ways and from different points of view, four essential and interrelated questions. What are the defining characteristics of the public intellectual? When and why did they first arise? Are they a good thing—both for society and for intellectual life? Are they now disappearing, as is often claimed, or only mutating into some other form?

The first five chapters concern the past and primarily describe the historical origin and development of the public intellectual. Arthur Melzer begins with a brief attempt to define the public intellectual and state what is historically unique about it. Thomas Pangle then takes us back to the Greek enlightenment, where the phenomenon essentially did not yet exist. Through an interpretation of the closest Greek analog to the intellectual—the Socratic "citizen philosopher" or the Platonic conception of "political philosophy"—he tries to show *why* it did not exist and how philosophy had to be fundamentally transformed in its relation to theology, as it began to be in the Renaissance, for something like the public intellectual to emerge. Paul Rahe picks up the story in the eighteenth-century Enlightenment, where the public intellectual and the attendant hope for a "Party of Reason" first come into their own. But the dangers of this new phenomenon—doctrinairism, the neglect of political prudence, revolutionary subversion—now become fully apparent, as Rahe shows through a discussion of the warnings issued by Burke, Hume, and Tocqueville. It was Rousseau, however, who engaged in the most complex exploration of the promise and especially the inner tensions and dangers of the modern intellectual, as Chris Kelly shows in his account of Rousseau's famous quarrels with Voltaire, Diderot, and the other philosophes. Finally, Gordon Wood shows how something like this whole history was recapitulated on the American scene: the Founding Fathers were not yet intellectuals but neoclassical, philosophical aristocrats. Yet they created a modern democracy in which people like themselves could not long endure—to be replaced, among other things, by public intellectuals.

The remaining chapters focus primarily on the present. Staying within the American context, John Diggins traces the history of intellectuals—their character, social role, and self-understanding—from the Founding Fathers to the present. Josef Joffe analyzes the present state and possible future of the American intellectual—whom he sees as representative of the whole species—in light of various social changes like the retreat of intellectual life into the universities, the increase in specialization, the growth of the "new class," and the spread of relativism.

Returning to the European scene, Pierre Hassner picks up the story where Rahe and Kelly left off, bringing us into the twentieth century. In particular, he continues the focus on the dangers and vices of intellectuals through an analysis of the "totalitarian temptation," the mystery of their slow-to-die flirtations with fascism and especially with communism. Tony Judt further explores these dangers but also focuses on one public intellectual who combated them in his case study of Raymond Aron. Finally, Adam Michnik, moving the scene to Eastern Europe, reminds us of the heroic role played by dissident intellectuals in the struggle against communism, while also warning of the danger that such heroes and moralists can pose in times of peace and reconstruction.

Implicit in all these discussions of the vices of intellectuals is a sense of what the public intellectual still could and ought to be. Explicit reflections on this question finally come to the surface toward the end of Michnik's essay. This is also the main subject of Ira Katznelson's discussion of Karl Mannheim, Robert K. Merton, and C. Wright Mills. Similarly, Martha Nussbaum presents a case study of how contemporary philosophy has a vital role to play in the alleviation of human suffering. One issue that emerges in these three pieces, although it has been a leitmotiv running throughout the volume, is the question of how the intellectual's public role can continue in a world dominated by relativism or the postmodernist rejection of universal truth.

Having discussed the promise of the modern intellectual as well as the tragic side, especially the totalitarian temptation, we conclude with the comic side. That is the theme of Saul Bellow's chapter (and of his novels). He begins with the question of why so many modern artists and intellectuals have been comic writers, but eventually brings the question around to why they are themselves such comic figures.

I

THEORY

1

What Is an Intellectual?

Arthur M. Melzer

Today, when we think of the term "intellectual," Sartre and Camus are probably the first examples to come to mind. But if we look to the historical origins and upper reaches of the phenomenon, Voltaire and Diderot are the classic representatives. To flesh out and localize the idea, one might also name Tom Paine, George Orwell, Dwight Macdonald, Lionel Trilling, Edmund Wilson, Hannah Arendt, Mary McCarthy, and more recently Irving Kristol, Edward Said, Betty Friedan, and Stanley Fish.

We surely know one when we see one. What, then, *is* an intellectual? We sense that there is something new or historically unique about the phenomenon—that it did not exist in the ancient or medieval worlds but is emblematic of the life of the mind in modernity. But in what does this uniqueness consist? How does the intellectual differ from the other species of "knowers" familiar to us: the prophet, the scientist, the expert, the scholar, the enlightened statesman, the philosopher, the sophist? All of these represent different postures toward knowledge and indeed different ways of life. What is the specific posture and way of the intellectual? What does he do and how does he understand himself? What strange turn of human consciousness or new ideological or historical conditions have given rise to the modern intellectual?

Generally speaking, "knowers" differ regarding the source of their knowledge (divine or human), regarding the subject matter of their knowledge, and regarding the ground for their valuing and pursuing knowledge. Concerning the last point, does the person seek knowledge as an end in itself or merely as a means—to the welfare of society, for example? How, in other words, does the love of knowledge relate to the other major sphere of human life, the moral-political? What should be—and, realistically speaking, *can* be—the relation of theoretical knowledge to social action, of reason to history?

Using these questions to make some obvious distinctions, the intellectual's knowledge is typically secular, deriving from the unassisted exercise of the human intellect; so in this respect he or she differs fundamentally from the priest or prophet (although we will see that, in other respects, he bears a peculiar resemblance to the priest). The intellectual, although secular, also differs from the scientist because his or her knowledge concerns the human world, the sphere of politics and culture. He is distinguished from the expert, the specialist, and the technician because his knowledge is not "technical" or "instrumental," merely a tool to some further end and therefore exact, narrow, and specialized. Rather, he is a generalist and a "person of ideas": someone who loves ideas largely for their own sake and therefore especially large and sweeping ideas. Yet—and here we approach the core—for all his love of ideas, he is not the scholar or academic because he has a vital concern for the practical application of ideas and the welfare of society. He writes op-ed pieces and magazine articles. He is "committed" and "engaged." The intellectual "takes a stand." Still, for all this emphatic practical concern, he is not the enlightened or intellectual statesman, like Woodrow Wilson, James Madison, Cicero, or even Plato's philosopher-king, for he holds resolutely to a posture of detachment, even "alienation," and regards direct political involvement as something that would compromise his very being as an intellectual. He is not part of the establishment. Being an outsider and a misfit is somehow an essential part of his identity and self-understanding.

It would seem, then, that the unique and defining characteristic—as well as the central paradox—of the public intellectual is an inner tension or contradiction on the crucial issue of theory and practice, contemplation and action. If he is primarily a lover and explorer of ideas, why is it so *essential* to him to take a public stand? But, if he is primarily concerned with the welfare of society, why is it so *essential* that he be an alienated idea lover who stands apart from and even disdains society? Does he embrace the world of ideas in order to *help* society—or to *escape* it? Somehow he necessarily claims *both* things. His characteristic stance toward society is both concerned and hostile, both attached and detached. Thus to answer the question, What is an intellectual? is to explain this strange contradiction at his core, this posture of "detached attachment." What is the origin and inner necessity of this stance, and why is it uniquely modern?

It may be useful to consider the one remaining type of "knower" that the intellectual, in some respects, most resembles: the philosopher, particularly the political philosopher. This intellectual ideal was most prevalent and most elaborately described in the classical world, especially in the dialogues of Plato. This knower too claims a nontechnical, sweeping, and secular knowledge of the world of politics and culture; and he too is somehow both political and yet detached from politics. Is the intellectual, then, the same as the classical political philosopher? Is Plato the archetype of the intellectual?

Somehow it strikes our ears (for many of us, at least) as anachronistic and wrong to call Plato an intellectual. Despite the resemblance, there are clearly important differences between the classical political philosopher and the intellectual, difficult as it may be to put one's finger on precisely what they are. A brief consideration of these differences—three in particular—will help clarify the specific character and origins of the detached attachment at the core of the modern intellectual.

First, although both types are marked by a well-advertised "detachment" from political engagement, there is a profound difference in the source and nature of their detachment. The philosopher, as distinguished from the intellectual, tends to avoid political action because he has attained—or at least seeks—a radical withdrawal from and transcendence of the practical realm as such. Impressed by the smallness, illusoriness, and ultimate futility of all the goals of political life, the classical philosopher endeavors to find his good in the realm outside of politics and practice, outside of the "cave," in the detached contemplation of the cosmos.[1]

To be sure, he takes men's political hopes and longings seriously, but primarily to ground and dialectically ascend to the transpolitical, theoretical life. Plato did speak of philosopher-kings and had his own political misadventures in Syracuse. But he also stated clearly that if a philosopher ever engaged in politics or agreed to rule, it would not be because he thought it a great and noble good but an unavoidable necessity: "No one willingly chooses to rule and get mixed up in straightening out other people's troubles; but he asks for wages." And the only "wage" the philosopher cares about is the avoidance of a great penalty: "The greatest of penalties is being ruled by a worse man if one is not willing to rule oneself. It is because they fear this, in my view, that decent men rule, when they do rule. . . . they enter on it as a necessity and because they have no one better than or like themselves to whom to turn it over."[2] Most thinkers in the classical tradition may not have been either so extreme or so blunt in their characterization of political involvement. But there was widespread agreement that, although theoretical knowledge is useful for practical life, and although practical life is necessary for us in various ways since we are not pure minds, still the wholly detached *vita contemplativa* is simply the highest. After all, in the classical view, the whole purpose of society—and of the practical life that serves it—is to promote human excellence, perfection, and happiness. And the latter is ultimately to be found in the philosophic or contemplative life. Clearly, then, the purpose of philosophy is not and cannot be service to society, but, if anything, the reverse. The detached, contemplative life is our final end.

The public intellectual, by contrast, is defined less by his escape from the cave than by his flight from the ivory tower. However much he may pride himself in his love of ideas and truth, he self-consciously rejects the contemplative ideal of withdrawal and detachment, and is vitally concerned to "make a difference," to "take a stand," to "help society." Given the depth of his practical concern and attachment, what the basis is of his famous posture of detachment remains unclear for the moment, but what is certain is that it does not stem from the radical, almost otherworldly transcendence of the practical sphere that is at the core of the classical philosophical ideal. The intellectual tends to regard that ideal and that sort of detachment as a fairy tale. His own stance is somehow an emphatically this-worldly detachment.

A second reason why it sounds wrong to call Plato—or the philosopher in general—an intellectual is that the former is a great genius, an original thinker of the first rank, whereas the latter typically is not. Almost any intelligent person, we sense, can become an intellectual. Philosophers are rare, singular occurrences, like saints, whereas intellectuals are numerous enough to form a class, an intelligentsia, a "priesthood," an ongoing institution with its own place and role within society. In short, the modern concept of "intellectual" generally denotes a larger and lower order of thinkers, intellectual retailers who, consciously or unconsciously, elaborate, apply, and popularize the thought of the great, epoch-making thinkers.

One might see an inner connection between these first two characteristics of the intellectual—concerning detachment and rank. When Plato discusses the character of the philosopher in the *Republic*, he puts primary emphasis precisely on what I have called detachment. The genuine philosopher is not merely someone who particularly delights in or excels at learning, but someone who has undergone a radical and wrenching "turning around of the soul" by which he sees through and separates himself from all the fond illusions and false hopes of ordinary life, of moral/political life. It is only by virtue of this difficult process of disillusionment and disengagement that he is able to make contact, for the first time, with the deepest and truest need of his soul: an erotic hunger to know and contemplate the truth for its own sake. The genuine love of truth, in other words, is not something that we all begin with—it is the rare achievement and the defining characteristic of the philosopher.

Now, this philosophic conversion is something that very few can undergo—but many can admire. And that is why, as Plato goes on to discuss, the philosopher always tends to produce in his wake a crowd of pretenders, imitators, and approximations—like the Sophists, rhetoricians, and other intellectually gifted nonphilosophers that populate the dialogues. The defining characteristic of these intelligent nonphilosophers is that, lacking genuine philosophic conversion and detachment, they have become "men of ideas" and professional knowers, not because they love the pure truth for its own sake and above all things, but because they love the honor, nobility, or social advantages that attach—within certain cultured societies—to the ideal of the truth lover. Thus it is precisely their attachment to certain goods of social life, especially honor, that leads them to mimic philosophic detachment. Permanently torn in this way between attachment and detachment, Plato's intelligent nonphilosophers would seem to be precisely what we mean by the class of intellectuals.[3]

The comparison is powerful and revealing but, in the end, not completely adequate or fair. For there is something that distinguishes the modern intellectual from the ancient rhetorician or Sophist no less than from Plato and the ancient philosopher. This difference—the third on our list—concerns the all-important modern idea, alien to classical times, of progress: the faith that the advance of theoretical knowledge and its public dissemination will lead to social and material progress for all—a new faith concerning the role and power of reason in history.

Faith in progress is rooted partly in the rise of modern natural science—and of its agent the "scientist," a uniquely modern species of knower with a fundamentally new intellectual stance. Unlike the ancient natural philosopher who sought to understand nature—in a posture of passive and loving contemplation—for the fulfillment and perfection of his own soul, the modern scientist actively probes and manipulates nature largely in order to conquer it for the physical well-being of humankind.

On the moral and political front, the belief in progress stems originally from the Enlightenment project: the concerted effort to subvert the ancien régime (indeed, all "traditional society," dominated by prejudice and superstition) and replace it with rational society ("modernization")—and all of this, not through direct rule but through the gradual transformation of consciousness or public opinion by the broad dissemination of philosophy and science ("enlightenment"). And just as modern natural science has its unique agent—the scientist—so the Enlightenment has an agent unique to it—the modern intellectual (in his original form). This is a completely new species of knower defined in terms of a fundamentally new intellectual project, a new conception of what a knower can do and be. The movement of enlightenment and progress, together with all of its epistemological and political presuppositions, forms the original basis and continuing background of the new concept "intellectual."

It is, for example, because of this essential, if often unarticulated, connection to the modern movements of progress and enlightenment that it feels not only wrong but *anachronistic* to apply the term "intellectual" to Plato or the Sophists—or, for that matter, to Chinese Mandarins, medieval scribes, and so forth. One can no more speak of intellectuals in fifth-century Athens than of missionaries—both are agents of a movement or project that did not exist in that time and place. This is also why, whereas "philosopher" clearly indicates a way of life of the individual, "intellectual" is more of a sociological term, denoting a particular social role or function. And it is with a view to just this social role that we intuit that intellectuals are and should be relatively numerous, constituting a class, and of a rank midway between the great minds and the people—so as to serve the function of transmitting and popularizing philosophic knowledge.

Above all, it is the link to the modern conception of progress that primarily explains the intellectual's unique posture toward society, his contradictory stance of detached attachment. First, the attachment.

Modern intellectuals are characterized by the fact that they have open to them a radically new employment for their talents, a novel mission for theoretical intelligence, a unique calling that simply did not exist in previous times: the world-historical role as enlighteners and agents of progress. They live in a world that takes for granted the existence of a whole dimension of reality unsuspected by earlier ages: "History" or "Progress" or the "historical process." And they are ineluctably drawn to orient their intellectual lives toward this new dimension—to *attach* themselves to the historical process and seek to "make a contribution." They are captivated by the idea that their inner mental experiences are not merely private events but can and should have grand historical consequences. This was not an idea or way of life available or imaginable to premodern knowers. A classical thinker like Cicero could occasionally aspire, through his writings and especially through his political action, to contribute to the welfare of Rome. But this remained on the level of ordinary politics: particular reforms, local in their reach, temporary in their application, and enacted through the prudence, power, and good luck of the particular individual, Cicero. Surely, he never dreamed of transforming the nature of politics, of making Roman society rational or enlightened—for example, by eliminating polytheism, superstition, and other prejudices. On the contrary, he attempted to rule Rome largely by means of those prejudices while also moderating them. But the way of life of the modern intellectual is based on an altogether new kind of hope or ambition. This hope—rooted in the belief in progress—contains at least the following elements, which dwell at the back, if not the front, of the intellectual's mind and condition his whole self-understanding and life activity.

First, the intellectual, as he sees himself, does not stand alone, relying on his own individual and uncertain powers, stymied at every turn by the age-old forces of custom and irrationality, but is a participant in a "movement" or force larger than himself, the onward march of enlightenment. He lives in the inspiriting belief that his own thoughts and insights, however small or partial, once "published" in the modern sense—with the help of the printing press and a vast social and material infrastructure designed for targeted as well as mass distribution—will reach out beyond him, combining additively with the contributions of thousands of others in order somehow to "make a difference" and improve society. Second, the historical process to which he is contributing will bring not mere reform, but fundamental transformations, altering the very character of society. Third, these changes are not temporary or fragile (like ordinary moral or political reform) but more or less a stable, permanent, even "thing-like" achievement, a new "stage" of "history." Fourth, this change comes through or involves the transformation of consciousness by the dispelling of prejudice and the spread of theoretical truth. Thus large, abstract ideas, the stock-in-trade of the intellectuals—as distinguished from ideas diluted and applied by the prudence of intelligent statesmen, like Cicero—play a direct and crucial role in the world of action. And fifth, this progress can lift nations, whole regions, perhaps eventually all mankind to new historical levels.

It is this radical new conception of what a knower can do and be in the world, this wholly new employment for theoretical intelligence, this lofty historical mission unimagined by earlier times, that induces the intellectual to be vitally and essentially *attached* to society and its future, unlike the classical philosopher. Indeed, he is more than attached: he tends to be highly public-spirited and idealistic, not to say moralistic. This is a phenomenon that we have grown used to and so take for granted. But through it, the modern, public intellectual stands in striking contrast to the Sophists and other intellectual nonphilosophers of the ancient world, who, seeing through and liberated from the way of life of ordinary citizens and yet lacking all notion of such a grand historical employment, most often inclined to open cynicism, self-seeking, and exploitation. The modern intellectual remains idealistic and attached to society because the faith in progress gives him something extremely important to do.

But, at the same time, the modern, Enlightenment idea of progress also explains the other half of the intellectuals' inner contradiction: the resolutely detached or apolitical posture strangely adopted by these highly attached, idealistic, and engaged individuals. The basis of this posture is the new conception, implicit in the idea of progress, of how reason or truth can be a force shaping politics and history.

The classical view was expressed by Plato: "Unless the philosophers rule as kings . . . and political power and philosophy coincide in the same place . . . there is no rest from ills for the cities" (*Republic*, 473d-e). This famous statement means that reason and truth can indeed shape history, can guide society—but only to the extent that rational individuals rule politically. Reason has no force of its own, no power in history other than the political power that rational individuals may chance to acquire. And Plato also knew that the political rule of the rational, of the philosophers, was extremely unlikely and, more, that the effort to make a rarified quality like "wisdom" or "truth" into a title to rule is, in practice, very dangerous: an open invitation to charlatanry and endless subversion. Therefore, he had little belief in the political force of truth or in the coming of a rational society. There may indeed be progress in knowledge among a few philosophers, but the political impotence of reason or truth is such that this does not translate, in any systematic or significant way, into progress for society at large.

The modern belief in progress could emerge only on the basis of a new conception of the workings of reason in the world, according to which it has a force of its own, independent of rulers and politics. Perhaps stimulated by the example of Christianity—which conquered without an army and changed the world using only Scripture and an apolitical clergy—philosophers like Hobbes conceived the hope to transform the politics of the West through a book and a new intellectual clerisy to teach and propagate it. Reason and truth could rule the world nonpolitically by shaping public opinion, by transforming public consciousness, in a word, by *enlightenment*. To be sure, earlier thinkers thought it possible, within limits, to mold public opinion—but not to make it fundamentally rational, not to "enlighten" it. Even Plato's philosopher-king, for example, who shapes the whole education of his subjects starting from birth, who oversees every game they will play, every song or poem they will hear, even he does not make them truly rational. That is why he needs to teach them "noble lies" and myths. Even he does not hope to rid public life of prejudice but only to rule by means of it. The wise man, according to Plato, cannot *spread* his wisdom to the people—that is precisely why he must *rule*. The unstated premise of philosopher-kings is the impossibility of enlightenment. Conversely, the idea of enlightenment—and of its agent, the intellectual—is premised on a rejection of the need and demand for the political rule of the wise. Reason can guide the world through public opinion—and so it can and should reject the ever troublesome title to rule of wisdom (in favor of consent), a title that has in fact been a great source of irrationality and strife in politics. The unique posture of the public intellectual is based on this modern understanding of the relation of reason and history, of the enlightening power of truth. And this new understanding provides the first key to the intellectual's particular "detachment": he is by no means indifferent to practice, but he is confident, as no knower before him was, that he does not need to rule or be politically engaged in order to help make the world rational and right.

We must go further: the intellectual believes that he must positively *avoid* political rule, for nonrule is one of the essential preconditions of his right and power to rule public opinion. Plato and other classical thinkers, with their highly political approach to human affairs and culture, emphasized that it was the political rulers, bathed in the majesty of public power and authority, who had the greatest power to mold public opinion. A community tends to follow the leader. But various phenomena, above all the rise of Christianity, dramatically demonstrated how, under the right circumstances, men without power—and thus without the stain of compromise and injustice that the attainment and exercise of power inevitably require—could claim a purity and moral authority that the politically powerful could never match. This is how the meek inherit the earth. The modern intellectual is largely based on this clerical model.

To be sure, unlike the Christian priest, the secular intellectual cannot bolster his power by claiming a connection to divine providence; but he can and does claim to be the agent or interpreter of "History." Again, he cannot attempt to subvert the authority of the politically powerful by appealing to the Christian doctrine of the sinfulness of worldly success and power, but he does make use of the antipolitical ethos of modern liberalism with its demotion or denigration of the public sphere, its deliberate separation of political power from moral and religious authority, its view of power as a necessary evil. Liberalism embraces something like the Christian transvaluation: the politically superior are no longer considered morally superior, but if anything the reverse. The liberal slogan is "power corrupts." It follows that we must look for moral guidance among those without power.

Yet not just anyone without power: not those who primarily seek wealth or position, for they will only speak for their class interests. But also not the "virtuous," on whom traditional society relied—the religious and secular moralists whose direct and proclaimed goal is the moral improvement of others—for, in the skeptical, liberal view, the virtuous "improvers of mankind" almost always wind up in the end (if not from the very beginning) trying to control others for their own honor or profit. The only one who can really be trusted is the detached truth-loving or beauty-loving intellectual, for he alone has found something in this world to love more than wealth and power and (perhaps) even more than the welfare of society itself. It is only this extreme detachment and withdrawal—founded on the love of ideas and a certain contempt for society—that can render a man relatively immune to the seductions of interest and partisanship and thus make him a worthy guide for society. Thus the public intellectual is *necessarily* defined by a posture of detachment, alienation, and nonconformity: he is the outsider, the misfit, the bohemian. He has not compromised, conformed, or sold out. It is this social and existential stance outside the system—more than any educational attainment or innate genius—that is the basis of his superiority, his credibility, his right to rule public opinion. Only the intellectual, by virtue of his *detachment* from society, is able to see and be willing to speak the truth to society.

In sum, it is the idea of progress—with its new conception of the relation of reason and history—that produces and explains the mind-set of the modern intellectual and the contradiction of detached attachment that defines him. It attaches the gifted nonphilosopher to society, as never before, by creating a new calling or mission for theoretical intelligence, by inviting the intellectual to be a crucial participant in the founding of a new social order. But at the same time, it necessarily forces the intellectual to detach himself and withdraw from society and political involvement—even to deny, on some level, his attachment and desire to lead society—for that is the precise condition of his credibility and influence. Not despite, but because of his overriding desire to help society, he must convince others and himself that what he really loves is truth and not society. The modern intellectual is that unique form of knower who ceremoniously disdains and turns his back on society—the better to serve it.

It would be more accurate to say that this is the first and most basic stratum of the modern intellectual. Significant variations were introduced as ideas changed regarding the precise relation of reason and history. To the Enlightenment view—that the power of reason in the world primarily depends on the conscious, if indirect or unpolitical, action of the intellectuals—were added more robust theories of history according to which reason is an impersonal force imbedded in the "historical process" itself and intellectuals are to be understood as interpreters, agents, and expressions of this larger process. Again, intellectuals, being agents of change and opposition, necessarily varied as their enemies varied. In the initial (and relatively unified) stage, they were defined against traditional society—against the superstition and privilege of the ancien régime. In triumphing over these enemies, however, they eventually acquired new ones (splintering in the process)—for some, it was the newly hegemonic bourgeoisie, for others, the antibourgeois movements of fascism and communism. And whichever side they took, increasingly their enemies included the intellectuals of the other side.

Having emphasized the crucial link between the modern intellectual and the idea of progress, it is necessary for me to speak briefly of that variant of the species—the "romantic" strain—whose extreme opposition to society culminates in the rejection of the belief in progress itself. The romantics, in this somewhat idiosyncratic sense, would include such varied figures as Flaubert, Stendahl, the early T. S. Eliot, Céline, Thoreau, and Kerouac. Among romantic intellectuals, the sense of being agents of social progress shrinks toward the vanishing point, while the sense—the cult—of alienation becomes the primary theme. This limit case is in a way the most revealing. Despite their explicit doubt of progress, the romantics may still be called intellectuals because their famous alienation does not lead them quietly to turn away from society to a purely contemplative life, or alternatively to revert to an exploitative posture. It drives them to *épater* the bourgeois, to *tell* society how hopeless and beyond all help it is—in the obscure hope that, in the end, this will in fact do some good. In other words, the romantics remain intellectuals in the decisive respect because they *cannot keep their thoughts to themselves.* They continue in the grips of the Enlightenment faith in the act of "publication." They remain addicted to the idea that their inner mental lives must ultimately have some public purpose, some larger historical meaning. They either find such a purpose or live in the anguished pursuit of one.

Again, the famous romantic concept of "alienation" is anything but a return to the classical philosopher's "detachment," for it implies that the intellectual's separation from society, while perhaps inevitable in the short run, is something essentially wrong that, in the course of history, should and must be overcome. That is why there is an element of bitter and rebellious disappointment in the alienation of the romantics. They are angry at society for not being something that they could love and believe in or for not being open to their guidance and aid. In sum, while rejecting the explicit belief in progress, the romantics still continue under the spell of the particular hopes and ambitions that that belief first set in motion. They continue to believe in—or to seek to believe in, or to rage against the inability to believe in—that uniquely modern way of life that harnesses together theoretical reason and fundamental social influence in the way promised by the idea of progress.

In fact, as time has gone on, the explicit belief in progress has become less and less necessary to ground the intellectual way of life. Today, primarily due to the rise of postmodernism, grand historical "narratives" are out of fashion and large numbers of intellectuals (not just anguished romantics) claim to reject progress (although faith in progress, like faith in God, is not so easily uprooted from the deeper recesses of the mind). But this has not, as one might have expected, significantly undermined the felt need for intellectuals. The explicit belief in progress was essential to the intellectual when he faced powerful and entrenched opponents in the form of organized religion and ancestral custom. He needed the theory of progress to help him convince society that it could and should be guided by theoretical reason instead. But today, the movements of progress and enlightenment have completely undermined traditional society, removing any alternative to something like the intellectual. In the modern world, the foundation of prevailing laws, principles, and practices is no longer sought in custom, tradition, and religion but in abstract, theoretical ideas. Ours is a post-traditional "age of ideology." We see no alternative to being ruled by humanly constructed theories—and by the men and women who construct them. To be sure, there are still plenty of people around who complain about the harmful influence of the intellectuals—but they themselves tend to be or to rely on intellectuals. There is nowhere else to turn.

This entrenched power of the intellectuals has been further strengthened by the rise of democratically ruled nation-states, which has put ultimate power in the hands of mass public opinion. In order to mobilize this diffuse power, large ideas, sweeping theories, intellectual "vision" have become politically essential, as they were not in aristocratic ages. Still another factor making intellectuals a practical necessity is the great dynamism and ever accelerating change characteristic of modern life, for this means that old traditions and customs and indeed even yesterday's ideologies quickly become obsolete. There is a constant need for new ideas, explanations, and theories—and for the suppliers of these. Amid all this flux, we are constantly interpreting our lives to ourselves, trying to get a fix on where history is taking us. Are we facing the "clash of civilizations"? Have we reached the "end of history"? Are we entering a postmodern era? We cannot stop asking such questions and so cannot stop needing intellectuals. In sum, we live in a new world in which an elaborate doctrine of progress or theory of history is no longer necessary in order to ground the role of the public intellectual. That role now answers to an obvious, pressing, and inescapable need rooted in the very structure of modern society.

Still, without a theory of progress or history, the question is, What will provide the intellectual with his standards? And without firm principles, how will he stand outside and against his society? Furthermore, the *need* for intellectuals that modern society now openly feels and acknowledges paradoxically poses a threat to their continued existence, for it makes real detachment and withdrawal ever more difficult. Intellectuals are becoming an institution, a profession. Bohemianism, "detachment," and a countercultural stance are becoming mainstream phenomena. Cut off from the idea of progress, it is unclear whether, in the long run, the public intellectual can survive.

NOTES

1. "Detachment" is, of course, a somewhat ambiguous term. In its broadest sense, it extends to a selfless indifference to one's own personal good. In this sense, the classical philosopher is (or understands himself to be) the *least* detached of men because

he alone lives for the true fulfillment of the human soul—philosophic contemplation. But doing so necessarily involves "detachment" in the narrower sense I am using: a transcendence of the material, social, and political attachments of ordinary life.

2. *Republic,* trans. Allan Bloom (New York: Basic Books, 1968), 346e–347d; see 520a, 540b, and Aristotle *Ethics* 1134b4–7.

3. See *Republic* 484a–497d. See also Leo Strauss, *Natural Right and History* (Chicago: University of Chicago Press, 1950), 115–17.

2

A Platonic Perspective on the Idea of the Public Intellectual

Thomas L. Pangle

There is, I am afraid, no idea of the public intellectual in Plato, and no place for any such idea. Indeed, I am under the impression that there is no place for the idea of the public intellectual in any text written prior to the modern era. The idea of the public intellectual is, I would contend, a distinctly modern idea. It is an idea born in, and inseparable from, the Enlightenment. But as soon as we confront this fact, we recognize how important it is to begin any comprehensive reflection on the idea of the public intellectual by considering precisely the absence of that idea from premodern thought, and especially from Plato. For only thus will we begin to grasp the most important earlier conception of the political responsibilities and social consequences of the life of the mind—the conception against which the idea of the public intellectual rose up in antagonism, or as a replacement.

If we ask what takes the place, in Plato, of the idea of the public intellectual, we notice immediately that at the center of the Platonic stage is the idea, or rather the figure, of the citizen-philosopher, personified in Socrates. More precisely, Socrates, as immortalized in both Xenophon and Plato, is generally acknowledged to have been the first political philosopher, the founder of political philosophy. As such, Socrates is distinguished from his fellow citizens, from the poets, and above all from the so-called pre-Socratic philosophers—along with the Sophists, who followed eventually in the wake of these last. But what substantively distinguishes the Socratic from the pre-Socratic? What is a "philosopher," in the strict Platonic sense, and why, according to the Platonic dialogues, were the philosophers and Sophists prior to Socrates not civic philosophers? What was it that Socrates initiated, as the first "political philosopher"?

We learn from the Platonic dialogues that philosophy in the strict sense arose when there emerged a quest to uncover the nature of the universe through unassisted reasoning, on the basis of evidence available to man as man. The philosophers sought the lasting causes of all things, particularly humanity and its doings. The philosophers meant to establish the true human good by clarifying those authentic needs whose genuine satisfaction constitute human flourishing. Despite the fact that some of the great pre-Socratics and their Sophist students may have played, from time to time, an active role as citizens and even as leaders in various cities, they were not citizen-philosophers. They were not political philosophers. Why not, or in what sense not?

The Platonic answer may be expressed in a nutshell as follows: the philosophic inquiry into nature as a whole, and into human nature as a part of the whole, convinced the pre-Socratics that the most fundamental beliefs on which any and all civic life must rest are in fact false illusions, having no basis in, and indeed contradicted by, the natural reality of things. In the words of Plato's Athenian Stranger: "And indeed they declare that some small portion of the political art is in partnership with nature, but most is artificial, and thus the whole of legislation, whose establishments are not true, is not by nature, but artificial" (*Laws* 889d-e).

Now this perspective is, as the Athenian Stranger and his statesman-interlocuter Kleinias stress, manifestly subversive of obedience to law. This outlook inevitably subjects its proponents—insofar as they and their doctrines become known—to the danger of understandable persecution, as corrupters of the city and of the family. It is therefore not surprising that, as the first great Sophist Protagoras stresses, in the Platonic dialogue of that name, all his predecessors "used covering wings," "made concealments," and "hid" their wisdom "behind veils" (*Protagoras* 316d6, 316e5). "I myself," he adds, "have taken other precautions" (317b6–7). As the dialogue proceeds, Protagoras conveys his critique of political life only by way of a richly allegorical "myth." Yet Protagoras proudly indicates that in this myth, and otherwise, he is much more open than were his great predecessors. And for this daring Protagoras paid a very heavy price. He apparently ended his life fleeing an Athenian court conviction for impiety, and the Athenians made his book on the gods the object of the first public book burning recorded in history. No writing of Protagoras survives, and, indeed, no writing of any Sophist or pre-Socratic philosopher has come down to us. The meager snippets and paraphrases that we do possess come largely from the works of Plato and Aristotle, and their commentators. We find the fullest and frankest presentations of some of the chief features of the anticivic arguments of the pre-Socratics in very special or peculiar texts: in Platonic passages where, in private conversations with Socrates, certain Sophists are so provoked by Socrates that they momentarily "spill the beans" or, perhaps more fully revealing, in Platonic passages where certain young citizens report arguments that they have heard from the Sophists—arguments that these youths find deeply troubling, powerfully attractive, or both.

Thus we find Plato's brother Glaucon, in the second book of the *Republic*, elaborating a fuller version of the outlook introduced by the Sophist Thrasymachus in the first book. The Sophists argue, Glaucon reports, that the true nature of civic justice is nothing other than a social contract. The laws and mores that define civil society's notions of right and wrong do not express what humans are naturally inclined toward, nor do humans find their natural fulfillment in following these moral laws. The moral rules are nothing more than artificial conventions, constructed over time by the mass of men who are individually weak and untalented. They seek through these rules to restrain one another's natural, mutually exploitative pursuit of selfish goods, as well as to prevent the strong and gifted from exercising their natural capacity to flourish, by dominating or at least using the rest. Justice, or the restraint of the pursuit of one's own true welfare in order to avoid injuring the welfare of others, is not intrinsically good for anyone, and indeed it blocks access to complete happiness for everyone; such behavior becomes qualifiedly good for the defective majority because it is a kind of mean between doing what is truly best—procuring happiness for oneself and one's loved ones at the expense of others—and suffering what is worst, namely, injury or neglect at the hands of others who can better succeed in obtaining happiness for themselves and their loved ones. Clear testimony to the truth of this insight is seen in the fact that human beings everywhere reliably obey the laws only when the laws have sanctions—when people are rewarded for obedience and punished for disobedience. Strip a man of his standing in the community and his reputation for justice, including his fame for having made what are called "sacrifices" for a just cause; leave a man with nothing but his having acted justly, at the cost of the conventional rewards for justice—that is, with the loss of his reputation and fame, as well as his life and the security of his property and loved ones—and no one would honestly say that justice was good for such a man.

Furthermore, as Thrasymachus earlier contended, those who make and enforce the laws always do so with a strong bias in their own favor, partly avowed and partly hidden—often even from themselves. When appeal is made to "the city," or to "the community," or to the rule of law, as to something that transcends particular interest—when the country is held up as something for the sake of which each citizen ought to be ready to sacrifice himself and his personal interests—what is obscured is the fact that the city is not a natural, let alone an organic, unity. Every human society is composed of rulers and ruled, and the ruling group—be it the majority in a democracy or a minority, as in other regimes—acts as an alliance or a coalition of predominantly self-concerned beings standing over and against the ruled. Human society is surely not like an ant colony or a beehive. The laws or rules may apply to all, and of course claim to be in the interest of all or of the so-called public; but the laws are made and enforced with a view to the interest of the ruling class or group.

Glaucon's eloquent restatement of the Thrasymachean position is supplemented and deepened by his brother Adeimantus, who stresses the moral incoherence of the typical arguments given by fathers in praise of justice.

Adeimantus complains especially about the appeal fathers make to the providential gods, which shows that even or precisely those who preach justice do so, not on the grounds that justice is intrinsically good, but only on the grounds that it is backed up by great extrinsic rewards and punishments.

Civil society's overwhelming dependence on religious belief, and the city's preoccupation with worshiping, placating, and beseeching providential deities, is, according to the pre-Socratics, the most massive sign of the illusory character of civic consciousness (see *Laws* 889eff.). For natural science reveals no evidence whatsoever for such providential gods. On the contrary: natural science reveals a world governed by unchanging and will-less necessities.

These and kindred arguments stem from the so-called Sophists, those itinerant professional teachers of rhetoric who are in Plato the most obtrusive, politically speaking, of the pre-Socratic thinkers. The first man to apply to himself the term "Sophist," in the sense which subsequently became famous, seems to have been Protagoras. In Plato's presentation, Protagoras boasts that by thus naming and proclaiming himself, he is declaring openly the project that has been the covert agenda of a long series of duplicitous wise men among the Greeks, starting with Homer and Hesiod and continuing notably with the great lyric poet Simonides. While pretending, on the surface, to be reverent respecters and promoters of the pious tradition, these poets and their intellectual heirs have implanted in their writings a hidden teaching that seeks to woo the best young men of Greece away from allegiance to their elders, and to the ruling elites, to become instead admirers and disciples of the poets themselves, as the avatars of wisdom (*Protagoras* 316c–317c).

This amazingly bold declaration is muted considerably in response to Socrates' rather demagogic questioning. In the first place, Protagoras distinguishes himself from other Sophists, who, he says, "corrupt the young" by teaching them science: Protagoras claims that he, in contrast, teaches a student only what the student comes to learn, namely, "good counsel in household affairs, so that he might best manage his own household; and also good counsel about civic affairs, so that he might gain the greatest power" (318d-e). When Protagoras accedes to Socrates' apparently benign reformulation of this to mean a claim to teach "the political art" and "to make men good citizens" (319a), Socrates springs his trap—laying down a challenge to Protagoras in the name of the basic principles of Athenian democracy. For in democracy every citizen is already presupposed to be a good citizen, and to know sufficiently the political art; elitist, not to say oligarchic, claims to teach special political wisdom, for large sums of money, are highly suspicious. Protagoras seeks to elude this Socratic net by retreating into the beautiful haze of an allegorical myth, which Protagoras then interprets to mean that all he does is teach the sons of the rich a little, tiny supplement to what they have already learned from their parents and schoolteachers—but, Protagoras must remind his clientele in the audience, this supplement is of course worth the enormous sums of money Protagoras charges. In other words, the sly young plebeian Socrates very quickly, and very easily, gets the great, old, but insufficiently cautious Protagoras on the ropes of incoherence. (Or at least that is the story Socrates rushes to tell outsiders immediately after the private indoor confrontation with the great Sophist. For we learn of Socrates' encounter with Protagoras only through overhearing a narration by Socrates to several nameless, idle, rich, and gossipy associates.) This and the rest of the conversation between the pesky young Socrates and the evasive and increasingly irritated old Protagoras allow us to discern clearly enough Protagoras's true agenda, an agenda that can be said to be more or less typical of the most prominent Sophists. Protagoras takes over the personally liberating theoretical insights of his poetic and philosophic predecessors, and establishes, on this basis, a practical teaching that guides the exploitative or at any rate self-aggrandizing careers of active political men. In the process, Protagoras wins for himself a comfortable fortune, and a vast fame—as the thinker who has had the manly daring to be the first to speak out as an independent teacher or Sophist.

But as the dialogue proceeds, we see that Socrates leads us to raise this searching question about Protagoras: Does not his passionate pride in his fame as a man of courage, as a Promethean spirit, indicate that his concern to be manly, and to be known as courageous, is not strictly controlled by his prudent wisdom about his own true good? In other words, does not Protagoras slip back into—or has he perhaps never fully escaped—the belief in a virtue which transcends prudent self-concern? But is such a virtue intelligible on the basis of the critique of civic virtue which Protagoras has taken over from the pre-Socratic philosophers? Does devotion to such virtue not entail an exaggerated conception of his own importance in the great scheme of things?

These questions are prompted not only by Socrates' stunning proof of Protagoras's self-contradiction on the issue of the unity of virtue, and especially on the separability of courage from wisdom or prudence; the questions are also prompted by the juxtaposition Socrates creates between the career of Protagoras as a Sophist, and the career of what one is tempted to call the Socratic Sophist—Simonides. For in the latter part of the dialogue, Socrates celebrates the sophistic wisdom of the poet Simonides. Socrates agrees with Protagoras's characterization of the wise Simonides as an esoteric writer, a poet with a complex hidden message. But Socrates suggests that Protagoras is far from having taken the measure of the wisdom and the greatness of Simonides, as expressed in this esoteric poetry. Simonides was at least as free and cosmopolitan a spirit as Protagoras, and as successful at obtaining fame and fortune. But Simonides—at least as Socrates presents him—put no serious stock in these external goods. The wise Simonides valued wealth and glory only as means, as tools, for obtaining a situation in life that would allow him the greatest feasible independence and the fullest access to the most promising young of his own and future generations. For the sake of those young, and for his own satisfaction, Simonides wrote subtle poetry, which Socrates declares he has "studied thoroughly." The hidden teaching of that poetry, as interpreted by Socrates, adumbrates an account of the fundamental, permanent—and permanently beautiful, if permanently austere—constituents of the human situation. It is this wisdom alone that the Socratic Simonides teaches to be the core of such happiness as is available to man as man: "for," as Socrates says, summarizing the teaching he attributes to the poetry of Simonides, "this alone is faring badly—to be deprived of scientific knowledge" (345b5). And to secure for himself and other kindred spirits the richly pleasing experience and display and contemplation of this thinking and knowing, Simonides was prepared to perform, when necessary, such unmanly deeds as the flattery of tyrants—without shrinking from the instructive, public, poetic confession of his lack of conventional manliness.

Socrates' evocation of Simonidean wisdom allows us to glimpse the decisive difference between the sophistic movement, initiated by Protagoras, and the previous philosophic and poetic wisdom on which this sophistry is parasitic. The Sophists would appear to have vulgarized, and, what is worse, rendered confused, the earlier wisdom—by diluting, if not abandoning, the pure passion for knowledge, and by making knowledge, instead, into a tool or weapon for the securing of fame and fortune.

Yet this is not Plato's last word on the thought of Protagoras. In the *Theaetetus* and the *Cratylus* we are shown Socrates in the last days of his life wrestling with the radically relativist and subjectivist teaching that is summed up in the most famous Protagorean remark: "man [meaning to say, each different, individual, human] is the measure of all things—of the things that are, that [or how] they are, and of the things that are not, that [or how] they are not." What is strange about the entire presentation is this: Socrates succeeds in so thoroughly discrediting this radical Protagorean relativism—by indicating its inner incoherence, by showing how it contradicts all the evidence of common sense, and by showing how it renders Protagoras's own life as a teacher absurd—that the reader is compelled to wonder why Socrates ever took the teaching seriously, and, what is more, how so intelligent a man as Protagoras could ever have proposed it seriously.

In seeking for an answer to at least the former question, we sooner or later are led to consider the dramatic setting Plato gives to his dialogue *Theaetetus*. At the end of the *Theaetetus*, Socrates says he must now go off to appear at his arraignment to answer Meletus's accusation of him on the charge of impiety. In the dialogue entitled *Euthyphro*, we learn that, while waiting his turn at the Stoa of the King, Socrates met Euthyphro and carried on with him the famous conversation on piety. In that conversation, Socrates heard from Euthyphro that to the latter it had been revealed, through repeated and unmistakable prophetic inspirations, that the gods, as the supreme powers in the universe, are at war over justice and injustice, and that only he who hears the truth from them can know what is pious and impious, what is right and what is wrong, in the most important respect (*Euthyphro* 5d–6b). Socrates repeatedly attempts to shake Euthyphro's confidence in these claims by demonstrating his, or their, incoherence; but the Socratic dialectic proves an almost complete failure in the face of the deeply moving and impressive experiences Euthyphro is convinced that he has undergone. In the *Cratylus*, whose dramatic date is not made precise, but which—given that the chief interlocutor is Hermogenes—evidently takes place near the time of Socrates' trial, Socrates reconsiders the Protagorean doctrine, but this time Socrates characterizes that doctrine in an amazing and arresting way: Socrates identifies the Protagorean thesis, and the entire philosophic tradition with which the thesis is associated—and this may mean all the philosophers with the exception of Parmenides, all the philosophers who hold that the universe exists only in motion or as becoming—as a version of what Socrates says he has heard from Euthyphro. In the *Theaetetus* itself (162d-e), Socrates indicates that the famous "man is the measure" asseveration must be considered together with a second, and almost equally famous—or infamous—Protagorean pronouncement: "I exclude from my speech and my writing the question of whether the gods exist or do not exist." If we put this evidence together with several other important clues we find in the *Theaetetus*, I believe we are led to entertain the following possibility: Protagoras sought, through his radical relativism, to bracket or neutralize the challenge to free thinking implicit in the testimony of the experience of revelation about warring gods offered by men such as Euthyphro. On the basis of Protagorean relativism, the truth of the experiences Euthyphro claims to have had may be said not to contradict the truth of the life experience of an honest atheist (such as Protagoras probably considers himself to be). For the truth about the world is, for each, simply however the world comes to sight for each.

If this is indeed the import of Protagorean relativism, it is hard to believe that Socrates regarded such relativism as an adequate response to the challenge of the purported revelation of warring gods. But the Protagorean position may make a serious contribution inasmuch as it expresses the impasse to which rationalism prior to Socrates had been brought by its incapacity to dispose of the challenge of revelation as represented most vividly by a man like Euthyphro. We may surmise that perhaps no one prior to Protagoras had faced so clearly how doubtful the purely theoretical life and the purely theoretical or scientific enterprise must become, in the face of philosophy's inability to exclude the possibility that the universe has no nature in the strict sense, but is instead the mysterious product of elusive, conflicting, and willful providential deities, who reveal themselves, for unfathomable reasons, to some humans and not to others.

This suggestion makes more intelligible what is perhaps the most important and unforgettable passage in the *Theaetetus* (172c): the long "digression" in which Socrates interrupts his examination of the Protagorean thesis in order to present his own conception of the character, and the reasons for the superiority, of the philosophic life. This account of Socratic political philosophy makes clearer than any other in Plato, I believe, that the chief purpose of the Socratic "turn" is the successful vindication of the theoretical life, or the reestablishment, on a firm basis, of the enterprise of Socrates' wise predecessors. The vindication of the theoretical-philosophic life is at the same time the critique of the political life. But the Socratic critique of the city and the civic is a very different kind of critique from that we have in the doctrines of the Sophists. Socrates does not base his critique on a theory or an account of human nature—an account whose basic premises, after all, are always contestable by a man like Euthyphro, or surely by more thoughtful defenders of the city and its gods. By the same token, Socrates does not base his critique solely or chiefly on the evidence afforded by empirical observation of the behavior of cities and citizens, of lawgivers and rulers; in particular, Socrates does not rest his refutation of the civic opinions on the observation that those opinions are contradicted by civic deeds. Socrates does not scorn such scientific evidence, but he does not find it to be decisive. What, then, is the character of the distinctively Socratic critique of the political life?

The Socratic critique proceeds by way of "dialectics," or what Socrates calls his "midwifing art"—activity that expresses what he calls his "terrible erotic passion for refuting." Socrates refutes in conversation the articulate young who begin by being firmly rooted in, and guided by, and able to express and argue clearly for, the fundamental civic opinions about justice and nobility. The Socratic refutation—for example, of Polemarchus—proceeds on the basis of those civic opinions, and on the premises underlying those civic opinions. The Socratic refutation succeeds by bringing to light grave contradictions in those opinions and premises. The Socratic critique is an immanent critique, and those who are refuted cannot question the premises of the refutation, because those premises are their own premises. What is most important, however, is not the refutation itself, but rather the consequence for the young person who is so refuted. The young who have the intelligence and the manliness, or strength of soul, truly to follow and grasp the meaning of the refutation undergo a profound change in spirit. The refutation of their opinions about justice and nobility entails or carries in its wake a refutation of their experiences, or of the way things appear to them (see esp. *Theaetetus* 161e4–8). The young who truly recognize that they have been refuted alter, fundamentally, their conception of the human situation. They become converted to philosophy, or to the conviction that the philosophic way of life and the philosophic vision of the world, or nature, divinity, justice, and nobility, is true. In bringing about and witnessing this conversion, Socrates reproduces, and thus confirms, the conversion that he himself must originally have undergone. And Plato, by preserving in his writings a record of the Socratic process of verification, conveys to future generations of potential philosophers indications of both the path of conversion and the reproducibility of that path.

To be sure, in his account of his own doings in the *Theaetetus*, Socrates makes it clear that only a very few of the young have the capacity to undergo a true or full conversion. Even among those with whom Socrates can converse at any length, the vast majority wind up refusing to listen—in one way or another. The conclusive confirming evidence that Socrates gathers is thus not copious; and this would seem to explain the fact that even at the very end of his life, Socrates speaks as if his gathering of confirming evidence is not simply a thing of the past. For Socrates, the theological question is never entirely closed, it would seem. This feature of the account in the *Theaetetus* also prompts us to wonder whether Socrates does not feel the need to gather supplementary evidence from truncated refutations of the unpromising—even, perhaps, refutations of some of the old, who can be assumed to be so settled in their convictions that it would be utterly unreasonable to expect them to undergo the conversion to philosophy. In the *Laws*, and especially in the opening pages of that long dialogue, we do indeed witness a remarkable theological outcome of a Socratic refutation of two shrewd old statesmen, born and raised in the most traditional and orthodox of all Greek cities. Those statesmen are not, as a consequence of the refutation, converted to philosophy; but they do react by spontaneously abandoning the cardinal theological tenet of their civic creeds.

The old statesmen are rewarded for this wrenching sacrifice by being shown a legal order far more reasonable and noble than any previously known to them, and by being allowed a vision of law-inspiring divinity far purer and more in accord with nature than any of which they have previously heard. This brings us to what we may call the politically constructive aspect of the Socratic critique of politics. This aspect is much more visible in the great political dialogues—the *Republic*, the *Laws*, and to a lesser extent the *Gorgias*. The theme of these dialogues is the "best regime by nature," or that "true political art" of which, Socrates boasts, he is one of the very few, not to say the only, practitioner in Athens. In elaborating the "best regime" of the *Republic*, or even the "second or third best regime" of the *Laws*, the Socratic philosopher brings out the diamonds hidden in the rough of actual politics. The Socratic critique of civic opinion, unlike the pre-Socratic critique, does not lead to the conclusion that the entire realm of civic opinion ought to be simply left behind, as hopelessly deluded. The Socratic critique leads to an immanent ascent within and from the civic, to the trans-civic and trans-moral; the Socratic critique leads to a self-transcendence of the civic rather than an abandonment of the civic. To put it another way: precisely by criticizing civic opinion for being contradictory, Socrates insists that we must try to decide which of the two contradictory premises in each crucial case can and must be maintained, and which abandoned. The ordinary civic opinions prove to be not simply false, but, so to speak, half false—and therefore half true.

This means, of course, that Socrates does not reveal the purer and more consistent notions of justice and nobility and divinity that are embedded in ordinary moral opinion without simultaneously laying bare the tawdriness and incoherence of ordinary moral opinion. Socrates cannot demonstrate why virtue and moral responsibility must be understood as centered on knowledge, and vice on ignorance, of the most important things—without casting severe doubts on retributive punishment and the idea of angry gods.

Socrates cannot show that we mean by true virtue an excellence choice worthy strictly for its own sake—without forcing us to confront the extent to which virtue is ordinarily motivated by a sense of shame, desert, and a hope for divine favor. We cannot be brought to recognize that our being is primarily defined by an erotic love of the beautiful that seeks from the start eternity, and that finds consummation in the contemplation of natural order and spiritual grace—without feeling some contempt for the mundane objects of mortal, corporeal need that constitute the main preoccupation of ordinary civic life and action. We cannot appreciate the austere divinities of the *Republic* without smiling at the childishness of our initial expectations or demands from divinity.

Yet none of this adds up to a program of civic reform. The chief practical implication of Platonic political philosophy is a kind of moderating, or indeed even a chastening, of political zeal, or of the ambitious hopes that animate and often inflame civic life. Even this lesson is not one that is welcome, or that can expect to meet with great success. The same reasons that make most of even the best young people turn away from the Socratic refutations ensure that the vast majority of citizens and statesmen will be unable and hence unwilling to follow very far the Platonic critique of civic life. To be sure, the *Laws*, and to a lesser extent the *Republic*, contain important useful general lessons in constitutionalism. For instance, the third and sixth books of the *Laws* provide the classic justification for, and institutional elaboration of, the mixed regime; the second and seventh books of the *Laws*, and to some extent the third book of the *Republic*, outline the classic principles of civic education, and reveal in particular the central role of music, or the fine arts, in such education; to take a final example, the ninth and tenth books of the *Laws* present a teaching on the principles of penal law that, in accord with the Socratic doctrine that traces virtue to knowledge and vice to ignorance, exemplifies and thereby promotes a tempering of punitive indignation. And everywhere in Plato we find a profound, if profoundly qualified, respect for political life: the Platonic dialogues promote a respect for politics that is centered on, and justified by, the hidden directedness of law toward that which transcends law. According to Plato, the call of citizenship draws men up and out of their narrow concerns for material, personal, and familial security and contentment; the experience of civic life awakens in the best men a longing for greatness, for excellence, for a responsibility and hence a fulfillment and a salvation that will give life meaning and dignity otherwise unknown. Politics centered on the quest for justice gives life seriousness. The political vocation has the potential to provoke in those who hearken to it an intense concern for the truth about the principles and hopes and dreams that inspire and are inspired by political action. But this rich potential, if it is to be fully realized, must encounter the bracing challenge of the philosophic or theoretical life. Only then does the political man begin to discover the cave-like character of civic life, and thus the life beyond the cave toward which civic life unknowingly gropes and which gives to civic life its ultimate high justification—and at the same time, its sense of limits. The ambition to rule does not find a good reason for stopping short of noble but ultimately self-corrupting imperialism unless that ambition is checked by some awareness, however dim or veiled, of the higher dignity and richer satisfaction of the leisured theoretical life. One of the most important ways in which the Socratic-Platonic philosophers have, down through the centuries, sought to inculcate this awareness is by their attempts to influence and modify the theology of their respective communities.

In the preceding, very sketchy suggestions as to the nature of the Socratic idea of political philosophy that takes the place, as it were, of the "idea of the public intellectual," I have selected especially features that allow one to appreciate the enormous difference between the Socratic conception of the civic role and responsibility of the life of the mind and the competing modern "idea of the public intellectual." Let me close by attempting to characterize briefly the central concern that is at the heart of the modern departure.

Socratic political philosophy, I have contended, has as its chief raison d'être the vindication of the rational theoretical life, and of the conception of divinity discovered by strict reasoning, in the face of the challenge posed by purported experiences of supra-rational and indeed contra-rational divine revelations and laws. Modern political philosophy, I would like to suggest, has something akin as its fundamental animating goal. But modern political philosophy is born out of a grave obfuscation: a loss of understanding or awareness of the theological import of Socratic dialectics. It may also be the case—but of this I speak with much less confidence—that modern rationalism lost sight, in addition, of the fact that the theoretical or contemplative life is the fullest possible answer to the deepest spiritual needs of human nature. Certainly this much is true: the moderns (with the possible exception of Spinoza) are defined by their conviction that the life of free reasoning and thinking can be vindicated only at the cost of ceasing to advance the claim that this life and this life alone fulfills human nature.

If I may be permitted to focus on the modern whom I know best, Montesquieu, I would try to formulate the modern enterprise in the briefest possible terms as follows. The moderns begin from a grand hypothesis to the following effect: the prevalence in the world of belief in supra-rational revelations of contra-rational divine laws is caused, not by the existence of the deities believed to reveal themselves in and through those laws, but instead by pathological political and social and economic conditions. Human beings are by nature largely satisfied by mundane prosperity. Humans turn to imaginary deities who demand the transcendence and even the sacrifice of worldly prosperity, only because worldly prosperity is so uncertain. If men's lives were made secure, and invested with a modicum of worldly dignity, men might well continue to imagine and worship supernatural deities who would help them assuage the fear of death, but one would find that those supposed deities and their purported commandments would cease to contradict in any significant way, would instead simply support, the rules and practices and institutions that reason showed were necessary for worldly prosperity. Religions and gods and commandments that stood in the way of this "progress" would either disappear or be reinterpreted by their believers so as to become practically unrecognizable shells of their former selves. And philosophy or science can and must be reconceived as politically and socially active in such a way as to direct this transmogrification of the conditions of human existence. As the transformation proceeds, the proof of the hypothesis should become plainer and plainer. But this means that philosophy must cease to present itself, and perhaps even to conceive of itself, as fundamentally theoretical or contemplative. Philosophy must replace the cave with the Enlightenment. Political philosophy must become lawgiving in the deepest sense. But immediately a practical difficulty is encountered: philosophy (in the strict sense) and philosophers (in the true sense) are very, very rare. Philosophy must therefore recruit a kind of spiritual army. Philosophy must debase its own name, lending that name to the officers of the new army—the "philosophes." The new rationalism must create cultural cadres: lesser lights who will obediently carry forward—not altogether self-consciously—the theological-political struggle of secularizing social transformation and humanistic cultural revolution. This is the deepest significance—the truly world-historical significance—of "the idea of the public intellectual." And this deepest, world-historical significance of "the idea of the public intellectual" is the important truth that we learn if, and only if, we approach the idea of the public intellectual from a Platonic perspective. There is no more telling sign of the decisive flaw in the Enlightenment and its "idea of the public intellectual" than that the deepest purpose of that idea has been lost sight of by all its living proponents—and that it is only those enlightened by the rediscovery of the undiminished intrinsic intellectual power of its enemies who can still appreciate the theological-political grandeur of the modern project.

NOTE

A different version of this essay appears as "The Platonic Challenge to the Modern Idea of the Public Intellectual," in R. Beiner and W. Norman, eds., *Canadian Political Philosophy at the Turn of the Century: Exemplary Essays* (New York: Oxford University Press, 2000).

3

The Idea of the Public Intellectual in the Age of the Enlightenment

Paul A. Rahe

That the public intellectual is a product of the Enlightenment we need not doubt. In the ancient and medieval worlds, there was no one comparable to Voltaire. Dénis Diderot, Jean Le Rond d'Alembert, and their *Encyclopédie* have no premodern analogues, and the same point can arguably be made concerning Anne-Robert-Jacques Turgot, Jacques Neckar, and the Marquis de Condorcet. Neither in antiquity nor in the Middle Ages was there a concerted attempt to make the general public cognizant of the fruits of science and philosophy. In the premodern world, theoretical expertise was in no way deemed a prerequisite, a qualification, or even a recommendation for high political office. Science was not considered the foundation for society.

In classical antiquity, of course, there was no dearth of philosophers, and men of letters such as Cicero, Seneca, Petronius, and Marcus Aurelius played a prominent role in public life. But they did not do so in their guise as philosophers or even as members of the republic of letters: they did not assert a claim to rule on that foundation and no one asserted anything of the kind on their behalf. Cicero's rise to power had much to do with his eloquence and his knowledge of Roman law and nothing to do with his training in philosophy. Nero no doubt found the erudition of Seneca and Petronius attractive but certainly not for its practical utility. In surrounding himself with such men, he was merely indulging his tastes as a dilettante. That a philosopher such as Marcus Aurelius became Roman emperor was a freak accident. In antiquity, statesmanship and philosophy remained distinct. Philosophy was judged quintessentially a private pursuit: as Plato's Socrates observes, a philosopher would never willingly reenter the cave.[1] Even if a concern for his own welfare somehow dictated that he intervene in the affairs of the city, he would not take as his task popular enlightenment. The opinion of Plato's Socrates that "it is impossible that a multitude be philosophic" was, in antiquity, never challenged by a philosopher of any note.[2]

The one piece of evidence most likely to be cited in support of the view that, in antiquity, there were philosophers who aspired to the position later occupied by the public intellectual arguably sustains the very opposite. In what may be the most famous passage in Plato's *Republic*, Socrates suggests to Glaucon that "unless either the philosophers rule as kings in the cities or those now called kings and lords *(dunastai)* genuinely and sufficiently philosophize, and political power and philosophy fall together into the same place . . . there will be no cessation of evils for the cities . . . nor for human kind." A bolder claim could hardly be made on behalf of theoretical wisdom, but Socrates is perfectly correct in acknowledging that, in advancing it, he risks being "inundated by laughter and ill repute" (5.473c-d).[3] Even if one were to discount the practical obstacles that stand in the way of identifying those in possession of such wisdom and the obstacles that stand in the way of persuading ordinary men to submit to their guidance, there is the far greater obstacle that it is doubtful whether there are any human beings at all genuinely graced with theoretical wisdom. In Plato's *Apology* (20c–24a, 29a-b, 33b-c, 41b), this same Socrates denies having ever met a man wiser than he is, and his wisdom, which is apparently the only wisdom available to man, consists in his recognition and acknowledgment of his own ignorance: such wisdom could hardly eventuate in a teaching that would elucidate and guide practice.

Of course, one might wish to argue that the Socrates of *The Apology* is by no means the same man as the Socrates of *The Republic*: the two dialogues, we are often told, were written at different times; and although, in terms of dramatic chronology, *The Republic* precedes *The Apology*, it is said to have been written well after the latter work and to represent a different phase in the development of Platonic thinking. The trouble with this argument is that it rests on quicksand: there is almost no philological evidence for determining the order in which the Platonic dialogues were composed; there is some suggesting repeated revision of existing dialogues; and the attempts to place the dialogues in order of composition all rely on circular argument. Put simply, they presuppose what they set out to prove: the stylistic criteria for determining which dialogues go together is always itself selected because it confirms a prior conviction as to the grouping of the dialogues. To make matters worse, Plato demonstrates in *The Symposium* and elsewhere a measure of stylistic control and a capacity for deliberately varying the manner in which he writes that calls into question the very possibility of finding a standard indicative of unconscious stylistic development over time.[4]

Even if one could so order the dialogues and even if that ordering opened up the possibility that Plato had changed his mind and that his representation of his master Socrates changed in accord with this alteration in views, there is evidence within *The Republic* itself suggesting that Plato was no Platonist: that he was persuaded that theoretical wisdom remains beyond human grasp and, in any case, provides no guarantee of practical control.

There are two pertinent passages. The first is especially poignant. In it, Socrates describes the emergence of the philosopher from the cave and the process by which he achieves enlightenment, looking first at the shadows as his eyes grow accustomed to the light, then at the reflections of human beings and the other things in the water, then at the things themselves, then at the stars and the moon by night, and finally gazing at the sun, "not its appearances in water or some alien seat, but the sun itself by itself in its own territory" (7.516a-b). What he does not say is that a human being who gazes into the sun goes blind. This fact was well known at the time: it is the sort of thing that would have puzzled virtually any careful contemporary reader of the dialogue. Elsewhere, Plato's Socrates and his Athenian Stranger make much of this phenomenon, and Xenophon's Socrates mentions it as well.[5] It was not esoteric knowledge. The use of this particular metaphor in *The Republic* by Plato's Socrates suggests that human beings cannot comprehend the idea of the good, that they cannot grasp the whole as a whole, that whatever wisdom they may possess will remain partial and limited at best, that the project laid out in the dialogue is, as Socrates on one occasion intimates (5.450c-d), more a prayer than an argument, and that Glaucon was right initially when he exclaimed that Socrates' description of the idea of the good was a "daimonic extravagance" (6.509c-d).[6] One must keep in mind that *The Republic* is a drama, replete with irony, in which a question is playfully explored—not a treatise in which a doctrine is solemnly elaborated.

In the second passage (8.545c–47c), Socrates describes for Glaucon just how the city that they have constructed in speech might be undermined in fact. The source of all revolutions, he suggests, is faction, and faction will come to the just city when, through ignorance of the mathematics dictating the management of breeding, the city's guardians allow a chaotic mixing of human types. What is striking is that no student of this passage—not even those skilled in mathematics and in textual criticism—has ever been able to make any sense of Socrates' description of the so-called nuptial number. This is arguably intended by the author as an indication that politics is a sphere from which fortune and the irrational cannot be banned. In short, the belief that there is a mathematics adequate to the management of a city would seem to be a delusion. Human affairs would appear not to be amenable to geometrical precision.[7]

This is certainly what Plato's most distinguished student took to be the case, for Aristotle insists that the knowledge of political matters is not and can never be an exact science. As he puts it,

> Precision is not equally to be sought after in all accounts *(logoi),* just as it is not equally to be sought after in all of the products made by craftsmen. The noble or beautiful *(ta kala)* and the just, which are the subjects into which political science makes inquiry, evidence so much diversity and instability *(plane)* that they seem to exist solely by convention and not by nature. Even the good evidences such instability because damage in many circumstances arises from that which is good: some are destroyed by wealth; others, by courage. Those discoursing concerning such matters and from such premises must be content to display the truth in a rough manner and by means of a sketch, and in discoursing concerning matters

> and from premises which are true for the most part, they must be content to reach conclusions of the same kind. One must, in the same spirit, take in each of the things said. For the well-educated man seeks as much precision with regard to each kind of study as the nature of the business allows. For to accept from a mathematician arguments aimed at persuasion is much like demanding formal proofs from an orator.[8]

Aristotle's point is that, strictly speaking, there can be no political philosophy and no political science. To approach political questions from a theoretical perspective is to distort them beyond recognition. In consequence, he consistently views politics from the perspective of the statesman. "It is necessary also to remember," he says,

> what has already been said and not to seek precision in a similar fashion in all investigations, but in each according to the underlying matter and as far as fits the mode of inquiry. For a carpenter and a geometrician seek the right angle in different ways: the one seeks it in so far as it is useful for the work he is doing; the other seeks what it is and what sort of thing it is, for he is a spectator of truth. In the same manner we must act also in other spheres—lest secondary concerns *(parerga)* outweigh the work at hand.[9]

The implication of these remarks is that, when the statesman and the philosopher investigate, say, the question of human responsibility, they are looking for different things altogether. The statesman is interested in the limits to a man's responsibility for his own action only insofar as they bear on the question of punishment and rewards, of blame and praise. Human freedom is something that he must take for granted; the citizen's presumption that he is an agent capable of choice and responsible for results the statesman must reinforce and exploit. The philosopher has no such needs and may, in fact, be inclined to treat all actions as caused in a manner that would obviate both the need for and the possibility of genuine statesmanship and citizenship. It is not only the case that the quest for theoretical wisdom does not eventuate in political prudence: this quest may, in fact, be antithetical to and subversive of political prudence. Plato, arguably, and Aristotle, certainly, set out to debunk the pretension to geometrical precision in political affairs and to defend the perspective shared by the statesman and citizen. In consequence, ancient philosophers tended not to pretend to any special, technical expertise in political affairs: at most they devoted themselves to elucidating the perspective of statesmanship and to fostering prudential deliberation thereby.

THEORY AND PRACTICE IN EARLY MODERNITY

I digress in this fashion in order to set off as distinct the public intellectuals of early modernity—for, in contrast with the philosophers of ancient times, they sought to subordinate practice to theory and even to subsume the one under the other. In the process, they treated as largely illusory the statesman's point of view.

Their ancient predecessors could sustain the integrity of this point of view because they conceived of philosophy in general as an attempt to "save the phenomena"—as an attempt to make sense of what seemed to be the case.[10] In consequence, they treated the opinions widely held by ordinary men, alongside the opinions of those reputed to be wise, with great respect, attempting to elicit sense from them all on the presumption that each of the conflicting opinions that exercised considerable sway or was issued from a source commanding respect was somehow perceptive—even though partial, quite possibly partisan, and certainly incomplete.[11] Plato's metaphor for what was presupposed by the procedure of beginning always with received opinion and attempting to make progress therefrom was recollection. To much the same purpose, the scholastic philosophers would later speak of innate ideas. Both expressions are shorthand for the shared conviction that there is a kinship, a fit, between the human understanding and the natural world and that human beings are, therefore, at least in principle, capable of approaching, if not attaining, moral and political rationality.

This kinship and the attendant possibility of achieving a measure of moral and political rationality the early modern philosophers were as one in denying. Sir Francis Bacon expressly rejected the notion that "true philosophy can be coaxed from the preconceptions of the intellect."[12] René Descartes did the same when, after adopting as his own both Galileo's contention that vision is a species of touch and his subsequent assertion that the "universe" is a "book . . . written in the language of mathematics," he then took that mathematics, with its peculiar claim to certitude, as the model for all truth. In effect, his celebrated method, grounded in universal doubt and predicated on the presumption that clarity and distinctness are the sole criteria for truth, is an instrument designed to justify the dismissal of popular opinion as completely bereft of insight.[13] The critique of innate ideas in the first book of John Locke's *Essay Concerning Human Understanding* served precisely the same function.

The significance of this epistemological maneuver is clearest in the political writings of Thomas Hobbes, who prefaced the first full statement of his political science with a categorical rejection of "those opinions which are already vulgarly received" and who then later joined Descartes in grounding his new science on an introspection which was informed by the implications of Galileo's analysis of vision as a species of touch and inspired by the Italian scientist's closely related critique of the notion that there is an identity or close correspondence between sensation and its cause.[14] The Englishman likewise shared with his French counterpart the project of achieving an absolute certainty like that attainable in mathematics.[15] In method, substance, and tone, Hobbes's political philosophy was so reminiscent of Descartes's publications and of the opinions he privately expressed that, not long after

De cive first appeared as an anonymous tract in 1642, Samuel Sorbière confronted the author of *The Discourse on Method* and the *Meditations* on the supposition that he had composed Hobbes's political treatise as well.[16]

When Bacon acknowledged that his new science was at odds with common sense, noting that "true philosophy" cannot "be coaxed from the preconceptions of the intellect," he expressed grave doubts as to whether it could "lower itself to the capacities of the multitude *(ad captum vulgi)* except through its utility and works," and so he insisted that "no one of greatly superior intellect" could safely present himself to those "inferior in intelligence" except when "wearing a mask."[17] To be effective, philosophical rule would have to be invisible—as was the case in Bacon's utopia *The New Atlantis*.

There is in Descartes no comparable discussion of the difficulties associated with the revolution that he and others were then undertaking. There are, however, indications that he agreed with Bacon. Not long after Galileo was tried in the courts of the Inquisition and condemned, Descartes alluded to the event in a letter to his close friend and fellow scientist Father Marin Mersenne. In that document, he drew attention to his own "desire of living in repose and of continuing the life [of philosophy] he had begun" some years before. To protect himself from suffering Galileo's fate, he remarked, he would henceforth conduct his affairs in accord with Ovid's device *bené vixit, bené qui latuit*: "He has lived well, he who has remained well hidden."[18] Accordingly, Descartes deliberately composed his "philosophy in such a manner as not to be offensive to anyone—so that it can be received anywhere, even among the Turks."[19] Mindful that "because of the corruption of our morals and manners *(moeurs),* there are few people who are willing to say all that they believe,"[20] the French philosopher made it his own "custom to refuse to write down" his "thoughts regarding morals." "There is," he explained, "no other matter from which men of malign purpose can so easily draw pretexts for calumny."[21]

Hobbes deserves close attention because, although he was no less firm an admirer of Galileo, he was far less timid than Descartes and because he demonstrated far greater confidence in the capacities of ordinary men than their common mentor Sir Francis Bacon. The true motive for propagating his political science was, arguably, his fury at "the suppression of True Philosophy, by such men, as neither by lawfull authority, nor sufficient study, are competent Judges of the truth."[22] Hobbes's ire was directed at the theologico-political order constituted by the alliance between Aristotelianism and Christianity, which he contemptuously dubbed "Aristotelity."[23] In contrast with the churchmen who had argued that secular learning should be made the handmaid of revelation, he contended that "in order that it might prosper, philosophy ought to be free and subject to coercion neither by fear nor by shame." To this end, he urged what Plato's Socrates had denied was possible: that "the multitude *(vulgus)* be gradually enlightened *(eruditur)*."[24] Consequently, in *Leviathan*, Hobbes not only declared war on the "Confederacy of Deceivers" who employ "Pious Frauds" on "them that have not much knowledge of naturall causes, and of the nature, and interests of men" and did battle with those who take advantage of "the ordinary ignorance, stupidity, and superstition of mankind" in order "*to obtain dominion over men in this present world.*"[25] He went further and elaborated a science of politics that he took to be exact.

POLITICAL GEOMETRY

The philosopher of Malmesbury's task was to elaborate with geometrical precision "the true and only foundation" of the "science" of "justice and policy." His purpose was to explain to men in general and to rulers in particular the "dictates of Reason," which is to say, the "Conclusions, or Theoremes concerning what conduceth to the conservation and defence of themselves."[26] He thought such an endeavor possible because the fundamental principles of the science of justice and policy and the institutions to which that science gives rise are artifacts of the human mind precisely akin to the definitions from which geometry begins.

Hobbes establishes his science by means of Galileo's resolutive-compositive method. Initially, he breaks the commonwealth into its constituent parts; then, he traces the manner in which the passions found in individual men account for its composition. Because human beings are capable of introspection, their knowledge of this causal process is certain. In one passage Hobbes writes, "Politics and ethics . . . can be demonstrated *a priori* because we ourselves make the principles—that is, the causes of justice (namely the laws and covenants)—whereby it is known what *justice* and *equity*, and their opposites *injustice* and *inequity* are." In another, he speaks of the political scientist as an

> artist . . . who, in his demonstration, does no more but deduce the consequences of his own operation. The reason whereof is this, that the science of every subject is derived from a precognition of the causes, generation, and construction of the same; and consequently where the causes are known, there is place for demonstration, but not where the causes are to seek for. Geometry therefore is demonstrable, for the lines and figures from which we reason are drawn and described by ourselves; and civil philosophy is demonstrable, because we make the commonwealth ourselves. But because of natural bodies we know not the construction, but seek it from the effects, there lies no demonstration of what the causes be we seek for, but only of what they may be.

Thus, while knowledge of the natural world can only be conditional or hypothetical, the sphere that Aristotle considered least subject to precise determination is for Hobbes an object of exact science.[27]

It is easy to underestimate the audacity of the Hobbesian project, for the English philosopher's boldness of expression obscures an even greater boldness of intention. As we have seen, in *The Republic*, Plato's Socrates had explored the possibility that political prudence might be reduced to calculation, and he had argued that "there will be no cessation of evils for the cities nor for human kind" until the day when "the philosophers rule as kings or those now called kings and lords *(dunastai)* genuinely and sufficiently philosophize, and political power and philosophy fall together into the same place." Such an eventuality he seems to have considered so unlikely as to be virtually impossible.[28] In contrast, Hobbes—without the slightest hint of irony—argued that his "Science of Naturall Justice" makes the achievement of philosophic rule not only possible but relatively easy. His own efforts would, he thought, enable men to convert the "Truth of Speculation, into the Utility of Practice." The consequences, he explained, would be just as Plato's protagonist had foretold:

> Though nothing can be immortall, which mortals make; yet, if men had the use of reason they pretend to, their Common-wealths might be secured, at least, from perishing by internall diseases. For by the nature of their Institution, they are designed to live, as long as Man-kind, or as the Lawes of Nature, or as Justice it selfe, which gives them life. Therefore when they come to be dissolved, not by externall violence, but intestine disorder, the fault is not in men, as they are the *Matter*; but as they are the *Makers*, and orderers of them.

Theoretical wisdom could be achieved; fortune could be conquered; and a "very able Architect," instructed in the Hobbesian school, could actually engineer the "constitution" of a commonwealth so skillfully as to make it "(excepting by externall violence) everlasting."[29] Thomas Hobbes was the Platonist that Plato was not.

Hobbes's constructive account was preceded by a critique—analogous to Descartes's deployment of universal doubt and Locke's repudiation of the notion of innate ideas. For Hobbes, as well as for his colleagues, the enemy was Aristotle and his understanding of *logos*.[30] From the undeniable fact that men—and philosophers in particular—find it notoriously difficult, if not impossible, to reach agreement concerning the advantageous, the just, and the good, Hobbes concluded that natural reason lacks the capacity to discern what these really are. This incapacity he traced to the relationship between thought and desire. In his *Leviathan*, the English philosopher argues initially that memory and imagination depend upon sensation; then, he suggests that reason is the slave of the passions. Where a man's "Trayne *of Imaginations*" or "Thoughts" is not a "wild ranging of the mind" but possesses a certain coherence reflecting guidance or direction, this coherence is rooted in "Passionate Thought" or "Desire." As the Wiltshire philosopher puts it, "From Desire, ariseth the Thought of some means we have seen produce the like of that which we ayme at; and from the thought of that, the thought of means to that mean; and so continually, till we come to some beginning within our own power." In short, "the Thoughts, are to the Desires, as Scouts, and Spies to range abroad, and find the way to the things Desired."[31] For Hobbesian man, theory is by its very nature not only subordinate to practice; it is the supreme form of practice.

If human desire were coherent and consistent, reason's enslavement might not be an obstacle to concord. But unfortunately, for man, there is no "*Summum Bonum.*" In Hobbes's estimation, human "Felicity" is not "the repose of a mind satisfied"; it is rather "a continuall progresse of the desire, from one object to another." Moreover, because desire is incoherent and men are insatiable, they "conceive the same things differently," and "the same man, in divers times, differs from himselfe." Though the true nature of what human beings contemplate may be the same, "the diversity of our reception of it, in respect of different constitutions of body, and prejudices of opinion gives everything a tincture of our different passions." More often than not, then, the words used by an individual tell us more regarding "the nature, disposition, and interest of the speaker" than they do of the subject he is talking about. Thus, what one man calls wisdom another man thinks of as fear, and what one describes as cruelty another terms justice; indeed, what a man calls prodigality on one occasion, he may later consider magnanimity; and what he thinks of today as gravity he may regard as stupidity tomorrow. As a consequence of the "*inconstant* signification" of the moral terms that men employ, "such names can never be true grounds of any ratiocination," and they can therefore hardly provide a foundation for political harmony.[32] To the extent that all pre-Hobbesian regimes rest on authoritative opinion regarding the advantageous, the just, and the good, they are built on quicksand and on that alone.

What might seem to be a misfortune, ruling out the very aspiration to moral and political rationality, turns out to be a godsend—for reason's dependence on desire makes precise political calculation possible and serves, thereby, as the foundation stone for the purportedly impregnable political edifice that Hobbes sets out to build. Hobbes begins by dividing the "Trayn of regulated Thoughts" into two species. The first type of coherent thinking takes place

> when of an effect imagined, wee seek the causes, or means that produce it: and this is common to Man and Beast. The other is, when imagining any thing whatsoever, wee seek all the possible effects, that can by it be produced; that is to say, we imagine what we can do with it, when wee have it. Of which I have not at any time seen any signe, but in man onely; for this is a curiosity hardly incident to the nature of any living creature that has no other Passion but sensuall, such as are hunger, thirst, lust, and anger. In summe, the Discourse of the Mind, when it is governed by designe, is nothing but *Seeking*, or the faculty of Invention, which the Latines call *Sagacitas*, and *Solertia*; a hunting out of the causes, of some effect, present or past; or of the effects, of some present or past cause.[33]

Put simply, Aristotle and the Greeks more generally were wrong: the capacity that distinguishes man from the animals is not *logos* per se; it has nothing to do with the application of reason to the question of justice and the human good; and it is in no way linked with the pursuit of virtue and the contest for immortal fame.[34] If man surpasses the animals, he does so not as *homo politicus* but as *homo faber*. He is by nature an inventor, a hunter of causes and effects, a fashioner of tools, and he alone is driven by "a Lust of the mind" to investigate the consequences of particular actions.[35] In short, he alone is capable of achieving a mastery over nature through the application of Galileo's resolutive-compositive method.

This fact has profound political implications. The lust of mind which distinguishes Hobbesian man from the beasts is not the idle curiosity of the contemplative: like the longing for riches and honor, this lust "may be reduced to . . . Desire of Power." Moreover, because human consciousness is above all else the awareness of consequences, man quite naturally conceives of himself first and foremost as the cause of future effects, as a creature endowed with power. In fact, for him, "all conception of future, is conception of power able to produce something." In short, his subjectivity is itself constituted by a "perpetuall solicitude of the time to come . . . So that man, which looks too far before him, in the care of future time, hath his heart all the day long, gnawed on by feare of death, poverty, or other calamity; and has no repose, nor pause of his anxiety, but in sleep."[36]

The absence of a summum bonum for man adds a further complication: because he is insatiable and human felicity is a haphazard progress of desire from one more or less whimsically selected object to another, the hunter of causes and consequences longs first and foremost not for any particular end, but rather for the means "to assure for ever, the way of his future desire." In short, he experiences a "perpetuall and restlesse desire of Power after power." The resulting quest for power eventually brings him face to face with his fellow human beings. Inevitably, given the incapacity of *logos* to provide a foundation for community, he treats these men, like everything else he encounters, simply as instruments for dominating nature; and, just as inevitably, they treat him in precisely the same fashion. Thereby, men discover that "the power of one man resisteth and hindereth the effects of the power of another"; and, in the end, they also come to recognize the preeminent political truth: that "power simply is no more, but the excess of the power of one above that of another."[37]

This recognition transforms "the life of man"—which ceases to be oriented by ordinary, bodily desire. Under its influence, human life becomes "a race" with "no other goal, nor other garland, but being foremost." Thus, for man, "Joy consisteth in comparing himselfe with other men," and he "can relish nothing but what is eminent." For him, "felicity" has no close connection with bodily need; it is a species of progressive conquest in which each individual strives "continually to out-go the next before." Thus, in practice, all the passions of man can be reduced to feelings of *relative* power and powerlessness. Vanity attains mastery as we maniacally struggle to sustain "the imagination or conception of our own power, above the power of him that contendeth with us." In the process, since "every man looketh that his companion should value him, at the same rate he sets upon himselfe," men squabble, come to blows, and then kill one another not only or even primarily because their material interests clash but "for trifles, as a word, a smile, a different opinion, and any other signe of undervalue." As Hobbes sums it all up, "Men from their very birth, and naturally, scramble for every thing they covet, and would have all the world, if they could, to fear and obey them."[38]

Hobbes took little pleasure in contemplating the struggle for preeminence. As he pointed out, in these circumstances, even pusillanimous men endowed with relatively moderate desires find it impossible to be confident that they will continue securely to possess in perpetuity "the power and means to live well"; ultimately, even they are driven constantly to seek "the acquisition of more." In a world ungoverned, in "that dissolute condition of masterlesse men, without subjection to Lawes, and a coërcive Power, to tye their hands from rapine, and revenge," mankind would inevitably be forced into a self-destructive war of all against all: "In such condition, there is no place for Industry; because the fruit thereof is uncertain: and consequently no Culture of the Earth; no Navigation, nor use of the commodities that may be imported by Sea; no commodious Building; no Instruments of moving, and removing such things as require much force; no Knowledge of the face of the Earth; no account of Time; no Arts; no Letters; no Society; and which is worst of all, continuall feare, and danger of violent death; And the life of man, solitary, poore, nasty, brutish, and short." Fortunately, men eventually learned how to escape their natural condition by submitting to someone stronger than they were or by banding together for common defense under a common leader or council—which is to say, by inventing the state. To this achievement, they were guided not by unassisted reason but by the fear of death and, in particular, by the fear of a violent and dishonorable death at the hands of their fellow men.

This fear concentrates the mind wonderfully, and it is able to do what reason can never accomplish on its own: it can silence all the other passions, put an end to the vain quest for glory, stop the incessant clash of opinions, and teach individual men the truth regarding their helplessness and vulnerability when left in isolation. It serves as the Archimedean point within nature from which nature can be overcome. It humiliates men; and under its benign influence, they are able to become parties to a contract and give mutual consent to the establishment of a "Leviathan" or "*Mortall God*" which will serve as "*King of all the children of pride.*" It is only out of fear that men, who are naturally vain, will humbly submit to the dictates of a sovereign and representative prince or assembly authorized to impose peace, empowered to settle all disputes, entrusted with the determination of principles, and thereby made strong enough to enforce its every command.[39]

THE CREED OF THE PUBLIC INTELLECTUAL

I outline in some detail Hobbes's political science not because the public intellectuals of the Enlightenment both before and after were in agreement with its exponent on every detail, for they were not. I focus on it, instead, because it is especially revealing. As we have seen, Sir Francis Bacon had cautioned his disciples that "true philosophy" would "not be of much use" in their dealings with "the common lot of men *(vulgus hominum).*" Because it could not "be coaxed from the preconceptions of the intellect," it could not "lower itself (except through its utility and works) to the capacities of the multitude *(ad captum vulgi).*" In consequence, he suggested that its advocates "appear masked" and continue to "employ" the political and moral philosophy of the ancients where "convenient." One must, he explained, "deal with nature in one fashion and with the people in another."[40]

This was the procedure initially followed by all but Hobbes: Bacon's onetime amanuensis recognized that the "first grounds of all science are not only not beautiful, but poor, arid, and in appearance deformed"; quite early on, he expressed the hope that "wiser men" than he might "digest" his political "doctrine as to fit it better for a public teaching." And throughout he was mindful "how much greater thanks will be due than paid me, for telling men the truth of what men are."[41] But he nonetheless insisted on making visible the "first grounds" of his political science; and in doing so, he laid bare the foundations for the efforts of his colleagues as well. Years later, in the course of a dinner party conversation, Benjamin Franklin would sum up the common presumption in claiming that man is by nature "a tool-making animal."[42]

This claim—which has, as its corollaries, a denial that man is by nature a political animal equipped with a capacity for rational speech *(logos)* and deliberation concerning the advantageous, the just, and the good and an assertion that human reason is the slave or instrument of the passions—provides the foundation for the pretensions of the public intellectuals of the age of the Enlightenment. It is the doctrine that they deploy against their rivals the priests; it enables them to debunk all theological disputation; and it provides them with a justification for their attempt to revolutionize society and redirect it from the pursuit of salvation toward the conquest of nature. Those who, after Hobbes, digested his "doctrine as to fit it better for a public teaching" (with James Harrington and John Locke preeminent in their number) may have rendered it more palatable and practicable by disguising it somewhat in the manner advised by Bacon, by recasting what began as a defense of absolute monarchy into a doctrine of republican political architecture, by demonstrating that it sometimes dictates resistance and revolution rather than obedience, and by introducing a host of prudential considerations qualifying what could be seen as its doctrinaire potential—but, in doing so, they retained and elaborated its central presumption, for it provides the grounds for asserting that politics can be reduced to calculation and that theory can therefore ground practice.[43] It was this claim that Edmund Burke recognized to be at the heart of the project espoused by the public intellectuals, and it was this claim that he contested in his *Reflections on the Revolution in France.*

RATIONALISM IN POLITICS

Burke's most famous work is of particular value, for it is among the very first critical analyses of the new social type represented by the public intellectual. To grasp what Burke is up to, one must keep three facts in mind. First, despite what was once thought, John Locke's *Two Treatises of Government* never had a quasi-official status: it was one tract among the many that were published in the wake of the Glorious Revolution; it represented a viewpoint at odds with the dominant Whig and Tory interpretations of that event; and it was distinguished from virtually all contemporary tracts by its resolutely rationalist bent. Virtually all the other Whig defenders of the Revolution appealed not just to reason but to history as well. Second, the appeal to tradition was the distinctive feature of the 1689 Declaration of Rights: that official document embodied no concessions to geometrical politics at all.[44] And third, after the Sacheverell Trial and the Tory reaction that followed, the dominant wing of the Whig party in the eighteenth century turned its back on Lockean politics and took as a central feature of its policy the claim that the Glorious Revolution was a restoration of sorts, reaffirming the traditional liberties of the English and making modest adjustments in political institutions as a means of providing for their defense.

Burke took it as his task to defend the Revolution Settlement of 1688 and 1689 and the Court Whig interpretation of that event against those among Locke's radical Whig heirs who conceived of the French Revolution as an opportunity to transform England itself in accord with the dictates of Locke's argument.[45] In taking on Richard Price, the leading English Lockean apologist for the French Revolution, Burke found it necessary to indict the class of which he was a member. At the center of his argument lay the claim that 1789 was, despite all appearances to the contrary, a recapitulation of 1649 and that the public intellectuals of eighteenth-century France had displaced the clergy in more ways than one.

Burke was not the first to draw attention to the manner in which modern philosophy, embodying as it did a quest to reduce politics to an exact science, tended to reproduce in a slightly different form the sectarian civil strife that had so long bedeviled Christendom and that modern political science was intended to eliminate. Earlier in the eighteenth century, with an eye to the growing influence of Thomas Hobbes's disciple John Locke, David Hume had sounded a similar warning. Hume shared Locke's loathing for priestcraft and his predilection for moderated monarchy, commercial society, and progress in the arts. He celebrated the fact that "liberty of thinking, and of expressing our thoughts, is always fatal to priestly power, and to those pious frauds, on which it is commonly founded." He rejoiced that "most people, in this island, have divested themselves of all superstitious reverence to names and authority" so that "the clergy have much lost their credit: Their pretensions and doctrines have been ridiculed; and even religion can scarcely support itself in the world." In his essays and in his philosophical works, he did what he could to further propagate and deepen the corrosive skepticism evident in Locke's *Essay*, in his religious works, and in his contributions to the debate on toleration. Moreover, with the help of Adam Smith and the other luminaries of the Scottish Enlightenment, Hume sought to elaborate a new science of practical politics capable of bringing to an end the long reign of superstition and enthusiasm.[46] Locke's goals he wholeheartedly embraced. It was Locke's philosophical partisanship that he deplored.

Like Bacon, Hobbes, and Locke, Hume attributed Christianity's propensity to give rise to religious warfare to the marriage of pagan philosophy and faith. "Parties from *principle*," he wrote, "especially abstract speculative principle, are known only to modern times, and are, perhaps, the most extraordinary and unaccountable *phænomenon*, that has yet appeared in human affairs." The emergence of such parties was partly due to Christianity's original character as an insurgent religion independent of the Roman state and to the resulting separation of ecclesiastical and civil authority, but the deeper cause lay in the fact that,

> as philosophy was widely spread over the world, at the time when Christianity arose, the teachers of the new sect were obliged to form a system of speculative opinions; to divide, with some accuracy, their articles of faith; and to explain, comment, confute, and defend with all the subtilty of argument and science. Hence naturally arose keenness in dispute, when the Christian religion came to be split into new divisions and heresies: And this keenness assisted the priests in their policy of begetting a mutual hatred and antipathy among their deluded followers. Sects of philosophy, in the ancient world, were more zealous than parties of religion; but in modern times, parties of religion are more furious and enraged than the most cruel factions that ever arose from interest and ambition.

Hume feared that natural rights theory would have a similar effect. Because they honored man's capacity to exercise *logos*, the republics of ancient times had been "furious and tyrannical," and for much the same reason, traditional Christianity had given rise to sectarian parties "furious and enraged." In principle, Locke's adaptation of Hobbes's public teaching should have been free from this malady. It was profoundly skeptical in its foundations; it was grounded on a rejection of the ancient notion that man is by nature a political animal; and it was hostile to the concomitant assertion of the primacy of politics.[47] And yet, because it purported to confer on men—albeit by a new method of political analysis—a capacity to distinguish and make clear to others what is advantageous, just, and good, it evidenced a formidable propensity to engender fury, rage, and tyranny as well. In England, it promoted faction: for, to the extent that they succumbed to Locke's influence, the Whigs were a party opposed to the Tories on "abstract speculative principle," and the opposition between the old political theology and the new contract theory fed on itself. Abroad, the rigid, juridical rhetoric deployed in the *Two Treatises of Government* and popularized by Locke's many disciples threatened to give rise to a doctrinaire politics incompatible with the only species of political order possible in most societies and quite likely to force the relatively moderate monarchies of Europe to resort to tyrannical measures in self-defense.[48] David Hume was among the first to recognize the dangers inherent in the reign of what came to be called *ideology*.[49]

Consequently, in much the same fashion as his friend Montesquieu,[50] Hume attempts to restore a measure of prudence and "moderation" to political affairs. In this spirit, the Scot defends the legitimacy of "civilized monarchies" such as the one in France and insists that such polities "are found susceptible of order, method, and constancy to a surprizing degree. Property there is secure; industry encouraged; the arts flourish; and the prince lives secure among his subjects, like a father among his children." But if Hume asserts that "a civilized EUROPEAN monarchy" is "a government of Laws, not of Men," he nonetheless concedes that such polities receive "their chief stability from a superstitious reverence to priests and princes" and "have commonly abridged the liberty of reasoning with regard to religion, and politics, and consequently metaphysics and morals." There can then be no doubt that republics and governments like that of Great Britain are superior in "gentleness and stability" and give much more effective encouragement to "commerce" and industry by making them "honourable." If Hume denies that consent can generally be the foundation of government, he still acknowledges that it is "surely the best and most sacred of any."[51]

Moreover, in his *Treatise of Human Nature*, though Hume seems to dismiss "the suppos'sd state of nature" as "a mere philosophical fiction," he nonetheless asserts that the one rational motive men have for honoring justice and preserving society is to "keep themselves from falling into that wretched and savage condition, which is commonly represented as the state of nature." Like Locke, he traces the origins of government to man's "numberless wants and necessities," to "the slender means" that nature affords him in "relieving these necessities," to his "selfishness" and "partiality," and to the fact that the "avidity" he evidences for "acquiring goods and possessions" turns out to be "insatiable, perpetual, universal, and directly destructive of society." He gives primacy to the preservation of property, and he asserts that self-interest rightly understood is the only foundation for government that will stand up to the test of reason; he concedes the legitimacy of resistance against tyranny, and he neglects even to canvass the possibility that government exists to make men pious and faithful or noble and good. In short, Hume's critique amounts to a restatement of Locke's account of the origins and purpose of government—albeit in a nonjuridical, noncontractarian disguise intended to make it more conducive to the promotion of domestic tranquillity.[52]

Thus, in one chapter of his *History of England*, the Scots philosopher can denounce Locke's *Two Treatises of Government* and Algernon Sidney's quite similar *Discourses Concerning Government* as Whig "compositions the most despicable, both for style and matter," which "have been extolled, and propagated, and read; as if they had equalled the most celebrated remains of antiquity"; and in another, he can remark that, in the latter work, Sidney "had maintained principles, favorable indeed to liberty, but such as the best and most dutiful subjects in all ages have been known to embrace; the original contract, the source of power from a consent of the people, the lawfulness of resisting tyrants, the preference of liberty to the government of a single person."[53]

Burke occupied much the same ground as Hume and displayed precisely the same ambivalence regarding the new philosophy of rights. In confronting Richard Price, who was a Presbyterian minister, he hammered away at the dangers posed by "truly christian politicians" and their "pious designs," speaking with dismay of "apostolic missionaries" who had "quit their proper character to assume what does not belong to them" by "dogmatically" asserting a "political gospel" composed of "abstract principle." These men are, he said, "wholly unacquainted with the world in which they are so fond of meddling, and inexperienced in all its affairs, on which they pronounce with so much confidence." They know "nothing of politics but the passions they excite," and they have reintroduced into the political arena "after so long a discontinuance" the "pulpit style" of the mid-seventeenth century, which Burke regarded as "a novelty not wholly without danger." Price's sermon he looked on "as the public declaration of a man much connected with literary caballers, and intriguing philosophers; with political theologians, and theological politicians both at home and abroad."[54]

Burke juxtaposed prudence to principle, denying that he could "give praise or blame to any thing which relates to human actions, and human concerns, on a simple view of the object, as it stands stripped of every relation, in all the nakedness and solitude of metaphysical abstraction." It was, he insisted, "circumstances" which in reality give "to every political principle its distinguishing colour, and discriminating effect," which "render every civil and political scheme beneficial or noxious to mankind."[55] In the same context, he then juxtaposed the prudential politics of John Somers and the revolutionaries of 1688 to the principled politics of those who had beheaded Charles I in 1649: where principle is not adjusted to circumstances by statesmanship, he contended, "competence and power" will "soon be confounded, and no law be left but the will of a prevailing force."[56]

In France, where the revolutionaries "have industriously destroyed all the opinions, and prejudices, and . . . all the instincts which support government," the first "moment any difference arises" between the national assembly and any part of the nation, there will have to be "recourse to force." In time, then, there will be "rule by an army," for the assembly, which itself usurped the authority that it exercises, will lack the authority to control that army. "This weapon will snap short, unfaithful to the hand that employs it. The assembly keep a school where, systematically, and with unremitting perseverance, they teach principles, and form regulations destructive to all spirit of subordination, civil and military—and then they expect that they shall hold in obedience an anarchic people by an anarchic army." Already in

1790, Burke saw that France would be destined to have a Cromwell all its own.[57]

According to Burke, Lord Somers and the revolutionaries of 1688 took the opposite tack, subordinating "their theoretic science" to "practical wisdom," and preferring a "positive, recorded, *hereditary* title" to "that vague speculative right, which exposed their sure inheritance to be scrambled for and torn to pieces by every wild litigious spirit." Burke applauded the policy which the Court Whigs adopted after the Sacheverell Trial of treating the upheaval as an unfortunate necessity providing no precedent for future action, the stratagem they then devised of papering over the elements of discontinuity involved in replacing James II with William III, and the pretense they thereafter sustained that the rights which they asserted in 1688 and 1689 were, in fact, all inherited. This politic, if somewhat mendacious, depiction of the Glorious Revolution he regarded as "the result of profound reflection" or, rather, as "the happy effect of following nature, which is wisdom without reflection, and above it." In his judgment,

> a spirit of innovation is generally the result of a selfish temper and confined views. People will not look forward to posterity, who never look backward to their ancestors. Besides, the people of England well know, that the idea of inheritance furnishes a sure principle of transmission; without at all excluding a principle of improvement. It leaves acquisition free; but it secures what it acquires. Whatever advantages are obtained by a state proceeding on these maxims, are locked fast as in a sort of family settlement; grasped as in a kind of mortmain for ever. By a constitutional policy, working after the pattern of nature, we receive, we hold, we transmit our government and our privileges, in the same manner in which we enjoy and transmit our property and our lives.[58]

The disaster approaching in France he blamed on "the shallow speculations of the petulant, assuming, shortsighted coxcombs of philosophy." These last constituted "a new description of men . . . the political Men of Letters"—so "fond of distinguishing themselves," so "rarely averse to innovation," so much inclined to make "the extreme medicine of the constitution its daily bread," and so caught up "with their theories about the rights of man that they have totally forgot his nature."[59]

Burke did not deny the existence or even the significance of natural rights. His point was that "government is not made in virtue" of these natural rights, "which may and do exist in total independence of it; and exist in much greater clearness, and in a much greater degree of abstract perfection." His point was that "their abstract perfection is their practical defect." When men are told that they have "a right to every thing they want every thing." But since "government is a contrivance of human wisdom to provide for human *wants*," among which is "the want, out of civil society, of a sufficient restraint upon their passions," men cannot have everything. It is a prerequisite for society that "the inclinations of men should frequently be thwarted, their will controlled, and their passions brought into subjection," which can only be accomplished "*by a power out of themselves*; and not, in the exercise of its function, subject to that will and to those passions which it is its office to bridle and subdue." The details of this subjection must inevitably "vary with times and circumstances, and admit of infinite modifications" which "cannot be settled upon any abstract rule." In the end, these arrangements are "a matter of convenience," and this makes "the constitution of a state and the due distribution of its powers, a matter of the most delicate and complicated skill." In other words, statesmanship "requires a deep knowledge of human nature and human necessities."[60]

Burke's greatest objection to the public intellectuals is that they neither possess nor see the need for such knowledge. Instead, "they despise experience as the wisdom of unlettered men; and as for the rest, they have wrought under-ground a mine that will blow up at one grand explosion all examples of antiquity, all precedents, charters, and acts of parliament."

> They have "the rights of men." Against these there can be no prescription; against these no agreement is binding; these admit no temperament, and no compromise: any thing withheld from their full demand is so much of fraud and injustice. Against these their rights of men let no government look for security in the length of its continuance, or in the justice and lenity of its administration. The objections of these speculatists, if its forms do not quadrate with their theories, are as valid against such an old and beneficent government as against the most violent tyranny, or the greenest usurpation. They are always at issue with governments, not on a question of abuse, but a question of competency, and a question of title.[61]

Their rights are, he says, "pretended rights." They are "all extremes; and in proportion as they are metaphysically true, they are morally and politically false." In and under government, he contends, the rights of men are "their advantages; and these are often in balances between differences of good; in compromises sometimes between good and evil, and sometimes between evil and evil." He is perfectly willing to concede that "political reason is a computing principle." But he insists that it adds, subtracts, multiplies, and divides, "morally and not metaphysically or mathematically, true moral denominations." Hobbes's Platonist vision of a geometrically precise politics cannot be sustained. There is no substitute for "the first of all virtues," which is "prudence."[62] Theory cannot ground practice.

HINDSIGHT

Burke's observations ought to be sobering, for events soon justified what must have seemed at the time to be the fears of a hysteric; and with the benefit of hindsight and careful study, Alexis de Tocqueville would later confirm his Irish predecessor's analysis. There was, he saw, something peculiar about the public intellectuals of eighteenth-century France. French "writers" displayed an "intellectual brilliance which won them worldwide fame." But, in contrast with English writers, they played no "active part in public affairs," and there was not that salutary cooperation between theorists and practitioners that enabled "the former" to set forth "their new theories" which the latter could then amend or circumscribe "in the light of practical experience." Instead, French writers kept "aloof from the political arena"—so that, "in a nation teeming with officials none of the men of letters held posts of any kind, none was invested with authority," and "precept and practice were kept quite distinct." And yet, in contrast with their German counterparts, these French writers did not devote themselves to "*belles lettres* and pure philosophy." Instead, they evidenced a keen interest in and even "an obsession" with "all that concerned the government of nations," discussing at length "questions such as the origin of human society, its earliest forms, the original rights of citizens and of authority, the 'natural' and the 'artificial' relations between men, the legitimacy of custom, and even the whole conception of law."[63]

According to Tocqueville, what emerged was an "abstract, literary politics"; and although "the political programs" advocated by the exponents of this new politics varied greatly, "all these various systems stemmed from a single concept of a highly general order," which these authors took as "their premise before venturing on their personal, often somewhat eccentric solutions of the problem of good government." What they had in common was a propensity for "ringing changes on this one idea"—that "what was wanted was to replace the complex of traditional customs governing the social order of the day by simple, elementary rules deriving from the exercise of the human reason and natural law." Circumstance endowed them with this propensity: "as a result of the total absence of any political freedom, they had little acquaintance with the realities of public life," and they therefore "lacked the experience which might have tempered their enthusiasms." This same absence of freedom denied their compatriots ordinary channels of the sort enjoyed by their ancestors by which to seek a redress of grievances. In the absence of any other outlet, "political ferment was canalized into literature," and France's writers "become the leaders of public opinion," there being "no one . . . to dispute their right to leadership."

Thus alongside the traditional and confused, not to say chaotic, social system of the day there was gradually built up in men's minds an imaginary ideal society in which all was simple, uniform, coherent, equitable, and rational in the full sense of the term. It was this vision of the perfect State that fired the imagination of the masses and little by little estranged them from the here and now. Turning away from the real world around them, they indulged in dreams of a far better one and ended up by living, spiritually, in the ideal world thought up by the writers.

One result was that the French adopted "the instincts, the turn of mind, the tastes, and even the eccentricities characteristic of the literary man" and then imported "these literary propensities . . . into the political arena." This had consequences which were "nothing short of disastrous; for what is a merit in the writer may well be a vice in the statesman and the very qualities which go to make great literature can lead to catastrophic revolutions."[64]

No one need doubt that Burke and Tocqueville had it right. To test their claims, one need only study the career and writings of that exemplary figure the Marquis de Condorcet.[65] Moreover, their analysis is of more than merely historical interest because the project to reduce practice to theory is still very much with us. In our century, the aspiration to reduce politics to an exact science and the various futile attempts to make it conform to what predictably, in every case, turned out to be pseudoscience produced mayhem on a scale unimagined even by Burke, and no matter how terrible the events that took place, there were always intellectuals ready, willing, and able to enter the public arena as ideologues—providing excuses, rationalizations, and even full-scale, elaborated justifications for all that transpired.[66] With the end of the Cold War, the fervor for an extreme rationalism in politics has abated somewhat, and the public intellectual seems to be fading from the scene, even in France. His natural antagonist, the principled proponent of prudence—the Hume, the Burke, the Tocqueville, the Raymond Aron—is less in evidence as well. One would, however, be ill advised to assume that we have seen the last of the rage to reorder political, social, and economic relations in light of the dictates of theory. As its name suggests, postmodernism is an appendage. We still live within modernity, and the impulse exemplified by Thomas Hobbes is its central feature.

NOTES

1. Consider Plato *Republic* 7.519b–21a, with an eye to 6.485d and 9.591d–92b.
2. Plato *Republic* 6.494a. Unless otherwise indicated, all translations are my own.
3. See also Plato *Republic* 6.499b-c.
4. See Jacob Howland, "Rereading Plato: The Problem of Platonic Chronology," *Phoenix* 45 (1991): 189–214.
5. Cf. Plato *Phaedo* 99d4–100a8 and *Laws* 10.897d-e, with Xenophon *Memorabilia* 4.3.14, 7.7.
6. Elsewhere, another Platonic interlocutor intimates that such a community presupposes the rule of a god over gods or demigods: Plato *Laws* 4.713e–714a, 5.739a-e.
7. This question is reexamined in a series of dialogues—*Theaetetus*, *Cratylus*, *Sophist*, and *Statesman*—with dramatic dates situating them in close proximity to the trial of Socrates and is given much the same answer: see Jacob Howland, *The Paradox of Political Philosophy: Socrates' Philosophical Trial* (Lanham, Md.: Rowman & Littlefield, 1998).
8. Aristotle *Nicomachean Ethics* 1094b12–28.
9. Aristotle *Nicomachean Ethics* 1098a26–b4.
10. Consider Aristotle *Eudemian Ethics* 1216b26–1217a18, 1235b13–18, *Nicomachean Ethics* 1145b2–7 in conjunction with the famous claim of Eudemus recorded by Simplicius *De Caelo* 488.18–24 (Heiberg); and see Harold Cherniss, "The Philosophical Economy of the Theory of Ideas," *American Journal of Philology* 57 (1936): 445–56; G. E. L. Owen, "*Tithenai ta phainomena*," in Suzanne Mansion, ed.,

Aristotle et les problèmes de méthode (Louvain: Publications Universitaires, 1961), 83–103; and Martha Craven Nussbaum, "Saving Aristotle's Appearances," in *The Fragility of Goodness: Luck and Ethics in Greek Tragedy and Philosophy* (Cambridge: Cambridge University Press, 1986), 240–63.

11. Cf. Aristotle *Topics* 100a18–101b4 (esp. 100b21–23) with *Nicomachean Ethics* 1098b9–12, 27–31, 1145b2–7, 1153b25–28; *Eudemian Ethics* 1216b26–1217a18, 1235b13–18; *Politics* 1280a9–25, 1281a42–b38; *Rhetoric* 1355a14–18, 1361a25–27, 1398b20–1399a6, 1400a5–14; *Metaphysics* 993a30–b19. Note, in this connection, Aristotle's attitude regarding that which has been sanctioned by time: *Politics* 1264a1–10, *Metaphysics* 1074b1–15. The stated principle of Aristotle is entirely in keeping with the practice of Socrates in the Platonic dialogues. In this connection, one should consider the significance of Socrates' "taking refuge in rational speech (*logous*)": cf. Plato *Phaedo* 96a–100b, with *Republic* 5.473a, and see *Laws* 12.950b-c; note *Politicus* 262a–263b; and see Leo Strauss, *The Political Philosophy of Hobbes: Its Basis and Its Genesis* (Chicago: University of Chicago Press, 1952), 142–45; Ronna Burger, *The Phaedo: A Platonic Labyrinth* (New Haven: Yale University Press, 1984), 135–60; and Seth Benardete, *Socrates' Second Sailing: On Plato's Republic* (Chicago: University of Chicago Press, 1989).

12. *Redargutio philosophiarum*, in *The Works of Francis Bacon*, ed. James Spedding, Robert Leslie Ellis, and Douglas Denon Heath (London: Spedding, Ellis & Heath, 1857–74), 3:562.

13. Consider René Descartes, *Discours de la méthode* 1–6, and *La recherche de la vérité par la lumière naturelle*, in Descartes, *Oeuvres et lettres*, ed. André Bridoux (Paris: Bibliothéque de la Pléiade, 1953), 125–79, 879–901, with an eye to *Discoveries and Opinions of Galileo*, trans. Stillman Drake (Garden City, N.Y.: Doubleday, 1957), 237–38, 273–79.

14. Thomas Hobbes, *The Elements of Law Natural and Politic*, ed. Ferdinand Tönnies, 2d ed. (London: Frank Cass, 1969), 1.13.3. For the manner in which the work done by Descartes and Hobbes on the optical foundations of vision shaped not only their understanding of matter as extension but also their understanding of human nature as a form of subjectivity, consider Hiram Caton, "On the Basis of Hobbes's Political Philosophy," *Political Studies* 22 (1974): 414–31, in light of Alan E. Shapiro, "Kinematic Optics: A Study of the Wave Theory of Light in the Seventeenth Century," *Archive for History of the Exact Sciences* 11 (1973): 134–266; and see Richard Tuck, "Optics and Sceptics: The Philosophical Foundations of Hobbes's Political Thought," in Edmund Leites, ed., *Conscience and Casuistry in Early Modern Europe* (Cambridge: Cambridge University Press, 1988), 235–63. It makes no difference whether Hobbes was the author of the *Short Tract on First Principles* or not: Richard Tuck, "Hobbes and Descartes," in G. A. J. Rogers and Alan Ryan, eds., *Perspectives on Thomas Hobbes* (Oxford: Clarendon, 1988), 11–42.

15. The critical fact about geometry is that it never gives rise to sectarianism: note Thomas Hobbes, *Leviathan*, ed. C. B. Macpherson (Harmondsworth, U.K.: Penguin, 1968), 4.46.11 (686); and *Six Lessons to the Professors of the Mathematics*, in *The English Works of Thomas Hobbes of Malmesbury*, ed. Sir William Molesworth (London: J. Bohn, 1839–45), 7:346. To make it easy for readers to find the pertinent passages in *Leviathan*, I cite the part and chapter numbers provided by Hobbes; the paragraph numbers added by Edwin Curley in Thomas Hobbes, *Leviathan*, ed. Edwin Curley (Indianapolis: Hackett, 1994); and finally, in parenthesis, the pertinent pages of the Macpherson edition. Hobbes agreed with Descartes in supposing that man's capacity

to achieve certainty in geometry is rooted in the fact that his knowledge is dependent on introspection alone: note Hobbes *Elements of Law* 1.5.14, *Leviathan* Introduction 3–4 (82–83) with 1.2.1 (87), and *Concerning Body* 1.6.7, in Hobbes *English Works* 1:73–75. For Hobbes's dedication to geometry and for his admiration of Descartes's capacities as a mathematician, see John Aubrey, *'Brief Lives,' chiefly of Contemporaries, set down by John Aubrey, between the Years 1669 & 1696*, ed. Andrew Clark (Oxford: Clarendon, 1898), 1:222, 332–33, 367.

16. Descartes denied that he was the book's author and added that "he would never publish anything on Morals." See Letter from Samuel Sorbière to Thomas de Martel on 1 February 1643, in Thomas Hobbes, *De Cive: The Latin Version*, ed. Howard Warrender (Oxford: Clarendon, 1983), 300.

17. *Redargutio philosophiarum*, in *The Works of Francis Bacon*, 3:562. Note *Novum Organum* Praef., in *The Works of Francis Bacon*, 1:153 (translated at 4:42).

18. Letter from Descartes to Mersenne in April 1634, in *Oeuvres de Descartes*, ed. Charles Adam and Paul Tannery (Paris: J. Vrin, 1964–1974), 1:284–91. For the Latin tag, see Ovid *Tr.* 3.4.25. Cf. Letter from Friedrich Nietzsche to Georg Brandes on 2 December 1887, in Friedrich Nietzsche, *Werke*, ed. Karl Schlechta (Munich: Carl Hanser Verlag, 1966), 3:1272. Initially, when he learned of Galileo's condemnation, Descartes had wanted to burn all his papers "or at least not let anyone see them." Regarding the doctrine for which Galileo was condemned—the claim that the earth actually moves—Descartes wrote, "I confess that if it is false, all the foundations of my philosophy are also. . . . It is so tied up with all the parts of my treatise *Le Monde* that I would not know how to detach it from the treatise without rendering the rest entirely defective." See Letter from Descartes to Mersenne at the end of November 1633, in Descartes, *Oeuvres et lettres*, 947–48. Descartes alerts his readers to the danger he faces by alluding to the Galileo case in the initial paragraph of the sixth part of his *Discourse on Method*; there, of course, he casts his own reticence in a somewhat less self-serving light: Descartes, *Oeuvres et lettres*, 167–68.

19. Conversation with Frans Burman on 16 April 1648, in *Oeuvres de Descartes*, 5:159.

20. Descartes, *Discours de la méthode* 3, in Descartes, *Oeuvres et lettres*, 141.

21. For his reticence, Descartes gives a second reason as well, but his claim to believe "that involvement in regulating the mores of others belongs to Sovereigns alone or to those who are authorized by them" is rendered suspect by the first reason he gives. See Letter from Descartes to Chanut on 20 November 1647, in *Oeuvres de Descartes*, 5:86–88. In the *Discourse on Method*, Descartes is similarly disingenuous. In one passage, he compares his project with the work of a legislator like Lycurgus: 2 (Descartes, *Oeuvres et lettres*, 132–35). In another, he first expresses his disapproval of "those of turbulent and restless humor who, though called to the management of public affairs neither by birth nor fortune, nonetheless never fail to have always in mind some new reformation." Then he asserts that his "design has never extended beyond trying to reform" his "own thoughts" and indicates that he would regret having published the work if it were to justify in any respect the suspicion that he had in mind "the folly" of some such reformation: 2 (Descartes, *Oeuvres et lettres*, 135). But, in the end, in the very last part of the treatise, Descartes announces a program of reform far more radical than anything that could be attributed to the legendary Spartan legislator: 6 (Descartes, *Oeuvres et lettres*, 167–79).

22. Cf. *Decameron physiologicum*, in Hobbes *English Works* 7:77, with *Leviathan* 4.46.42 (703); and see Thomas Hobbes, *Behemoth, or The Long Parliament*, ed. Ferdinand Tönnies, 2d ed. (New York: Barnes & Noble, 1969), 95–96; and *De cive* 2.10.3 n.

23. Hobbes *Leviathan* 4.46.13 (688).

24. Cf. *Lux mathematica* Ep. Ded., in *Thomas Hobbes Malmesburiensis opera philosophica quae Latine scripsit omnia in unum corpus*, ed. William Molesworth (London: J. Bohn, 1839–45), 5:92, with *De homine* 14.13, in Hobbes *Opera philosophica* 2:119.

25. Hobbes *Leviathan* 3.37.10–12 (474–75); 4.44.1 (627–28); 47.20 (712).

26. Hobbes *Elements of Law* Ep. Ded.; and *Leviathan* 1.15.41 (216–17). Hobbes would later deny that "Civil Philosophy" is "older . . . than my own book *De Cive*." See *Concerning Body* Ep. Ded., in Hobbes *English Works* 1:vii–xii. See also *A Minute or first Draught of the Optiques*, in Hobbes *English Works* 7:471. For the possibility of achieving progress in the science of politics, see *Leviathan* 2.30.5 (377–78).

27. Cf. Hobbes *De homine* 10.5, in Hobbes *Opera philosophica*, 2:93–94; and *Six Lessons to the Professors of the Mathematics* Ep. Ded., in Hobbes *English Works* 7:184, with Aristotle *Nicomachean Ethics* 1094b10–1095a14. Consider Hobbes *Elements of Law* 1.6.1, 8.3, *De cive* Ep. Ded. [6], Praef. [9], [19], 3.17.28, 18.4, *Leviathan* 1.5.17 (115), 7.1–7 (130–34), 12.8 (171), 2.20.19 (261), 30.25 (392), 4.46.1–6 (682–83), in light of *Concerning Body* 4.25.1, 26.11 (at the end), 30.15 (at the end), in Hobbes *English Works* 1:387–89, 444, 531. On this question, see Leo Strauss, *Natural Right and History* (Chicago: University of Chicago Press, 1974), 169–74. See also Arthur Child, *Making and Knowing in Hobbes, Vico, and Dewey* (Berkeley: University of California Press, 1953), 271–310 (esp. 271–83), and Richard Ashcraft, "Ideology and Class in Hobbes's Political Theory," *Political Theory* 6 (1978): 27–62 (esp. 33–41). It should be clear from the hypothetical character of man's knowledge of the natural world that Hobbes's political vision can in no way depend on his mechanical conception of nature; both are, in fact, derivative from the same root: Hobbes's conviction that reason is enslaved to desire, and his conclusion that man can therefore understand the universe and everything within it (himself included) only in terms of cause and effect. See Michael Oakeshott, "Introduction to *Leviathan*," in *Hobbes on Civil Association* (Berkeley: University of California Press, 1975), 15–28. One might even say that Hobbes's philosophy—civil and natural alike—is nothing more than an elaboration of the implications of this doctrine.

28. Cf. Plato *Republic* 7.519c-521a, 540d-e, with 9.591d-592b: the establishment of such a city could result only from "divine chance"; philosophers concerned solely with "their own city" would certainly have no motive for bothering themselves with such a task.

29. Cf. Hobbes *Leviathan* 2.29.1 (363–64), 30.5 (378), 31.41 (407–8), with *Behemoth* 70–71. Hobbes divided his *Leviathan* into four parts and underlined the importance of his statement concerning the possibility of converting "this Truth of Speculation, into the Utility of Practice" by placing it at the very end of the second part—which is to say, as close as possible to the boundary marking the book's center. Consider David Johnston, "Plato, Hobbes, and the Science of Practical Reasoning," in Mary G. Dietz, ed., *Thomas Hobbes and Political Theory* (Lawrence: University Press of Kansas, 1990), 37–54.

30. See, for example, Hobbes *Leviathan* 1.12.31 (182), 2.21.8–9 (267–68), 4.44–47 (esp. 46.11–37 [686–700]). See also Hobbes *Elements of Law* 2.6.9, 9.8. On this point, see Shirley Robin Letwin, "Hobbes and Christianity," *Daedalus* 105 (1976): 1–21.

31. See Hobbes *Leviathan* 1.1–3 (esp. 3.4 [95–96]), 8.14–16 (139). In this connection, see Jeffrey Barnouw, "Hobbes's Causal Account of Sensation," *Journal of the History of Philosophy* 18 (1980): 115–30.

32. See Hobbes *Leviathan* Introduction 3 (82–83), 1.4.24 (109–10), 11.1 (160–61), 15.40 (216–17). See also *Elements of Law* 1.5.1–14, 7.3, 6–7, and *De homine* 11.11–15, in Hobbes *Opera philosophica* 2:100–103.

33. Hobbes *Leviathan* 1.3.4–5 (96).

34. See Paul A. Rahe, "The Primacy of Politics in Classical Greece," *American Historical Review* 89 (1984): 265–93.

35. See *Leviathan* 1.6.35 (124). See also 1.5.6–7 (113–14), 12.1–5 (168–69), 4.46.1–2 (682). One should read Hobbes *Elements of Law* 1.3.1–5.4 in light of 1.9.18. In one place, the preeminent twentieth-century student of the subject identifies this claim as "the simple leading thought of Hobbes's teaching about man"; in another, he speaks of it as "the nerve of Hobbes's argument." One should read Leo Strauss, "On the Basis of Hobbes's Political Philosophy," in *What Is Political Philosophy?* (New York: Free Press, 1959), 170–96 (esp. 176 n. 2), in light of Strauss, *Hobbes politische Wissenschaft* (Neuwied am Rhein: Hermann Luchterhand Verlag, 1965) 8; and *Natural Right and History*, vii.

36. Hobbes *Leviathan* 1.8.13–16 (139), 11.1 (160–61), 12.1–6 (168–70), and *Elements of Law* 1.8.3. See 1.9.18. In this regard, Hobbesian and Cartesian introspection are indistinguishable: see Annette Baier, "The Idea of the True God in Descartes," in Amélie Oksenberg Rorty, ed., *Essays on Descartes's Meditations* (Berkeley: University of California Press, 1986), 359–87.

37. Hobbes *Leviathan* 1.11.2 (160–61); and *Elements of Law* 1.8.4.

38. Hobbes *Elements of Law* 1.9.1–21 (esp. 1 and 21); *De cive* 1.1.5, 12; *Leviathan* 1.13.4–6 (185); 2.17.8 (226); *Decameron Physiologicum*, in Hobbes, *English Works*, 7:73. See *Elements of Law* 1.7.7, 9.19, 16.11, 2.8.3; *De cive* 3.15.13; and *De homine* 11.11–15, in Hobbes *Opera philosophica* 2:100–103. If Hobbes gives human vanity less prominence in *Leviathan*, his reasons are rhetorical rather than philosophical. It is not because he is beginning to doubt whether vanity is the root of man's contentiousness: in fact, in *Leviathan* (2.17.6–12 [225–26]), and there only, he traces the pursuit of material goods, a pursuit that sets men at odds, to the fact that "man . . . can relish nothing but what is eminent." If, in *Leviathan*, Hobbes to some extent emphasizes gain at the expense of vainglory, it is because he is eager to draw the attention of his readers away from the ambitions that they will have to abandon for the sake of peace to the commodities that they will have access to thereby. Cf. F. S. McNeilly, *The Anatomy of Leviathan* (London: Macmillan, 1968), 137–72, with William Mathie, "Reason and Rhetoric in Hobbes's *Leviathan*," *Interpretation* 14 (1986): 281–98 (esp. 292–98).

39. Cf. Hobbes *Leviathan* 1.11.2 (161), 13.9 (186), 2.18.20 (238) with 1.14 (189–201), 2.17.13 (227–28), 28.27 (362–63). The virtual certainty that death will come through defeat makes the prospect intolerable: see Michael Oakeshott, "Introduction to *Leviathan*," 34 (esp. n. 59).

40. *Redargutio Philosophiarum*, in *The Works of Francis Bacon*, 3:562–63.

41. Hobbes *Leviathan* 2.18.9 (233); *Concerning Body* Ep. Ded., 1.1.1; and *Six Lessons to the Professors of the Mathematics*, in Hobbes *English Works* 1:vi–xii, 1–3, 7:335–36 (with 344–45).

42. *Boswell's Life of Johnson*, ed. George Birkbeck Hill (Oxford: Clarendon, 1887), 3:245: 7 April 1778. This passage caught the keen eye of Karl Marx; see *Das Kapital: Kritik der politischen Ökonomie* (Frankfurt: Verlag Ullstein, 1969–71), 1:289 n. 13. See also 1:150.

43. See Paul A. Rahe, *Republics Ancient and Modern: Classical Republicanism and the American Revolution* (Chapel Hill: University of North Carolina Press, 1992), 364–541. In this connection, note also Paul A. Rahe, "Antiquity Surpassed: The Repudiation of Classical Republicanism," in David Wootton, ed., *Republicanism, Liberty, and Commercial Society: 1649–1776* (Stanford: Stanford University Press, 1994), 233–69.

44. See Michael P. Zuckert, *Natural Rights and the New Republicanism* (Princeton: Princeton University Press, 1994).

45. This is even more evident in Burke, "An Appeal from the New to the Old Whigs" (1791), in *The Writings and Speeches of the Right Honourable Edmund Burke* (Boston: Little, Brown, 1901), 4:57–215.

46. See David Hume, "Whether the British Government Inclines More to Absolute Monarchy, or to a Republic," "Of Parties in General," "Of the Parties of Great Britain," and "Of Superstition and Enthusiasm," in Hume, *Essays Moral, Political, and Literary*, ed. Eugene F. Miller (Indianapolis: Liberty, 1985), 47–79 (esp. 51, 65–66), 611–19; and see James Farr, "Political Science and the Enlightenment of Enthusiasm," *American Political Science Review* 82 (1988): 51–69.

47. After reading Rahe, *Republics Ancient and Modern*, 28–54 and 364–98, see 445–520.

48. Consider Hume, "Of the Social Contract," "Of Passive Obedience," and "Of the Coalition of Parties," in Hume, *Essays Moral, Political, and Literary*, 465–501, in light of "Of Parties in General," in Hume, *Essays Moral, Political, and Literary*, 60–63, and note "Of Civil Liberty," in Hume, *Essays Moral, Political, and Literary*, 88. In this connection, see Donald W. Livingston, *Hume's Philosophy of Common Life* (Chicago: University of Chicago Press, 1984); "Hume's Conception of True Religion," in *Hume's Philosophy of Religion: The Sixth James Montgomery Hester Seminar* (Winston-Salem, N.C.: Wake Forrest University Press, 1986), 33–73; and "David Hume: Ambassador from the World of Learning to the World of Conversation," *Political Science Reviewer* 18 (1988): 35–84.

49. See Mark Goldie, "Ideology," in Terence Ball, James Farr, and Russell L. Hanson, eds., *Political Innovation and Conceptual Change* (Cambridge: Cambridge University Press, 1989), 266–91.

50. See Paul A. Rahe, "Forms of Government: Structure, Principle, Object, and Aim," in *Montesquieu's Science of Politics: Essays on the Spirit of Laws*, ed. David W. Carrithers, Michael A. Mosher, and Paul A. Rahe (Lanham, Md.: Rowman & Littlefield, 2001), 69–108.

51. See Hume, "Of Civil Liberty," "Of the Rise and Progress of the Arts and Sciences," and "Of the Social Contract," in Hume, *Essays Moral, Political, and Literary*, 87–96, 111–37 (esp. 115–54), 465–87.

52. David Hume, *A Treatise of Human Nature*, ed. L. A. Selby-Bigge (Oxford: Clarendon, 1888), 3.2.2–10. In this connection, see Duncan Forbes, *Hume's Philosophical Politics* (Cambridge: Cambridge University Press, 1975), 91–101, 125–92; Martyn P. Thompson, "Hume's Critique of Locke and the 'Original Contract,'" *Il Pensiero Politico* 10 (1977): 189–201; James Coniff, "Hume on Political Parties: The Case for Hume as Whig," *Eighteenth Century Studies* 12 (1978–79): 150–73; David Miller, *Philosophy and Ideology in Hume's Political Thought* (Oxford: Clarendon, 1981), 19–98; and David Gauthier, "David Hume—Contractarian," *Philosophical Review* 88 (1982): 3–38.

53. Cf. David Hume, *The History of England* (New York: Harper, 1878), 6:365–66 (chap. 70), with 6:271 (chap. 69). Note also "New Hume Letters to Lord Elibank, 1748–1766," ed. Ernest Campbell Mossner, *Texas Studies in Literature and Language* 4 (1962): 431–60 (at 437–38): 8 January 1748.

54. See Edmund Burke, *Reflections on the Revolution in France*, in Edmund Burke, *Reflections on the Revolution in France* and Thomas Paine, *The Rights of Man* (Garden City, N.Y.: Doubleday, 1961), 17–27.

55. Burke, *Reflections*, 19.

56. Burke, *Reflections*, 32.

57. Burke, *Reflections*, 238–43.

58. Burke, *Reflections*, 44–46.

59. Burke, *Reflections*, 64, 75, 77, 124.

60. Burke, *Reflections*, 72–74.

61. Burke, *Reflections*, 71.

62. Burke, *Reflections*, 75.

63. Alexis de Tocqueville, *The Old Regime and the French Revolution*, trans. Stuart Gilbert (Garden City, N.Y.: Doubleday, 1955), 138, 145–46.

64. Tocqueville, *The Old Regime and the French Revolution*, 139–47.

65. See Keith Michael Baker, *Condorcet: From Natural Philosophy to Social Mathematics* (Chicago: University of Chicago Press, 1975).

66. In this connection, see Aleksandr L. Solzhenitsyn, *The Gulag Archipelago: An Experiment in Literary Investigation* (New York: Harper & Row, 1973–78), 1:173–75.

4

Rousseau's Critique of the Public Intellectual in the Age of the Enlightenment

Christopher Kelly

If the word *public* is emphasized in the term "public intellectual," which is the theme of this volume, we must grant Rousseau a central position because he was the first intellectual to perfect the art of being a celebrity. He wrote works that reached an unprecedented popular audience. For example, as soon as it appeared, *Julie* was quite simply the most popular novel that had ever been written, reprinted more than a hundred times in less than forty years. Among the byproducts of the fame deriving from this and other works was a very powerful public image of their author. Rousseau received an enormous quantity of fan mail from adoring readers who felt a personal relationship with a writer whom they felt had put onto paper their own deepest feelings and aspirations. They named their children after him and the characters in his books, just as sports fans name their children after athletes and presidents of the United States name their children after popular songs. Shortly after his death Rousseau's image even appeared on playing cards. In short, he is in some sense the prototype for the modern celebrity, whether intellectual or not.

At the same time Rousseau is also the most private of intellectuals. Unlike the ancient Socrates, who said at his trial that he spent his whole life in public, the modern Socrates says that (after an initial mistake that brought him into the public eye) he spent his whole life trying to escape it. He is the author of the *Reveries of a Solitary Walker,* which he said was written for himself alone. There is no contradiction between these two aspects of Rousseau's career. In fact they are the two sides of a single coin. One of the most compelling things about Rousseau is his ability to invest the most private events with universal significance and make every public issue into a personal dilemma.

One personal aspect of Rousseau's life that took on a great public significance was the series of bitter quarrels he had with other intellectuals. He fought with people like Grimm, Diderot, Hume, d'Holbach, d'Alembert, and Voltaire; in short with the vanguard of the Enlightenment in the eighteenth century. These quarrels became public events because the partisans of the Enlightenment shared with Rousseau the perception that public opinion could become a potential force in the world and the desire to shape this new force. Each of the participants in these quarrels rushed to present his case in a published or widely circulated open letter or pamphlet. They mobilized public opinion so successfully that their defenses engendered an additional host of letters and pamphlets supporting one side or the other.[1]

Anyone who reveres the intellectual life who examines these quarrels must be dismayed by the petty vindictiveness, refusal to tolerate differences of opinion, outright paranoia, and unscrupulous actions that characterized them. In this regard the intellectual quarrels of the eighteenth century hardly differ from those with which we are familiar today. Nevertheless, if we can move beyond mere indulgence in gossip about famous people or, at least, if we try to learn from such gossip as we indulge in it, we can see that fundamental issues lay at the base of these quarrels. Without denying the personal side of these bitter clashes, I would like to clarify the extent to which they concerned which vision of the public intellectual would predominate. I will focus on Rousseau's stormy relations with Voltaire, Diderot, and d'Alembert in the hope of showing that they illustrate well-considered alternatives on the issues of individual responsibility, partisanship, and intellectual independence: issues that must always be central to consideration of the public intellectual.

NAMING NAMES

A series of entanglements between Rousseau and Voltaire around questions of anonymity, false attributions, and naming names offers a prime example of the mixture of bitterly personal and generally significant issues.[2] It began with a prank played by Voltaire shortly after Rousseau fled from France in 1762 following the condemnation of *Emile*. Among the many people who wrote to Rousseau to express admiration and seek spiritual guidance was a pious woman who had been impressed by the "Profession of Faith of the Savoyard Vicar." Not knowing where he had settled and believing in the solidarity of men of letters, she addressed her letter to Rousseau in care of Voltaire, who responded by sending her a copy of a scandalous antireligious work he had published anonymously the year before and had publicly denied writing. Because he did not indicate whom the pamphlet was from, the astonished woman assumed that Rousseau had sent it and may have thought that he was its author. Reassuring her caused him a certain amount of trouble at a difficult time.

Rousseau retaliated when he published the *Letters Written from the Mountain* some months later. There Rousseau put into Voltaire's mouth a speech in which the latter admits that he was the author of the very work he had sent to the pious woman. Voltaire reacted with total rage. While his opinion of Rousseau had never been high, he now decided that the author of the *Letters Written from the Mountain* was not only insane, but also a traitor of the worst sort, or as he sometimes put it, a modern Judas. To the terms of ridicule Voltaire had frequently used in referring to Rousseau he now added the new one of police informer *(délateur)*. Not satisfied with accusing Rousseau of being an informer, he decided to become one himself and took the remarkable step for a champion of toleration of writing to Genevan authorities implying that they should sentence Rousseau to death in absentia because of his failure to be an orthodox Christian. In fact, there is no reason to believe that Voltaire seriously wished to have Rousseau executed. Nevertheless, he did want him to be publicly discredited. Within days he also published (anonymously of course) a pamphlet in which he revealed personal secrets about Rousseau, told half-truths, and fabricated scandalous stories. Eventually, after Rousseau settled in England, Voltaire struck again with the *Lettre de M. de Voltaire au Docteur Jean-Jacques Pansophe*.[3] When Rousseau's complaint against this work was made public, Voltaire published a denial that he was its author and accused Rousseau of being a liar for attributing it to him.

Both Rousseau and Voltaire behaved very consistently throughout this sequence of events. On the one hand, in a book published under his own name Rousseau named Voltaire as the author of a work that the latter had in fact written. On the other hand, Voltaire consistently denied writing works he had written and was eager to have them attributed to others. While it might be tempting to dismiss this lamentable comedy by referring to Rousseau's characteristic paranoia and Voltaire's typical vindictiveness, we should not embrace a picture of a rather naive Rousseau in contrast to a sophisticated Voltaire. Behind their behavior lies a profound disagreement about authorship and anonymity and their relation to responsibility. In fact each of them had a well-considered view of the social responsibility of authors arrived at through careful reflection on the circumstances in which they found themselves. In fact, contemporary writers such as d'Alembert and Diderot also were compelled to reflect deeply about their own position in the world and each arrived at a different strategy for combining safety and effectiveness. D'Alembert, for example, wrote an *Essai sur la société des gens de lettres et des grands* analyzing many of the same problems identified by Rousseau and Voltaire.[4]

To an American in the twenty-first century Voltaire's behavior requires more of an explanation than Rousseau's does. This is so because we tend to regard it as natural for an author's name to appear on a book. In fact, however, Voltaire was simply one of the most conspicuous examples of a rather common practice. Most of the seminal works of the Enlightenment, including works by Descartes, Spinoza, Locke, Hume, Montesquieu, and Diderot, were published anonymously. Concealment of one's identity (or at least what we could call preserving deniability) was accepted as one of the conditions of authorship, even in the comparatively liberal climate in which Rousseau began his literary career.[5]

Voltaire, who had spent time in the Bastille and narrowly escaped other jail terms, regularly used pseudonyms, false attributions, and anonymity. Not only did he issue statements denying authorship of books he had in fact written, he also made denials to friends so that they would spread the lie without knowing that they were doing so. While Voltaire was the most expert practitioner of this type of behavior, he was far from the only one. He incessantly counseled his followers that "one must never give anything under one's name."[6] His outrage at Rousseau's public breach of his anonymity indicates his belief in the possible danger in spite of the fact that his authorship of the works in question was a fairly open secret. It should be noted that Rousseau does not seem to have thought that he was putting Voltaire into any danger (any more than Voltaire subsequently really tried to have Rousseau executed for impiety) and that, in fact, there were no repercussions for Voltaire. On the other side, however, it should also be noted that Voltaire's fearfulness was the outcome of a lifetime of hard lessons about the vulnerability of authors. He regarded Rousseau's openness as both imprudent and wickedly irresponsible.

In correspondence with Helvétius, Voltaire explained his reasons for his policy clearly. He insisted that, far from any disharmony between devotion to truth and concern for one's own safety, service to enlightenment depends on attending to one's own interest.[7] Enlightenment will be served well only if it wins and the strength of its opponents depends on their influence with the powerful. To undermine this influence one must make opponents look ridiculous through satire and even libelous attacks. This policy obviously runs the risk of running afoul of the censors or prosecutors. Moreover, one's own reputation can suffer if one is known as the author of such works. Voltaire's analysis leads directly to his avowed maxim, "Strike and conceal your hand."[8] In sum, in the face of repression, anonymity is required for both safety and effectiveness in the cause of Enlightenment.

In Rousseau's view every part of Voltaire's analysis is wrong. Under the influence of Diderot who had just been released from a prison term brought about by his own writing, Rousseau had commenced by publishing the *First Discourse* anonymously. As he became famous, however, he started to reflect on all aspects of his celebrity[9] and decided to use his fame to set an example of behavior. Thenceforth he never published anonymously. In contrast to Voltaire and his indignant denials, Rousseau obsessively set the record straight, publicly owning even works that had been published without his permission. Thus Rousseau is responsible for bringing to the fore the public role of the author.[10] He explained his decision to put his name on title pages by saying, "Every honorable man must acknowledge the books he publishes."[11] Given the implication that other writers (such as Voltaire and Diderot but also, for example, Descartes, Spinoza, Hume) were dishonorable, it is no wonder that Voltaire and others understood Rousseau's policy of naming names as a declaration of war.

Rousseau spelled out his position on numerous occasions. He claims that only two types of authors thrive in the current system: those who flatter the prejudices of the powerful and those who hide behind anonymity. It is obvious that truthfulness cannot be expected from the first type of writer,[12] but Rousseau is no more hopeful about the second. The sort of boldness that derives from a concern for protecting oneself is not likely to be disinterested. In a thinly veiled reference to Voltaire in the *Letters Written from the Mountain,* Rousseau says that these cowards use anonymity to give vent to "the poison of calumny and satire."[13] Rather than inspire boldness in expressing the truth, the shield provided by anonymity allows the freedom to pursue personal vendettas with impunity. For both officially approved and anonymous writers, the system of censorship promotes irresponsibility, hypocrisy, self-seeking, and venom. Only "clumsy" and "imprudent" authors like Rousseau who put their names on their books ruin the charade.[14]

While Voltaire justified anonymity as combining effectiveness with safety, Rousseau names himself as an author in order to combine effectiveness with responsibility. Anonymous authors could object that such a project reduced both because it makes the censors more diligent and gives them an easy target. Thus Voltaire could alternately attack Rousseau for imprudently endangering the cause of philosophy and for hypocritically making concessions to established religion in order to see his name in print. Rousseau can respond that the success of his books owes much to his *persona* as an author in that the presence of his name on books made readers flock to them because their author embodied boldness in defying injustice.[15] Rousseau spends so much time justifying himself because he makes it impossible to separate his books from their author. In the end he was able to make himself into a symbol of all victims of oppression in the way that those who published anonymously while living safely in high society could not.

THE CITIZEN AND THE PHILOSOPHER

My first story was about names; the second is about nicknames. The first of two disputes that precipitated the rupture between Rousseau and his closest friend and literary associate, Diderot, concerns the question of whether either one of them was entitled to his nickname. Rousseau was familiarly addressed as "Citizen," a title that he regularly used on his works. Diderot was known to his friends as "Philosopher," or sometimes as "Plato" or anagrammatically as "Tonpla." These nicknames encapsulated the public persona of each, a commitment to civic republicanism, and a commitment to intellectual life, respectively.

When Diderot sent Rousseau a copy of his recently published play *The Natural Son*, Rousseau took great offense at the line "Only the wicked man is alone," which he took as a public rebuke of his decision to leave Paris for a life in the country. One could attribute this reaction to Rousseau's hypersensitivity, and Diderot seems to have received his friend's complaint in this light.[16] He responded with a rather breezy dismissal and the reassurance that Rousseau is the one hermit whom he would clear of this charge. Nonetheless, there is reason to believe that Rousseau's conviction that Diderot had intended the application to his friend was not a mere misunderstanding.

Numerous commentators have seen a resemblance between the temperament and opinions of Rousseau and those of the character Dorval, to whom the remark is made. Also, the speech containing the offending statement refers to "unfortunates waiting for a father" who will not be rescued if Dorval abandons them, which could be taken as a reference to Rousseau's decision to put his children into a foundling hospital. As the title of the play indicates, one of its major themes is illegitimate birth. Moreover, the speech in question argues that people of unusual talents have a particular obligation to use those talents for the good of society, an obligation they cannot fulfill if they remove themselves from society.[17] Finally, in the letter answering Rousseau's complaint Diderot repeats this argument, pointing out the possible harm to others coming from Rousseau's retirement. He concludes the letter by saying, "Farewell Citizen! Nevertheless a hermit makes a very peculiar citizen."[18] Thus Diderot questions Rousseau's title to the nickname on which he prided himself.

Rousseau responded by citing the good he did for his neighbors in the country and concluded, "You are amusing, you philosophers, when you regard all the inhabitants of the cities as the only men to whom your duties connect you. It is in the country that one learns to love and serve humanity: one learns only to despise it in the cities."[19] Those like Diderot who commit themselves to the society of large cities are poor philosophers in that they fail to understand humanity as a whole, which leads them to the moral failing of despising it. It is, then, Diderot rather than Rousseau who betrays his nickname because he substitutes a spurious combination of philosophy and sociability for the genuine version of either.

The issue here concerns the ancient problem of how moral and intellectual virtue can be combined. Diderot's nickname conceals the fact that he offers a new solution to the problem or denies that it really exists. We can most easily grasp this new position, which Diderot was thought by many to embody, by looking at the article "Philosophe" in the *Encyclopédie*. Although Diderot was not the original author of this piece, he selected it for inclusion in the *Encyclopédie*. Those who gave him the nickname understood him to be the embodiment of this sketch, which had circulated for some time. The article is clear about the novelty of the idea of philosophy it is defending and seeks to correct a traditional view that regards philosophers as ill suited to sophisticated society. It argues that a philosopher is the antithesis of the gloomy misanthrope who seeks his wisdom by fleeing society; rather, he "is a decent man who wishes to please and make himself useful." He does this by participating in social life in all senses of the term. In short, this view of philosophy emphasizes both freedom from vulgar prejudices and urbane participation in social life. It makes philosophy fashionable by portraying the philosopher as a perfected man of fashion.[20]

Thus Diderot claims that philosophers become useful by actively participating in social life. This immersion in society could be accomplished in a number of ways. Recently there has been much discussion among historians about the efforts of intellectuals in the years before the Revolution to fashion a "public sphere" independent of the government using things such as the periodical press and literary salons.[21] It should not be forgotten, however, that as part of their effort to construct and guide public opinion they were also eager to co-opt existing institutions and practices such as academies and royal pensions. Over a period of years d'Alembert made use of his position as Secretary of the Academie Française to see that this venerable institution became dominated by figures friendly to the Enlightenment. Pensions allowed one both to gain the sort of independence that comes with a guaranteed income and to enhance one's prestige and secure ties to the powerful. Thinkers varied in their commitment to each of these tactics: for example, Diderot was no great frequenter of salons headed by women and d'Alembert had a very healthy suspicion of close association with the rich and powerful. Nevertheless, it is fair to say that the Enlightenment endorsed a two-pronged tactic of creating new centers of power and penetrating existing ones. Through the use of the press, salons, academies, and pensions the new philosophers could become insiders.

Rousseau was suspicious of these efforts and consistently expressed and acted on his reservations. He turned down the offer of a lucrative position with an important periodical on the grounds that he could not write "as a trade as all the other literary people did."[22] He objected to salons because they required submission to the tone established by the wealthy people who led them. He politely declined several invitations to become an academician.[23] Finally, he turned down pensions from three different kings at least in part because the acceptance of a pension would make it impossible for him to present himself as standing for truth, freedom, or courage without being an ingrate.[24] Few other intellectuals willingly worked for a living. David Hume acknowledged the singularity of Rousseau's insistence upon living on money earned through his own labor by calling it "a kind of phenomenon in the republic of letters."[25] The same comment could be made about Rousseau's reluctance to participate in the other institutions and practices promoted by the Enlightenment. In each case he rejected engagements with wealth and power as entanglements that might compromise his independence, which he regarded as the necessary underpinning of his boldness.[26] To be sure, individual instances could be cited to show Rousseau's willingness to break his rule, but both his general policy and its contrast with that of other intellectuals are clear.

Rousseau's critique of the Enlightenment policy is the complement of his own policy. Self-proclaimed philosophers like Diderot assume their own impartiality and possession of the knowledge of what is best for their society and, guided by this assumption, seek to co-opt or create positions of influence to make their knowledge effective. In fact, however, their perspective on things is tainted by their immersion in the corrupt society they profess to want to reform. They identify the world with the social world they are striving to occupy. Consequently their pursuit of influence is hardly as benevolent as they claim. It turns into, or reveals itself as having always been, simply self-promotion. As Rousseau once said, "Behold authors and Philosophers: Always some private interest as their motive, and always the public good as a pretext."[27] The project of enlightening the world reduces itself to the project of securing privileges for those who enlist in the party of enlightenment.

In the *Dialogues* Rousseau explicitly extends this critique to Diderot's remark, "Only the wicked man is alone."[28] In this discussion he also emphasizes the novelty of this doctrine, which he says Diderot was the first to state. Moreover, in this passage he bitterly refers to his former friend as "the philosopher Diderot" four times in the space of three paragraphs. Rousseau both defends the taste for solitude and attacks the attempt to combine goodness with success in the social world. He says, "Whatever motive might animate someone who wants to join the crowd and be noticed, he must summon up the vigor to repel those who push him, push aside those who are in front of him, divide the crowd and make his way."[29] Even those with the best motives are necessarily corrupted by this sort of activity.

Although he emphasizes the novelty of Diderot's approach to the union of philosophy and morality, Rousseau's alternative is not simply a return to a traditional one. Rather, it is a radically new approach that demands a complete break with the centers of society. One can see the point of Rousseau's charge that the desire to please the sophisticates of Paris can harm philosophy by limiting the philosopher's vision, but Diderot's claim that hermits make peculiar citizens retains some force even if Rousseau was a good neighbor while living in the country. After all, he was not only living in the country but was doing so hundreds of miles away from his fatherland. How can he claim to be living up to his civic responsibilities? Rousseau chose to live in the French countryside for a number of reasons. By living in one country (France), being a citizen of a second (Geneva), and publishing his books in a third (Holland), he thought he could maximize his freedom to write what he wished. In particular, this position as a citizen who was also an outsider allowed him to publish works relating to Genevan politics without submitting them for prior censorship in Geneva.[30] Ordinary citizenship requires that the citizen live in his community, but the citizenship of the public intellectual may be most effective if he lives somewhere else. A hermit is indeed a peculiar citizen, but in Rousseau's case he can be a good one. This claim that an intellectual can best have a public effect by being an outsider to his own community stands in radical opposition to Diderot's claim that intellectuals should strive to be insiders.

AUTHORS AND PHILOSOPHERS

A different quarrel between Diderot and Rousseau, which led to their final rupture, shows their perspectives on the relation between intellectuals and their community from a different angle. Rousseau confided in Diderot when he fell in love with Sophie d'Houdetot, the mistress of their mutual friend Saint Lambert. Diderot left their conversation believing that Rousseau had resolved to confess this love and his efforts to resist it to Saint Lambert. Although there is room for disagreement about his reasons for doing so, it was not Rousseau but Diderot who acted and told Saint Lambert and others as well.[31] As a result of what he regarded as a breach of confidence, Rousseau decided to announce a break with Diderot by inserting notice of it into the *Letter to d'Alembert,* which was in press at the time. For this purpose he inserted a quotation from Ecclesiasticus presenting the "disclosing of secrets" as one of the few unforgivable acts one can commit against a friend.[32]

Although this passage may seem to have little to do with the subject of the *Letter*, it points to a theme running throughout the work—the question of what sort of things should be made public and what sort should be kept private. For example, Rousseau addresses questions such as the appropriateness of female modesty and the public display of private passions in theatrical performances. In each case Rousseau, the supposed lover of transparency, aligns himself with those who oppose public openness. This should give pause to those who argue that Rousseau's insistence on transparency with respect to authorship "casts suspicion on those who refuse to show and tell all" and promotes "the practice of surveillance and social control."[33] In fact Rousseau wishes to combine openness about who is speaking with discretion about what is being said.

To clarify his position, it is useful to focus on one specific example. Rousseau begins the *Letter* by stopping just short of making a charge against d'Alembert similar to the one he makes against Diderot: that he has betrayed the confidence of the Genevan clergy by publicly revealing things he had been told in confidence. In the article "Geneva," d'Alembert had held up the Genevan clergy as models on the grounds that many of them had rejected the intolerance that had plagued Geneva because of the influence of Calvin. D'Alembert finds the source of their new toleration in their disbelief in doctrines such as the existence of hell, the divinity of Jesus, and other doctrines depending on revelation. In fact d'Alembert asserts that these ministers "have no religion other than a complete Socinianism."[34] Geneva excels other communities in toleration because it is unusually open to philosophic inquiry, as is shown by its acclaim for Voltaire's works, including the ones that attacked Calvin, the founder of Geneva's religion. D'Alembert contrasts the enlightenment of Geneva with other countries "in which pusillanimous writers, who are called prudent, respect prejudices which they could combat with as much propriety as security."[35] Thus d'Alembert's standard of praise is the extent to which a society encourages attacks on prejudices and is willing to abandon its own prejudices when they have been successfully attacked. Moreover, he makes it clear that all doctrines based on revelation are to be numbered among these prejudices.

By making public the extent to which the clergy were dissenters from traditional Calvinism, d'Alembert clearly hoped to further the cause of enlightenment by destroying what he regarded as a few lingering prejudices. He clearly believed that he could further this process by making it publicly known, as we might say today, by "outing" the clergy. The leaking of confidential information appears to be one of the characteristic practices of the Enlightenment, just as it is of American society today. The publication of his description of the beliefs held by Genevan clergy did indeed cause a public stir, but not the sort he had been hoping for. Although d'Alembert meant his characterization as praise, its implication that the official Calvinism of Geneva had been covertly replaced by a long-standing opponent, Socinianism, opened the clergy to the charge of treason.[36] The clergy responded by hastily denying d'Alembert's claims and affirming their commitment to Calvinism.

Rousseau's response was rather different. He did not so much deny the truth of d'Alembert's claim as he contested his right to make it. He points out that the clergy publicly claim to be good Calvinists and argues that d'Alembert could have solid knowledge about their departures from orthodoxy only through private conversations, which he would be honor bound to keep secret. He speculates about the possibility that the clergy might have told d'Alembert that they were Socinians, but concludes that they would have done this only "in secret, in the decent and frank expansiveness of philosophic intercourse; they would have said it to the philosopher and not to the author."[37] D'Alembert's error is to confuse philosophy and authorship and to make philosophy political in a purely partisan manner.

D'Alembert replied that he had derived his characterization only from well-attested public statements. He goes on to capture the essence of Rousseau's very peculiar defense of the clergy: "I do not know whether the Genevan ecclesiastics whom you wished to justify concerning their belief, will be much more satisfied with you than they have been with me, and whether your laxity in defending them will please them more than my frankness. You seem to accuse me almost solely of *imprudence* with regard to them."[38] Because Rousseau said nothing that disagreed with d'Alembert about the real beliefs of the Genevan clergy, d'Alembert considered the difference between himself and Rousseau to be a trivial one and praised Rousseau's defense of freedom of conscience. Rousseau, on the contrary, regarded their difference as more than merely prudential in that it concerns the desirability of maintaining a separation between private belief and public avowal in certain matters.

Rousseau objects to d'Alembert's campaign of publicity on two grounds. First, he argues that instead of furthering toleration, d'Alembert is opening up to public debate theological conflicts that cannot be settled precisely because they are unsuitable for rational discussion. Second, he claims that instead of having genuine toleration as his goal, d'Alembert is seeking to end conflict by promoting the victory of a sectarian dogma: that of Enlightenment. He dogmatically sets up his own skepticism on matters of revelation as the measure of what should be publicly accepted.

In Rousseau's view d'Alembert's attempt to combat prejudices and thereby make politics more philosophic is dangerous because it threatens to make theological issues into matters of public dispute. While writers like d'Alembert and Voltaire attempt to combat prejudices and replace them with what they consider to be reason, Rousseau argues that they, in fact, are merely seeking to replace one form of intolerant dogmatism with another. Rousseau and the Genevan ministers, as he portrays them, respect prejudices about which they have private reservations because (unlike d'Alembert) they understand the role of such prejudices as sentiments of sociability that hold the community together. Rather than seek the public victory of the Enlightenment position as d'Alembert does, Rousseau seeks to support both a public religious doctrine that can unite Geneva and a private freedom of conscience. Thus he rejects the attempt to replace public opinion with philosophy.

CONCLUSION

The characteristics of a Rousseauian intellectual emerge from these anecdotes and can be contrasted with the characteristics of an Enlightenment intellectual as seen by Rousseau. The quarrel between Rousseau and Voltaire about naming names represents a disagreement about both the meaning of personal integrity and the potential importance of taking a public stand. The dispute between Diderot and Rousseau over nicknames concerns the temptations and opportunities provided by direct participation in the social world. In both of these instances Rousseau rejects the view that intellectuals can form a party whose private interest is identical to the public interest. Instead, he argues that people should pay heed only to a solitary intellectual who ignores both party spirit and his own advancement. The permanent outsider should be preferred to the aspiring insider. Rousseau's charge of betrayal of confidence leveled against both Diderot and d'Alembert shows his view that certain political issues as not susceptible to being settled by reasoned and open political debate. Both intellectual independence and political health require an appreciation of the role that prejudices play in society at large.

In sum, the philosophers of the Enlightenment saw themselves as temporary outsiders whose intellectual independence was guaranteed by their naturalization into a cosmopolitan party of progress or republic of letters. From this vantage point they sought to transform the narrower societies to which they belonged by becoming insiders at the center of power. Rousseau questions both the reality of their intellectual independence and the compatibility of their concern for gaining personal power with genuine public spiritedness. In exposing the problems with the Enlightenment practice he makes the extreme demands that the public intellectual stand permanently alone in a personal public stand, that he show his good faith by constantly arguing against his own interest, and that he never allow his commitment to philosophy to make him forget his participation in a nonphilosophic community. Somehow personal responsibility, radical intellectual independence, and communal solidarity must combine as his preeminent virtues. It is, of course, possible to have reservations about Rousseau's picture. It is based on an extreme view of the gap between intellectual life and the good of the community and, in addition, an equally extreme view of the need for those devoted to intellectual life to subordinate this side of their existence to their commitment to a particular community. It may well be vulnerable to a radical anti-intellectualism and immersion in what are known to be irrational prejudices.[39] Nevertheless, I have attempted to show that Rousseau's view is well thought out and not merely a product of his personality quirks, however real those might be.

Since Rousseau there have been many examples of intellectuals who have adopted one or more of the features of his portrait of the public intellectual. When we see individuals take a public stand at great personal risk instead of working behind the scenes, when we see intellectuals keeping a distance from positions of influence, and when we see them insisting on their links with the common man rather than with their fellow intellectuals we are witnessing a Rousseauian strain in modern intellectual life. Of course, frequently these elements are adopted as a self-conscious pose rather than an honestly held conviction. There are people who seek out "controversial" public stands containing no real risk and solely for the purpose of cultivating an image of independence. There are others who denounce the "system" while parasitically profiting from university posts and publishing opportunities. Finally, there are plenty of spokesmen for the common man who make no genuine effort to share in the real concerns of their fellow citizens. Rousseau's exposé of the potential phoniness of the Enlightenment idea of the public intellectual has engendered its own array of charlatans. The difficulty of combining the qualities he exalts without cheapening them is exceeded only by the potency of this combination when it happens as is shown by the astonishing impact of Rousseau himself and his works.

NOTES

1. For an interesting account of this result of the quarrel between Rousseau and Hume, see Dena Goodman, "The Hume-Rousseau Affair: From Private *Querelle* to Public *Procès*," *Eighteenth Century Studies* 25, no. 2 (1991–1992): 171–201.

2. The details of this sequence of events can be found in Henri Gouhier's excellent study of the relations between Rousseau and Voltaire, *Rousseau et Voltaire: Portraits dans deux miroirs* (Paris: J. Vrin, 1983), 195–234. While acknowledging that the

difference of opinion over anonymity played a role in Voltaire's behavior, Gouhier does not give it the same importance I do here.

3. For the details of the intervening events, which also deal with questions of authorship and anonymity, see Gouhier, *Rousseau et Voltaire*, 289–304.

4. For a good treatment of the literary strategies of Rousseau, Diderot, and d'Alembert in particular, see Rémy G. Saisselin, *The Literary Enterprise in Eighteenth-Century France* (Detroit: Wayne State University Press, 1979).

5. For a more elaborate account of Rousseau's quarrel with Voltaire and of censorship in the eighteenth century, see Christopher Kelly, *Rousseau as Author: Consecrating One's Life to the Truth* (Chicago: University of Chicago Press, 2003).

6. See, for example, the letters to Helvétius in May and September 1763 in *Les Oeuvres de Voltaire*, ed. Theodore Besterman (Banbury, U.K.: Voltaire Foundation, 1973), 110:199, 228, 404. On this point see John N. Pappas, *Voltaire and Diderot* (Bloomington: Indiana University Press, 1962), 37.

7. The account that follows is drawn mainly from *Les Oeuvres complètes de Voltaire*, 110:199–200, 227–28, esp. 403–5. It is meant only to show the elements in Voltaire's strategy that shed light on Rousseau's opposed strategy. A book-length study would be necessary to provide a full explication of Voltaire's understanding of the social role of an author. For a some useful preliminary remarks, see Reinhart Koselleck, *Critique and Crisis: Enlightenment and the Pathogenesis of Modern Society* (Cambridge: MIT Press, 1988), 60, 113–17.

8. Quoted in P. N. Furbank, *Diderot: A Critical Biography* (New York: Alfred A. Knopf, 1992), 167.

9. *Confessions* in *Collected Writings of Rousseau*, ed. Roger D. Masters and Christopher Kelly (Hanover, N.H.: University Press of New England, 1990–), 5:303–8. Additional references to this edition will be made as C.W. with volume number.

10. In this regard consider Michel Foucault's claim that "Speeches and books were assigned real authors, other than mythical or important religious figures, only when the author became subject to punishment." "What Is an Author?" in *Language, Counter-Memory, Practice*, ed. Donald F. Bouchard (Ithaca, N.Y.: Cornell University Press, 1977), 124.

11. *Julie*, C.W., 6:5. The term translated as "honorable" here is *honnête,* which also means honest or decent. For an alternative translation and discussion of this passage, see Victor Gourevitch, "Rousseau on Lying: A Provisional Reading of the Fourth *Reverie*," *Berkshire Review* 15 (1980): 97. Gourevitch points out that, while Rousseau always blamed the practice of publishing anonymously, he did not always name anonymous authors.

12. *Social Contract*, C.W., 4:146–47. For a discussion of this, see Gérard Namer, *Rousseau Sociologue de la connaissance* (Paris: Editions Klincksieck, 1978), 72.

13. This occurs in the same section of the *Letters Written from the Mountain* in which Rousseau revealed that Voltaire was the author of the *Sermon* discussed above. See C.W., 9:219.

14. C.W., 9:219.

15. For a brief account of the intensity of readers' reaction to Rousseau and their identification with him, see Robert Darnton, "Readers Respond to Rousseau: The Fabrication of Romantic Sensitivity," in *The Great Cat Massacre and Other Episodes in French Cultural History* (New York: Basic Books, 1984).

16. Rousseau himself strenuously objected to having opinions expressed by characters in his works attributed to him. See *Dialogues*, in C.W., 1:70.

17. *Le Fils naturel*, 4.3.

18. *Confessions*, in C.W., 5:558.

19. *Confessions*, in C.W., 5:385.

20. See *Confessions*, in C.W., 5:67–68, for a statement from Rousseau contrasting one of the traditional meanings of philosophy with the newly fashionable sense.

21. This discussion stems in large part from Jürgen Habermas, *The Structural Transformation of the Public Sphere: An Inquiry into a Category of Bourgeois Society*, trans. Thomas Burger with Frederick Lawrence (Cambridge: MIT Press, 1989). For an argument for the importance of salons in promoting this public sphere, see Dena Goodman, *The Republic of Letters: A Cultural History of the French Enlightenment* (Ithaca, N.Y.: Cornell University Press, 1994).

22. *Confessions*, in C.W., 5:430.

23. *Confessions*, in C.W., 5:435. See also "Preface to Narcissus," in C.W., 2:197.

24. *Confessions*, in C.W., 5:319.

25. *Correspondance complète de Rousseau*, ed. R. A. Leigh (Geneva: Institut et Musée Voltaire, 1967), 15:85. This edition will be cited as Leigh.

26. Preface to a Second Letter to Bordes, in C.W., 2:182.

27. Letter to Vernes, July 1759, in Leigh, vol. 5.

28. In the *Dialogues* the remark is misquoted as "Only the wicked person is alone" (C.W., 1:99).

29. C.W., 1:99.

30. *Confessions*, in C.W., 5:341.

31. Diderot always claimed that he spoke assuming that Rousseau had already made his confession to Saint Lambert. Maurice Cranston has made a solid case for the position that Diderot's accounts are self-contradictory and that he knowingly violated the confidence. See *The Noble Savage: Jean-Jacques Rousseau, 1754–1762* (Chicago: University of Chicago Press, 1991), 131.

32. *Letter to d'Alembert on the Theatre* in *Politics and the Arts*, ed. Allan Bloom (Ithaca, N.Y.: Cornell University Press, 1959), 7. Cited below as *D'Alembert*.

33. Dennis Porter, *Rousseau's Legacy: The Emergence and Eclipse of the Writer in France* (Oxford: Oxford University Press, 1995), 33.

34. *D'Alembert*, 146–47.

35. *D'Alembert*, 146.

36. On the opposition between Calvinism and Socinianism with particular reference to the issue of dissimulation and persecution, see Perez Zagorin, *Ways of Lying: Dissimulation, Persecution, and Conformity in Early Modern Europe* (Cambridge: Harvard University Press, 1990), 63–82.

37. *D'Alembert*, 11.

38. Jean Le Rond D'Alembert, *Oeuvres complètes*, 5:457, emphasis in original. He goes on to indicate that Rousseau's later defense of dancing is more shocking to orthodoxy than his own defense of the theater. See also his "Avertissement sur la justification de l'article 'Genève' de *l'Encyclopédie,*" in *Oeuvres complètes*, 5:423.

39. For a reply to the view that Rousseau's position leads to either withdrawal from politics or a fanatical unwillingness to compromise, see Ruth W. Grant, *Hypocrisy and Integrity: Machiavelli, Rousseau, and the Ethics of Politics* (Chicago: University of Chicago Press, 1997).

5

The Founding Fathers and the Creation of Public Opinion

Gordon S. Wood

The intellectual caliber of the Founding Fathers has never been questioned. Praises of their qualities of mind have been sung so often that we are hard put to find new ways of describing them. In the last quarter of the eighteenth century, one historian has written, America "boasted a galaxy of leaders who were quite literally incomparable." "These leading representatives of the American Enlightenment," another historian has said, "were a cluster of extraordinary men such as is rarely encountered in modern history."[1] No one, it seems, can look back without being overawed by the brilliance of their thought, the creativity of their politics, the sheer magnitude of their achievement. They are indeed more marvelous than even those they emulated—the great legislators of classical antiquity—precisely because they are more real. They are not mythical characters but authentic historical figures about whom there exists a remarkable amount of historical evidence. For our knowledge of the Founding Fathers, unlike that of many of the classical heroes, we do not have to rely on hazy legends or poetic tales. We have not only everything the Revolutionary leaders ever published but also an incredible amount of their private correspondence and their most intimate thoughts, being made available with a degree of editorial completeness and expertness rarely achieved in the Western world's recovery of its documentary past.

Despite the extent and meticulousness of this historical recovery, however, the Founding Fathers still seem larger than life, and seem to possess intellectual capacities well beyond our own. The awe that we feel when we look back at them is thus mingled with an acute sense of loss. Somehow for a brief moment ideas and power, intellectualism and politics, came together—indeed were one with each other—in a way never again duplicated in American history.

There is no doubt that the Founding Fathers were men of ideas and thought—the leading intellectuals of their day. But they were also the political leaders of their day, politicians who competed for power, lost and won elections, served in their colonial and state legislatures or in the Congress, became governors, judges, and even presidents. Yet, of course, they were neither "intellectuals" nor "politicians," for the modern meaning of these terms suggests the very separation between them that the Revolutionaries avoided. They were intellectuals without being alienated and political leaders without being obsessed with votes. They lived mutually in the world of ideas and the world of politics, and shared equally in both in a happy combination that fills us with envy and wonder. We know that something happened then in American history that can never happen again.

But there is no point now, more than two centuries later, in continuing to wallow in nostalgia and to aggravate our deep feelings of loss and deficiency. What we need is not more praise of the Founding Fathers but more understanding of them and their circumstances. We need to find out why the Revolutionary generation was able to combine ideas and politics so effectively and why subsequent generations in America could not do so. With the proper historical perspective on the last quarter of the eighteenth century and with a keener sense of the distinctiveness of that period will come a greater appreciation of not only what we have lost by the passing of that Revolutionary generation but, more important, what we have gained. In the end, what made subsequent duplication of the remarkable intellectual leadership of the Revolutionaries impossible in America was the growth of what we have come to value most—our egalitarian culture and our democratic society. One of the prices we had to pay for democracy was a decline in the intellectual quality of American political life and an eventual separation between ideas and power. As the common man rose to power in the decades following the Revolution, the inevitable consequence was the displacement from power of the uncommon man, the man of ideas. Yet the Revolutionary leaders were not merely victims of new circumstances; they were in fact the progenitors of these new circumstances: they helped create the changes that led eventually to their own undoing, to the breakup of the kind of political and intellectual coherence they represented. Without intending to, they eagerly destroyed the sources of their own greatness.

There is no denying the power and significance of the intellectual products of the Revolutionary era. Samuel Eliot Morison and Harold Laski both believed that no period of modern history, with the possible exception of the Civil War decades of seventeenth-century England, was so rich in political ideas and contributed so much in such a short period of time to Western political theory.[2] In the Americans' efforts to explain the difference of their experience in the New World and ultimately to justify their Revolution and their new governments, they were pressed to speak and write both originally and extensively about politics, using a wide variety of eighteenth-century instruments: newspapers, pamphlets, state papers, poetry, plays, satire, and, of course, letters. Indeed, their phenomenal reliance on personal correspondence for the communication of their thoughts made the Revolutionary years the greatest letter writing era in American history. (Without Jefferson's letters, what would we know of his mind?) It is a remarkable body of political literature that the Revolutionaries created, and what is most remarkable about it is that this political theory was generally written by the very men responsible for putting it into effect.

Despite the intellectual creativity and productivity of the Revolutionary leaders, however, it is obvious that they were not professional writers. They bore no resemblance to the Grub Street scribblers hired by government officials to turn out political propaganda. Nor were they only men of letters, "intellectuals" like the eighteenth-century French philosophes or the Tory satirists of Augustan England, writers fully engaged in political criticism and using their pens to gain money and position. To be sure, there were American writers like John Trumbull and Philip Freneau who sought to make careers as litterateurs, but they were exceptions. Most of the intellectual leaders of the Revolution were amateurs at writing—clergymen, merchants, planters, and lawyers deeply involved in their separate occupations.

No doubt writing was important to them. Indeed, it was often through their writing that they first gained a reputation. Both John Adams in the Stamp Act crisis and Jefferson in 1774 captured the attention of their peers by something they wrote. Even Washington became well known only with the publication of his journal in 1754 recounting his adventures with the French and Indians in the West. Still, they were not writers by profession. Writing was simply a byproduct of their careers and one of their many accomplishments or duties as gentlemen. Because they were gentlemen, they never wrote for money and often avoided putting their name on what they wrote for publication. They thought of their writing, even the belletristic sort, as a means to an end, either to make a polemical political point or to demonstrate their learning and gentlemanly status.

Yet men like James Otis, Richard Bland, Thomas Jefferson, and John Adams were not only amateur writers; in an important sense they were amateur politicians as well. For all the time and energy these Revolutionary leaders devoted to politics, most of them cannot accurately be described as professional politicians, at least not in any modern meaning of the term. Their relationship to public life and their conception of public service were different from those of today: their political careers did not create but rather followed from their previously established social positions; their political leadership, like their intellectual leadership, was a consequence, not a cause, of their social leadership. Some of them even refused salaries for their offices, protesting that it was unbecoming for gentlemen to be paid for public service.

As gentlemen, they thought they had a duty to lead the society, serve in government, and build consensus. Franklin certainly felt this obligation. "Let not your love of philosophical amusements have more than its due weight with you," he admonished his friend and New York royal official Cadwallader Colden in 1750. Public service was far more important than science. In fact, said Franklin, even the "finest" of Newton's "Discoveries" could not have excused his neglecting to serve the commonwealth if the public had needed him.[3]

Because public office was seen as an obligation, the Founding Fathers often described it—sometimes wrongly, of course, but sincerely—as an unhappy burden, as a wretched responsibility thrust upon them by the fact of their high social rank. Few of Jefferson's letters are as revealing and filled with emotion as his 1782 protest to Monroe over the social pressures making him engage in public service despite the miseries of office and his longing for private repose.[4] We smile today when we hear politicians complaining about the burdens of public office, but precisely because the eighteenth-century leaders were not professional politicians such disavowals of public office and such periodic withdrawals from politics as they habitually made possessed a meaning that is difficult for us today to recapture.

What ultimately enabled the Revolutionary leaders to be amateur politicians and amateur writers, and to be both simultaneously, was their status as gentlemen—the dominant social distinction of the eighteenth century that has since lost almost all of its earlier significance. The Founding Fathers took their gentlemanly status seriously and accepted the privileges and responsibilities of the rank without guilt and without false humility. Compared to the English gentry of the eighteenth century, some of the colonial leaders may have been uncertain about their distinctive status, but none doubted the social importance of their separation from the common people, which was expressed in various ways—through speech, dress, demeanor, learning, taste, and one's acquaintances and friends.[5] Eighteenth-century leaders took it for granted that society was a hierarchy of finely graded ranks and degrees, divided into vertical interests and lines of personal influence rather than as today into horizontal cleavages of class and occupation. In such a society men generally were acutely aware of their exact relation to those immediately above and below them but only vaguely conscious, except at the very top, of their connections with those at their own level. It was believed that the topmost rank, that of a gentleman—the horizontal social division that had most significance to the eighteenth century—ought to be made up of special sorts of men, the "better sort," men of property no doubt, but more—men of "politeness" and "good character." Members of the elite debated endlessly over what constituted the proper character for a gentleman—John Adams and Thomas Jefferson were still going at it in their correspondence at the end of their lives—but they never questioned the leadership of the society by an aristocracy of some sort.

Because prominent gentlemen saw themselves as part of an organic social community linked through strong personal connections to those below them, for all their attitudes of superiority and elevation they had no sense of being in an adversarial relationship to the populace; they never saw themselves standing apart from the society in critical or scholarly isolation. They were individuals undoubtedly, sometimes assuming a classic pose of heroic and noble preeminence, but they were not individualists, men worried about their social identities. They were enmeshed in the society and civic-minded by necessity; thus they hid their personal feelings for the sake of civility and sociability. Someone like Benjamin Franklin never thought that his characteristic behavior—his artful posing, his role-playing, his many masks, his refusal to reveal his inner self—was anything other than what the cultivated and sociable eighteenth century admired.[6] Today we are instinctively repelled by such calculation, such insincerity, such willingness to adapt and compromise for the sake of society; yet our distaste for such behavior is only one more measure of our distance from the preromantic eighteenth century.

Because the Revolutionary leaders were cultivated gentlemen with special privileges and responsibilities, tied to the people through lines of personal and social authority, they believed that their speeches and writings did not have to influence directly and simultaneously all of the people but only the rational and enlightened part, who then in turn would bring the rest of the populace with them through the force of deferential respect. The politically minded public in eighteenth-century America may have been large compared to contemporary England, but most of the political literature of the period, unlike much of the religious literature, showed little evidence of a broad reading public.[7] The Revolutionary leaders for the most part wrote as if they were dealing with reasonable and cultivated readers like themselves. Of course, by publishing their writings, they realized they were exposing their ideas to the vulgar, which is why they often resorted to pseudonyms; but before the Revolution they made very few concessions to this wider public. They were aware of the term "public opinion"—which had first arisen in the English-speaking world in the early 1700s—but they conceived of the public as a very limited sphere.[8]

For many gentlemen this sphere was in fact the limited arena where gentlemanly affairs of honor took place. Honor was an aristocratic conception: it essentially meant reputation, but the only reputation that counted was the one that existed in the eyes of one's fellow gentlemen. Gossip was everywhere, and every gentleman was fearful of being slandered by other gentlemen. Consequently, insults to one's honor provoked responses that sometimes ended in duels. Although ritualized affairs of honor became very common in the last quarter of the eighteenth century, most of them did not result in actual duels. Alexander Hamilton, for example, was directly involved in eleven affairs of honor but actually fought in only one.[9]

It was this genteel public that the Revolutionary leaders generally thought of when they wrote and spoke—a public that was roughly commensurate with their social world. "When I mention the public," wrote John Randolph in a 1774 political pamphlet, "I mean to include only the rational part of it. The ignorant vulgar are as unfit to judge of the modes, as they are unable to manage the reins of government."[10] Such bluntness in public was rare and became even rarer as the Revolution approached. Although few of the Revolutionaries shared Randolph's contempt for the mass of the populace—indeed, most had little reason as yet to fear or malign the people—they vaguely held to a largely unspoken assumption that the only public opinion worth worrying about was that of their cultivated peers.[11]

Actually the reading public for genteel literature in the mid-eighteenth century may have been more limited than we have generally assumed. Certainly the prevalence of literacy is no measure of it. The price of both newspapers and pamphlets was itself restricting. Although a pamphlet cost no more than a shilling or two, even that put it beyond the reach of most. Indeed, the practice of reading some pamphlets before groups of Sons of Liberty or town meetings indicates not the general breadth but the usual limits of their circulation. Even members of the elite relied extensively on passing pamphlets from hand to hand as if they were letters.[12]

Yet there is no doubt that the intellectual climate was changing in the half century before the Revolution. In the 1720s there were fewer than a half dozen newspapers in the colonies, with a limited number of subscribers; by 1764 there were twenty-three newspapers, each with double or triple the earlier circulation. Between 1741 and 1776 men had experimented with at least ten magazines, and although none of them lasted longer than a few years, the effort was promising. Since most of the publications emphasized governmental matters, there was bound to be some raising of political consciousness, and printers were becoming more important public figures. The number of political pamphlets multiplied at an ever increasing rate, and in some urban areas in the years before the Revolution such writings were being used with particular effectiveness in election campaigning.[13] All these developments were bringing Americans to the edge of a vast transformation in the nature and size of their politically conscious reading public.[14]

Regardless of the actual extent of the American reading public, what is crucial is the Revolutionary leaders' belief that the public for which they wrote was cosmopolitan and cultivated. We know they conceived of their audiences or readership as restricted and aristocratic, as being made up of men essentially like themselves, simply by the style and content of what they wrote. They saw themselves and their readers as mutual participants in an intellectual fraternity, "the republic of letters," a view that gave them a confidence in the homogeneity and the intelligence of their audience, which in turn decisively influenced the particular qualities of their literary productions.[15]

First of all, a large amount of the Revolutionary literature was extraordinarily learned, filled with Latin quotations, classical allusions, and historical citations—multitudes of references to every conceivable figure in the heritage of Western culture from Cicero, Sallust, and Plutarch, to Montesquieu, Pufendorf, and Rousseau. They delighted in citing authorities and in displaying their scholarship, sometimes crowding or even smothering the texts of their pamphlets with quantities of footnotes.[16] Often the newspaper essays and pamphlets were mere extensions of the kind of speeches that political leaders might present in legislative halls, devices by which gentlemen, in the absence of published reports of legislative debates, might tell other gentlemen what they said, or would like to have said, within the legislative chamber. Thus Stephen Hopkins's *The Rights of Colonies Examined* was first read before the assembly of Rhode Island, which then voted that it should appear in pamphlet form.[17] Or even more indicative of the limited elitist conception of the audience was the extraordinary reliance on personal correspondence for the circulation of ideas. It is often difficult to distinguish between the private correspondence and the public writings of the Revolutionaries, so much alike are they. Sometimes the published writings even took the form of letters, or, like John Adams's pamphlet *Thoughts on Government*, grew out of what were originally letters to colleagues and friends.[18]

It is not just the prevalence of scholarship and the personal form of the literature that reveal the limited and elitist nature of the audience. Even the character of the invective and polemics suggests a restricted reading public in the minds of the authors. Much of the polemics was highly personal, a succession of individual exchanges between gentlemen who were known to one another, quickly becoming unintelligible to an outsider and usually ending in bitter personal vituperation. Since such abuse was designed to destroy the gentlemanly reputation of one's enemies, no accusation was too coarse or too vulgar to be made—from drunkenness and gambling to impotence and adultery.[19] The vitriolic burlesques, like those satiric closet dramas of Mercy Otis Warren, derived much of their force from the intimate knowledge the author presumed the audience or readers had of the persons being ridiculed or satirized. Without such familiarity on the part of the audience, much of the fun of the pieces—the disguised characterizations, the obscure references, the private jokes, the numerous innuendoes—is lost.[20]

Indeed, it is the prevalence of satire in the Revolutionary literature that as much as anything suggests the elite nature of the audience. For satire as a literary device depends greatly on a comprehensible and homogeneous audience with commonly understood standards of rightness and reasonableness. Since the satirist can expose to instantaneous contempt only what is readily condemned by the opinion of his readers, he must necessarily be on intimate terms with them and count on their sharing his tastes and viewpoint. If this intimacy should break down, if the satirist's audiences should become heterogeneous and the once shared values become confused and doubtful—if the satirist has to explain what his ridicule means—then the satire is rendered ineffectual.[21] But most Revolutionary writers, at the outset at least, presumed the existence of these universal principles of right behavior and expected a uniformity of response, supposing that their audience either was, or would like to be, part of that restricted circle of men of good taste and judgment.

Nearly all the literature of the Revolutionary leaders thus suggests—in its form, its erudition, its polemics, its reliance on satire—a very different intellectual world from our own, a world dominated by gentlemen who were both amateur writers and amateur politicians, essentially engaged, despite their occasional condescension toward a larger public, in either amusing men like themselves or in educating men to be or think like themselves. More than any of these characteristics, however, what decisively separates the literature of the Revolutionary generation from that of our own was its highly rhetorical character. It was in fact the Revolutionaries' obsession with rhetoric and with its requirement of effectively relating to the audience that in the end helped contribute to the transformation of American intellectual life.

Rhetoric today no longer means what it meant in the eighteenth century. To us rhetoric suggests at best elocution, or at worst some sort of disingenuous pleading, hyperbolic bombast lacking the sincerity and authenticity of self-expression that we have come to value so highly. But to the Revolutionary generation rhetoric—briefly defined as the art of persuasion— lay at the heart of an eighteenth-century liberal education and was regarded as a necessary mark of a gentleman and an indispensable skill for a statesman, especially for a statesman in a republic.[22] Language, whether spoken or written, was to be deliberately and adroitly used for effect, and since that effect depended on the intellectual leader's conception of his audience, any perceived change in that audience could alter drastically the style and content of what was said or written. Already in the mid-eighteenth century theorists of rhetoric were responding to the need for a language that could move and influence the passions of audiences, calling for a more natural speech that would avoid ornamentation and formality and would express the plain and naked truth of the speaker's inner feelings.[23]

We can see these changes in rhetorical style in the oratory of Patrick Henry and in the writing of Thomas Paine. Both Henry and Paine sought to reach out to wider and deeper layers of the population, and in doing so they aroused the awe and consternation of the gentlemanly elites. Henry was a failure as a planter and storekeeper, but at the age of twenty-three he taught himself law and soon emerged as the gentlemanly spokesman in the Virginia House of Burgesses for the poor and middling farmers and religious dissenters of southwest Virginia. Like the evangelical preachers he listened to as a youth, Henry was the master of the oral culture in which most ordinary people still lived.

Paine's rise was even more dramatic. He was a one-time English corset maker and schoolteacher and twice-dismissed excise officer who had only arrived in America in 1774—thirty-seven years old and filled with rage at the establishment that had pressed him down. Paine looked for readers everywhere, but especially in the artisan- and tavern-centered worlds of the cities. His publication of *Common Sense* in 1776 electrified America and made Paine an instant celebrity. The pamphlet went through dozens of editions and sold at least 150,000 copies at a time when most pamphlets sold in the hundreds or a few thousand at best.

Both Henry and Paine deliberately rejected the usual classical apparatus of persuasion and sought to express to ordinary people the kinds of feelings—

both revulsions and visions—that the traditional elitist conventions of speech and writing did not allow. Both lacked formal schooling, and both were accused of using ungrammatical language and coarse and vulgar idioms. Henry ignored all the criticism of his pronunciation and speaking style, for, as his fellow Burgess Edmund Randolph pointed out, he discovered that an irregular and homespun language "which might disgust in a drawing room may yet find access to the hearts of a popular assembly."[24]

Paine was even more contemptuous of convention. His pamphlet contained few of the traditional genteel references to learned authorities and few of the subtleties of literary allusions and techniques known to the Augustans. "As it is my design to make those that can scarcely read understand," he said, "I shall therefore avoid every literary ornament and put it in language as plain as the alphabet." He scorned "words of sound" that only "amuse the ear" and relied on simple and concrete—some critics said barnyard—imagery drawn from the commonplace world that could be understood even by the unlearned. Both Henry and Paine aimed to break through the usual niceties and formalities of rhetoric and counted on their audiences or readers being familiar with only the Bible and the English Book of Common Prayer. They meant to declare, as Randolph said of Henry, that "it was enough to feel."[25] Fancy words and learned citations no longer mattered as much as honesty and sincerity and the natural revelation of feeling.

Henry remained throughout his career firmly attached to the world of the gentry, but Paine was different. Paine seemed to be unconnected to society, a man who came out of nowhere and was tied to no one, a man without a home and even without a country. Many of America's gentry were frightened by Paine, and they accused him of many things, one of the most common being that he lacked "connections." Paine was free-floating, and in this respect he was very different from the other Founding Fathers. He was in fact America's first modern intellectual, an unattached social critic, who, as he said in 1779, knew "but one kind of life . . . and that is a thinking one, and of course, a writing one."[26]

Henry's and Paine's remarkable success showed that the eighteenth-century neoclassical world of civic-minded philosopher-statesmen was passing even as it expressed itself most forcefully and brilliantly. While the Revolutionary gentry were still busy creating their learned arguments to persuade reasonable men of the need for resistance or of the requirements of government, there were social processes at work that would in time undermine both their political and intellectual authority. A new democratic society was developing, becoming both a cause and a consequence of the Revolution. As egalitarian as American society was before 1776, as broad as the suffrage was in the several eighteenth-century colonies, the republican society and culture that gradually emerged after the Declaration of Independence were decidedly different from what had existed earlier. The older hierarchical and homogeneous society of the eighteenth century—a patronage world of personal influence and vertical connections whose only meaningful horizontal cleavage was that between gentlemen and common people—this old society, weaker in America and never as finely calibrated as in England, now finally fell apart, beset by forces released and accelerated by the Revolution, to be replaced over the subsequent decades with new social relationships and new ideas and attitudes, including a radical blurring of the distinction between gentlemen and the rest of society. New men, often obscure ordinary men, were now touched by the expanding promises of opportunity and wealth in post-Revolutionary America and clamored for a share in the new governments and in the economy. The "people" were now told repeatedly that they rightfully had a place in politics, and lest they should forget, there were thousands of new rising popular tribunes, men who lacked the traditional attributes of gentlemanly leaders, to remind them, cajole them, even frighten them into political and social consciousness. Under such pressures, within a generation or so after Independence the old eighteenth-century world was transformed. The gentry, at least outside the South, gradually lost its monopoly of politics and intellectualism as the audience for politicians, writers, and orators ballooned out to hitherto unimaginable proportions.

Although few of these changes actually began with the Revolution, it was during the Revolution that they became evident. Before the Revolutionary movement only a few Americans, mostly royal officials and their connections, had worried about the expanding size of America's political society. But the imperial controversy had the effect of making all Americans more conscious of the power of the people out of doors. Political leaders, in their contests with royal authority, vied with each other in demonstrating their superior sympathy with the people—and in the process considerably widened and intensified their public audiences.[27] Given the Whig tradition of celebrating the people against the Crown, it was a tendency that most American leaders found difficult to resist. In 1766 the Massachusetts House of Representatives erected a public gallery for the witnessing of its debates—a momentous step in the democratization of the American mind. The Pennsylvania Assembly followed reluctantly in 1770, and eventually the other legislatures too began to reach out to a wider public, usually provoked by the desire of Whig leaders to build support among the people for opposition to Great Britain.[28]

Yet old habits died hard, and it was difficult to shed the conception of assembly proceedings being in the nature of private business among gentlemen. Votes in the legislatures continued to remain unrecorded and reports of debates were rarely carried to the outside world. When in 1776 the Revolutionaries met in their conventions to discuss the forms of their new state constitutions, they felt no need either to report what they said or to extract vows of secrecy to prevent leaks of what they said to the people out of doors. As a result we know very little of what went on during those momentous closed meetings in the months surrounding the Declaration of Independence. Apparently the leaders believed that nearly everyone who counted and ought to hear what was said was within the legislative or convention halls.

A decade later, however, by 1787, the situation had become very different. In many of the states, particularly in Pennsylvania and Massachusetts, legislative debates had begun to be reported by a growing number of newspapers (which now included dailies), and political leaders had developed a keen, even fearful, awareness of a larger political society existing outside of the legislative chambers. Politics no longer seemed an exclusively gentlemanly business, and consequently gentlemen in public discussions increasingly found themselves forced to concede to the popular and egalitarian ideology of the Revolution, for any hint of aristocracy was now pounced upon by emerging popular spokesmen eager to discredit the established elite leaders. Under these changed circumstances the delegates to the Philadelphia Convention in 1787 felt it necessary to take extraordinary measures to keep their proceedings private: no copies of anything in the journal were allowed, nothing said in the Convention was to be released or communicated to the outside society, and sentries were even to be posted to prevent intruders—all out of a sensitivity to a public out of doors that had not existed ten years earlier.

By the late 1780s gentlemen in the Convention had become convinced not only that this public ("the too credulous and unthinking Mobility," one delegate called it) was now interested in what went on within doors but that, if allowed access to the debates through publication by "imprudent printers," this hovering presence of the people would inhibit the delegates' freedom of expression.[29] Events bore out the significance of this deliberate decision to impose secrecy. The delegates to the Philadelphia Convention showed a remarkable degree of candor and boldness in discussing what were now sensitive issues, like aristocracy and the fear of popular power, that was notably missing from the debates in the various ratifying conventions held several months later. Since the ratifying conventions were open and their proceedings widely publicized in the press, the difference in the tone and character of the respective debates is revealing of just what a broader public could mean for the intellectual life of American politics. Madison later reportedly declared that "no Constitution would ever have been adopted by the convention if the debates had been public."[30] As it was, the defenders of the proposed Constitution knew very well that "when this plan goes forth, it will be attacked by the popular leaders. Aristocracy will be the watchword; the Shibboleth among its adversaries."[31] Hence the proponents of the Constitution found themselves in the subsequent public debates compelled to stress over and over the popular and "strictly republican" character of the new federal government. Men who only a few months earlier had voiced deep misgivings over popular rule now tried to outdo their opponents in expressing their enthusiasm for the people. "We, sir, idolize democracy," they said in answer to popular critics of the Constitution.[32]

Although aspects of this public exuberance by the Federalists over the democratic character of the Constitution appear disingenuous and hypocritical to us in light of their private fears of popular power and majority rule, in the debates they were only doing what their liberal education in rhetoric had taught them: adapting their arguments to the nature and needs of their audience. Yet the demands of rhetoric were not supposed to lead to dishonesty and duplicity by the intellectual leader, particularly if his audience was the people. Such a gap between private and public feelings as was displayed in the debates over the Constitution only raised in a new form an issue that had been at the heart of American public discussions throughout the eighteenth century, and never more so than at the time of the Revolution.

During that entire century, and even earlier, enlightened men everywhere had been obsessed by what was often called "Machiavellian duplicity," the deliberate separation between men's hidden feelings or motives and their public face—an obsession that the rhetorical attitude only enhanced. It was often feared that some dishonest men would assume roles and play falsely with their audience or public. The worst villain was the one who, like Iago, achieved his end through plots and dissembling; indeed, the enlightened eighteenth century was incapable of locating evil anywhere else but in this kind of deceiving man.[33]

Assumptions like these lay behind the character of American political life in the eighteenth century and eventually became central to the decision to revolt in 1776. Time and time again, opposition spokesmen against royal authority in the colonies had emphasized the duplicity and flattery of courtiers who selfishly sought the favor of great men while they professed service to the public. Dissimulation, deception, design were thus accusations quickly made, and suspicion of men in power pervaded the political climate. The alternative to the courtier, opposition spokesmen said, was the true patriot, a man like themselves who did not need to dissemble and deceive because he relied solely on the people. As the conventional theory of mixed government pointed out, the people may have lacked energy and wisdom, but they made up for these deficiencies by their honesty and sincerity. Hence writers and critics, themselves gentlemen, delighted in posing as simple farmers in attacking the aristocratic pretensions and duplicity of other gentlemen who had acted condescendingly or who seemed to possess privileges and powers they had no right to have—all the while citing in support of their arguments eighteenth-century writers from Richardson to Rousseau who were increasingly celebrating the moral virtue of sincerity, or the strict correspondence of appearance and reality, action and intention.

At the beginning of the Revolution few American Whig gentlemen had any deep awareness that, in drawing these contrasts between the aristocratic guile and pretensions of the rank they belonged or aspired to and the sincerity and honest hearts of the body of common people, they were unleashing a force they could not control. In 1776 many of them, including the likes of John Adams and Thomas Jefferson, watched with equanimity and indeed enthusiasm the displacement in political office of proud and insolent grandees by new men "not so well dressed, nor so politely educated, nor so highly born. . . ." There was little to fear from such a "political metamorphosis," to use Jefferson's term, for these new men were "the People's men (and the People in general are right). They are plain and of consequence less disguised . . . less intriguing, more sincere."[34]

Out of these kinds of changes in values, fed by the vast social transformation taking place on both sides of the Atlantic, developed a new sentimentalization of the common man and of natural and spontaneous speech. In this atmosphere the use of Greek and Latin as the exclusive property and ornament of gentlemen was disparaged, and the written and spoken word itself became suspect, as men, taking off from Locke's mistrust of imagery, increasingly urged that what was needed in communication were things, not words.[35] And since words, not to mention the classical languages, were associated with cultivated learning and with aristocracy, it was the common man, the simple untutored farmer or even, in the eyes of some like Jefferson, the uncorrupted Indian with his natural gift of oratory, who became consecrated. It was not long before all gentlemen, those "lawyers, and men of learning and money men, that talk so finely, and gloss over matters so smoothly," were brought into question.[36]

By the final decade of the eighteenth century the implications of what was happening were becoming clear to some American gentry. Growing apprehensions over the abuses of popular power had contributed to the movement to create the new federal government, and such fears of democracy eventually became the fixation of the Federalist Party in the 1790s. Most Federalist leaders, at least those who were old enough to be politically conscious at the time of the Revolution, had not anticipated becoming afraid of the people. Like other good Whigs, they had assumed that the people, once free of English influence, would honor and elevate the country's true patriots and natural aristocracy in ways that the English Crown had not. But when in the decades following the Revolution the people seemed to succumb to the deceit and flattery of mushroom demagogues, who were the popular counterparts of courtiers, the Federalists became bewildered and bitter. All respectability, all learning, all character—the very idea of a gentleman as a political leader—seemed to be under assault.

The Federalist writers and speakers of the 1790s responded as eighteenth-century gentlemen would—with the traditional elitist weapons of satire and invective, saturating the political climate with vituperation and venom the likes of which have never been equaled in our national history. But such verbal abuse and ridicule—against democracy, demagoguery, vulgarity—were rhetorical devices designed for a different culture than America was creating. Such calumny and invective as the Federalists expressed were supposed to be calculated and deliberately exaggerated, not a genuine expression of the satirists' inner emotions, and were justifiable because they were the result of the righteous indignation that any gentleman would feel in similar circumstances.[37] Hence, to be effective such rhetorical anger and abuse were dependent on an instantaneous uniformity of recognition by the audience of the universal principles of truth and reasonableness to which the satirist appealed.

But the democratization of American society and culture that was occurring in these years was not only broadening and diversifying the public, weakening those common standards of rightness and good behavior that underlay the potency of satire, it was also destroying the ability of the Federalist writers to maintain a rhetorical detachment from what was happening. The Federalists thus groped during the next decade or so to discover a rhetoric that could persuade their audience without at the same time alienating it.

The Federalists found it increasingly difficult to publicly speak the truth as they saw it and not get punished for it. Anonymity was now resorted to, less because it was unseemly for a gentleman in the eyes of other gentlemen to expose his writings to the vulgar than because it was harmful for a gentleman's public career in the eyes of the vulgar (who could vote) to be caught writing, especially if that writing contained anything unpopular.[38] "In democracies," the Federalists concluded, "writers will be more afraid of the people, than afraid for them," and thus the right principles of political science, like those that had been discovered by the Revolutionary leaders, would become "too offensive for currency or influence" and America's intellectual contributions to politics would cease.[39]

Some Federalists took a stubborn pride in their growing isolation from the public, regarding scorn by the people as a badge of honor and counting on posterity to vindicate their reputations.[40] Other Federalists, however, could not easily abandon their role as gentlemanly leaders and sought desperately to make their influence felt, some eventually concluding that they too must begin flattering the people, saying that if they could not achieve their ends "but by this sort of cant, we must have recourse to it." They came to realize, in Hamilton's words, that "the first thing in all great operations of such a government as our is to secure the opinion of the people." But in competition with their Republican opponents, the Federalists, said Fisher Ames, were like "flat tranquility against passion; dry leaves against the whirlwind; the weight of gunpowder against its kindled force."[41] They could not shed fast enough their traditional eighteenth-century rhetorical and elitist techniques. They continued to rely on a limited audience of reasonable gentlemen like themselves who alone could respond to their satirical blasts against democracy and vulgarity. And they preferred private correspondence among "particular gentlemen" to dealing with the unlettered multitude through the newly developing media of communication, especially the newspapers.[42]

In the 1790s both the Federalists and their opponents recognized the changing role popular media of communication were coming to play in American public life.[43] The sale of every sort of printed matter—books, pamphlets, handbills, periodicals, posters, broadsides—multiplied, and through new channels of distribution these publications found their way into hands that were not used to such literature. In New York City alone the number of booksellers increased from five in 1786 to thirty by 1800.[44] No vehicle of communication was more significant than newspapers; in time men of all persuasions came to believe that the press was almost single-handedly shaping the contours of American political life. The number of newspapers grew from fewer than 100 in 1790 to over 230 by 1800; by 1810 Americans were buying over 22 million copies of 376 newspapers annually, the largest aggregate circulation of newspapers of any country in the world.[45] With this increase in readership came a change in the newspaper's style and content. Although much of the press, especially that in Federalist control, retained its eighteenth-century character, other papers began responding to the wider democratic public. Prices were reduced, new eye-catching typography was used, cartoons appeared, political information replaced advertisements on the front pages, political speeches, debates, and rumors were printed, editorials were written, and classical pseudonyms were dropped as "a friend of the people" or "one of the people" became more attractive signatures. In most public writing there was a noticeable simplification and vulgarization: the number of footnotes, the classical and literary allusions, the general display of learning, all became less common, as authors sought, in the way Paine had, to adapt to the new popular character of their readers.[46]

Not all gentlemen in the 1790s became Federalists, of course, nor did all gentlemen become apprehensive over what was happening. Jefferson and the other gentlemen who came to constitute the Republican leadership retained a remarkable amount of the earlier Whig confidence in the people and in what Jefferson called the "honest heart" of the common man. Part of this faith in democracy on the part of Jefferson and his Republican colleagues in the South can be attributed to their very insulation from it, for most of the southern planters remained comparatively immune to the democratic electoral politics that were beginning to seriously disrupt northern society and to eat away the popular deference to "the better sort" that the southern gentry took for granted.[47] Moreover, because these democratic developments in the North—not only the new popular literature and the broadened public but also the expanded suffrage, the new immigrants, the mobilization of new men into politics—all tended to support the Republican cause, they seemed unalarming to Republican gentlemen everywhere and only vindications of their trust in the people and fulfillments of the Revolution.

Nevertheless, the Republican intellectual leaders at first showed little more knowledge than the Federalists in dealing with an expanded American public. To be sure, Jefferson, in good Enlightenment manner, had always favored the full exchange of ideas and almost alone among the Founding Fathers had disliked the Philadelphia Convention delegates' "tying up the tongues of their members"—a decision, he said, which only reflected "their ignorance of the value of public discussion." And right at the outset of the 1790s Madison had urged as being favorable to liberty and republican government the development of "whatever facilitated a general intercourse of sentiments," such as roads, commerce, frequent elections, and "particularly a circulation of newspapers through the entire body of the people."[48] But during the 1790s, when the popularization of American culture was proceeding rapidly, Jefferson continued to rely extensively on private correspondence for the dissemination of his views, and Madison continued to write learned pieces, like his "Helvidius" essays, for a restricted audience of educated gentlemen.

Others, however, dozens of writers and speakers, common, ordinary obscure men, men without breeding, without learning, without character—in short, persons who were not gentlemen—were now presuming "without scruple, to undertake the high task of enlightening the public mind." By 1800, wrote the Reverend Samuel Miller in his elaborate compendium of the Enlightenment entitled *A Brief Retrospect of the Eighteenth Century*, much of the intellectual leadership of America had very recently fallen into "the hands of persons destitute at once of the urbanity of gentlemen, the information of scholars, and the principles of virtue."[49] And these intellectual upstarts were for the most part supporting the Republican Party, and in their literature were exceeding even the Federalists in scurrility and vituperation and reaching out to touch an audience as obscure and ordinary as themselves.

To the Federalist this upstart nature of both authors and audience was precisely the point of their frenzied response to the literature of the 1790s. It was one thing to endure calumny and abuse from one's own social kind. That had been a constant part of Anglo-American political life for a century or more. But it was quite another thing to suffer such invective from social inferiors, from nongentlemen, from "uneducated printers, shop boys, and raw schoolmasters," and to have such criticism and vituperation carried down to the lowest levels of the society.[50] Like freethinking and deistic religious views, such personal abuse was socially harmless as long as it was confined to the gentlemanly ranks. But when it spread to the lower orders, as it was doing in the 1790s at the hands of Republican publications, it tended to destroy the governing gentry's personal reputation for character and the deferential respect for the rulers by the common people on which the authority of the political order was based.

It was these considerations—the belief that the channels of communication between governors and governed were rapidly becoming poisoned by mushroom intellectual leadership and the fear that the stability of the entire political order was at stake—that lay behind the Federalists' desperate resort to coercion, the sedition law of 1798—an action that more than anything else has tarnished their historical reputation. The Federalists' attempt to stop up the flow of malice and falsehood from the Republican presses by the use of state power may have been desperate, but it was not irrational, as the subsequent debate over the Sedition Act showed. For at issue in the debate was not simply freedom of the press but the very nature and structure of America's intellectual life.

The debate over the Sedition Act marked the crucial turning point in the democratization of American intellectual life. It fundamentally altered America's understanding not only of its intellectual leadership but of its conception of public truth. The debate, which spilled over into the early years of the nineteenth century, drew out and articulated the logic of America's intellectual experience since the Revolution, and in the process it undermined the foundations of the elitist eighteenth-century classical world on which the Founding Fathers stood.

The English had celebrated freedom of the press since the seventeenth century, but had meant by it, in contrast with the French, no prior restraint or censorship of what was published. Under English law people were nevertheless held responsible for what they published. If a person's publications were slanderous and calumnious enough to bring public officials into disrespect, then under the common law the publisher could be prosecuted for seditious libel. The truth of what was published was no defense; indeed, it even aggravated the offense. Furthermore, under the common law judges, not juries, had the responsibility to decide whether or not a publication was seditious. Although this common law view of seditious libel had been challenged by the Zenger trial in New York in 1735, it had never been fully eradicated from American thinking or practice.

The Federalists in their Sedition Act of 1798 thought they were being generous by changing the common law conception of seditious libel and enacting the Zenger defense into law. They not only allowed juries to determine what was seditious but also they made truth a defense, stating that only those statements that were "false, scandalous, and malicious" would be punished. But the Republican polemicists would have no part of this generosity. In the debate over the sedition law the Republican libertarian theorists rejected both the old common law restrictions on the liberty of the press and the new legal recognition of the distinction between truth and falsity of opinion that the Federalists had incorporated into the Sedition Act. While the Federalists clung to the eighteenth century's conception that "truths" were constant and universal and capable of being discovered by enlightened and reasonable men, the Republicans argued that opinions about government and governors were many and diverse and their truth could not be determined simply by individual judges and juries, no matter how reasonable such men were. Hence, they concluded that all political opinions—that is, words as distinct from overt acts—even those opinions that were "false, scandalous, and malicious," ought to be allowed, as Jefferson put it, to "stand undisturbed as monuments of the safety with which error of opinion may be tolerated where reason is left free to combat it."[51]

The Federalists were incredulous. "How . . . could the rights of the people require a liberty to utter falsehood?" they asked. "How could it be right to do wrong?"[52] It was not an easy question to answer, as we continue to discover. The Republicans felt they could not deny outright the possibility of truth and falsity in political beliefs, and thus they fell back on a tenuous distinction, developed by Jefferson in his first inaugural address, between principles and opinions. Principles, it seemed, were hard and fixed, while opinions were soft and fluctuating; therefore, said Jefferson, "every difference of opinion is not a difference of principle." The implication was, as Benjamin Rush suggested, that individual opinions did not count as much as they had in the past, and for that reason such individual opinions could be permitted the freest possible expression.[53]

What ultimately made such distinctions and arguments comprehensible was the Republicans' assumption that opinions about politics were no longer the monopoly of the educated and aristocratic few. Not only were true and false opinions equally to be tolerated but everyone and anyone in the society should be equally able to express them. Sincerity and honesty, the Republican polemicists argued, were far more important in the articulation of ultimate political truth than learning and fancy words that had often been used to deceive and dissimulate. Truth was actually the creation of many voices and many minds, no one of which was more important than another and each of which made its own separate and equally significant contribution. Solitary individual opinions may thus have counted for less, but in their numerous collectivity they now added up to something far more significant than had ever existed before. When mingled together they resulted into what was called "public opinion." But this public opinion was no longer the small intimate entity it had been for the Revolutionary leaders; it was huge and impersonal, modern and democratic, and it included everyone's opinion. This new expanded idea of public opinion soon came to dominate all of American intellectual life.[54]

Public opinion is so much a part of our politics that it is surprising that we have not incorporated it into the Constitution. We constantly use the term, seek to measure whatever it is and to influence it, and worry about who else is influencing it. Public opinion exists in any state, but in our democracy it has a special power. The Revolution in America transformed it and gave it its modern significance. By the early years of the nineteenth century, Americans had come to realize that public opinion, "that invisible guardian of honour—that eagle eyed spy on human actions—that inexorable judge of men and manners—that arbiter, whom tears cannot appease, nor ingenuity soften and from whose terrible decisions there is no appeal," had become "the vital principle" underlying American government, society, and culture.[55] It became the resolving force not only of political truth but of all truth—from disputes among religious denominations to controversies over artistic taste. Nothing was more important in explaining and clarifying the democratization of the American mind than this conception of public opinion. In the end it became America's nineteenth-century popular substitute for the elitist intellectual leadership of the Revolutionary generation.

Although the will of the people, the vox populi, was an old idea in Western culture, it took on an enhanced significance in the latter half of the eighteenth century in response to the steady democratization of Western society. During the Revolutionary era many American leaders, echoing Hume and other enlightened thinkers, had become convinced that public opinion ought to be "the real sovereign" in any free government like theirs. Yet when Madison in 1791 referred to public opinion he was still thinking of it as the intellectual product of limited circles of gentlemen-rulers. Which is why he feared that the large extent of the United States made the isolated individual insignificant in his own eyes and made easier the counterfeiting of opinion by a few.[56] Other Americans, however, were coming to see in the very breadth of the country and in the very insignificance of the solitary individual the saving sources of a general opinion that could be trusted.

Because American society was not an organic hierarchy with "an intellectual unity," public opinion in America, it was now argued, could not be the consequence of the intellectual leadership of a few learned gentlemen. General public opinion was simply "an aggregation of individual sentiments," the combined product of multitudes of minds thinking and reflecting independently, communicating their ideas in different ways, causing opinions to collide and blend with one another, to refine and correct themselves, leading toward "the ultimate triumph of Truth." Such a product, such a public opinion, could be trusted because it had so many sources, so many voices and minds, all interacting, that no individual or group could manipulate or dominate the whole.[57] Like the example of religious diversity in America, a comparison many now drew upon to explain their new confidence in public opinion, the separate opinions allowed to circulate freely would by their very differentness act, in Jefferson's word, as "a Censor" over each other and the society—performing the role that the ancients and Augustan Englishmen had expected heroic individuals and satiric poets to perform.[58]

Americans' belief that this aggregation of individual sentiments—this residue of separate and diverse interacting opinions—would become the repository of ultimate truth required in the end an act of faith, a faith that was not much different from a belief in the beneficent workings of providence. In fact, this conception of public opinion as the transcendent consequence of many utterances, none of which deliberately created it, was an aspect of a larger intellectual transformation that was taking place in these years. It was related to a new appreciation of the nature of the social and historical process being developed by Western intellectuals, particularly by that brilliant group of Scottish social scientists writing at the end of the eighteenth century. Just as numerous economic competitors, buyers and sellers in the market, were led by an invisible hand to promote an end that was no part of their intent, so too could men now conceive of numerous individual thinkers, makers and users of ideas, being led to create a result, a public opinion, that none of them anticipated or consciously brought about.

In such a world, a democratic world of progress, providence, and innumerable isolated but equal individuals, there could be little place for the kind of extraordinary intellectual leadership the Revolutionary generation had demonstrated. Because, as Americans now told themselves over and over, "public opinion will be much nearer the truth, than the reasoning and refinements of speculative or interested men," because "public opinion has, in more instances than one, triumphed over critics and connoisseurs" even in matters of artistic taste, because, as the Federalists warned, public opinion was "of all things the most destructive of personal independence & of that weight of character which a great man ought to possess," because of all these leveling and democratizing forces, it was no longer possible for individual gentlemen, in their speeches and writings, to make themselves felt in the way the Founding Fathers had.[59]

In the new egalitarian society of the early nineteenth century, where every man's opinion seemed as good as another's, either "men of genius" (they could no longer be simply educated gentlemen) became "a sort of outlaws," lacking "that *getting-along* faculty which is naturally enough the measure of a man's mind in a young country, where every one has his fortune to make." Or, in trying to emulate the civic consciousness of the Founding Fathers, such would-be intellectual leaders ended up being "fettered by fear of popular offense or [having] wasted their energies and debased their dignity in a mawkish and vulgar courting of popular favor."[60] It was not a world the Founding Fathers wanted or expected; indeed, those who lived long enough into the nineteenth century to experience its full force were deeply disillusioned by what they had wrought. Yet they had helped to create this popular world, for it was rooted in the vital principle that none of them, Federalists included, ever could deny—the people. In the end nothing illustrates better the transforming democratic radicalism of the American Revolution than the way its intellectual leaders, that remarkable group of men, contributed to their own demise.

NOTES

This is a retitled, revised, and updated version of an article written nearly twenty-five years ago, "The Democratization of Mind in the American Revolution," in *Library of Congress Symposia on the American Revolution: Leadership in the American Revolution,* 3d (Washington, D.C.: Library of Congress, 1974), 63–89.

1. Henry Steele Commager, "Leadership in Eighteenth-Century America and Today," *Daedalus* 90 (1961): 652; Adrienne Koch, ed., *The American Enlightenment* (New York: Braziller, 1965), 35.

2. Samuel Eliot Morison, ed., "William Manning's "*The Key of Libberty*," *William and Mary Quarterly*, 3d ser., 13 (1956): 208.

3. Franklin to Colden, October 11, 1750; Leonard W. Labaree et al., eds., *Papers of Benjamin Franklin* (New Haven: Yale University Press, 1961), 4:68.

4. Jefferson to Monroe, May 20, 1782, in Adrienne Koch and William Peden, eds., *The Life and Selected Writings of Thomas Jefferson* (New York: Random House/Modern Library, 1944), 56.

5. Gordon S. Wood, *The Radicalism of the American Revolution* (New York: Alfred A. Knopf, 1992), 24–42; Richard L. Bushman, *The Refinement of America: Persons, Houses, Cities* (New York: Alfred A. Knopf, 1992).

6. Robert F. Sayre, *The Examined Self: Benjamin Franklin, Henry Adams, Henry James* (Princeton: Princeton University Press, 1964), 12–43.

7. David D. Hall has contended that eighteenth-century evangelical religious writing was already popular and designed to reach a wide readership. No doubt he is correct about the early transformation of evangelical writing, but most of the political literature remained part of the cosmopolitan "system" that "presumed hierarchy and

privilege." Hall, *Cultures of Print: Essays in the History of the Book* (Amherst: University of Massachusetts Press, 1996), 152.

8. For the intimate nature of the networks of communication in the eighteenth century, see Richard D. Brown, *Knowledge Is Power: The Diffusion of Information in Early America, 1700–1865* (New York: Oxford University Press, 1989), 89–90, 271, 278. This public sphere is essentially the polite and clubby world David S. Shields has reconstructed so brilliantly in his *Civil Tongues and Polite Letters in British America* (Chapel Hill: University of North Carolina Press, 1997). Although Shields emphasizes the ways the "discursive manners" of this world crossed social ranks and spread throughout American society, it seems evident that in comparison to what followed in the nineteenth century the eighteenth-century world he describes was still at heart an aristocratic one.

9. Joanna B. Freeman, "Dueling as Politics: Reinterpreting the Burr-Hamilton Duel," *William and Mary Quarterly*, 3d ser., 53 (1996): 289–318; Freeman, *Affairs of Honor: National Politics in the New Republic* (New Haven, Conn.: Yale University Press, 2001).

10. [John Randolph], *Considerations on the Present State of Virginia* (n.p., 1774); quoted in Merrill Jensen, "The Articles of Confederation," in *Library of Congress Symposia on the American Revolution: Fundamental Testaments of the American Revolution,* 2d (Washington, D.C.: Library of Congress, 1973), 56.

11. On the refined and restricted nature of classical rhetoric in the eighteenth century, see Kenneth Cmiel, *Democratic Eloquence: The Fight over Popular Speech in Nineteenth-Century America* (Berkeley: University of California Press, 1990), chap. 1.

12. Homer L. Calkin, "Pamphlets and Public Opinion during the American Revolution," *Pennsylvania Magazine of History and Biography* 64 (1940): 30, 35.

13. Frank Luther Mott, *American Journalism: A History, 1690–1960*, 3d ed. (New York: Macmillan, 1962), 3–64; Mott, *A History of American Magazines, 1741–1850* (New York: D. Appleton, 1930), 13–67; Arthur M. Schlesinger, *Prelude to Independence: The Newspaper War on Britain, 1764–1776* (New York: Vintage, 1965), 51–66, 303–4; Philip Davidson, *Propaganda and the American Revolution, 1763–1783* (Chapel Hill: University of North Carolina Press, 1941). Charles Evans's great bibliography of American publications between 1639 and 1799 numbers twelve volumes. Three volumes cover publications from the first 125 years of American history up to 1764; the remaining nine volumes contain the publications of the last thirty-four years of the century—a graphic measure of the explosion of reading material in the Revolutionary era.

14. By assuming that a large and impersonal public sphere existed well before the Revolution and that the participants in this sphere were unknown and unknowable, Michael Warner seems to be anticipating the future too quickly. Although a public sphere was certainly growing quite rapidly in the eighteenth century, many authors continued to write as if they and their readers were known to one another. See Warner, *The Letters of the Republic: Publication and the Public Sphere in Eighteenth-Century America* (Cambridge: Harvard University Press, 1990), chaps. 1–2. That different scholars emphasize different public spheres seems to stem from the fact that the boundaries of cultural change can never be sharply demarcated: the future is always present in the past and the past is always present even after the future arrives.

15. References to the republic of letters are common in the Revolutionaries' writings. See, for example, Brooke Hindle, *The Pursuit of Science in Revolutionary America, 1735–1789* (Chapel Hill: University of North Carolina Press, 1956), 384.

16. Bernard Bailyn, *The Ideological Origins of the American Revolution* (Cambridge: Harvard University Press, 1967), 23.

17. Calkin, "Pamphlets and Public Opinion," *Penn. Mag. of Hist. and Biog.* 64 (1940): 28, 35.

18. John Adams, *Diary and Autobiography*, ed. L. H. Butterfield et al. (Cambridge: Harvard University Press, 1961), 3:331–32.

19. Bailyn, *Ideological Origins*, 4–5, 17.

20. John J. Teunissen, "Blockheadism and the Propaganda Plays of the American Revolution," *Early American Literature* 7 (1972): 148–62. It was no easy matter for women to participate in the public sphere. They were prohibited from speaking in public, and only a few, like Warren, were able to get their writings published, and then only anonymously. On Warren, see Rosemarie Zagarri, *A Women's Dilemma: Mercy Otis Warren and the American Revolution* (Wheeling, Ill.: Harlan Davidson, 1995).

21. Maynard Mack, "The Muse of Satire," in Richard C. Boys, ed., *Studies in the Literature of the Augustan Age: Essays Collected in Honor of Arthur Ellicott Case* (New York: Gordian, 1966).

22. On eighteenth-century rhetoric, see Wilbur Samuel Howell, *Eighteenth-Century British Logic and Rhetoric* (Princeton: Princeton University Press, 1971); Peter France, *Rhetoric and Truth in France: Descartes to Diderot* (Oxford: Clarendon, 1972); Warren Guthrie, "The Development of Rhetorical Theory in America, 1635–1850," *Speech Monographs* 13 (1946): 14–22; 14 (1947): 38–54; 15 (1948): 61–71.

23. Jay Fliegelman refers to these changes as "the elocutionary revolution." See his *Declaring Independence: Jefferson, Natural Language, and the Culture of Performance* (Stanford: Stanford University Press, 1993), 20–35.

24. Rhys Isaac, *The Transformation of Virginia, 1740–1790* (Chapel Hill: University of North Carolina Press, 1982), 267–69; Arthur H. Shaffer, ed., *Edmund Randolph: History of Virginia* (Charlottesville: University of Virginia Press, 1970), 179–81.

25. Eric Foner, *Tom Paine and Revolutionary America* (New York: Oxford University Press, 1976), 82–86; Bernard Bailyn, "Common Sense," in *Library of Congress Symposia on the American Revolution: Fundamental Testaments*, 2d (Washington, D.C.: Library of Congress, 1943), 7–22; John Keane, *Tom Paine: A Political Life* (New York: Little, Brown, 1995), x; Thomas Paine, *Common Sense* (1776), in *The Complete Writings of Thomas Paine*, ed. Philip S. Foner (New York: Citadel, 1969), 1:8; James T. Boulton, *The Language of Politics in the Age of Wilkes and Burke* (London: Routledge & Kegan Paul, 1963), chap. 7.

26. David Freeman Hawke, *Paine* (New York, 1974), 53, 101; Keane, *Paine*, 179.

27. Gary B. Nash, "The Transformation of Urban Politics, 1700–1765," *Journal of American History* 60 (1973): 605–32.

28. J. R. Pole, *Political Representation in England and the Origins of the American Republic* (London: St. Martin's, 1966), 9–70, 277–78.

29. Alexander Martin to Governor Caswell, July 27, 1787, in Max Farrand, ed., *The Records of the Federal Convention of 1787* (New Haven: Yale University Press, 1911–37), 4:64.

30. Jared Sparks, Journal, April 19, 1830, in Farrand, *Records of the Federal Convention,* 3:479.

31. John Dickinson, in Farrand, *Records of the Federal Convention,* 2:278.

32. John Marshall (Va.), in Jonathan Elliot, ed., *The Debates in the Several State Conventions on the Adoption of the Federal Constitution*, 2d ed. (Washington, D.C.,

1836–45), 3:222; Gordon S. Wood, *The Creation of the American Republic, 1776–1787* (Chapel Hill: University of North Carolina Press, 1969), 524, 526–64.

33. Gordon S. Wood, "Conspiracy and the Paranoid Style: Causality and Deceit in the Eighteenth Century," *William and Mary Quarterly* 39 (1982): 403–41.

34. John Adams to Patrick Henry, June 3, 1776, in *The Works of John Adams . . .*, ed. Charles Francis Adams (Boston: Little, Brown, 1850–56), 9:387–88; Thomas Jefferson to Benjamin Franklin, August 13, 1777, in *The Papers of Thomas Jefferson*, ed. Julian P. Boyd et al. (Princeton: Princeton University Press, 1950–), 2:26; Roger Atkinson to Samuel Pleasants, November 23, 1776, quoted in James Kirby Martin, *Men in Rebellion: Higher Governmental Leaders and the Coming of the American Revolution* (New Brunswick, N.J.: Rutgers University Press, 1973), 190.

35. Meyer Reinhold, "Opponents of Classical Learning in America during the Revolutionary Period," *Proceedings of the American Philosophical Society* 112 (1968): 221–34; Linda K. Kerber, *Federalists in Dissent: Imagery and Ideology in Jeffersonian America* (Ithaca, N.Y.: Cornell University Press, 1970), 95–134.

36. Amos Singletary (Mass.), in Elliot, *Debates*, 2:102.

37. George L. Roth, "American Theory of Satire, 1790–1820," *American Literature* 29 (1958): 399–407; Roth, "Verse Satire on 'Faction,' 1790–1815," *William and Mary Quarterly*, 3d ser., 17 (1960): 473–85; Bruce I. Granger, *Political Satire in the American Revolution, 1763–1783* (Ithaca, N.Y.: Cornell University Press, 1960), 2.

38. Robert E. Spiller et al., *Literary History of the United States*, 3d ed. (New York: Macmillan, 1963), 175; Benjamin Spencer, *The Quest for Nationality: An American Literary Campaign* (Syracuse, N.Y.: Syracuse University Press, 1957), 65.

39. Fisher Ames, "American Literature," *Works of Fisher Ames*, ed. Seth Ames (Boston: Little, Brown, 1854), 2:439–40.

40. Richard Buel Jr., *Securing the Revolution: Ideology in American Politics, 1789–1815* (Ithaca, N.Y.: Cornell University Press, 1972), 113; Gerald Stourzh, *Alexander Hamilton and the Idea of Republican Government* (Stanford: Stanford University Press, 1970), 95–106.

41. John Rutledge Jr. to Harrison Gray Otis, April 3, 1803, quoted in David Hackett Fischer, *The Revolution of American Conservatism: The Federalist Party in the Era of Jeffersonian Democracy* (New York: Harper & Row, 1969), 140; Alexander Hamilton to Theodore Sedgwick, February 2, 1799, in *The Works of Alexander Hamilton*, ed. Henry Cabot Lodge (New York: Putnam's, 1903), 10:340; [Fisher Ames], "Laocoon. No. 1," in *Works*, 2:113.

42. Thomas Truxtun to John Adams, December 5, 1804, quoted in Fischer, *American Conservatism*, 133–34.

43. Donald H. Stewart, *The Opposition Press of the Federalist Period* (Albany: State University of New York Press, 1969), 634, 638, 640.

44. Sidney I. Pomerantz, *New York: An American City, 1783–1803* (Port Washington, N.Y.: Ira J. Friedman, 1965), 440.

45. Mott, *American Journalism*, 167; Merle Curti, *The Growth of American Thought*, 3d ed. (New York: Harper & Row, 1964), 209; Stewart, *Opposition Press*, 15, 624.

46. Fischer, *American Conservatism*, 129–49; Stewart, *Opposition Press,* 19; Jere R. Daniell, *Republicanism: New Hampshire Politics and the American Revolution, 1741–1794* (Cambridge: Harvard University Press, 1970), 235–36.

47. Buel, *Securing the Revolution*, 75–90.

48. Jefferson to John Adams, August 30, 1787, in Farrand, ed., *Records of the Federal Convention*, 3:6; Madison, "Public Opinion," *National Gazette*, December 19,

1791, in *The Writings of James Madison*, ed. Gaillard Hunt (New York: Putnam's, 1900–1910), 6:70.

49. Samuel Miller, *A Brief Retrospect of the Eighteenth Century* . . . (New York: T. and J. Swords, 1803), 2:254–55.

50. Fisher Ames to Jeremiah Smith, December 14, 1802, quoted in Fischer, *American Conservatism*, 135.

51. [George Hay], *An Essay on the Liberty of the Press* . . . (Philadelphia: Printed at the Aurora office, 1799), 40; Jefferson, Inaugural Address, March 4, 1801, Koch and Peden, eds., *Writings of Jefferson*, 322.

52. Samuel Dana, Debates in Congress, January 1801, quoted in Buel, *Securing the Revolution*, 252.

53. Jefferson, Inaugural Address, March 4, 1801, Koch and Peden, eds., *Writings of Jefferson*, 322; Rush to Jefferson, March 12, 1801, *Letters of Benjamin Rush*, ed. Lyman H. Butterfield (Princeton: Princeton University Press, 1951), 2:831.

54. Tunis Wortman, *A Treatise Concerning Political Enquiry, and the Liberty of the Press* (New York: G. Forman, 1800), 118–23, 155–57.

55. William Crafts Jr., *An Oration on the Influence of Moral Causes on National Character, Delivered before the Phi Beta Kappa Society, on Their Anniversary, 28 August,* 1817 (Cambridge: University Press/Hilliard & Metcalf, 1817), 5–6; Wortman, *Treatise*, 180.

56. Madison, "Public Opinion," *National Gazette*, December 19, 1791, in Hunt, *Writings of Madison*, 6:70.

57. Wortman, *Treatise*, 118–19, 122–23.

58. Jefferson to John Adams, January 11, 1816, in Lester J. Cappon, ed., *The Adams-Jefferson Letters* (Chapel Hill: University of North Carolina Press, 1959), 2:458.

59. Samuel Williams, *The Natural and Civil History of Vermont*, 2d ed. (Burlington, Vt.: Samuel Mills, 1809), 2:394; Joseph Hopkinson, *Annual Discourse, Delivered Before the Pennsylvania Academy of the Fine Arts* . . . (Philadelphia: Bradford and Inskeep, 1810), 29; Theodore Sedgwick to Rufus King, May 11, 1800, quoted in Richard E. Welch Jr., *Theodore Sedgwick, Federalist: A Political Portrait* (Middletown, Conn.: Wesleyan University Press, 1965), 211.

60. [Richard Henry Dana Sr.], "Review of the Sketch Book of Geoffrey Crayon, Gent.," *North American Review* 9 (1819): 327; Theron Metcalf, *An Address to the Phi Beta Kappa Society of Brown University, Delivered 5th September, 1832* (Boston: n.p., 1833), 6.

6

The Changing Role of the Public Intellectual in American History

John Patrick Diggins

A discussion of the role of the public intellectual in American history begins with a question: What do we mean by the term "intellectual"? Generally it has referred to those with the superior gifts to wield the power of the written word. Yet many who are regarded as such would want to deny the term's being applied to themselves. Once the British philosopher Bertrand Russell was asked for his definition of an intellectual. "I have never called myself an intellectual, and no one has dared to call me one in my presence," replied Lord Russell. "I think an intellectual may be defined as a person who pretends to have more intellect than he has, and I hope this definition does not fit me."[1] The late Richard Hofstadter once quipped that an intellectual is a person who likes to turn easy answers into harder questions.[2] However much intellectuals themselves shy away from providing a definition, the term came into prominence in its noun form at the time of the Dreyfus affair (1893–1906), when the radical French intellectual community rose to defend the republic from its reactionary enemies. Observing that affair, the American philosopher William James issued a warning about the role of intellectuals in society. "We 'intellectuals' in America must all work to keep our precious birthright of individualism and freedom free from these institutions [church, army, aristocracy, royalty]. Every great institution is perforce a means of corruption—whatever good it may do. Only in the free personal relation is full ideality to be found."[3] A half-century later, when the American intellectual was less interested in preserving his individuality than engaging in collective protest, the literary scholar Lionel Trilling described the phenomenon as the "adversarial culture," implying that the writer and artist relished the thought of always assaulting the status quo. In recent times the term "intellectual" connotes the critic who would rather deny than affirm, the estranged outsider at once negative and antagonistic.

The term "public intellectual" has a different connotation entirely. First coined by the historian Russell Jacoby, the term was meant to distinguish an almost lost species from the more newly emerging academic scholar.[4] The earlier public intellectual wrote for a general readership and often became a notable speaker addressing topics of popular interest. Many of these figures worked in journalism and believed that accessible communication was as important as rigorous analysis. The academic scholar, however, chose to specialize and write in a prose weighted with technical jargon and on subjects that only a handful of specialists find interesting. Jacoby had in mind the pre–World War II period when he saw public intellectuals like Walter Lippmann and Reinhold Niebuhr flourishing. Yet the role of the intellectual as a public figure has far deeper roots in American history, so much so that one might suggest that in the beginning American history and the American mind were inseparable.

THE FUSION OF POWER AND INTELLECT AND ITS BREAKDOWN: SEVENTEENTH AND EIGHTEENTH CENTURIES

In the earliest episode of American intellectual history—New England Puritanism—men of knowledge and learning were indispensable. During this period, roughly between 1630 and the advent of the Enlightenment toward the end of the century, life was conceived primarily in theological terms. All aspects of Calvinist theology required the most rigorous analysis and interpretation: the nature of the covenant with God, faith and reason, predestination and moral responsibility, original sin, and the meaning of true virtue. As members of the "elect," those who had been blessed with grace and had undergone some inward mystical-spiritual experience, intellectuals enjoyed the status of minister and moral guardian. The role of leaders and philosophers like John Winthrop and Jonathan Edwards was to interpret the meaning of existence by explaining the ways of God to man.

New England Puritanism, however, lasted but two generations. Its decline could be seen in such episodes as the Half-Way Covenant (1661), when the children of first-generation settlers were allowed to become church members without having undergone a conversion experience; and in the Salem witchcraft hysteria (1690–1694), when Puritan theology came to be seen by some as too medieval and superstitious to deal with the stresses and strains of daily life. With the advent of the Enlightenment in the early eighteenth century, America began to leave the world of John Winthrop to embrace the world of Benjamin Franklin, turning from faith and scripture to learn from science and nature. The purpose of life was now conceived to be not so much salvation as success, not the inner mysteries of the soul but the external "pursuit of happiness."

During the imperial crisis of the 1760s and 1770s, Calvinism still played an important role. In the American Revolution, unlike the French and many other revolutions, many churchmen sided with secular philosophers in opposing British rule in the colonies. Although a few ministers like Jonathan Boucher preached the religious duty of submission to sovereign authority, most Americans followed John Wise in advocating resistance to unpopular government as an obligation to uphold the Puritan covenant and preserve America from the corruptions of Europe. Even more influential were Thomas Paine and Thomas Jefferson, liberal thinkers who drew on the laws of nature and of God to lay down the foundation for the natural rights of man. Whether or not the American Revolution was *made* by those who enter history from "the bottom up," by the workers, artisans, and small farmers that are the subjects of Marxist historians, few can deny that it was *led* by intellectuals and scholars, by those capable of articulating the reasons that give philosophical legitimacy to the right of revolution.

In America during the era of the Founding Fathers we have what might be regarded as the most complete fusion of power and intellect. The Revolution called on the founders to demonstrate why illegitimate authority must be opposed and why not only reason and argument but also power and even violence may be resorted to in order to preserve liberty. The drafting of the Constitution required its framers to demonstrate somewhat the opposite; to show why the new federal system required the enlargement of centralized power in the new national government and why Americans should render obedience to the new system as the best means of safeguarding their liberties and protecting their interests. In this role the framers performed as scholars as well as statesmen. Most had been highly educated in America or abroad, and among those who participated in the heated debates at the Philadelphia Convention were two university presidents and three college professors. Indeed, John Adams's *A Defense of the Constitutions of the Government of the United States of America* was an attempt to answer the French critics of America's new system of government, and he did so by displaying his keen knowledge of ancient and modern traditions of political philosophy from Machiavelli to Montesquieu. Alexander Hamilton and James Madison displayed similar feats of intellect in *The Federalist.* They had to demonstrate why it was necessary to come forth with a "new science of politics" that would depart from the classical heritage of "civic virtue" and still preserve liberty by other means. We need not explore the arguments of the Federalists and the anti-Federalists, those who sought to convince Americans to reject the new "experiment." It suffices to note that both those who supported and those who opposed the Constitution subscribed to the Enlightenment assumption that the man of ideas had a responsibility to use his superior mental prowess to grasp the lessons of history in order to control the movement of power. Never again in American history would the political intellect shine so brilliantly as in this golden age of the founding. Yet at the very moment of America's political founding there existed a kind of hidden irony that has gone almost unnoticed in modern historical and political science scholarship.[5] What would be the role of the intellectual in this "new science of politics"? More precisely, would he have any role?

In *Federalist* 10 Madison addresses this question directly. The anti-Federalists had been arguing that many of the structural mechanisms of the new Constitution were not needed to control power and adjudicate clashing interests, for such problems could be handled by men of superior learning. "It is in vain," Madison replies to this argument, "to say that enlightened statesmen will be able to adjust these clashing interests, and render them all subservient to the public good. Enlightened statesmen will not always be at the helm."[6] What Madison is saying, in effect, is that although his generation of the framers are men of reason and virtue, they must use their ability to construct a Constitution that will not have need of men of such caliber, for America can never again count on their appearance. Henceforth it would be not the moral qualities of man but the "machinery of government" that would perpetuate the Republic. Thus, unlike the twentieth-century sociologist Karl Mannheim, the American framers did not see the intellectual as the one member of society who was capable of rising above economic interests and political passions to offer a "disinterested" perspective on matters of government. John Adams even suggested that men of superior wealth and intellect be subject to "ostracism" by being isolated in the Senate so that they would not be able to prey on the weaker and less intelligent members of the lower House of Congress.[7]

In some respects it could be said that in the political founding of America the intellectual elite was likened to the idle aristocracy of Europe, creatures whom both the Federalists and anti-Federalists looked on with varying degrees of distrust. But the disturbing irony is that it took the intellectual man of letters to conceive of a new system of government that would not require the activity of intellect to perpetuate it. What became known as "liberal pluralism" in political science, the competitive clash of interest group politics, would be self-regulating and find its own equilibrium.[8]

THE ALIENATION OF THE INTELLECTUAL: THE NINETEENTH CENTURY

The role of the intellectual shifted considerably in the nineteenth century: no longer was he the nation's spiritual guardian or political mentor. Several developments took place in the pre–Civil War years that tended to regulate the man of learning to the periphery of society.

Evangelicalism

The religious revivals that swept America beginning in the 1830s struck out against the authority of the intellect in favor of the prompting of the heart. As emotion replaced reason as the foundation of belief, the idea of a learned minister gave way to the popular orator with a flair for pulpit theatrics. Soon preachers and their followers became convinced that one could get closer to God without a college education.

Jacksonianism

The advent of mass democracy with the election of Andrew Jackson in 1828 seemed to discredit the intellectual as statesman. Jackson ran against John Quincy Adams, a deeply learned and refined man who wanted to see America develop culturally as well as economically. But Jackson was a military hero from the War of 1812, and the election pitted "the man who can write against/the man who can fight," as one wit put it. Adams embodied the older elitist tradition of politics, which his opponents associated with the decadent idleness of aristocracy. Jackson signified the egalitarian folk hero gifted with a common wisdom that had no need of formal education. Beginning with Jacksonian democracy, the American who ran for political office would be handicapped if he displayed his superior intellect and praised if he could boast of his humble origins, whether a log cabin or a flat above the grocery store. Politics was no longer the domain of the gentlemanly class.

Transcendentalism

In the 1830s and 1840s the most powerful, brilliant flowering of the American mind radiated out of New England and came to be known as transcendentalism, in some ways a counterpart to European romanticism. Several leaders of this movement, especially Ralph Waldo Emerson and Henry D. Thoreau, rejected the life of politics and religion for the "higher" life of poetry and philosophy. If the American intellectual had a role in society, it was not in public affairs. Although many transcendentalists supported the abolitionist crusade against slavery and spoke out against the injustices of capitalist society and the Mexican-American War of 1846, few looked on politics as a noble calling. In their essays on "The American Scholar," "Politics," "Civil Disobedience," and "The Future of the Republic," Emerson and Thoreau explained why the Constitution and the government it sustained had done little to elevate the people, further the spirit of freedom, develop the West and build the country, and, above all, stimulate the intellect and waken the "Oversoul." Against a Lockean philosophy that permeated America with commercialism and materialism, Emerson and Thoreau urged their countrymen to turn to Eastern wisdom and meditate on the sublime truths of Buddhism and Hinduism. Against the pressures of social conformity and the needs of government, they called for a life of solitude and the separation of the self from the state. The intellectual would not be a responsible citizen dedicated to public affairs but a philosopher of ethical insight committed only to the voice of conscience.

As one surveys the role of the intellectual in American history, it is tempting to say that anyone who warrants such a label must have been on the right side of a given political controversy. Surely anyone gifted with a superior mind must be capable of seeing things as they ought to be seen. Such was the assumption of the eighteenth-century Enlightenment, when it was commonly believed that the faculty of reason would bring forth virtuous thinkers who would dedicate themselves to the promotion of freedom. The "mind of the South" in the pre–Civil War years, however, stands as an embarrassment to that assumption. During those years southern thinkers became intensely conscious of their "peculiar institution," slavery. In the face of attacks by northern intellectuals they used their talents to defend a unique way of life that violated the egalitarian principles of the Declaration of Independence, which Abraham Lincoln regarded as the "sheet anchor" of the American republic.

Such southern political thinkers as John C. Calhoun, George Fitzhugh, and William Gilmore Simms constituted a "sacred circle" who justified the South as a superior civilization. Calhoun had to show that the Constitution framed in 1787 had failed to preserve the rights of minorities, and he had in mind not black slaves, of course, but the southern states whose vested interest in chattel labor as property was being threatened by the growing numerical majority of the northern and western states. Southern intellectuals drew on the Bible and ancient history to claim that slavery was a "natural" condition. Fitzhugh in particular has attracted the attention of contemporary Marxist historians for claiming that the slave was better off in the "paternalistic" plantation aristocracy of the South than was the northern wageworker who was being exploited by industrial capitalism. The unique role of the southern intellectual was that he had to deny what was being affirmed elsewhere in American: reason, progress, equality, and justice.[9]

After the Civil War the northern as well as the southern intellectual continued to feel alienated from the center of power. Although the Southerner had been fighting a lost cause in defending slavery and the virtues of plantation aristocracy, the Northerner also came to feel that his cause was hopeless in the postwar era. With the triumph of northern industrial capitalism, the nouveaux riches began to command power and prestige. In the Gilded Age of the 1880s, observed Oliver Wendell Holmes, "the man who commands the attention of his fellows is the man of wealth. Commerce is the great power. The aspirations of the world are those of commerce."[10] The historian Vernon L. Parrington labeled the Gilded Age "the great barbecue," so squalid was its unabashed materialism. The American republic, lamented Parrington, would sell its soul to get rich. The hero of America was not the productive worker, the earnest statesman, or the man of letters; he was the idle rich, the subject of Thorstein Veblen's splendid satire, *The Theory of the Leisure Class* (1899). In a commercial society dominated by the power of wealth and the pleasures of consumption, there would be no central place for the intellectual, and no one felt this more painfully than did Henry Adams.

THE TWENTIETH CENTURY: FROM PROGRESSIVISM TO MARXISM

Woodrow Wilson was the first modern president to qualify as a genuine intellectual. Like the founders John Adams, Thomas Jefferson, and James Madison, Wilson was a man of thought and reflection before he became a man of political action. A professor of jurisprudence and political economy, president of Princeton University, author of seminal books on America's political institutions, Wilson seemed to reverse the widespread prejudice against the intellectual as too bookish and abstract to succeed in the calculating world of politics. He seemed to be the living embodiment of what had then been referred to as "the Wilsonian idea," a school of thought started by Governor Robert La Follette, who believed that the academic scholar could extend his services to the state as a specialized "expert." Yet Wilson failed to capture the imagination of America's intellectual community; his commitment to laissez-faire economics seemed reactionary and his rhetoric too religious and moralistic. Far more appealing was Theodore Roosevelt, the famous "trust-buster" who would use the power of the federal government to discipline big business, the "Rough Rider" who hated the deceits of political corruption as much as he disdained the creature comforts of bourgeois capitalism. Many of America's young college graduates thrilled to Roosevelt's idea of a "New Nationalism," a strong political state that would render industrial capitalism subservient to the public good. To regenerate the American republic by political means also required that citizens participate in public affairs, even if they become involved in machine politics and associate with party bosses. Unlike Henry Adams and Max Weber, Roosevelt did not see modern politics as structurally fated to thwart the fulfillment of political ideals. On the contrary, Roosevelt called on young Americans to immerse themselves in the rough-and-tumble of local politics, the seamy world of saloonkeepers, aldermen, ward heelers, and other fixers and brokers. "Our more intellectual men," Roosevelt complained, "often shrink from the raw coarseness and the eager struggle of political life as if they were women," as if, that is, refinement and delicacy were tantamount to virtue and duty. Whatever threatened the public good—political corruption, *incivisme*, class conflict, racial hatred, corporate power, acquisitive individualism—threatened the future of the republic. Roosevelt was convinced that the young intellectual could prove his masculinity and "virility" by fighting against such forces.[11]

Many of the intellectuals who had a hand in starting the *New Republic* in 1914 had been inspired by Roosevelt's message. Several had written influential books: Herbert Croly, the liberal magazine's editor, had published *The Promise of American Life*; Walter Weyl published *The New Democracy*; and Walter Lippmann produced two texts for the American people to consider, *A Preface to Politics* and *Drift and Mastery*. All had opposed Wilson and his commitment to Jeffersonian individualism, a stance that would have subordinated the intellectual to the "new freedom" to be enjoyed by the entrepreneur and budding capitalist. Instead they sought to save American politics from the Jeffersonianism that had determined the political culture of American history. In addition to overcoming the debilities of individualism, they would transform the mechanistic system of politics bequeathed by *The Federalist* authors, the legacy of liberal pluralism that conceived government as almost a self-regulating "routine" that required no leadership on the part of the intellectual class. They believed that from the philosophy of pragmatism developed by William James and John Dewey they could establish a more empirical approach to politics so that government could be an instrument of social control guided by the canons of science. Croly and Lippmann in particular were elitist and would sometimes refer to the philosopher George Santayana's idea of a "socialistic aristocracy." Because they preferred the leadership of the enlightened few to the unreliable many, some historians have suggested that the *New Republic* intellectuals' nationalistic elitism carried the seeds of "fascism."[12] It is true that *New Republic* writers wanted to see a strong centralized state and believed in the revivifying power of nationalism and the rule of the best and brightest. But they were also pro-labor and still believed in the values of reason and science. Actually they saw themselves as something of an intellectual *samurai*, a superior learned class that would use the power of its mind to fight for social justice. In the final passage of *The Promise of American Life* Croly called on common citizens to rise to "nobility" and "virtue" by imitating "the ability of exceptional fellow-countrymen" who will "offer him acceptable examples of heroism and saintliness." The hero and saint Croly had in mind was Abraham Lincoln. Impressed by Lincoln's willingness to criticize America for its political and moral failings, especially in regard to slavery, Croly praised "the sincerity and depth of his moral insight" that enabled a political leader to approach history with feeling and compassion. "The quality of being magnanimous is both the consummate virtue and the one which is least natural."[13]

But Croly's Lincolnesque Christian concept of politics would be undermined by the nationalism that had forged it. Croly believed that the patriotism and community spirit that had supposedly flowered in ancient Greece and Renaissance Italy could be the historical analogue for American nationalism. Thus when World War I erupted, he used the *New Republic* to advocate intervention; when Wilson went before Congress to ask for a declaration of war in 1917, Croly and other editors were ecstatic. Now the future of the American republic came to be identified as the intellectual responsibility of the *New Republic*, and the journal in turn identified the fate of Progressivism with the future of nationalism. With the Versailles settlement, these equations collapsed as nationalism came to be seen—as Randolph Bourne and Thorstein Veblen had warned—as reactionary rather than progressive. The *New Republic* grew bitterly disillusioned with Wilson and the whole effort to save the world by controlling the forces of history. With the rise of right-wing dictatorships in Italy, Hungary, Poland, and elsewhere in the 1920s, it seemed that liberalism had made the world "safe" for fascism.

While World War I undermined the idea of liberalism, the Russian Revolution undermined the idea of socialism, transforming it from a democratic dream into a party monstrosity that would later become a totalitarian nightmare. Max Eastman, Floyd Dell, and John Reed, editors of *The Masses*, had all applauded Lenin's seizure of power in 1917. With Reed's death in 1920 and the coming to power of Stalin in 1924, the remaining members of what I have called "the Lyrical Left" of the Greenwich Village generation either renounced Bolshevism or lost all interest in politics and revolution.

The antipolitical mood continued in American history through the 1920s, the period of the "Lost Generation" that saw artists and writers fleeing America for Europe. Few thinkers saw themselves as public intellectuals dedicated to the American republic. Instead they saw America as having been burdened by three conditions: a Puritan founding that bequeathed a legacy of repression; a frontier environment that failed to nurture the life of the mind; and a business civilization that turned all value into capitalist exchange relations. Malcolm Cowley's *Exile's Return*, an intimate account of the literati who expatriated to France and Italy, made it clear that the intellectual would find no constructive role in America. Only in Europe could the intellectual achieve some kind of redemption through art and aesthetic adventure.

But the aesthetic spirit of the Lost Generation collapsed with the Wall Street crash and the onset of the Great Depression at the end of the decade. The intellectual was now called on to rejoin the world and commit himself to political struggle. In the early 1930s many of America's leading intellectual figures were attracted to communism. Such writers as John Dos Passos, Granville Hicks, and Edmund Wilson supported the Communist Party in 1932, although few intellectuals became party members. Also during the 1930s a new group of radical intellectuals emerged who came from Jewish and east European immigrant backgrounds. The new journals *Partisan Review* and *Modern Monthly*, unlike the more native and Protestant (liberal) *New Republic* and *Nation*, articulated a Marxist perspective on literature and politics and supported Leon Trotsky as the true heir of the October Revolution. Several intellectuals also began to write books in an attempt to reconcile Marxism with America's political and cultural traditions. In historical scholarship America's past emerged as an industrial battleground seething with class conflict. Journals on the left bristled with arguments over Hegel and the dialectic. The young philosopher Sidney Hook wrote *Toward an Understanding of Karl Marx* in order to explain to Americans why Marxism and the pragmatism of John Dewey had their epistemological foundations in the same principle of "praxis," the testing of all ideas in practical experience. The role of the intellectual was to serve as the "vanguard" of the workers as both pushed America closer and closer to the great moment of revolution.

It would be a mistake to leave the impression that all American intellectuals became radicalized in the 1930s and committed themselves to the cause of communism or Trotskyism. A sizable number of academic intellectuals took leave of their positions as professors to work for the New Deal under President Franklin D. Roosevelt. Legal scholars like Rexford G. Tugwell and A. A. Berle became part of Roosevelt's "Brain Trust," an unofficial cabinet of economists, lawyers, professors, and social workers who wanted to see their expertise used to fight the Depression. It was during the New Deal that the American intellectual became politically institutionalized as a number of government agencies and bureaucracies grew in response to the need for public works, social security, energy and reclamation, budget analysis, and economic planning. Indeed government work proved a godsend for college graduates in search of a job. One college newspaper described the plight of the "locked-out generation":

> I sing in praise of college
> Of M.A.'s and Ph.D.'s
> But in pursuit of knowledge
> We are starving by degrees.

During the World War II years American intellectuals continued to work in government agencies or joined the Office of Strategic Service as translators, ideological advisers, or counterespionage specialists. So did numerous European refugee intellectuals, whose own contribution to the war effort and to American culture in general was enormous. It was the scientific intellectuals, physicists like the Dane Niels Bohr, the German Albert Einstein, and the Italian Enrico Fermi, who were instrumental in the development of the atomic bomb. But the close relationship between the government and the intellectual community collapsed after World War II. Karl Marx once declared that whoever controlled the means of production controlled all power. The scientific intellectual now controlled the means of destruction. With the advent of the Cold War in the late 1940s, the American people grew nervous and suspicious. Was the intellectual to be trusted?

THE COLD WAR, MCCARTHYISM, AND THE FATE OF THE INTELLECTUAL

One of the consequences of the Cold War and the anticommunist hysteria of the post–World War II era was to render the intellectual suspect as a loyal citizen and naive and impractical as a potential statesman. In the 1950s the two-time defeat of Democratic candidate Adlai Stevenson by the Republican Dwight D. Eisenhower seemed a replay of John Quincy Adams's loss to Andrew Jackson in 1828—once again the American people chose a military warrior over a brilliant, witty intellectual. It was against this background, as well as Senator Joseph McCarthy's attack on Ivy League liberals as subversives, that Richard Hofstadter wrote *Anti-Intellectualism in American Life*. If the lost generation of the 1920s rejected America and left for Europe; the generation of the postwar era felt rejected by America and had no place to go. The latter phenomenon was commented on by America's leading weekly, *Time*. Eisenhower's victory, *Time* announced, "discloses an alarming fact long suspected: there is a wide and unhealthy gap between the American intellectuals and the people."[14]

That "gap" began to develop with the onset of the Cold War in 1945, when the secrets of the Yalta Conference were made public and intellectuals were forced to take sides. Conservative Republicans and ex-communist intellectuals charged that Roosevelt had "sold out" the eastern Europeans at Yalta. Liberal Democrats replied that Roosevelt conceded no area that had not already been occupied by the Red Army. But pro-Soviet Democrats like Commerce Secretary Henry Wallace went much further and argued that America's and England's "get-tough" policy would only provoke Stalin to respond in kind. The Cold War debate polarized the intellectual community. Right-wing intellectuals insisted that the Soviets were intent on conquering the world, the thesis of the ex-Trotskyist James Burnham's *The Struggle for the World*. The left wing was just as sure that the Soviets were devoted to peace and security, the position of those Americans who joined Wallace and the Progressive Party movement of 1947–1948. To a certain extent liberal intellectuals were divided among themselves, as indicated by the debates between George Kennan's theory of "containment" and Walter Lippmann's critique of it.[15]

The Cold War years were a period of accusation, guilt, and self-recrimination for American intellectuals. In part these emotions were due to the fact that many intellectuals had flirted with various expressions of radicalism in their younger, student years, and some would continue to harbor illusions about the Soviet Union until the moment of truth came—1939 and the nonaggression pact, 1945 and Yalta, 1948 and the "rape" of Czechoslovakia. But American intellectuals have been the object of two particular accusations that need to be considered. During the McCarthy era intellectuals were regarded as either closet communists who covertly supported the Soviet Union, perhaps even as spies, or liberal "dupes" whose innocence about the realities of Stalinism misled their readers and students into accepting a benign view of Russian developments during and after the war. During the 1950s American intellectuals, as writers, teachers, and public figures, had to defend themselves against such charges, and it has been estimated that several thousand lost their jobs for refusing to cooperate with various "un-American activities" investigating committees.[16] The second accusation emerged a decade later with the Vietnam War. The New Left of the 1960s charged the Old Left of the 1930s with having made the Cold War inevitable by trying to "outdo the right in its anticommunist zeal" in the 1940s and 1950s and even collaborating with the CIA in its counterrevolutionary efforts. Ironically, while the Old Right claimed the American intellectual was soft on communism, the New Left claimed he was too hard, so hostile that the American people were preconditioned to respond favorably to McCarthy and his witch hunts. Both of these accusations lack the accuracy of historical sequence.

The intellectuals who opposed communism took their stand long before the McCarthy era. Many had been radicalized in their college years in the early 1930s, but by the end of the decade they had become disenchanted with the Soviet Union. Thus, during World War II, while the American people were being told about the wonders of the Soviet Union and the heroic leadership of Joseph Stalin in *Life* magazine and in such films as *Mission to Moscow,* an emergent anticommunist left composed of various ex-communists or consistent democratic socialists tried in vain to warn Americans about Soviet totalitarianism in their small and obscure publications. They were hardly surprised, as were Roosevelt, Truman, and the American people, by the conduct of the Soviet Union after the war.

Ever since the eighteenth-century Enlightenment many Western intellectuals had regarded themselves not as advocates of narrow patriotism and nationalistic chauvinism, but as "citizens of the world." In the late nineteenth and early twentieth centuries Marxism reinforced the conviction that the intellectuals, "the engineers of the soul," would be internationalist in orientation and dedicated to the universal values of truth, freedom, and justice. This great hope, always more dream than reality, crashed like a house of cards at the meeting that took place in April 1949 at New York's Waldorf Astoria Hotel, the Conference of Scientific and Cultural Workers for World Peace.

Some of the world's most illustrious intellectual figures attended the conference. The American participants, led by the philosopher Sidney Hook, the anarchist wit Dwight Macdonald, and the old Greenwich Village radical Max Eastman, demanded that the conference address itself to the issue of cultural freedom, specifically to the fate of the Russian novelist Boris Pasternak, whose writings had been suppressed by Stalin. To the dismay of American composer Aaron Copland, Russian composer Dimitri Shostakovitch responded by defending the Soviet attacks on Igor Stravinski and other musicians experimenting with new symphonic compositions whose abstract notations were incomprehensible to "the broad masses." American scientists like H. J. Muller, Nobel Prize–winner in genetics and once a friend of Russian geneticists, challenged the dominance in the Soviet Union of the teachings of T. D. Lysenko, an agronomist who insisted that evolution proceeds from inherent genetic mechanisms, a thesis at odds with the latest findings in molecular biology. Henry Wallace, to his credit, expressed some skepticism of Lysenkoism at the conference, and Hook declared from the floor that the laws of science are universal and know no national boundaries or political requirements. But American intellectuals were not allowed to present their own papers at the conference. When it became clear that intellectual freedom was being suppressed for the sake of world peace, most American participants charged that the meeting was being dominated by the communists, and a small group withdrew and held their own meeting at Macdonald's house. Out of this nucleus grew the American Committee on Cultural Freedom (ACCF), a counterpart to the Congress of Cultural Freedom that had been started in Berlin by writers like Arthur Koestler, author of *Darkness at Noon*, a penetrating psychological novel on the Moscow trials, and contributor to *The God That Failed*, a collection of essays by American and European ex-communists, among them the black novelist Richard Wright.

Meanwhile another group of intellectuals had been organizing, the Americans for Democratic Action (ADA), which consisted of former New Deal liberals, labor leaders, legal scholars, and academic specialists. ADA could agree with the Wallace Progressives about the need to expand the welfare state, develop a full-employment economy, and extend civil rights to blacks and other minorities. ADA broke sharply with Progressives on the issue of the Soviet Union. Progressives claimed that the Soviet Union had been on the right road to progress, peace, and prosperity until America's "aggressive" foreign policy caused Stalin to respond militantly and silence liberty. ADA intellectuals like Reinhold Niebuhr and Arthur Schlesinger Jr. refuted that claim in *The Irony of American History* and *The Vital Center*. They argued that Stalin's totalitarian system emerged from the utopian illusions of Marx and the organizational tactics of Lenin, both of which denied the Russian people liberal political institutions through which authority can be resisted and power controlled.

Most ACCF and ADA intellectuals were anti-Stalinists who felt the need to defend America in its confrontation with the Soviet Union. Few, however, believed the containment policy should be extended to Asia, and several had reservations about the wisdom of America's intervention in the Korean War. What drove the anticommunist left apart, however, was McCarthyism, an issue that became the focus of bitter debate among intellectuals of all persuasions.

The McCarthy hysteria forced ACCF and ADA members to take a stand on such controversies as the loyalty oath, the right of communists to teach, the propriety of invoking the Fifth Amendment, and the security cases of fellow intellectuals like Robert Oppenheimer and Owen Lattimore. The question of taking a public stand on McCarthy himself proved even more divisive. The majority of the members of the two organizations believed it was necessary to denounce McCarthy as a menace not only to civil liberty but to the cause of anticommunism itself. The trouble with McCarthyism, observed *Partisan Review* editor Philip Rahv, was that it misled people into thinking that communism posed a threat primarily *in* America rather than *to* America. Other members, especially the ex-Trotskyists Burnham and Eastman, saw the threat as internal, at least in part. Thus while they found McCarthy himself repugnant they believed that anticommunist pressures should be kept up against possible subversives in government and other institutions. Still others, such as Irving Kristol, denied that McCarthy was jeopardizing civil liberties, and Hook justified the Smith Act (requiring members of the Communist Party to register as agents of a foreign government) and the right of universities to fire communist teachers. Soon a great debate arose: which represented the greater danger to American freedom, communism or McCarthyism? The literary scholar Diana Trilling and the sociologist David Riesman concluded that both did. By 1955 the ACCF suffered defections from both the left and right. Historian Schlesinger resigned after protesting that ACCF had lost sight of cultural freedom in its obsession with anticommunism long after the threat of internal conspiracy had passed. Burnham and Eastman resigned for the opposite reasons, whereupon they joined young Yale graduate William Buckley Jr. in launching the new conservative weekly *National Review*.

The phenomenon of McCarthyism continued to haunt as well as divide America's intellectual community, as indicated in Arthur Miller's play *The Crucible* (1953). Where did it come from? Miller strongly implied that McCarthyism had its analogue in the witch trials of seventeenth-century Puritan New England. The historian Richard Hofstadter traced it to nineteenth-century populism and rural America's bias against the East, its conspiratorial view of history, and its "paranoid style" of politics. The sociologists Daniel Bell and Seymour Martin Lipset undertook a study of "The New American Right," disturbed by the intolerance of the working class and the "status politics" of aspiring middle-class businessmen susceptible to McCarthy's attacks on government and the eastern establishment. The poet and historian Peter Viereck regarded McCarthy as a vulgar rabble-rouser who violated all the cultivated human values that conservativism stands for: moderation, civility, decency, and tradition. But those who claimed to speak for the "New American Conservatism," William Buckley, L. Brent Bozell, and Willmoore Kendall, defended McCarthy against his many critics. To the new conservatives, McCarthyism simply represented the desire of Americans to render their country inhospitable to communism; it was a legitimate sanction against subversion that indicated America's limits for tolerance.[17]

Aside from McCarthyism, the experience of World War II, the dark night of European totalitarianism, the Holocaust, and the Cold War led American intellectuals to reappraise their own heritage. In 1952 *Partisan Review* ran a symposium, "Our Country, Our Culture," one of the most important documents in the intellectual history of that era. In the 1920s the Lost Generation rejected America for its cultural shortcomings; in the 1930s the Old Left expected a capitalist America to succumb to Marx's prophecies. But when America's economy performed so efficiently during World War II, and when its free political institutions survived the war intact, the American intellectual could not help but be impressed. For the first time in the twentieth century the American writer and artist felt it was no disgrace, no shallow provincialism, to accept America and admire it. The celebration of America by some of the very intellectuals who had once disparaged it influenced a variety of disciplines. In literature it led to a resurgence of cultural nationalism, in political theory an emphasis on the stability of liberal pluralism, in sociology demonstrations of mobility and opportunity in an allegedly open-class society, in history explications of consensus rather than conflict as the key to the past, and in philosophy an emphasis on an older pragmatism or a newer European existentialism, both of which stressed freedom of will against the supposedly deterministic cast of Marxism. Some intellectuals may have subjected America to criticism on matters pertaining to culture, entertainment, and the problem of mass society. But few if any saw the persistence of problems requiring a political solution. "There are no problems on this side of the depression with which the American economy cannot, if it must, contend," wrote economist John Kenneth Galbraith in 1952. Sociologist Lipset was certain that "the fundamental political problems of the industrial revolution have been solved." Yet while intellectuals were optimistic about the achievements of modern America, they could also be pessimistic about the possibility of a revival of political hope. Perhaps the mood was best expressed in Niebuhr's paradoxical injunction that the intellectual must "seek after an impossible victory and adjust himself to an inevitable defeat." Sociologist Daniel Bell wrote *The End of Ideology* to convey the sense of exhaustion. "Ours, a 'twice-born' generation, finds its wisdom in pessimism, evil, tragedy, and despair. So we are both old and young before our time."[18]

Daniel Bell was one of a few from the Old Left who could be classified as a public intellectual. He worked for *Fortune* magazine before turning to the academic world, and his writing style remained free of technical jargon. During the administration of President Jimmy Carter in the late 1970s, Bell was invited to Camp David to proffer advice on the state of the nation. At the same time, however, there developed a growing hostility toward the allegedly soft-headed liberalism of the Carter presidency and the academic radicalism that pervaded American campuses, a residue of the tumultuous 1960s many of whose New Left activists went on to graduate school and became professors and thereby earned the epithet "tenured radical." With the rising critique directed at the left, the role of public intellectual now fell to the neoconservatives.

Neoconservatism is a dire reaction to what its adherents regard as the excesses of the 1960s and 1970s in domestic programs and naive illusions in foreign affairs.[19] The neoconservative intellectual believes that the assault on America's economic and political institutions launched by the radicals of the 1960s created a crisis of authority and a slackening of conviction based on older values. But while radicals attacked government, they also demanded from it a vast array of reform programs to improve the conditions of the poor and of minorities, and such demands, according to the neoconservatives, have made government "the victim of overload" as more and more people feel they are entitled to whatever they ask from the political system.

Neoconservatism can also be interpreted as an angry reaction to the drift of events in foreign affairs. In this field its major voices were former Senator Daniel P. Moynihan (although he remains a liberal Democrat) and former United Nations Ambassador Jeane Kirkpatrick. As public intellectuals, both were severely critical of President Carter for allowing defense expenditures to decline in the guilt-strickened mood of the post–Vietnam War period. Particularly upsetting to the neoconservatives was Carter's commencement speech at Notre Dame University in May 1977. Here the president told Americans that we were not "free of that inordinate fear of communism which once led us to embrace any dictator who joined us in that fear." He called on the Soviets to join America in the "great adventure" of closing the economic gulf that separates North from South and putting the East versus West rivalry behind us. In response, Moynihan wanted to see concrete evidence that the Cold War was coming to an end ideologically as well as militarily. Kirkpatrick also responded to the Carter administration in a now famous essay that was read by presidential candidate Ronald Reagan, "Dictatorships and Double Standards," which appeared in *Commentary* in November 1979. She focused specifically on two countries to dramatize to Americans the illusions of Carter's foreign policy: Iran and Nicaragua.

Both the shah's Iran and Somoza's Nicaragua were dictatorships, Kirkpatrick concedes. Both leaders did not come to power through free elections; both often relied on martial law and even arrested and occasionally tortured their opponents; and neither attempted to alter fundamentally either property or power relations. At the same time Iran and Nicaragua were limited dictatorships to the extent that the shah and Somoza tolerated opposition parties and rival newspapers, and both regimes were reliably anticommunist. Yet the Carter administration allowed both to fall on the naive assumption that there existed democratic alternatives. Kirkpatrick believes that such liberal assumptions are historically groundless. As evidence she points out that there is "no instance of a revolutionary socialist or communist society being democratized," while right-wing autocracies have the capacity to respond to pressure and undergo some form of liberalization. The present governments of Vietnam, Cambodia, and Laos are much more repressive than those of the despised previous rulers, as is Red China compared to Taiwan and North Korea to South Korea, she concluded, and perhaps recent events in the Philippines and Haiti would provide further evidence for her argument. Where then did America's erroneous assumptions come from? "Only intellectual fashion and the tyranny of Right/Left thinking prevent intelligent men of good will from perceiving the facts that traditional authoritarian governments are less repressive than revolutionary autocracies, that they are more compatible with U.S. interests."[20]

What is interesting about Kirkpatrick's argument, at least for the purpose of this chapter, is not so much its validity. Her thesis that a communist regime is permanent and cannot be changed and reversed would, to be fully convincing, have to consider that the peoples of Poland, Hungary, and other Eastern European countries would have enthusiastically thrown off their communist governments if it were not for the presence of Soviet tanks at their borders. When Mikhail Gorbachev announced, in the late 1980s, that the Soviet Union would no longer intervene in Eastern Europe, that is exactly what occurred, and a phenomenon that was once regarded as "irreversible" collapsed like a house of cards. But what was interesting about the argument is that Kirkpatrick attributed the wrong-headedness of American policy to "intellectual fashion," to the brain merchants of ideas who have misled their country with false categories and ideologies. Thus in some respects we have come full circle in surveying the position of the intellectual in American society. In the eighteenth century those who opposed the French Revolution, philosophers like Edmund Burke and statesmen like Alexander Hamilton, also questioned whether there existed a viable democratic alternative to monarchism, and they too blamed intellectuals like Thomas Paine for misleading Americans into believing that democracy could simply arise like a fresh flower from the bowels of despotism.

Today neoconservative intellectuals enjoy the support of a new rising phenomenon in American cultural and political life—think tanks. The Heritage Foundation and the American Enterprise Institute in Washington, D.C., house many conservative writers and sponsor their publications, as does the more internationally oriented Hoover Institution at Stanford University. When the Department of Education was under Secretary William Bennett in the Reagan years, it also took up many conservative causes. As policy advisers, neoconservatives see themselves as shielding government from populist pressures, reasserting the idea of authority and the value of family and religion, and in general lowering the expectations of people and their blatant interest-group politics.

With the end of the Cold War, and with the spectacle of both political parties falling all over each other to rush to occupy the center of American electoral politics, the role of the public intellectual has diminished. Perhaps the last new effort to bring the life of the mind to bear on American politics was the founding of the *Weekly Standard* by William Kristol, son of the Old-Left-turned-New-Right Irving Kristol. Both Kristols became convinced that the American people would be horrified to discover how permissive liberals were on gay lifestyle, abortion rights, unmarried mothers, infidelity, and other so-called sins against the moral conscience. But when President William Clinton survived an impeachment trial, brought on grounds of perjury and sexual escapades on the premises of the White House, and when his poll ratings actually increased to make him one of the most popular presidents in American history, conservative intellectuals learned how weak would be their voice in any effort toward the reformation of America. As to liberal and radical intellectuals, they had learned this dispiriting truth long ago.

NOTES

1. Bertrand Russell is quoted in Russell Kirk, "The American Intellectual: A Conservative View," in *The Intellectuals: A Controversial Portrait*, ed. George B. de Husar (New York: Free Press, 1960), 309.

2. Richard Hofstadter, *Anti-Intellectualism in American Life* (New York: Knopf, 1962).

3. *The Letters of William James*, ed. Henry James (Boston: Atlantic Monthly, 1920), 101–2.

4. Russell Jacoby, *The Last Intellectuals: American Culture in the Age of Academe* (New York: Basic Books, 1987).

5. An exception is Martin Diamond, "Democracy and the *Federalist*," *American Political Science Review* 53 (1962): 52–68.

6. *Federalist* 10.

7. On Adams, see John Patrick Diggins, *The Lost Soul of American Politics: Virtue, Self-Interest, and the Foundations of Liberalism* (New York: Basic Books, 1984).

8. For an excellent analysis of the theoretical assumptions of the framers, see Arthur O. Lovejoy, *Reflections on Human Nature* (Baltimore: Johns Hopkins University Press, 1961).

9. Drew Gilpin Faust, *A Sacred Circle: The Dilemma of the Intellectual in the Old South, 1840–1860* (Baltimore: Johns Hopkins University Press, 1977).

10. Holmes is quoted in Arthur Schlesinger Jr., "The Intellectual and American Society," in *The Crisis of Confidence: Ideas, Power, and Violence in America Today* (New York: Bantam, 1969), 54.

11. Theodore Roosevelt, "Citizenship in a Republic," in *The Works of Theodore Roosevelt*, ed. Herman Hagedon (New York: Scribner's, 1926), 13:27–35.

12. Charles Forcey, *The Crossroads of Liberalism: Croly, Weyl, Lippmann, and the Progressive Era, 1900–1925* (New York: Oxford University Press, 1961), 30–39.

13. Herbert Croly, *The Promise of American Life* (New York: Dutton, 1963), 90–94, 427, 453–54.

14. Hofstadter, *Anti-Intellectualism,* 4.

15. Christopher Lasch, "The Cold War and the Intellectuals," in *Dissenting Essays in American History*, ed. Barton J. Bernstein (New York: Pantheon, 1965); Christopher Lasch, "Liberal Anti-Communism Revisited," *Commentary*, September 1967, 64.

16. Joseph P. Lash, "Weekend at the Waldorf," *New Republic*, April 18, 1949, 10–12.

17. *The Meaning of McCarthyism*, ed. Earl Latham (Lexington, Mass.: D. C. Heath, 1973).

18. Galbraith, Lipset, and Bell are quoted in John Diggins, *The American Left in the Twentieth Century* (New York: Norton, 1973).

19. Peter Steinfels, *The Neo-Conservatives: The Men Who Are Changing American Politics* (New York: Simon & Schuster, 1979).

20. Jeane Kirkpatrick, "Dictatorships and Double Standards," *Commentary*, November 1979, 34–45.

7

The Decline of the Public Intellectual and the Rise of the Pundit

Josef Joffe

I

"Where have all the intellectuals gone?" asked Melvin Lasky, the editor of the now defunct *Encounter*, at a conference in 1967.[1] His question merely echoed the plaintive query put forth by Harold Stearns in 1921: "Where are our intellectuals?"[2] The problem, then, is hardly new; it seems to reemerge with every new generation.[3] And yet, though the question stays the same, the answer does not.

Harold Stearns thought that America's intellectuals had wandered off to Europe. But today's intellectuals have not gone AWOL to Paris, London, and Berlin. If they did, they might not find a critical mass of colleagues over there. Nor would they know whom to search out once they got past, say, Isaiah Berlin in Oxford (who died in 1997), Jürgen Habermas in Munich, Umberto Eco in Bologna, or the not so philosophical *nouveaux philosophes* in Paris. The point here is not the disappearance of Europe's intellectuals but their parochialism. There is one critical exception, the French "deconstructionists" or "postmodernists" like Michel Foucault, Jacques Derrida, and Jacques Lacan, whose influence has probably been stronger in the United States than in France, let alone in the rest of Europe. Each national group addresses its national audience, and if they publish abroad, they would rather do it in the *New York Review of Books* than in *Commentaire*, *Merkur*, or *Granta*. At the "low-brow" level, there is the same phenomenon. Europeans would rather watch American (and so some extent, British) movies and read American books than each other's.

Certainly, Berlin is no longer the cultural capital of the world, and neither is London or Paris, pace Derrida and Lacan, who have scored their greatest triumphs in American lit-hum departments. Today's culture capitals are more likely New York, Los Angeles, and Cambridge, Massachusetts, if one accepts a broad definition of culture that encompasses not only the literate arts but also cinematography, television, fashion, architecture, and painting. It is Harvard and Hollywood, the great university presses and DellBantamWarner, MOMA and Microsoft, DKNY and Tommy Hilfiger, the Met and Michael Jackson, the *New York Review of Books* and *Calvin and Hobbes* that shape the terms of the global culture. And these producers of icons and ideas, upmarket or down, are American. George Orwell and T. S. Eliot, Karl Jaspers and Ernst Jünger, Karl Kraus and Arthur Koestler, Jean-Paul Sartre and Raymond Aron, Benedetto Croce and Ignazio Silone, Fritz Lang and Federico Fellini, Europeans all, are the past, glorious as it was.

So let us talk about America first and foremost—for some obvious reasons. First, the United States has inherited the mantle of cultural dominance from a long line of predecessors ranging from Athens to Berlin. The tilt in the balance of cultural power goes back to the 1930s—to the forced exodus of talent and ambition from its previous locus that was Central Europe: Berlin, Prague, Vienna, Budapest, and beyond, to Vilna and Czernovic. The rise of Hitler and Harvard, not to put too fine a point on it, constituted two sides of the same coin. This author sometimes muses that, without Hitler, his four most important teachers at Harvard—Stanley Hoffmann, Judith Shklar, Karl Deutsch, and Henry Kissinger—would have taught, respectively, at Vienna, Riga, Prague, and Berlin. Would Kissinger have ended up running the Wilhelmstrasse? Perhaps. Walther Rathenau, a Jew and a public intellectual par excellence, became foreign minister in 1922. He was murdered twenty weeks later.

Second, the influx came at the right time: when America's rise to world power, both militarily and economically, acted like an insatiable sponge that continues to sop up talent to the present day. The anti-Nazis, the Jews, and the victims of communism were just the beginning. Even in the absence of persecution and revolution, they are being followed by the best and the brightest from all four corners of the globe, and with no end in sight.

Third, this is not an accident. America, like Rome and Berlin (c. 1871–1933) before, is a culture that not only draws but also liberates the genius of the outsider, whether from abroad or from below. How much talent goes untapped in the *banlieux* of Paris or the Turkish ghettoes of Berlin? European societies seem peculiarly unwilling to harness the energies of the newcomer. The move from Orchard Street to Columbia, accomplished in one generation, is not the European way; the son of a Turkish greengrocer in Kreuzberg will hardly teach at Berlin's Humboldt University thirty years after his father's arrival from Anatolia. How much skill and ambition, the raw material of all creativity, lies fallow in the non-, indeed, anticompetitive culture of Europe while they continue to flourish in America?

Add to this, in America, the best universities in the world, the biggest libraries, a vast array of private and public research facilities. Mix in a system of tertiary education that encompasses half of all high school graduates, as compared to about one-third in the large countries of Europe. Blend with a culture that thrives on novelty and debate (the scurrilous as well as the earnest), whereas Europe seems to cherish stability and predictability. Count the innumerable forums of published discourse—from the *New York Review of Books* to the *New England Journal of Medicine*—which are diligently read abroad whereas *Les temps modernes* barely radiates beyond the Left Bank.

The point of this excursion need not be labored. To expatiate on the place of intellectuals at the turn of the millennium is to talk about their role in America. For good or bad, the center of gravity of Western culture has shifted across the Atlantic, and the process is speeding along with the help of a worldwide lingua franca that is English, more precisely, its American-accented version. Also, there is the unwritten "five-year rule" that says: whatever happens in the New World will establish at least a bridgehead in Europe five years later. Only sixty years ago, and certainly up to the end of World War II, the key cultural forces traveled east to west.

II

So, "where have all the [public] intellectuals gone," if they are no longer ensconced on the Left Bank, in Bloomsbury, or in the cafes of Vienna and Prague? Melvin Lasky's five-word reply is: "into the groves of Academe."[4] Thirty-five years later, that is still one of the best answers.

Surely, this is a paradoxical solution to the puzzle. One might think that the enormous postwar expansion of tertiary education in the United States (as elsewhere in the West) would have triggered Marx's fabled leap from quantity to quality. Between 1920 and 1970, the U.S. population doubled from 106 to 203 million, but the number of college and university teachers multiplied tenfold, rising from 50,000 in 1920 to a bit less than 500,000 in 1970. A quarter-century later, there were 870,000 such teachers, an increase of 75 percent, which is still more than twice as much as population growth.[5] The student population has exploded as precipitously. In 1900 there were 232,000; in 1940, 1.4 million; in 1946, 2.4 million; in 1960, 3.2 million; in 1970, 7.5 million. At the end of the twentieth century, the number approached 10 million.[6]

The "old" public intellectuals—say, Lewis Mumford, Dwight Macdonald, Edmund Wilson, born around the turn of the past century—made their mark outside the academy. So did the next generation, the likes of Daniel Bell, Nathan Glazer, Irving Howe, Michael Harrington, Alfred Kazin, Bill Buckley, Irving Kristol, and Norman Podhoretz, who were born in the 1920s. But they were already part of the cohort that left behind Brooklyn and Greenwich Village and traveled to tenured positions in Columbia and Harvard (as did Bell and Glazer).

Liberation from economic uncertainty, one might think, should have unleashed intellectual creativity on a grand scale. Also, as the platoons bound for academia burgeoned into battalions, and thence into divisions, "more" should have begotten "better." But this does not seem to be the case, though we should beware the oldest trap of them all when looking back at the recent past. "Things aren't what they used to be," is the universal complaint of the middle-aged who saw only giants walking the earth when they were young. Having grown in age and stature, they compare themselves with their contemporaries and discover only stunted growth. Karl Marx, writing in 1859, tried to put it more objectively: "Just as our opinion of an individual is not based on what he thinks of himself, so can we not judge . . . a period of transformation by its own consciousness."[7]

Let us then stay with Marx for a while and look at the "material life" and the "modes of production" that characterize the vocation of the "New Class." This term is often attributed to Daniel Bell. Bell, though, refuses to accept the honor: "It was initiated by David Bazelon and popularized by Irving Kristol" (in a letter to the author, April 21, 1997). (This is, of course, not the "New Class" of communist functionaries and power holders in the Soviet realm described by Milovan Djilas.) These are the "brain workers" who populate the universities, the think tanks, the consulting outfits, the planning staffs of governmental and private bureaucracies. They have grown into the millions as not only the higher education sector but also America's role in the world expanded with a vengeance in the postwar period. Hungry for expertise and analysis, public and private bureaucracies recruited an ever-increasing army of information producers and managers who manipulate not tools and matter but words and symbols. What must they do to excel and advance? How do they acquire status, income, and power?

First, they must consider their "objective position." They are sheltered from the market in many ways—by tenure or public employment. Ironically, that is both liberating and enslaving. Ensconced in vast bureaucracies, they cannot celebrate their "alienation" or glory in nonconformism. By contrast, ponder Christopher Lasch's definition of the intellectual as "critic of society" whose role "is presumed to rest on a measure of detachment from the current scene."[8]

The members of the "New Class" must obey "professional standards" and heed the rules and rituals of their institutions. They are recruited by committees representing the consciousness and consensus of the field; to acquire peer status, they must show credentials that indicate appropriate socialization. That will ensure efficiency but not necessarily originality.

Second, they must secure a high level of proficiency in their field. Ideally, the academically trained expert wants to capture a monopoly on information. He wants to sit on a pile of knowledge that only he controls—just like any businessman who would dearly love to corner a part of the market where he, and only he, can sell what others want. In that position he can reduce output and raise prices to extract maximal profit from his enterprise.

Third, to scale that exalted position, the expert will be drawn to ever more specialized knowledge. By definition, he can extract maximal rent from a product that only he can offer. That will surely cut down on the competition.

A general practitioner, up against many of his kind, will not command the fees of a surgeon who excels in the excision of pachydermal kidney cancers. A political scientist who offers the full range of comparative government may land a modestly paid job in a junior college. But to make the tenure track in a great research university, he is better off with "The Political Economy of Health Regulation in the Food-Processing Industry of the Developing World," especially since there are so few in the field who could poke holes in his expertise. Stanley Hoffmann satirizes this as follows: "What s/he has to do is 'compare' a given attribute (say public policy concerning the health regulation of noodles) in 77 countries, none of which s/he has ever visited, in order to 'explain' her/his dependent variable (noodle policy) through such hypotheses as principal-agent theory, bureaucratic politics, electoral cycle theory etc. All this through equations and regressions, and preferably rational choice."[9] Hence the tendency toward ever greater specialization that is only counterbalanced by the imperative of marketability. The product cannot be so specialized that it finds no takers.

Fifty years ago, "political science" broke down into five subdisciplines: American government, public law and administration, political theory, comparative government, international relations. By 1996, there were 104 such subfields, according to the APSA (American Political Science Association). APSA's official program for the 1996 convention covered 120 pages, each listing about fifty events, paper givers, and discussants. Some of the paper topics may reveal how specialized things have become, for example, "Openly Gay and Maverick: The Activist Roles of Canadian MP Svend Robinson," "The Diaristic Films of JFK: An Inaugural Event in Campaign Film and Elite Control," and "The 6.7% Solution: An Analysis of Theories of Representation as It Applies to African-American Women Legislators."[10]

With the specialization of the field comes the specialization of the vocabulary. Since time immemorial, any priesthood—shamans, physicians, or management consultants—has used special garb, vernacular, and ritual to command deference and to armor itself against the intrusive scrutiny of laypersons. "You shall bring Aaron and his sons forward . . . Put the sacral vestments on Aaron . . . then bring his sons forward, put tunics on them. . . . This, their anointing shall serve them for everlasting priesthood." [11] To speak of "dilutional natremia," and to do so in the white vestment of the physician, is more impressive than saying: "You should have drunk less water and eaten more salt."

At least "dilutional natremia" can be translated with a bit of effort. But how should the intelligent layperson interpret the title of a paper delivered at the 1996 APSA convention: "World Politics and the Internationalization of Ethnicity: The Challenge of Primordial and Structural Perspectives"? Thirty, forty years ago, an educated person could read much of what was contained in the *American Economic Review* or the *American Political Science Review,* the two premier journals of these two disciplines. Today he will be stumped and, worse, not too interested as he faces an endless array of mathematical models that try not so much to elucidate economic events as to find the best fit between algebraic functions and a set of data frequently chosen for their heuristic rather than explanatory value.

Similarly in political science where only the twenty-five-hundred-year-old field of political philosophy seems reasonably immune against the "numbers crunchers" and "rational choicers." As models matter more and more, and politics less and less, political science climbs from one meta-level to the next into an ever more rarified atmosphere. Up there, the basic question of politics (Who gets what when where and why?) is lost in the fog of factor analysis and multiple regressions. And so, the race for theory and terminology in the humanities and the social sciences tends to replace rather than explain literature, politics, economics, and so forth.

Given the exponential expansion of academia and hence the competitive quest for differentiation and specialization, more and more is asked about less and less in ever more arcane ways. Professionalization is the watchword, and this has led Stanley Hoffmann, Harvard's doyen of international relations, to muse: "Today, I would not get tenure."[12] Nor would Daniel Bell get a Ph.D. for a series of magazine articles and academic papers that came together in *The End of Ideology*. Bell recalls that this was not unique in those days. "Robert Lynd got his Ph.D. for *Middletown* a number of years after he came to Columbia."[13] Surely, nobody would earn a Ph.D. today if the dissertation were written in the spirit of Lionel Trilling, who recalled his "determination that the work should find its audience not among scholars but among the general public."[14]

But the modern academic—the descendant of Kazin, Wilson, Trilling, et al., or in Europe, of Koestler, Camus, and Croce—does not write for the general public. Their successors may still know "real" English (or German, French, Italian), but a nice turn of phrase, a powerful metaphor, a gripping dramaturgy will not serve them well with their "reference groups." Instead, it will earn them the epithet "high-class journalist." They *have* to write for refereed journals; they have to put out the tightly circumscribed monograph that fits into just as narrow an open niche. And why? Because too many like them crowd the field, because advancement and income depend on the respect and goodwill of specialists just like themselves.

To mark the difference between the Then and Now, there is the wonderfully revealing story of the war of the Modern Language Association against Edmund Wilson, yesterday's man of letters par excellence. After Wilson faulted the scholarly editions sponsored by the MLA as compilations of pedantry and pettifoggery, the MLA shot back with a booklet of replies. Its gist was that Wilson represented yesterday's amateurism. And so Wilson's attack "derives in part from the alarm of amateurs at seeing rigorous professional standards applied to a subject in which they have a vested interest. . . . [A] similar animus . . . has been discredited in field after field from botany to folklore. *In the long run professional standards always prevail.*"[15]

That it is the long and the short of it: professional standards will prevail. Since these standards imply—and enforce—ever higher specialization and differentiation (cf. APSA's 104 subdisciplines), the forums grow more insular, and the language more arcane. Inevitably that does not favor the public intellectual. By definition, the public intellectual must speak a *public* language and address the public at large. When self-contained (or worse, self-referential) expert communities define the supply side of the market, there will be a dearth of those either polyglot or capable of transcendence. In a world of such archipelagoes, the public intellectual literally has no ground to stand on. Either he remains on his little island or he drowns.

III

What about the public, the demand side, so to speak? By definition, a public intellectual requires an intellectual public. What are we to make of the demise of *Encounter, Preuves*, and *Monat*, the waning of once powerful reviews with names such as *Partisan, Edinburgh*, *Westminister*, the nonbirth of a "Berlin Review of Books," and the failure to establish *Transatlantik*, a German version of the *New Yorker*, which folded after a few years?[16] All this suggests two possible explanations: Either the "intellectual public" has also contracted, or it, too, has "specialized."

Again, there is the paradox of quantity already noted in the context of an exploding tertiary education sector. On the producer side, as was argued, the exponential expansion of the professoriat surely has not made for more public intellectuals. Similarly, the new mass-educated public, emerging in the late 1950s in the United States and in the late 1960s in Europe, apparently has not lifted, pari passu, the demand for the wares of the traditional intellectual. Bemoaning that fact, here is Melvin Lasky's classic *Kulturkritik* in a new guise: "In our mass-literate environment, saturated with words and images, appetites are being constantly whetted, minds prepared, tastes cultivated." But what does the consumer really buy? "The mediocre fare of the runway bestseller, the easy-to-read digest, the high-priced serialization, the with-it art movement, the talked-about show." And so, we may well have "reached a point where culture will be forced to exist without a coherent intellectual community."[17]

True enough—as far as it goes. Just take a walk through the Frankfurt Book Fair, the largest in the world. Each year in October, it will display even more acres of books. But a quick sweep will also reveal an increasing proportion of self-help and coffee table tomes, pulp literature, and the fads of the day between covers—books that have a shorter shelf life (at home) than had the *Westminster Review* of yore. The complaint that high culture is going to hell is of course as old as Plato's familiar invective against the ignorance and insolence of the young. Hence, beware of arguments that would descry secular descent where there is only generational recurrence. Nonetheless, here too a larger market has not bred more discriminating takers. Or actually, it has—in a different meaning of the term. Just as the producers of intellectual goods have differentiated, so have the consumers.

To make the point in all its baldness, look at the fate of the middle-brow magazines in the United States. *Look, Life,* and *Saturday Evening Post,* which used to sell millions, have gone to the Great Shredder in the Sky. They have been shouldered aside by countless specialty and subspecialty magazines—just as the once dominant national networks are being crowded out by special-audience channels that will soon number in the hundreds. The same phenomenon obtains at the top of the high-brow market.

Fifty years ago, there were only two magazines dealing with international affairs: *Foreign Affairs* for the general up-market audience, *World Politics* for the academics. Today, there is the *National Interest*, *Foreign Policy*, *Washington Quarterly*, *International Studies Quarterly*, just to mention the better-known ones. And on the academic side, there is *International Security*, *International Organization*, *Security Studies*, the *SAIS Review*, *Survival*, the *Strategic* This and the *Military* That. Nary a university institute or think tank does not have its own periodical, and where there was once only "The Quarterly of X," there are now the "Southern," "Western," or even "Southwestern Quarterly of X." In the 1970s, notes George Will, four hundred journals were founded just in modern languages and literature to accommodate the "publish or perish" pressures of modern academia.

At a minimum, think tanks and university centers will put out a newsletter by mail, fax, or Internet. Each will cater to a slightly different audience, differentiated by ideology, interest, taste, or region. The audience has "deconstructed," to use an expression of the day. And so, the public intellectual has no "agora" in which to hold forth, as more and more separate audiences congregate in ever more—and smaller—public squares. In the age of the specialist, when we would rather go to a nephrologist or at least to an internist; the GP is a vanishing breed. And the public intellectual is the general practitioner of the mind.

Yet the problem of "deconstruction" goes deeper than the segmentation of the culture. Here is another paradox: Though the traditional public intellectual was a freelancer and Bohemian (in the sense of standing apart from the behavioral and intellectual conventions of his time), his vocation was predicated on a *regulated culture*. Plato took on the Sophists, Jesus the Pharisees, Melanchton the popists, Galileo the geocentrists, Voltaire the foes of reason and of *le bon sens*,[18] Burke the revolutionaries, Marx the bourgeoisie, Keynes the classical economists, and Milton Friedman the Keynesians.

To persuade in a public language in a public place, there has to be a paradigm asking to be cracked. For the outsider to bash in the gate, there has to be a locked portal in the first place, and something worth overturning in the realm beyond. In smiting the controllers—philistines and schoolmen, clerics, kings, and capitalists—the manifesto wielder and movement monger wants to dethrone the reigning authorities so as to become a controller himself. After the bourgeoisie is smashed, the protagonists of the novus ordo seclorum—the "vanguard" of the proletariat, Fauvists, Aquarians—want to set the rules for the greater good of all.

No capitalism, no Communist Manifesto; no David, no pointillism. And without a Culture (in the sense a "canon" flanked by a set of binding standards and tastes), no Culture Wars. But after the long run of antitraditionalism, beginning with the quattrocento, we are stuck in the dragonless world of postmodernity—for the time being, at least. There are no barriers to be smashed with rousing manifestoes that would ring in the new dawn in arts and politics. Transient agitation has shouldered aside the revolution; anybody can join the fight because "anything goes," as the postmodern creed has it.

Add to this the other mainstay of postmodernity: the ancient temptation of relativism that has reappeared in the guise of multiculturalism and deconstructionism. If my "text" is just as good as your "literature," if your invocation of "reality" or your interpretation of history is but a mask that conceals your gender-, class-, or race-based hold on power (even from yourself), then there is no debate. For a debate, the alpha and omega of the intellectual life, presupposes common rules—"objective" criteria that help us to discern Truth, Beauty, and Justice, even as we fight each other.

If there are no barriers and no criteria, if everybody can wade in and anything goes, then the public intellectual has lost his forum and his foundation. If Dostoevsky were still among us, he would be flummoxed. What would enable postmoderns to debate the "eternal questions" that have tortured the intellectuals of all ages? As he put it in the *Brothers Karamazov,* they have always been "talking about the eternal questions . . . What do you believe, or don't you believe at all? . . . of the existence of God and immortality. And those who do not believe in God talk of socialism or anarchism, of the transformation of all humanity on a new pattern."

IV

If the public intellectual is declining, the pundit is on a roll. While the waning of the latter remains, and will always remain, a matter of inconclusive debate, the ascendancy of the latter can be quantified. Fifty years ago, the *New York Times* had two columnists: Arthur Krock and James ("Scotty") Reston. In 1994 it had eight: Anthony Lewis, Bob Herbert, Thomas Friedman, Frank Rich, William Safire, Maureen Dowd, Abe Rosenthal, and Russell Baker. That is an increase of 400 percent, and a similar pattern holds in the *Washington Post* as well as in most American papers from the *Arizona Republic* to the *Wichita Eagle.*

The columnist is not quite as old as the public intellectual. If we define Plato as the original public intellectual, then the first columnist, literally, was Simeon Stylites of Syria, who spent thirty years preaching from a column until his death in 459 A.D. So his craft is about a thousand years younger. But as the explosion of numbers indicates, it has flourished most in the past forty years.

Indeed, the "modes of production" in both fields—academia and journalism—have engendered a reversal of fortunes for its protagonists. As the "New Class" grew in response to surging demand for its expertise, the number and/or importance of public intellectuals has dwindled in relation. On the other side, as American newspapers were being decimated, and town after town succumbed to the "one-paper" syndrome, fewer papers meant more columnists.

Notes Karl E. Meyer: "The surviving dominant newspapers in bigger cities found it both equitable and expedient to adopt a more ecumenical policy on opinion features. Conservative papers like the *Chicago Tribune* and the *Los Angeles Times* sought greater balance, as did less conservative survivors like the *New York Times* and *Boston Globe*. When the *Washington Post* absorbed its morning rival, the very conservative *Times Herald* in 1954, the new owners kept . . . right-wing columnists like George Sokolsky in the combined paper."[19]

And thus forty-odd years later: Abe Rosenthal versus Anthony Lewis in the *Times*, George Will and Charles Krauthammer, on the one hand, and William Raspberry and E. J. Dionne, on the other, in the *Post*. This both-and phenomenon is more than just "equitable and expedient." It fits in very nicely with the mood of the times and the requirements of the readers.

Open the op-ed page and behold a supermarket of the zeitgeist. There is no need to burn with indignation or to engage your mind in a battle of wits. "You need not commit, you can have it all," is the medium's message—much like the 1996 acceptance speech of Bill Clinton, the first postmodern president. He offered to conservatives more police protection, fiscal probity, and discipline in the schools; to the center more middle-class entitlements; and to the left more social spending and more war on pollution.

Just as this shopping basket of political goods allows the voter to pick and choose, "left and right together" on the op-ed page spares both readers and editors the necessity of commitment. If you don't like Bill Safire's contrecoeur conservatism, here is Tony Lewis's bleeding-heart liberalism. And if you like neither, go to the Living, Home, or Arts section. If "anything goes," then nothing matters. You can literally believe "six impossible things before breakfast," as the Black Queen told Alice.

Ideology has not ended, as the title of Daniel Bell's 1960 book suggested; it has scrambled. And the bigger the omelet, the more cooks can, and must, stir the pan. It isn't just that papers want to balance left and right. "Right" breaks down into cultural conservatism, religionism, and market liberalism. "Left" encompasses statism, environmentalism, lifestyle choice politics. But we also need black voices, women's issues, different sexual preferences. There have to be isolationists of the left and the right, and interventionists from both camps. Let neo- and paleoliberals speak. And the elder statesman, but only if we can also find a voice from the "new generation." So the twice-weekly regular is bracketed by the ad hoc opinionist of the day. But this is not all. Add a legion more to account for the pundits ensconced in the weeklies and monthlies—from *Newsweek* to the *Nation*, from *Harper's* to *George*. And let's not forget a few score specialty magazines where opinion leaders on trucks, computers, and sidearms hold forth.

Yet the New Catholicism of ideology, lifestyle, and consumerism is but one growth factor of the punditry industry. As noted earlier, the public intellectual requires an intellectual public. That is an audience which can suffer an argument of some length and complexity—five thousand or ten thousand words. Such willing victims have not multiplied along with the number of pundits and magazines. Even classic stemwinders like the *New Yorker* have cut down on length and increased the number of short takes. Eight hundred words, the attention span demanded by a column, seems to be the coin of the intellectual realm.

George Will once said about column writing: "The amazing thing is that something this much fun isn't illegal."[20] Actually, he works quite hard at his stuff (without snorting coke between paragraphs), and so does William Safire, when he pens his disquisitions "On Language." But "fun" is not a bad word to describe the mind state of writers and readers. The author does not have to sweat footnotes and chisel a sustained argument. The reader does not have to run a three thousand-meter course or scale Mount Rushmore. He can hop on the elevator for a short ride. After all, as Walter Lippmann has put it, a column is produced by a "puzzled man making notes . . . drawing sketches in the sand, which the sea will wash away."

It is fun and futility, and not too much toil and trouble—and yet there are morsels of meaning in between. Perhaps this is the spirit of our age, the age of journalism. Caught off balance between the pap and sound bites of television and the enamel-breaking fare of academia, even the intelligent and educated are only too happy to gorge on the finger food laid out on the pundit's buffet. This is also the age of grazing, and though journalism may be the fast food of the mind, make no mistake about it: it is filling and nourishing.

And yet. Just as the sparse prettiness of nouvelle cuisine has given way to lean but heartier stuff, the ebbing of the public intellectual discourse may well leave a void asking to be filled. For those who would grieve about the decline of the public intellectual, there is the consoling voice of Harold Rosenberg, himself an emblematic representative of the species. "Rosenberg did not share the worry that intellectuals might disappear; he believed that intellectuals assumed various guises and disguises and that they regularly showed up after being consigned to the historical dustbin."[21]

V

Rosenberg predicted salvation in 1965. Has Phoenix risen again? Perhaps, and if so, in a different guise—as is his wont. The classic paradigm of the public intellectual in the past century, as represented by the Wilsons,

Trillings, and Sontags was (literary) criticism, but these protagonists brought two qualities into the arena. They had something to say, and they knew how to say it. Analysis, judgment, and prescription came with a distinctive sensibility; not only did they see things differently, they also saw different things. And they described them in a language that transcended the ordinary.

A *tour d'horizon* of the contemporary American scene reveals a changed landscape. First, the public intellectual has shifted from "criticism to cultural studies,"[22] or from literature as thing-in-itself to literature as emanation-of-something-else. To sharpen the point, the center of gravity has moved toward the ground occupied by political and social theorists and their commercially much more successful imitators, the pop sociologists and psychologists. On the "left" there are Richard Rorty, Ronald Dworkin, Charles Taylor, Michael Walzer, Martha Nussbaum, Catharine MacKinnon, Albert Hirschmann, Amitai Etzioni, Robert Putnam—academics all, but known to a larger audience outside the university. The discourse ranges from serious political philosophy to sheer ideological agitation. On the "right" there are (or were) Allan Bloom, E. D. Hirsch, Leszek Kolakowski, Milton Friedman, Samuel Huntington, William Bennett, Martin Feldstein, Francis Fukuyama, Thomas Sowell, plus the academics and think-tankers who write for *Commentary*, *National Review,* and occasionally the *New Republic*.

The locus has shifted, too. Some of the most interesting contributions to the public debate come not from the universities but from research institutions—the Brookings Institution, the American Enterprise Institute, or the Manhattan Institute. Indeed, as the universities have succumbed to relentless "scientifization," these institutions, with their different ideological colorations, have offered a home and a salary to those who continue to deal with the "big issues" in a public language. There is something missing, though, when we compare them to the two previous generations. Let's call it "sensibility" or the "aesthetic element": the originality of style, perception, and language that even today distinguishes, say, the political reportage of a V. S. Naipaul from the best efforts of scholars and journalists.

Au fond, Harold Rosenberg had it right two generations ago: Phoenix always rises, in one way or another. But what if journalism, the newly dominant currency in the market of ideas, continues to rise? Then we might take heart from J. B. Priestly, the novelist, playwright, and public intellectual par excellence: "We are always led to infer that [the journalistic enterprise] is a new and reprehensible practice, the mark of a degenerate age. The truth is . . . that all the best essays in the language have first seen the light in the periodical press."[23]

True enough. Karl Marx was a relentless pundit, and so was Mark Twain. Marx also wrote *The Eighteenth Brumaire,* and Clemens published *Huckleberry Finn*—classics both. But these two set formidable standards for journalists who would want to transcend their craft. They expanded our understanding of the world: this is how it is. To the meaning, they added a message: this is how it should be. And finally they enclosed both in a "memorable form," as Jacques Barzun put it when musing about the task of art. At its highest, the challenge is to bond the meaning, the message, and the medium—the last implying the ability to rise above the vernacular and sensibility of the day. The models are in place. Are their should-be successors too? Not yet. But then let's await tomorrow's prophets and profiteers of hindsight who might cheer the giants of this generation and ask once more: Where have all the intellectuals gone?

NOTES

The author is indebted to the following people for their critical input: Daniel Bell, Stanley Hoffmann, Ronald Rogowski, Robert Silvers, George Will, and Fareed Zakaria.

1. "The Idea of an Intellectual Public," opening address at the conference on "The University and the Body Politic," University of Michigan, 1967. Reprinted in Melvin J. Lasky, *On the Barricades, and Off* (New Brunswick, N.J.: Transaction, 1989), 335.

2. Thus the heading of a chapter in his book *America and the Young Intellectuals* (New York: George Doran, 1921), 46–51.

3. See, twenty years after Lasky, Russell Jacoby, *The Last Intellectual: American Culture in the Age of Academe* (New York: Basic Books, 1987); all subsequent citations are from the 1989 paperback edition published by Noonday Books/Farrar, Straus and Giroux, from which I have profited greatly.

4. Lasky, *On the Barricades, and Off*, 335.

5. National Center of Education Statistics, *Digest of Education Statistics, 1995* (Washington, D.C.: U.S. Department of Education, 1995), 13. The figure for 1997 represents an estimate by the Center.

6. Anne Matthews, *Bright College Years: Inside the American Campus Today* (New York: Simon & Schuster, 1997), 127.

7. Preface to *The Critique of Political Economy*, in Karl Marx and Frederick Engels, *Selected Works* (New York: International Publishers, 1968), 183.

8. *The New Radicalism in America, 1889–1963: The Intellectual as Social Type*, p. ix, as cited in James Seaton, *Cultural Conservatism, Political Liberalism: From Criticism to Cultural Studies* (Ann Arbor: University of Michigan Press, 1996), 4.

9. In a correspondence to the author, April 28, 1997.

10. *American Political Science Association: APSA* (San Francisco, 1996), 165, 96, 135, 101.

11. Exodus 40:12–15.

12. His more science-minded colleagues in the field of course call him a "high-class journalist," as he has published widely in the *New York Review of Books*, the *New Republic*, and the *New York Times*.

13. In a correspondence with the author, April 21, 1997.

14. "Some Notes for an Autobiographical Lecture," in *The Last Decade: Essays and Reviews, 1965–75* (New York: Harcourt Brace, 1979), 239. As quoted in Jacoby, *Last Intellectual*, 18.

15. Gordon N. Ray, *Professional Standards and American Editions: A Response to Edmund Wilson* (New York: Modern Language Association, 1969), p. i. As recounted and cited in Jacoby, *Last Intellectual*, 194–95; emphasis added.

16. Interestingly, there is a new British journal, *Prospect*, which deals with "Politics, Essays and Reviews." It is a lively, controversial publication that covers a wide ideological spectrum. For a favorable review of the magazine's first year in existence, see John O'Sullivan, "Prospect," *Times Literary Supplement*, March 7, 1997.

17. Lasky, *On the Barricades, and Off*, 341.

18. Isaiah Berlin's take on Voltaire is perhaps the best definition of the public intellectual. "As a *philosophe* he is part moralist, part tourist and *feuilletoniste*, and wholly a journalist, albeit of incomparable genius." "The Sciences and the Humanities," in Berlin, *Against the Current* (London: Hogarth, 1979), 92.

19. Karl E. Meyer, *Pundits, Poets, and Wits: An Omnibus of American Newspaper Columns* (New York: Oxford University Press, 1990), xxxix.

20. In a column for the *Washington Post*, December 18, 1983.

21. Jacoby, *Last Intellectual,* 111, summing up Rosenberg's "The Vanishing Intellectual." First published in 1965, the essay was reprinted as "The Intellectual and His Future," in Jacoby, *Discovering the Present* (Chicago: University of Chicago Press, 1973).

22. Thus the subtitle of James Seaton's *Cultural Conservatism, Political Liberalism.*

23. As quoted in Karl E. Meyer, *Pundits, Poets, and Wits*, xii.

8

The Public Intellectual and the Experience of Totalitarianism

Pierre Hassner

This chapter starts with a warning that may seem excessively defeatist and an excuse that may seem excessively immodest: the author knows in advance that he will not be able to do justice to the complexity of the subject. Ideally it should cover the varieties of the intellectuals' experience both in time (before, during, and after totalitarian rule) and in space (the direct experience of totalitarianism as a reality and its image as seen from outside). It should cover both Marx and Havel, both Sartre and Solzhenitsyn. It attempts to do so, but some aspects will be much more developed than others. One experience—that of French intellectuals during the Cold War—gets much more emphasis than it probably deserves, for a simple biographical reason: the author's experience as a young student emerging out of communist Romania and undergoing the shock of the contrast between his own perceptions and attitudes and those of his French fellow students or teachers.

The excuse for not being able to put into coherent and comprehensive perspective the objective and the subjective, the reality of fascist or communist totalitarianism, the hope, attraction, and disappointment they produced among many Western intellectuals, and the author's own polemical reactions to both is that the same criticism applies to two important books, to which the present chapter is essentially a footnote. They are *L'opium des intellectuels* by my teacher Raymond Aron[1] and *Le passé d'une illusion* by my friend François Furet.[2] The theme of both books is the mystery of intellectuals' fascination with totalitarianism, particularly communism. But both cover simultaneously a narrower and a broader ground. They are based primarily on observations of French intellectuals, and they inevitably offer, directly or indirectly, an interpretation of communist totalitarianism itself.

Both works are based on deep reflection and scholarship with which I substantially agree. What I add, besides a few personal observations, is a look at the same phenomenon, however brief, that encompasses an even more extended period. I go back in time and follow the story beyond the end of the Cold War and the disappearance of the two great totalitarian ideologies into the present time.

A DREAM FOR THE FUTURE: TOTALITARIANISM AS THE INTELLECTUALS' UTOPIA

The most convenient starting point may be an even greater and earlier French thinker, Alexis de Tocqueville, on whose thought both Aron and Furet built. The first chapter of book 3 in Tocqueville's classic *L'ancien régime et la révolution* is entitled: "How, toward the Middle of the Eighteenth Century, Men of Letters Became the Country's Leading Politicians, and the Effects Which Resulted from This." In it he argues that eighteenth-century France was the most cultivated and literary nation in Europe and the least free politically: "We had kept one freedom amid the ruins of all others; we could philosophize almost without constraint on the origins of societies, on the essential nature of governments and on the primordial rights of the human race." Intellectuals in France, unlike those in England, had no practical political experience; but unlike those in Germany, they were interested in politics, in "a kind of abstract and literary politics." They all agreed on one starting point: "All think that one should substitute simple and elementary rules, drawn from reason and natural law, for the complicated and traditional laws that rule the society of their time." Hence, "the political world got to be divided into two separated provinces without any contact with each other. In one, administration was practiced; in the other the abstract principles on which any administration should have been founded were established." An "imaginary society, in which everything seemed simple and coordinated, uniform, equitable, and in conformity with reason was built." The American Revolution appeared as its confirmation and its application. This "literary politics" soon became passionate, for "general theories, once accepted, inevitably come to be transformed into political passions." Conversely, "each public passion was disguised in philosophy; political life was violently converted into literature and the writers, taking the leadership of opinion into their hands, found themselves for a while occupying the place that party leaders hold in free countries. Nobody was any longer in a position to challenge this role."

The consequence, Tocqueville says, is that "the French revolution was conducted in precisely the same spirit that presided over the writing of so many abstract books of government." But what is a virtue in a writer is sometimes a vice in the statesman. "The language of politics itself adopted some of the features of that spoken by the authors; it became full of general expressions, of abstract terms, of literary turns. This style, helped by the political passions that were using it, penetrated all the classes and filtered down with incredible ease into the lowest ones."[3]

Whereas in this chapter Tocqueville focuses on literature and "the literary spirit," in the following chapter, which examines the consequences of the antireligious passions, he announces the birth of "a kind of a new religion" (which Aron later called a "secular religion") that produced some of the noblest effects of the great religions but also led to the appearance of "revolutionaries of an unknown type, who carried daring to the point of madness, whom no novelty could surprise, whom no scruple could slow down, and who never hesitated in front of the execution of a design."

These were no longer men of letters. Their true ancestors are indicated in the following and third chapter: "Toward the middle of the (eighteenth) century, one witnesses the appearance of a number of writers who deal specifically with questions of public administration, and who, on the basis of several common principles, were given the name of *economists* or *physiocrats*. The economists shine less in history than the philosophers; they have perhaps contributed less to the coming of the revolution. But I believe that it is above all in their writings that one can best study its true nature. The philosophers have hardly gone beyond very general and abstract ideas about government; the economists, without leaving the theories, have nevertheless descended closer to the facts. The former have said what could be imagined, the latter have sometimes indicated what was to be done" (uncannily Tocqueville anticipates the title of Lenin's famous manifesto). And what is to be done is to suppress all the past ("The past is, for the economists, the target of a limitless contempt") and to change human nature through the means of an omnipotent state in the name of the people.

"The state, according to the economists, should not only lead the nation, but mold it in a certain fashion. . . . In reality, there are no limits to its rights nor to what it can do; it not only reforms men, it forms them; perhaps it would be in its power to produce other men! 'The State does what it wants with men,' says [abbé] Bodeau. This sentence sums up all their theories."

Tocqueville points out that this huge social power imagined by the economists is not only greater than any other but different in origin and in character. "It is impersonal: it is no longer called the king, but the state, it is the product and representative of all, and must bend the right of each under the will of all."

This is what Tocqueville calls "democratic despotism: a people composed of individuals who are almost alike and completely equal, this confused mass recognized as the only legitimate sovereign, but carefully deprived of all the powers that would enable it to lead or even to supervise its government by itself. Above it, a unique representative, whose mandate is to do everything in its name without consulting it. To control this representative, a public reason deprived of any organ; to stop it, revolutions, not laws; in principle, a subordinate agent; in fact, a master."[4]

I apologize for the length of these quotations. They seem to me, however, to indicate with unsurpassed and prophetic lucidity a number of distinctions and paradoxes that the reality of totalitarian regimes and intellectual attitudes in the twentieth century were to illustrate. First, the double face of the assertion of the critical, universalistic spirit, protesting against the irrationality or the immorality of the existing order: the virtue of standing up for truth and human rights and the danger of abstract utopianism. Second, the duality of the romantic man of letters and of the fanatic and doctrinaire "economist" or revolutionary. Third, the double role of the totalitarian state, as a servant of the people and as its godlike master. The convergence of these three oppositions explains, in our time, the paradoxical situation of the public intellectual, which I later describe, as tyrant or slave, as martyr or slayer of the totalitarian regime.

Before and after Tocqueville, from the late eighteenth to the early twentieth century, warnings denouncing the role of intellectuals in the French Revolution and announcing their fate in future ones abounded. The link between abstract blueprints and the unleashing of terror was denounced from Burke to Arendt via Hegel and Heine. Another illustrious Frenchman, Napoleon Bonaparte, coined the term "ideology" to denounce the political role of the "ideologues," a philosophical school that drew its name from its doctrine on the origin of ideas but represents the left-wing intellectuals of the time. In a familiar development, Napoleon broke with the ideologues after having come to power with their help: "It is to ideology, to this obscure metaphysics which, through looking with subtlety into first causes, wants to build the legislation of peoples on this basis instead of adapting laws to the knowledge of the human heart and to the lessons of history, that one must attribute all the misfortunes of our beautiful France. These errors were bound to bring about the reign of men of blood and they actually did. Who flattered the people by proclaiming its entitlement to a sovereignty it was incapable of exercising? Who has destroyed the respect and sanctity of laws, by basing them not upon the sacred principles of justice, of the nature of things and of civil justice, but only upon the will of an assembly composed of men alien to the knowledge of civil, criminal, administrative, political and military principles?"[5]

The irony is that Napoleon himself was seen by Hegel as "the world soul," the representative of the "world spirit," precisely because he was standing for universal rationality against decaying traditions, and because he was introducing in actual legislation this extraordinary innovation ("the most fantastic one since the earth rotates around the sun") brought about by the French Revolution, the attempt to make society stand on its head—to build it on thought.[6] But the universal principles needed a strong prince and a competent administration to put them into practice, or they would lead to anarchy, hostility toward government as such, or terror.

A similar view on the ambiguity of the role of revolutionary intellectuals is found in Heinrich Heine's *History of Religion* and *Philosophy in Germany*. On the one hand, Kant is the Robespierre of philosophy; the German philosophical revolution is even more important than the French political one. But the welcome liberation from dogma that it represents can lead to unprecedented terror, through the negation of recalcitrant realities and the elimination of all moral doubts or restraints. Heine adds, however, a new and important element when he announces that "most of all to be feared would be the philosophers of nature were they actively to mingle in a German revolution and to identify themselves with the work of destruction. For if the hand of the Kantian strikes with a strong unerring blow, his heart being stirred by no feeling of traditional awe; if the Fichtean courageously defies every danger, since for him danger has in reality no existence; the philosopher of nature will be terrible in this, that he has allied himself with the primitive powers of nature, that he can conjure in him the demoniac forces of old German pantheism."[7]

Isn't this a premonition of the "anti-intellectual intellectual" that found its fulfillment in fascism, in the affirmation of the prevalence of vital forces, of "soil and blood," over abstract ideas, of war over humanitarianism, of action over thought? From the Thomas Mann of the *Betrachtungen eines Unpolitischen* to the Heidegger of the *Rektoratseede* we find the same post-Nietzschean attack against the "civilization intellectual" and the same submission of the intellectual to the deeper or nobler powers of youth, force, life, and nature.[8]

But the opposite ideology, communism, presents an even more paradoxical reversal in the position of the intellectual. Both Marxism as a doctrine and communism as a regime can be seen as the triumph of the intellectual and as his abdication, self-sacrifice, or prostration in front of not the victors but the victims, not natural hierarchy but absolute equality. The Polish anarchist Machajski, in his criticism of Marx and in his proposed remedy, is a good prophet of both tendencies.

> He argued that Marx's idea of socialism specifically expressed the interests of intellectuals who hoped to attain a position of political privilege by means of the inherited social privilege of knowledge, which they already possessed. As long as the intelligentsia were able to give their children advantageous opportunities of acquiring knowledge, there could be no question of the equality which was the essence of socialism. The working class, which was at present at the mercy of intellectuals, could only achieve its ends by depriving them of their chief capital, namely education.[9]

Finally, the rule of the infallible guide in the name of a primitive and dogmatic ideology based on the *Volk* or the proletariat was to carry both the triumph of a simplified idea, the power of one former intellectual, and the destruction of intellectual activity as such to their logical extreme.

FROM PARADISE TO HELL: THE INTELLECTUALS' UTOPIA AS A REALITY

There is a sociological view sometimes propagated by dissident intellectuals, according to which Machajski's prophecy has indeed come true. In their book *The Intellectuals on the Road to State Power*,[10] György Konrád (a famous independent Hungarian writer, the inventor of the term "antipolitics") and Istvan Szelenyi (an independent sociologist) described the communist regime as the one that, being based on ideology and central planning, gave intellectuals the greatest power as distinct from either capitalists or workers. But by "intellectuals" they, like Machajski, meant "the technicians, organizers, administrators, educators, and journalists."[11] If the party apparatus, as well as the opponents of the regime, is included within the broad category of the intelligentsia, then the intellectuals are by definition both rulers and oppressed. It is important to distinguish both types of intellectual (using Tocqueville's distinction between "philosophers" or writers on the one hand and "economists" or men of action on the other) and types of relation to power. A Ukrainian author has enumerated five categories of the latter: (1) the ideologist intellectuals (or the communists in power); (2) the supernumerary clerks (or the sympathizers who were the reservoir from which the first category was selected); (3) the conformist intellectuals; (4) the marginalized intellectuals; and (5) the independent intellectuals or dissidents.[12]

Combining the two types of classification points to interesting paradoxes. For instance, the planners are constantly caught between the rigidity of the ideology, the arbitrary decisions of the leader, and the resistance of social and economic reality. Hence, the need for scapegoats to justify their failure. The scientists were to some extent (except in the most extreme ideological moments as when Stalin imposed his dictates on biology) protected from these perils and enjoyed a privileged material status; yet the very exercise of their task called forth frustrations and demands that could put them in conflict with the regime. Andrei Sakharov's critique started by asking for the freedom to communicate with Western fellow scientists; from there it developed into a plea for reform and tolerance and finally into a general stance based on human rights and moral responsibility. The ideological intellectuals proper were faced with the paradox of a regime based on ideology, hence on ideas, but whose particular ideology affirmed the subordination of ideas and of truth to a non- or anti-intellectual point of view, that of the elected race in one case, of the proletariat in the other, of the tyrant's power in both. Their task was to substitute, through terror and manipulation, belief in an imaginary world for the exercise of thought and the experience of reality. As Pasternak put it in *Doctor Zhivago*: "People had to be cured, through any possible terroristic means, of the habit of thinking and judging with their own head, and constrained to see something which did not exist."[13]

Intellectuals were indeed to be, as Stalin put it, "the engineers of the soul," but the classical question was never forgotten: Who will engineer the engineers? Fortunately, however, the totalitarian attempt at exercising total control over the human mind has never been totally successful any more than the attempt to direct and control the evolution of societies. The difference between phases of totalitarian regimes and the resistance offered by different forces or traditions in different societies provide in some cases a fragile protection to marginal and independent intellectuals or even an opportunity to strike back. This is particularly the case in the beginning of totalitarian regimes and during their decline. When totalitarianism is in full swing, however, the activity of the independent intellectual can only be that described and practiced by Solzhenitsyn—the "underground writer" whose work is hidden and sometimes not even written but only learned by heart; he cannot dream of publishing it. His hope is that somehow a copy will reach future generations.[14] Yet a few years later, to his own surprise, Solzhenitsyn himself was banging his head against the imposing trunk of the totalitarian oak to the point of shaking it until being expelled. Even during the time of terror, however, some authors like Ilya Ehrenburg were spared and could exert an ambiguous role, partly as court jesters, partly as false witnesses destined to give phony reassurance to the outside world, but partly, too, as forces for change. In later times, Gorbachev's "glasnost," which was originally motivated by a desire to revitalize and modernize the regime, tried to create artificially a partly fake "loyal opposition" that he could use against the resistance of the party apparatus, only to find that the genie of freedom could not easily be brought back into the bottle and could endanger his very rule and the survival of the regime itself.

In other countries where the regime's control over intellectual life was less complete, alternations of limited tolerance, brutal repression, and general relaxation produced an even greater variety of individual and collective experiences. Here I can only mention some of them.

In Nazi Germany, almost all critical intellectuals chose exile, while illustrious thinkers linked to the "conservative revolution" started by supporting the regime before choosing (or being driven to) a position of more or less silent detachment while continuing their own work. This was the case of Martin Heidegger, Carl Schmitt, and Ernst Jünger.

A similar phenomenon occurred in communist East Germany. Illustrious writers who had spent the war years as refugees in the United States chose, after their return, to lend their name to the prestige or propaganda of the regime that they considered the more democratic or at least the more hopeful part of Germany. Well-known playwright Bertolt Brecht likened the socialist Germany and the capitalist one to a young pregnant prostitute and an old vicious and refined *roué*, with the implication that the former deserved being helped to survive rather than the latter. Novelist Stefan Heym, philosopher Ernst Bloch, and, from a greater distance, Thomas Mann himself made the same choice. They occasionally and discreetly distanced themselves from the worst excesses of the regime before either emigrating again, like Bloch, or becoming official and tolerated mavericks, like Heym.

The secret police was playing a cat-and-mouse game with many others. Some apparently independent intellectuals were in reality spies or "agents provocateurs" of the Stasi; others, like Wolfgang Templin, went from being Stasi informers to being critics who were genuinely persecuted by it. Still others, like the poet and singer Wolfgang Biermann, permanently combined both roles, criticizing the regime and reporting to the Stasi[15] until they were expelled. Finally, some dissidents found a refuge under the protection of the church; they were the ones who started the demonstrations that led to the downfall of the regime.

In Poland, the paradoxes were even sharper. Many of the best intellectuals started as true believers who went on to raise, like Leszek Kolakowski, the banner of free criticism and moral responsibility and lead the "revisionist" movement of 1956. After the half failure of their revolution, which nevertheless led to a regime that was never as truly totalitarian as its neighbors, they abandoned the attempt to reform communism and started, sometimes under the protection of the church, an outright opposition to the regime in the name of civil society. Some were temporarily imprisoned or expelled from the country during the period of repression in 1968. Others (at home or abroad) continued their work half clandestinely.

In the late 1970s, a new development emerged. On the one hand, détente and increased communication with the West, combined with the less repressive rule of Gierek (who wanted, for economic reasons, to gain the West's goodwill), opened a space of freedom, or at least toleration, for dissident intellectual activity. On the other hand, this space was filled with the intense activity of the group of intellectuals gathered in KOR (Committee for the Defense of Workers), who participated in the creation of a series of parallel activities: a semiclandestine press, a parallel "flying" university meeting in private apartments, and so on.

They conceptualized the theory of their practice under the name of the "new evolutionism" (Michnik) or the "self-limiting revolution" (Kuron). The idea was to build a civil society facing the totalitarian party-state or rather turning its back on it. The idea was not to unseat the totalitarian power but to live as if it did not exist, first by refusing the permanent lie of the party "doublespeak" (an inspiration that they had in common with Solzhenitsyn and Havel, who both insisted that the main task was to "live in truth") and second by creating as many ties and activities at the social level as possible, so as to build an alternative parallel society that let the official communist one continue as an empty shell whose only function was to let the *nomenklatura* keep their privileges and to prevent Soviet troops from intervening.

This conception had a tactical side, trying to circumvent communist power without engaging a frontal battle that would be lost in advance, and a deeper moral and philosophical one, the search for integrity, truth, and autonomy over the search for power. The result at least in Poland (and indirectly for the whole Soviet empire) was as much a surprise for the dissidents as for the communist leaders. As Marcin Krol, a leading Polish intellectual, later put it in an oral communication with humor and insight: "We thought it made no sense to try to overthrow the regime since, being totalitarian, it could not collapse from within, and Gierek thought the same: he let us 'do our thing' in a kind of Indian reservation because he was confident that the regime, being totalitarian, could not be endangered by our activities." Yet, in the very year when a talented writer, Tadeusz Konwicki, wrote a novel, *The Little Apocalypse*, describing the slide of the Polish people into apathy and cynicism, Solidarity, a mass movement of 10 million people, dealt the first and decisive blow to the Soviet empire. It was a workers' movement but was heavily influenced by dissident intellectuals who ironically took up the role of "organic intellectuals," both advisers and cheerleaders of the people, assigned to them by Marxist theory.

This is not the place to retrace the story of Solidarity, the Jaruselski coup, and the years of repression in which the regime was unable to "normalize" Poland and finally had to negotiate with the same leaders it had imprisoned for six years, like Adam Michnik. Suffice it to say that, as in the Catholic doctrine of the three churches—the suffering, the militant, and the triumphant—they emerged from the state of victims through that of fighters into that of victors.

The Polish story is the most edifying and important one in the whole of Eastern Europe. It has been replicated elsewhere but without the support of a mass movement and with a positive *dénouement* which, in the later cases, owed much more to external circumstances.

In Hungary both the revisionist phase and the popular revolution initiated by the intellectuals of the Petöfi circle had taken place much earlier, in 1956. After a period of particularly harsh repression, the Kadar government adopted the not very totalitarian slogan "Who is not against us is for us." Instead of the Stalinist total suppression of intellectual dissent and civil society, instead of Poland's protracted and limited confrontation between the system and the society, Hungary lived through a much more complex game in which at different times various degrees of cooptation, corruption, seduction, and interpenetration were tried. Prestigious intellectuals like György Lukács alternated between attempts at independence and submission to the party line, between esoteric writing and intellectual abdication. Lukács's students were sometimes tolerated as unreliable but not too dangerous, sometimes forced to choose exile. In later years, a group of real dissidents was formed; János Kis, Miklós Haraszti, Gaspar Miklos Tamás are the best known. They were cosmopolitan, westernizing philosophers caught by the communist leadership's offer of dialogue and participation while on sabbaticals in the United States. As one of them (László Bruszt) put it: "They call me to discuss the future of Hungary and I haven't even spent six years in prison like Adam Michnik!"

In Czechoslovakia, as in Hungary, there was no mass movement of the Solidarity type but also no conciliatory communist government. The Prague Spring of 1968 was led by revisionist intellectuals, mostly former communists looking for a third way or a "socialism with a human face." Their fate was either exile or twenty years of survival as window cleaners or stokers. For nearly a generation, the regime lived with an almost complete abolition of intellectual life. But in the late 1970s, a movement, close in its inspiration to Solzhenitsyn and Sakharov, and to the Polish intellectuals of KOR, was born around Charter 77. It enjoyed neither a popular following as in Poland nor government overtures as in Hungary. But it was led by some of the most thoughtful and eloquent advocates of "living in truth." Václav Havel and the philosopher Jan Patocka, a creative disciple of Husserl and Heidegger, were seeing in totalitarianism the most extreme form of dehumanizing tendencies present in the world of modernity and technology. They adopted some of Heidegger's themes but with the crucial difference of stressing an ethical position, precisely what was lacking in Heidegger.

Romania offers an alternative road. Intellectual opposition or dissent was almost nonexistent. Adaptation (sometimes with tongue in cheek) to successive orthodoxies and dictatorships as well as sycophantic praise of the leader were the almost universally followed rule. Yet toward the end of the Ceausescu era something interesting occurred. A well-known philosopher, Constantin Noica, who had been a sympathizer of the pro-Nazi Iron Guard and had spent several years in prison under the communists, gathered around him a number of young, talented students with whom he was reading the great philosophers while teaching them about the ontological and cosmic value of everything Romanian, from the peasant way of life to the language. He was discouraging his disciples from becoming dissidents because in his view the important task was the maintenance of culture. It was not clear, however, if what was meant by that was devotion to, and knowledge of, philosophy or a national and nationalist mythology. Nationalism, at any rate, provided a common ground with Ceausescu's dictatorship as well as with earlier fascist or militarist ones and allowed Noica to be tolerated and used by the regime. From a philosophical point of view, one may argue that belief in communist utopia had long been dead and that the intellectual case for or against the regime was presented in terms of either universal morality (as for Patocka or Sakharov) or national identity, which in turn could lead either to collaboration with the regime in the name of the national interest (as in Noica's case) or to opposition in the name of fighting its betrayal of the nation's traditions and dignity (as in Solzhenitsyn's).

THE GREAT MISUNDERSTANDING: MURDEROUS TYRANNIES AS UTOPIAS FOR FREE INTELLECTUALS

If communist utopia had died long ago among those who had direct experience of its translation into reality, at least in Europe, it survived much longer among those who lacked direct experience and were comparing the reality of their Western societies with the claims or stated purposes of totalitarian regimes. This was particularly the case in important segments of the West European (above all French and Italian) left.

If I may be excused for being personal again, my own political experience, roughly between 1948 and the mid-1970s, was the gap between what I knew about communist regimes and the notions of my fellow students or teachers, including those who were not communists. My discovery of Raymond Aron came in 1948, a few months after my arrival in Paris, when I read a few newspaper articles that for the first time described Eastern Europe as I knew it. The great Polish poet Czeslaw Milosz describes a similar experience with Albert Camus:

> Camus was one of those few Western intellectuals who offered me a welcoming hand when I left Stalinist Poland in 1951, while others were avoiding me, as they considered me an untouchable and a sinner against the future. Hegelian intellectuals will never understand what consequences their ratiocinations could have at the level of human relations, and what gap they were creating between them and the inhabitants of Eastern Europe, whether or not the latter were knowledgeable about Marx. Philosophy is something very physical: it makes your look icy or, like with Camus, it introduces into a man the cordiality of a brother.[16]

Sixteen years later, Raymond Aron wrote a magnificent counterpart to this article by showing the fundamental impossibility of a dialogue between Solzhenitsyn and Sartre.[17] He comments on the passage of *The Oak and the Calf,* in which Solzhenitsyn explains his refusal to meet Sartre when the latter expressed the desire to see him during a visit to Moscow, and the bafflement of Simone de Beauvoir, Sartre's companion, at this refusal. Solzhenitsyn says he hesitated but thought that Sartre—who had just insulted genuine Russian literature by promoting the official Stalinist writer Sholokov for the Nobel Prize—would never understand what he had to tell him and might misuse their conversation while he, the persecuted and clandestine writer, would have no way to set the record straight. Aron shows how Solzhenitsyn's message (the return to basic decency, the refusal of the ideological lie that justifies any criminal act) is at the other extreme compared to Sartre's attitude. In spite of being a great thinker and basing his choices on a moralistic attitude that made him divide the world into good guys and bad guys or oppressors and victims, Sartre was the prisoner of what Aron called a "distorted practical reason" due precisely to the ideological commitment that made him excuse or condemn the same crimes according to the side that was perpetrating them.

Paradoxically, less than two years after this article was written, Sartre and Aron were pleading the cause of Vietnamese boat people with France's president, Giscard d'Estaing, prompted by the "new philosopher" André Glucksmann, who had been successively a student of Aron and a Maoist. In 1977, while Giscard d'Estaing was greeting Brezhnev in Versailles, all important French (predominantly left-wing) intellectuals were greeting Soviet dissidents in a small theater at a counterreception. After thirty years of bitter debate, left-wing and conservative intellectuals were finally united in criticizing the détente policies of their governments and competing for the attention of the victims and opponents of communist totalitarianism.[18]

How could this happen? Space does not permit us to examine the four-cornered struggle between communists and former communists (which, according to former communist intellectual Ignazio Silone, one of those who renounced "the God that failed" in a well-known book,[19] would be the most decisive struggle on the world scene) or between "half virgins" (the fellow-traveling left) and "fallen angels" (the refugees and former communists who had a direct experience of the Soviet utopia) according to the formula of Arthur Koestler, another of the famous antitotalitarian intellectuals who founded the Congress for Cultural Freedom. Much of this story has been told by Pierre Grémion in his book on the French left and the Prague events of 1968[20] and his history of the Congress for Cultural Freedom.[21] Here we are limited to a few suggestions, based largely on Aron and Furet, about the sources of many intellectuals' attraction to totalitarian regimes and a few thoughts about possible explanations for the belated conversion of most of them to antitotalitarianism.

The phenomenon to be explained includes three dimensions: the disaffection of Western intellectuals, their belief in revolution or in utopia, and their identification of the latter with a particular totalitarian regime.

Aron's *The Opium of Intellectuals* addresses all three. He expresses his disagreement and wonder about many intellectuals' tendency to be deeply pessimistic about the present, Western society, and wildly optimistic about the future, a postrevolutionary world. But he attacks even more strongly their identification of "the recognition of man by man" (an ideal that, as an abstract regulatory idea in a Kantian sense, he tends to share) or of "the end of history" (an idea that, also on Kantian grounds, he strongly dismisses) with a particular regime, that of the Soviet Union. He reproaches them both with judging this regime, contrary to Marx's prescription, according to what it claims rather than what it does, and with making its success or failure the test of the meaning or absurdity of history.

Furet puts less stress on conceptual inconsistencies and more on sociological and psychological explanations. Following a line that goes from Tocqueville to Daniel Bell's *Cultural Contradictions of Capitalism*[22] via Schumpeter's *Capitalism, Socialism, and Democracy,*[23] he stresses, like Aron, the trend toward the alienation of intellectuals from the bourgeoisie. But, more than Aron, he traces it to the weakness of the bourgeoisie as a ruling class (whose legitimacy, based on wealth, those who are inferior in this respect but feel superior in others find difficult to accept) and, even more, to the self-hate of the bourgeoisie itself.

The theme of antibourgeois passions, which opens *Le passé d'une illusion,* is one of the most powerful of the book. Furet finds in this hatred (and self-hatred) of the bourgeoisie the common root of fascism and communism. While he is certainly right and insightful in this emphasis on revolutionary passions and on the identification of their common enemy, he might, as many critics have argued, distinguish more clearly between the respective passions inspiring the two totalitarian ideologies.

Bourgeois attitudes, with their emphasis on self-interest, calculation, and material goods, can be attacked, either in the name of an aristocratic, warlike, or Nietzschean morality—in the name of greatness, nobility, heroism, and artistic creativity—or in the name of a Christian morality—that of the Sermon on the Mount, compassion, solidarity, the thirst for total equality or the essential right of the suffering, the oppressed, and the poor. While both emphasize struggle and stress sacrifice and violence as opposed to the bourgeois quest for security and comfort, one could say with Gaston Fessard, a Jesuit theologian who was a student of Kojève and a friend of Aron, that Nazism was a pagan heresy, derived from the point of view of the master, and communism a Christian one, derived from that of the slave.

These two passions turned against each other with at least as much intensity as against their common bourgeois enemy. Furet, building on what Aron called "the dialectic of the extremes," shows how anticommunism and antifascism fed on each other, how the struggle against communism misled some intellectuals toward fascism and how antifascism became, even more, the great legitimizer and the great alibi of communism or at least the great psychological inhibition against an anticommunist stand that might give aid and comfort to the fascist enemy.

We have, then, the two basic ingredients of the totalitarian temptation endlessly analyzed by Aron, of which Sartre was the prototype: on the one hand, a passionate desire to oppose the bourgeois conservative order and to identify with its victims and on the other hand, a conceptual mystification that consisted in a chain or succession of abstract identifications. From the proletariat to the young, via the colonized masses of the Third World, Sartre and his followers led a tireless search for the causes in the name of which to rebel against their own social and cultural origins. In a sense, they remained faithful to a vision of society and politics well summed up by Sartre in his definition of the left: "A man of the left is someone who looks at society from below." The real scandal is the justification of oppressive organizations and regimes in the name of the oppressed. One of Sartre's most famous dicta is the one according to which Soviet concentration camps, while real, should not be made the target of a public campaign in order not to "reduce Billancourt to despair," Billancourt being the site of the biggest Renault car factory. To be against the bourgeoisie one had to be for the working class; to be for the working class one had to be for the Communist Party, which spoke in its name (and, at the time, was getting a great part of its votes); to be for the Communist Party one had to be for the Soviet Union to which it proclaimed its loyalty.

This did not necessarily prevent criticism of Soviet policies. Sartre's relations with the Stalinists, whether Russian or French, went through various phases, from close association to violent polemics. The invasion of Hungary in 1956 and of Czechoslovakia in 1968 prompted eloquent denunciations. But in both cases, Sartre concluded that "this blood-soiled monster was still socialism," and Marxism remained "the ultimate horizon of our time." He stuck much longer than his associate Maurice Merleau-Ponty to the strange idea expressed by the latter in a book on the Moscow trials published in the late 1940s: if the Soviet experiment failed, history was in Macbeth's terms "a tale told by an idiot, full of sound and fury, signifying nothing."[24]

Yet, fail it did, and that basic truth progressively penetrated the consciousness of Western left-wing intellectuals. For many, the occasion was some particularly revolting action of the Soviet Union that could no longer, for the particular individual, be rationalized by ideology: the Moscow trials, the Stalin-Ribbentrop pact, the interventions in Hungary and Czechoslovakia. Each of these events took its toll of true believers, who, in general, remained nostalgic or, on the contrary, became ideologues of the right. The case of François Furet, who left the party in 1956 and remained moderate ever since, was rather exceptional. More surprising (or is it?) is the fact that what most made left-wing intellectuals turn against, or at least away from, the Soviet Union was that it became less totalitarian.

Stalinist terror fascinated—it had, for would-be revolutionary intellectuals, the somber appeal of the witches' chant in *Macbeth:* "Fair is foul and foul is fair." When the ideological "supersense" (to use Hannah Arendt's expression) started to dissolve, and the Soviet Union started to become a more normal regime, it ceased to fascinate. Diplomats were looking forward to the day when it would become "less of a cause and more of a country." For intellectuals, it could no longer be utopia incarnate. Khrushchev's secret speech, which was only repeating what anticommunists had known all along, produced a sharp decline in interest toward the Soviet Union. Revolutionary intellectuals started looking for a more romantic and exotic incarnation of the socialist utopia: Cuba, China (with which the same phenomenon repeated itself: intellectuals were carried away by the madness of Mao's cult and of his grandiose and criminal enterprises—the Great Leap Forward, the Cultural Revolution, etc.—and turned away when Deng started it on the road to *embourgeoisement*); even Albania represented, for some, the purity of the revolutionary ideal. For others, the struggle of decolonization played the same role, but the aftermath of independence in the Third World was equally disappointing.

This again was a passing phase: the cult of Guevara or the student movements of the 1960s more and more represented revolution for its own sake, the appeal of community and action, almost totally emptied of any specific social content or of any vision of history. Marcuse's "great refusal" was the expression of this mood. In some cases, as in Italy, this led to almost senseless terrorism against "the system." In others, particularly in France, the break with revolutionary Marxism, however diluted, was more complete. It led, at least among a group of French intellectuals, who usually had been Maoists, to two unexpected developments.

One was the renouncement of ideology in favor of humanitarianism. The "new philosopher" André Glucksmann and the founder of "Doctors Without Borders" Bernard Kouchner presented what they called the "ethics of extreme emergency." Instead of working or hoping for a radiant future, one should fight suffering (whether hunger or torture) immediately wherever it occurs and without accepting national or political choices and limitations. This had, and still has, a real appeal among the young, who could be called *the orphans of Marxism and Realpolitik,* who no longer wanted to believe either the official establishment, which had lost credibility with Vietnam and similar adventures, or the communist counterestablishment, which had discredited itself through both crime and *embourgeoisement.* They wanted to follow their urge to solidarity, compassion, and action without being fooled once again.

A related but even more unexpected development is the one I already mentioned—the belated discovery of totalitarianism.[25] For some revolutionary intellectuals, often the same ones (in particular André Glucksmann) who needed not only a cause but an enemy, Soviet totalitarianism, just when it was declining and when American sovietology was abandoning the concept altogether, took the place of American imperialism. By the same token, the victims of the Gulag took the place of those of colonialism, and the "heroic struggle of the Polish workers" replaced that of the Cuban or the Vietnamese people.

For the first time, then, Western left-wing intellectuals took an interest in Eastern Europe, started a dialogue with its dissidents, and found themselves competing for their attention both with traditional anticommunists and with another faction of the left (the so-called antitotalitarian left represented by organizations like the Christian Union CFDT or the periodical *Esprit* that liked Solidarity better than the socialist-communist alliance in France).

What happened was in great part due to Solzhenitsyn (whose impact, at least in France, particularly through his televised appearance in the crucial year 1977, was immense) and to Walesa and Solidarity. For the first time, left-wing intellectuals could become anticommunists without having, as Sartre had always feared, to rally the ranks of the bourgeoisie. Always faithful to the idea that the right cause was that of the deprived masses, they found in the inmates of the Soviet camps the substitute for the Western working class or the Third World peasants and in Solzhenitsyn a prophet who through his suffering, his eloquence, and his criticism of the West provided the romantic appeal to which a bourgeois thinker like Aron could never aspire.

All this did not go without new misunderstandings. Both French and East European intellectuals tended to dismiss or underestimate the decline of Soviet totalitarianism—the former because they just discovered the notion or because if the Soviet Union no longer represented the absolute good it had to represent the Absolute Evil, the latter because they at last had a chance to discuss it. Orwell and Arendt, even though they depicted the phase of acute terror, still pointed to a truth those who had lived through it could recognize, unlike the banal jargon of American social sciences. More important, Western left-wing intellectuals still projected some of their categories on the different realities of the East. Some of them were shocked to discover that Walesa was against abortion and that Solzhenitsyn was a traditionalist rather than a man of the left. Conversely, certainly not Solzhenitsyn but many of the Eastern European dissidents tended to tell their Western interlocutors what they wanted to hear. As Gaspar Miklos Tamás has argued with some exaggeration,[26] they adopted concepts like "civil society" but gave them a different meaning from that of Western authors, or they stressed universal ideas and human rights because that could more easily attract the goodwill and the help of Western friends of an open society. Although détente and communication with the West undoubtedly gained them precious moral and material support, it converged with their chosen strategy toward communist power of replacing political analysis with a moral or legal but somewhat abstract discourse.

AFTER VICTORY: POSTTOTALITARIAN BLUES

The new convergence between Western and Eastern intellectuals risks having a double face, on the one hand liberation (from pernicious myths in one case, from oppressive tyranny in the other), mutual recognition, and dialogue, but on the other, a convergence into a common letdown and a common fear of becoming irrelevant. For the first time, the problems of Western and Eastern societies are similar: those of capitalist societies where the message of intellectuals has little resonance and relevance and is drowned by the chaotic multiplicity of contradictory messages, the stringency of technical constraints, and the power of money. Those features are felt even more strongly by former dissidents who, in general, have to struggle with new rules of the game, more brutal and corrupt than in the West, and enjoy neither the privileged position of official intellectuals nor the psychological boost of suffering and fighting for a noble cause and representing their whole people. Some of them, like Solzhenitsyn, become voices in the desert. Others chose to emigrate or remain in the West, and still others become politicians with varying degrees of success. Their marginalization is much less total than indicated by Tamás. They may even, in some cases, enjoy a comeback, as Havel's "revanche" over Klaus's arrogant dismissal of intellectuals and civil society would seem to indicate. But the structural problem—the disaffection of intellectuals in societies where there is no alternative to capitalism and liberal democracy but where the level of political discourse, particularly under the influence of the media, is more and more stultifying—remains.

The problem is compounded by the fact that in the West, as in the East, not only do public intellectuals find it hard to get a hearing, but it is not certain that they have something to say. The legacy of ideological politics and of antipolitics is an obstacle to be overcome. Ideology consisted of giving political answers to metaphysical questions and metaphysical answers to political questions. This is fortunately behind us; the temptation, then, is that of a total separation between philosophy and politics. This would condemn both to sterility and would be the best way to resurrect the totalitarian temptation. A new articulation between theory and practice, between philosophy and politics—based on both their distinction and their mutual need of each other—is the new and indispensable task for public intellectuals.

NOTES

1. Raymond Aron, *L'opium des intellectuels* (Paris: Calmann-Levy, 1955).
2. François Furet, *Le passé d'une illusion* (Paris: R. Laffont, 1995).
3. Alexis de Tocqueville, *L'ancien régime et la révolution,* bk. 3, chap. 1.
4. Tocqueville, *L'ancien régime*, bk. 3, chap. 2.
5. Napoleon Bonaparte, Speech to the Conseil d'Etat (1805).
6. Friedrich Hegel, *Philosophy of History* (New York: Dover, 1956), 412. See also *Philosophy of Right,* para. 258.
7. Heinrich Heine, *Religion and Philosophy in Germany* (Albany: State University of New York Press, 1986), 159–60.
8. Allan Bloom, *The Closing of the American Mind* (New York: Simon & Schuster, 1987), 311.
9. Leszek Kolakowski, *Main Currents of Marxism* (New York: Oxford University Press, 1978), 3:162.
10. György Konrád and Istvan Szeleni, *The Intellectuals on the Road to State Power* (New York: Harcourt Brace Jovanovich, 1949).
11. Daniel Bell, *The End of Ideology* (New York: Collier, 1961), 355.
12. Volodymir Polokhalo, "Intellectuals and Power in Postcommunist Societies," in *The Demons of Peace and the Gods of War* (Kiev: Political Thought, 1997), 186–200.
13. Quoted by Victor Zaslavsky, *Storia del Sistema Sovietico* (Rome: La Nuova Italia Scientifica, 1995), 119.
14. Alexander Solzhenitsyn, *The Oak and the Calf,* Section 1, "The Underground Writer," 8–9 of the French translation.
15. See his "Auch ich war bei der Stasi," *Die Zeit,* 1990.
16. C. Milosz, "L'interlocuteur fraternel," *Preuves,* April 1960. Reproduced in *Preuves, une revue européenne à Paris,* ed. P. Grémion (Paris: Julliard, 1989), 389.
17. Raymond Aron, "Alexander Solzhenitsyn and European Leftism," *Survey 100–101,* Summer-Autumn 1976.
18. See Hassner, "Western European Attitudes towards the Soviet Union," in "Looking for Europe," *Daedalus,* Winter 1979, 113–50.
19. Ignacio Silone, *The God That Failed* (New York: Harper, 1949).
20. Pierre Grémion, *Paris-Prague: La gauche face au renouveau et à la régression tchécoslovaque, 1868–1978* (Paris: Julliard, 1985).
21. Pierre Grémion, *Intelligence de l'anti-communisme: Le Congrès pour la liberté de la culture à Paris, 1950–1975* (Paris: Fayard, 1995).
22. Daniel Bell, *The Cultural Contradictions of Capitalism* (New York: Basic Books, 1976).
23. Joseph Schumpeter, *Capitalism, Socialism, and Democracy* (London: George Allen & Unwin, 1947).
24. Maurice Merleau-Ponty, *Humanisme et terreur* (Paris: Gallimard, 1947).
25. See Hassner, "Communist Totalitarianism: The Transatlantic Vagaries of a Concept," *Washington Quarterly,* Fall 1985.
26. Gaspar Miklos Tamás, "The Legacy of Dissent: Irony, Ambiguity, Duplicity," *Uncaptive Minds,* Summer 1994.

9

The Peripheral Insider: Raymond Aron and the Wages of Reason

Tony Judt

When Raymond Aron died in 1983, he had achieved a unique status in French public life. He was almost universally admired and respected; his writings and opinions had been elevated to near-canonical standing across a broad swath of academic, intellectual, and public opinion. As the only prominent French thinker of his generation who had taken a consistent liberal stand against all the totalitarian temptations of the age, Aron represented not just a symbol of continuity with the great traditions of French thought but also a beacon of light pointing to the future at a time of confusion and doubt within the intellectual community. Where a few years earlier Aron had been, for the '68 generation, the vile and vilified incarnation of all that was wrong with the French mandarin elite, so by 1983 he was—in the opinion of some of the same people, now shorn of their illusions and ideals—the best hope for a revival of liberal thought. Institutes and journals sprang up to continue his work and pursue his objectives. Upon the funeral pyre of Sartrian radicalism a new generation of French intellectuals began to erect a monument to Aronian reason.

To anyone who recalls the hostility that Aron encountered in the French academic and intellectual "establishment" over the course of nearly three decades following the end of World War II, this was a striking reversal of fate. Raymond Aron lived just long enough to experience this transformation—hastened by the publication of his *Mémoires* in the year of his death—which gave him some pleasure and much cause for ironic reflection. Having knowingly chosen the discomforts of honesty and clarity in a political and intellectual culture marked by confusion and bad faith, Aron never complained at his exclusion from the mainstream intellectual community. But despite his widely acknowledged impact upon generations of students, his respectful audience among the readers of his column in *Le Figaro,* and his admirers in the fellowship of scholars across four continents, Aron was largely excluded from the company of his peers in France. He lived much of his adult life on the periphery of his natural home.

There is, of course, something mildly counterintuitive about describing Raymond Aron as "peripheral." He was, in one sense, a consummate insider, an exemplary Frenchman of his generation and pedigree. Born in 1905 (the same year as Sartre), he followed the career path of an outstandingly successful scholar, surpassing his peers at every stage. He attended the elite classes of the Lycée Condorcet, was admitted to the Ecole Normale Supérieure at a time when it was still the leading Grande Ecole of the country, took the national *agrégation* in philosophy in 1928 and was awarded first place. He prepared and defended a doctoral thesis in philosophy and was universally regarded as the most promising philosopher of his generation when World War II put a temporary end to his academic career.

After the war he postponed his return to the university for a while, turning his attentions instead to journalism—he would write some four thousand editorial articles for *Le Figaro* and other papers in the course of the postwar decades—but in 1954 he was appointed to the Sorbonne Chair (albeit in sociology) for which he had long seemed destined. From then until his belated election to a chair at the Collège de France in 1971, Aron's progress was consistently blocked by a de facto alliance of opponents from left and right, but he was nonetheless elected to membership of the Institut in 1964 and taught a regular seminar at the Ecole des Hautes Etudes en Sciences Sociales. By the time of his death he was widely regarded, in the words of François Furet, as "not just a great professor, but the greatest professor in the French University."[1]

There is little doubt that of all the accolades awarded him, this is the one that best fits both Aron's talents and his deepest aspirations. His natural disposition to think and write as a scholar, together with his often attested qualities as a teacher, were complemented by the pleasure he took throughout his life in the company of ideas and men of ideas. In his memoirs, composed shortly before his death, he reflected on his feelings upon entering the Ecole Normale for the first time, sixty years earlier: "My first impression, on entering the rue d'Ulm was, I confess at the risk of appearing ridiculous, one of wonder. Even today, if I were asked: why? I would reply in all sincerity and innocence that I have never met so many intelligent men gathered in such a small space."[2]

Moreover, and alongside his scholarly writings and teaching, Aron was a characteristically French "insider" in another sense. His contacts at the Ecole, his years with the Free French in London where he spent the war, his decades of political journalism had provided him with a broad range of contacts and friends throughout the upper reaches of French public life. It was his unusually good connections in government, public administration, and parts of the business world, for example, that gave Aron's editorial writings their special authority.

In addition to the moral authority and rigorous argument conventionally associated with the upper reaches of French intellectual journalism, Aron's articles had the air of credibility that derived from the author's evident command of his subject. Aron always seemed to know what he was talking about, and his authority in this respect derived in large measure from his close acquaintance with the men who were making the decisions he was analyzing. Without ever being a man "in" the French establishment (Raymond Aron only served once in government, as chef de cabinet in a short-lived Ministry of Information in 1946, and that was under André Malraux), Aron was very close to the political elites of France for many years (as he was to those of the United States, Germany, and Britain at various times). He thus wrote from the outside, but with an insider's sense of realities and limits.

There is another dimension to Aron's qualities as a man very much at home in and part of the French public world of his day. For in addition to being an academic "mandarin," a confidant of men of power and a prominent journalist, Raymond Aron was also an intellectual. This does not necessarily follow from his scholarly ambitions or attainments—many French intellectuals of his time were not scholars or teachers, and relatively few of his fellow academics were "intellectuals" in the sense usually understood. But Raymond Aron unquestionably was. He took an active lifelong interest in public matters beyond his sphere of professional expertise (although, as we shall see, he made a point of knowing more than most of his fellow intellectuals before intervening in public debate), and he took very seriously the responsibility of intellectuals to be involved in important public debates. But most of all, he came to the role of the public intellectual from the same starting point as that of many other well-known French intellectual activists—that of the philosopher.

For his contemporaries this was no surprise. To Claude Lévi-Strauss as to many others, Aron was and remained above all the author of "Introduction à la philosophie de l'histoire," his doctoral thesis on the nature and limits of historical knowledge, first defended in front of a disapproving audience of Sorbonne philosophers and sociologists in March 1938. The striking originality of Aron's argument, and the impact of his philosophical rigor, is muted for us today. He was building a case against the historical positivism then dominant in the French university but now long defunct. His argument was that historical understanding cannot be separated from the position and limits of the person seeking that understanding and that a consciousness of one's own place in the process one is seeking to describe and explain both deepens and restricts the scope of all such explanation. Shorn of its epistemological rigor and empirical illustration this claim now forms the core of much of what passes for "relativism" in modern academic cant, and we have some difficulty seeing just how original and even courageous it was at the time.

That Aron was courageous, even provocative, in his reasoning is made very clear if we recall the context. Academic philosophy in France in the 1930s was a long way behind that of Germany or Austria. History and the social sciences were practiced on unselfconsciously realist principles, to the extent that they recognized any methodological concerns at all. What Aron called the "dialectic" had hardly made its presence felt within the university, and the new philosophical thinking of Husserl and Heidegger or the sociological revolution of Max Weber, with their implications for all forms of social investigation and political action, were virtually ignored. Even Hegel was a largely unknown quantity, and those young radicals who did study him, at the feet of Alexandre Kojève, did so with more than half an eye to his contribution to the thought of Marx. To claim, as Aron did in his thesis, that history was something we construct as we live ("Everyone, according to his idea of himself, chooses his past"), was a radical departure from all that his teachers held most dear.[3]

Of course there were others in France at the time who were also breaking out from the straitjacket of French academic positivism—Marc Bloch and Lucien Febvre, the founders and editors of *Annales*; or Marcel Mauss, Maurice Halbwachs, and others who were beginning to shape the distinctively French school of cultural anthropology. But Aron was different, precisely because he was not abandoning old schools of thought but engaging and dismantling them on their own ground. He was not ignoring the objectives of any good social science, the need "above all to establish necessary connections through the observation of regularities." Nor was he suggesting for a moment, in contrast to his contemporary *normalien* Paul Nizan, that facts and truths were somehow class- or context-dependent.

Aron merely wished to argue, in an exercise whose analytical rigor was itself something unusual for its scholarly era, that there are limits, epistemological limits, to historical objectivity; that we come closer to the latter, paradoxically, by recognizing these limits; that these limits arise from the *situated* position of the historical actor himself; and that this dilemma cannot be overcome by some sort of philosophical sleight of hand but by the uncomfortable recognition of the necessary duality of the past: "Thus a dual knowledge of the past would be possible, one dealing directly with the mind as inscribed in the material world, the other with the consciousness of a person or group accessible through such objectifications; an alternative deriving not only from the situation of the historian, but also from the essential structure of reality."[4]

Here Aron was leading his audience toward the delicate balance that would shape his thinking for the rest of his life. There *is* reason in history, just as there is knowledge about the past. But whether or not there is *ultimate* reason and *absolute* knowledge is beside the point, since we cannot have access to them—our own place within the story deprives us of that Archimedean point from which to see the whole. A quarter of a century later he made essentially the same point: "Theoretical elaboration, in our view, should serve to sharpen awareness of the plurality of goals and aims, rather than favoring the tendency to monoconceptual interpretations, always arbitrary and partisan."[5]

For Aron's admiring contemporaries, his thesis and his energetic defense of it before an audience of skeptical senior professors taught three important lessons. First, that there is a plurality of possible interpretations of men and their works, and the decision to privilege one of them above the others is and must be an act of choice. Second, which follows from this, nothing is determined—the past and the present are composed of choices, and while these choices have consequences, they represent directions that might under other circumstances not have been taken. Third, though men are free to choose how to make their world (and how to interpret it, which also counts), the actions they take have real outcomes, for which they must accordingly take responsibility.

Taken together, these conclusions justified the response to Aron by his contemporaries and peers: that he had elaborated, for his generation, the outline of a properly *existential* philosophy of history. Sartre himself was in no doubt. When, a little later, he presented his college friend with a copy of his own new work, *Being and Nothingness*, he described it as merely an "ontological introduction" to Aron's work. And he was not mistaken. Aron had presented his thesis as an attempt to get beyond morality and ideology and determine the "true content of possible choices, limited by reality itself"; the Sartrian existentialist project, if one can write thus, would consist in accounting for the situation Aron had laid bare and behaving accordingly.

Aron's immersion in the philosophical concerns of his generation and the crucial role he played in introducing phenomenology and existentialist reasoning to his French contemporaries, hitherto ignorant of such matters, have been largely forgotten. After 1945, as Aron became actively engaged in political journalism and the academic social sciences, and he and Sartre took opposite sides in the Cold War, their common critique of philosophical idealism and historical positivism was obscured by their disagreements. And yet it was Aron, even more than Sartre and his fellow intellectuals, who remained loyal to the demands of his own reasoning. In recognizing that man is always *in* history and makes it himself, he wrote, we do not have to give in to relativism or nihilism, abandoning any hope of understanding our world. "On the contrary, we affirm thereby the power of the man who makes himself by assessing his place in the world and in making choices. Only thus can the individual overcome relativity through the absoluteness of decision, and only thus can he take possession of the history that he carries within him and which becomes his own."[6]

There is another sense in which Aron was absolutely at one with the French intellectual world of his day. He was obsessed, for much of his adult life, with Marxism. In contrast with most French intellectuals, including most French Marxists, Aron was a careful reader of Marx—and his obsession with Marxism derived in some measure from his frustration at the ignorance and inconsistencies of what passed for Marxist thought in French hands. Moreover, some of Aron's interest in the writings of Marx has to be understood through the vector of his concern with the Soviet Union—again, something he shared with his political opponents. But it remains a striking fact about Aron that he returned again and again to the subject of Karl Marx, so much so that in his memoirs he pauses at one point to wonder whether he didn't perhaps spend too much time on debating that "secular religion." Some of his best analytical writings and all his most powerful polemical essays deal with Marxism and Marxists, and it is tempting to agree with Aron that his interest in combating the error of his era amounted to a form of transposed "anticlericalism."[7]

Nonetheless, Aron's interest in Marx and his followers was consistent with his earlier philosophical concerns. His best-known and most influential critique of *marxisant* delusions among the left intelligentsia, *L'opium des intellectuels*, is in certain respects a companion volume and successor to his *Introduction à la philosophie de l'histoire*. And Marx himself interested Aron in part for his place in the story of modern social thought, in part for his trenchant observations on nineteenth-century capitalism, but above all for his *own* unsuccessful efforts to construct a philosophy of history at once "objective" and open to decisive human intervention. Aron could not help but admire this Promethean project, all the more so since it had informed his own initial writings, and his empathy for Marx's ambitions provided him with greater insight into the strengths and failings of the Marxist undertaking than was the case for most would-be Marxists among his fellow intellectuals. The irony of this was not lost on Aron himself.

If Aron shared many of the salient characteristics of the French intellectual of his day, and was in most respects a leader in his generation and recognized as such, in what ways was he not "one of them"? The simple answer, of course, was that after 1947 he took a firm stand in support of the Western alliance at a time when most French intellectuals either favored the Soviet bloc or else dreamed of a neutral "third way." Although it is true that for thirty years the Cold War shaped the configuration of public intellectual life in France as elsewhere, it is not enough to note that Aron took an unpopular position and paid the price for it within his natural community.

The question is, Why did he choose thus? He was by his own account a socialist; in 1945 he had joined the editorial board of *Les Temps Modernes* with Sartre, de Beauvoir, and others; his philosophical inclinations and intellectual tastes were not strikingly at variance from those of his contemporaries on the intellectual left, and the lifelong polemics he exchanged with them suggest that in spite of being the best-known liberal commentator in France (which in practice defined him for most of his audience as a conservative), he remained at heart a member of the left-leaning community. The reasons for his choices, the ways in which he became the Raymond Aron known to a later generation, must be sought not in his political choices but in the ways in which he came to those choices. And it is here that he distinguishes himself, in every sense and in a variety of keys.

To begin with, Aron was the most cosmopolitan French intellectual of his time. I have already noted his interest in German thought, first acquired during his extended period of study in Germany during the dying years of the Weimar Republic, 1930–1933. Indeed, until he became interested in Tocqueville and Montesquieu in the 1950s, most of Aron's intellectual debts were to German thinkers. From reading Husserl in particular he derived the shape of his philosophy of history. From Max Weber, about whom he wrote in a number of essays, he developed his complex vision of the relation between understanding and action. At odds with the dominant (Durkheimian) strain of French social theory, with its prejudice in favor of the identification of "scientific" laws and processes, Aron was attracted to Weber's careful interrogation of the relationship between consciousness and choice, his appreciation of the *responsibilities* of the social scientist toward both his subject matter and his own epoch. In *La sociologie allemande contemporaine*, first published in 1936, he introduced French readers to a tradition of social reasoning and criticism radically different from that inherited from Comte and Durkheim and far better attuned, as it seemed to Aron, to the needs and predicaments of the hour.

The crucial difference lay in Weber's famous distinction between conviction and responsibility. The task of the social scientist (or intellectual) could not be restricted to the business of understanding social processes, in the past or in the present. For the reasons Weber gave, which were not so different from those Aron himself offers in his philosophical writings, the intellectual must always face the decision of how to act in a given situation—understanding is not sufficient. But it was at least in principle possible to choose between acting either *in* history or else in the *light* of history—to engage in the debates and conflicts of one's time from a feeling of conviction or from a sense of responsibility.

In later years Raymond Aron would come to question Weber's own presentation of this option: the temptation to find necessity or even inevitability in a given historical moment, something to which Max Weber, like Carl Schmitt, was always prone, could lead men of conviction and responsibility alike to abdicate to History choices that should have been left to men.[8] But the Weberian calculus, the sense that we can behave coherently and responsibly without making partisan commitments—or else that a partisan engagement may under certain circumstances be the responsible option—lay behind many of Aron's own public utterances, as he explicitly recognized when approving the title of a book of interviews with him late in life—*Le spectateur engagé*.

After the war, the center of gravity of Aron's interests shifted steadily away from German thought toward the great social commentators of an earlier French tradition. But here, too, Aron was at odds with his contemporaries, who were as unconcerned with Montesquieu or Tocqueville as they had been with the great Germans (Marx always excepted).[9] What seems to have brought Aron to the writers of what he called, following Elie Halévy, the "English school of French political thought," was his frustration with the meta-scale of analysis characteristic of German thought—as early as 1936 he would remark that the value of even Weber's "bird's-eye view" of history was uncertain, however seductive. What distinguished Montesquieu and his heirs, by contrast, was their understanding of the *political,* and their willingness to accord politics an autonomous and important place in social and historical explanation.[10]

Montesquieu, however, posed a difficulty. His approach, which assigned governments and institutions to different social and geographical and historical milieus, seemed to run the risk of abdicating (moral) judgment. If each society has, and can only have, one appropriate form of government or leadership, from what perspective may the observer or analyst ever hope to criticize or condemn such "natural" institutions? Aron understood why the question in that form would not have troubled Montesquieu, but it troubled *him.* Nevertheless, in his two-volume study of Clausewitz, a work of which he was particularly proud, Aron made the point that what he most admired in the nineteenth-century German strategist—his capacity to treat each historical problem or choice in its singular context—was distinctively Montesquieu-like in its clarity and honesty. "Clausewitz's thinking resembles that of Montesquieu more than anyone has ever suggested, much more than it does that of Kant or Hegel." The challenge was to combine an appreciation of historical particularity—whether in military strategy or sociological description—with the call for conceptual explanation. The modern world sorely missed Montesquieu's grasp of the place of *les lois et les moeurs* in the human condition; the contemporary disposition to simplify, to attribute "the misfortunes of some to the advantages of others" served only, in Aron's view, to give nationalism a clean conscience![11]

In Tocqueville, Aron found a kindred spirit, a man whose grasp of both social *and* political explanations gave him a platform from which to see farther into the historical and contemporary sources of the problems of his time than any of his peers. Of the three social theorists of the nineteenth century who interested Aron most, it was Toqueville whose vision "most resembles west European societies in the nineteen-sixties."[12] Tocqueville's account of French instability since the ancien régime, in which elites proved consistently unable to agree on the forms of political life, and his insights into the "querulous satisfaction" of modern societies helped shape Aron's understanding of his own age. But perhaps more important, Aron could not help seeing, in Tocqueville's isolation amid the ideological currents of the nineteenth century, a foretaste of the difficulties of the liberal thinker in a later age: "Too liberal for the side from which he came, not enthusiastic enough about new ideas for the republicans, he was taken up neither by the right nor the left, but remained suspect to them all. Such is the fate reserved in France to the English or Anglo-American school."[13]

It was from his reading in French and German social thought alike that Aron would thus forge his distinctive critique of historicized interpretations in general, and Marxism in particular. It did not follow, he would argue, that because a particular political system, or even a system of reasoning, could be located in a given social context or historical moment, that one could derive from this knowledge any judgment as to its suitability or value in general terms. But, conversely, it was equally mistaken to attempt to assess the value of different political systems or ideologies without reference to their truth or falsity (an error he attributed to Karl Mannheim). If one wished to understand politics and political ideas, it was necessary *both* to situate these in their proper context *and* to measure them against criteria of good and evil, true and false, which could not be derived from those contexts alone. Immune, thanks in part to his Weberian sympathies, to the appeal of abstract neo-Kantian evaluations of political choice, Aron was unusual in his equally rigorous dismissal of the genetic fallacy.

Accordingly, Aron's polemical engagements with the Marxism of his contemporaries reflected the complexity and range of his concerns. Since he saw the Soviet ideological project as a device for saving Reason-in-History at the price of reason itself, the latter was his chief weapon. Why, he asked, even supposing that human history possesses a purpose and a goal, would the crucial test of that goal take place in the mid-twentieth century, in a country curiously unsuited for such a "sublime role"? And who authorized us to draw such definitive conclusions anyway? "Either History is the ultimate tribunal, and it will not pronounce sentence until the day of judgment; or conscience (or God) is the judge of History, and the future has no more authority than the present." No observer—historian, sociologist, or whoever—can hope to know the *meanings* of actions, institutions, and laws. History is not absurd, but no living being can grasp its final meaning.[14]

The danger of holistic historical reasoning, in Aron's view, lay less in the damage it does to men's minds than in the threat it would pose to their bodies: "Ministers, commissars, theorists and interrogators . . . will try to make men what they would spontaneously be if the official philosophy were true." Where the cunning of History fails, men will intervene on its behalf. For the same reasons, the simple category error of confusing economic competition ("class struggle") with political conflict—the mistake of identifying the struggle over the instruments of power with the struggle for power itself—substitutes for power (which is a human relationship) arbitrarily chosen determinants of that relationship.[15]

This conflation of the social (or the economic) with the political permits a confusion of political language that not only defeats its own purpose—to reveal the world to itself—but also contributes fatally to the very political outcomes it purports to oppose. Political argument of this kind is at once arrogantly overambitious—since it fails to grasp the partial and historically determined quality of all understanding, its own included—and dangerously foreshortened, in its unwillingness to engage the world not as it should be but as it is.

In later years Aron would come to wonder whether he had not squandered his energies in such polemics, bringing a powerful epistemological and empirical artillery to bear on debates "whose scientific value seems to me thin. . . . Men, and especially intellectuals, believe what they want to believe—me as well, perhaps—and are, in the final analysis, impervious to arguments."[16] But it is significant that for at least twenty years, from 1947 to 1968, the debate over Marxism—or rather the exchange of polemics, since no debate ever took place—seemed to Raymond Aron to merit his full attention. Were it not for his sense that the errors of Marxism were part of a larger, more interesting set of problems in social analysis and historical explanation, it is unlikely that he would have attended to them quite so fully or written about them with such moral and analytical intensity.

The difference between Aron and many of his contemporaries, on both sides of the political divide, was that for Aron these matters of high theory spoke directly to real, and in his view urgent, political worries. Ever since his student years in Germany, Aron was absorbed with, perhaps even obsessed by, the fragility of liberal polities and the threat of anarchy and despotism. This marked his writings in a way that nothing about his comfortable childhood and youth could have predicted, and it sets him apart from almost every other intellectual of his generation. It accounts for his remarkable prescience during the 1930s, when most French politicians and intellectuals alike were tragically slow to grasp the meaning of Hitler's revolution, and for his response to almost every major crisis in postwar French life, from the turmoil of the Liberation to the events of May 1968.

Writing from Cologne in 1931, Aron described to Jean Guéhenno a Germany "on the edge of the abyss" and expressed his sense of despair at French *insouciance* and at the hopelessness of trying to arouse the public to awareness of the crisis. "If you read both French and German newspapers, if you live in both countries, it is awful. Where are we heading?" By 1933 he had given up the effort to convince his correspondents or readers of the danger of a Nazi revolution already on the verge of consummation, and focused instead upon the (equally forlorn) task of arousing a degree of political realism in French policymaking.

In an article published that year in *Esprit*, Aron called for an end to "idealist aspirations" in French foreign policy and for a recognition that with the defeat of Weimar the Versailles era had come to an end. Disarmament and negotiation could no longer substitute for defense: "Left-wing Frenchmen use a sentimental language (justice, respect) which shields them from harsh realities. In their desire to make amends for our mistakes they forget that our policies must take into account not the past, but Germany today. And it is no reparation of past faults to commit new ones in the opposite direction. . . . A good policy is measured by its effectiveness, not its virtue." A typically Aronian sentiment.[17]

No one was listening, of course, and even antifascist intellectuals in France as elsewhere preferred to speculate about revolution at home (or in Spain) than to recognize the inevitability of a coming war with Germany. Raymond Aron thus lived the 1930s in anxious frustration, watching the slow unraveling of civil society and the political system in France as he had first observed it in Germany. His second experience of civic disorder and collapse, in the spring of 1940, confirmed his growing understanding of the workings—and vulnerability—of democracies, and accounts for his (strictly conditional) support for de Gaulle in the early years of the Fourth Republic. Thereafter he interpreted events, and decided his own stance, with constant reference to these formative experiences of his own early adult life—even his attitude to the Vichy regime was shaped by them: until November 1942 he was willing to allow that it had at least contributed to preventing civil conflict between the French.[18]

Thus, in the postwar years Aron was a vigorous critic of those who sought a "catastrophic" solution to the social woes of postwar France (or anywhere else). As he recognized, this taste for violent, "definitive" solutions, as though the road to utopia *necessarily* lay through destruction, was in part born of the experience of war. But he opposed it energetically, and when France came as near as it ever has in the twentieth century to a real peacetime civil conflict, at the time of the communist-led strikes of 1948, Aron took an uncharacteristically hard line: "The inevitable struggle will be muted only to the extent that the state has strengthened its means of action. It is just not acceptable that in the mines and electrical plants of France people are more afraid of the communists than of engineers, directors, and ministers combined."[19]

His argument in favor of Algerian independence, as we shall see, was similarly driven by a concern for French civil stability and order. But it is in Aron's reaction to the events of 1968 that the salience of this theme is most obvious. Despite his general sympathy with the students' criticism of French higher education, and his growing dislike of the authoritarian Gaullist state and its policies (domestic and foreign alike), he took an absolutely uncompromising line against the student movement, its intellectual supporters, and the public disruption it brought about. Like Edgar Morin and other professorial enthusiasts for student radicalism, Aron saw that the order of modern societies is inherently fragile.

Unlike them, he found this to be a source of anxiety. Once a carnival turns into anarchy, he wrote, it rapidly becomes less tolerable than almost any form of order. Analogies with revolutions past were misconceived, he noted: "To expel a president elected by universal suffrage is not the same thing as expelling a king." Even the university, whatever its well-recognized defects, depended upon a degree of *order*: "The university, any university, requires a spontaneous consensus around respect for evidence and for unforced discipline. To break up this social unit without knowing what to replace it with, or in order to break up society itself, is aesthetic nihilism; or rather, it is the eruption of barbarians, unaware of their barbarism.[20]

Aron's criticism of French intellectuals, and their student followers, was thus driven as much by what he came to see as their political irresponsibility as by their philosophical or moral errors. Writing in 1969, he assimilated the French "existentialists" to the "Marxists and para-Marxists of the Weimar Republic" and held them implicitly responsible for any political crisis they helped bring about—a point he had made explicitly thirty years earlier in an article accusing German and Italian socialists of having contributed in different ways to their own nemesis. In the introduction to *Les désillusions du progrès*, also written in 1969, he makes the link quite explicit: "Violence, even in the name of ideas diametrically opposed to those of interwar fascism, risks dragging liberal societies toward the same tragedy as that of thirty years ago. . . . Self-proclaimed noncommunist Marxists actively helped bring down the Weimar Republic: some of them speak and act as though they dream of repeating that achievement."[21]

The link in Aron's thought between political stability, civil order, and public liberties is thus clear, and as with Tocqueville, it was in essence a product of experience and observation rather than theory. This helps us understand his way of thinking about liberty in general, and the totalitarian threat to it. Unlike social commentators in the United States, for example, Aron was not an especially enthusiastic advocate of the term "totalitarian" as a general category covering various modern threats to the open society. His distaste for grand theory extended to anticommunist rhetoric as well, and his thoughts about totalitarianism derived in the first instance from his concern for its opposite—the partial, always imperfect reality of liberty, constrained and threatened by necessity and history. If the United States was to be preferred in the global conflicts of the day, it was not because it represented some higher or more logically satisfying order of life, but because it stood as the guarantor, however defective, of public liberties.

The Soviet Union, on the other hand, was marked by the very extremism of its system—the way in which all its particular defects were integral to its general project. This distinguished it from the authoritarianism of Franco, for example: the prison camps of Spain were a weapon of repression, but not part of the very workings of a slave economy in the manner of the camps of the KGB or the SS. It was this same integrated quality that paradoxically made truly totalitarian systems so appealing to utopian intellectuals, as Aron understood: the dialectic of a "violence that overcomes violence itself" was what appealed to someone like Maurice Merleau-Ponty in the early postwar years. And just because imperfect, intermediary, partial institutions were the main bulwark of political freedom, so they were most vulnerable to the revolt against "alienation," the search for final, logical solutions to what was in practice the human condition.[22]

In Aron's thinking, then, there was an intimate link between the French revolutionary myth—that desire to "bridge the gap between moral intransigence and intelligence" as he put it—and the distinctively *total* threat to freedom represented by a certain kind of repressive society. Hence the remarkable capacity of highly intelligent men and women to deny the evidence of their eyes; writing in 1950, at a time when the appeal of Stalin extended well beyond the boundaries of those parties and countries under his direct control, Aron commented that "the ludicrous surprise is that the European left has taken a pyramid builder for its God." The fault lay in the disposition of intellectuals to take words for things. "It requires the naïveté and remoteness of the Christians of *Esprit* or the humanists around Saint Germain des Prés to be taken in by the phraseology of Stalinist Marxism."[23]

But it was not enough to lay bare the unpalatable facts about totalitarianism. There were some uncomfortable truths about free societies, too, that intellectuals were equally disposed to ignore. For Aron's generation in the 1920s and 1930s, the widespread appeal of the writings of the philosopher Alain (Emile Chartier) had lain in his treatment of *all* political authority as incipiently, potentially tyrannical. Aron vigorously rejected Alain's innocent nostrums: "Alain's doctrine can only be applied just where it does more harm than good. Where it is really needed, against the ravages of fanaticism, there is no one left who can put it to work." All the same, he recognized a central truth in Alain's thought: that the adoration of all powers—any powers—and their wish to *be* adored lay at the root of modern tyranny.[24]

But Aron reasoned that it is absurd to propose that the sole task of the theorist of freedom *in a free society* lies in opposing and restricting authority wherever it may touch him. For resisting and denying the moderate claims and capacities of government in a free society is precisely the way to clear the path for the immoderate variety (Weimar, again). The lesson of totalitarianism, in short, was the importance of order and authority under law—not as a compromise with freedom nor as the condition of higher freedoms to come, but simply as the best way to protect those already secured.

In the years following World War II it was axiomatic for Aron that the totalitarian threat came from the Soviet Union and not from some hypothetical future revival of fascism. In his own words, "Every action, in the middle of the twentieth century, presupposes and involves the adoption of an attitude with regard to the Soviet enterprise. To evade this is to evade the implications and constraints of historical existence, however much one may invoke History." But he was always perfectly aware—again, in contrast to some of his friends and admirers across the Atlantic—that even though "totalitarian" might be a necessary description of Stalin's state, it was hardly sufficient. There were real differences between communism and fascism/nazism: "For those who wish to 'save the concepts,' there remains a difference between a philosophy whose logic *is* monstrous, and one which lends itself to a monstrous interpretation."[25]

Aron's preoccupation with liberty—its sources, its fragility, the threats to it and the ways in which these might be understood and thwarted—colored all his other concerns, just as his philosophical turn of thought and his sympathy for a certain style of social explanation shaped his responses to those concerns. His own sense of "responsibility," and his lifelong prejudice against posing questions for which he was unqualified to offer an answer, led him to study a number of topics to which other French thinkers of his day paid little attention. As early as 1937 he spelled out his reasons: "It isn't every day that a Dreyfus Affair allows you to invoke truth against error. If intellectuals want to offer their opinions on a daily basis, they will need knowledge of economics, diplomacy, politics, etc. Whether it concerns deflation and inflation, Russian alliance or *entente cordiale*, collective contracts or wage rates, the point at issue is less about justice than about effectiveness."[26]

One outcome of this desire to engage the real was a preoccupation with the idea of "industrial society." For most other French thinkers, of left or right, "society" was either capitalist or socialist, the forms of production and property ownership determining all other features. The Soviet Union and the West were categorically different systems, and there was widespread agreement across the political spectrum that it was a serious *political* mistake, as well as an analytical error, to suggest that the two antagonistic political systems shared certain fundamental modern elements in common.

Aron took a rather different position. He regretted the neglect of a question that had preoccupied early nineteenth-century writers: What is the meaning, what is the nature of a society shaped by science and by industry? Unlike a number of "industrial society" theorists in the United States, he did not want to claim that the "East" and the "West" were somehow converging, their distinctive ideological disagreements being cast in the shade by a common drive toward the social, managerial, and rationalist goals of an industrial economy. He was too conscious of politics—of the contrast between societies where state and society were collapsed into one and those where they were distinct—and too well informed about the place of ideology in Soviet thinking to make this elementary mistake.

That error merely reflected the Marxist one of concluding from a similarity of forces of production to an identity of political institutions and beliefs. But from as early as 1936 Aron had already observed an aspect of the Soviet "experiment": while freedom and private enterprise had been essential to the *origins* of industrial production, the latter might *now* thrive under Soviet-style conditions of planning and public ownership (although he also noted that to the extent that East and West *were* converging in certain respects, this undermined communist claims based on the necessary incommensurability of the two economic systems).[27]

In later years Aron modified this position, concluding that technical developments could at best attenuate certain formal differences between political regimes. Nevertheless, those technical changes were a fact of the modern world, and Aron was caustically dismissive of those French critics who fondly imagined that the rationalist and economistic traits of all modern (Western) societies were something gratuitously foisted upon Europeans by the United States for its own purposes. In his view the problems of modernity could not be cast in the simple old ways: private property versus public ownership, capitalist exploitation versus social equality, market anarchy versus planned distribution. Accordingly these themes of socialist doctrine and left-right polemic had largely lost their meaning. The paralysis of the French state—what Aron in 1954 called the "French disease"—lay at the heart of French political and economic stagnation, and could neither be understood nor addressed in the terms of an outdated partisan debate over the impropriety or otherwise of industrial modernization.[28]

In order to enter the discussion on the nature of and prospects for industrial society, Aron taught himself economics. For the purpose of becoming an influential commentator on foreign affairs, he familiarized himself with the language and arguments of nuclear strategy and international relations. He almost certainly had very little respect for international relations as a discipline, and his own forays into it—notably *Paix et guerre entre les nations* —were not a source of great satisfaction to him. But a combination of cool realism and copious information stood him in good stead. For thirty years Aron commented regularly on almost every aspect of French foreign policy and international affairs, and his opinions and projections stand up better today than those of almost anyone else, in France or abroad.

Raymond Aron was among the first in his generation to grasp the truth about post–World War II politics: that domestic and foreign conflicts were now intertwined and the traditional distinction between foreign policy and domestic policy had thus disappeared. "The truth is that in our times, for individuals as for nations, the choice that determines all else is a global one, in effect a geographical choice. One is in the universe of free countries or else in that of lands placed under harsh Soviet rule. From now on everyone in France will have to state his choice." In the late 1940s Aron laid out a two-track explanation of Soviet international strategy that would become conventional wisdom by the 1970s but was original and provocative in its time. According to this there was a fundamental continuity of Soviet goals, but these might be sought either by the tactic of alliances—as in the era of the Popular Front, or for a brief moment after Hitler's defeat—or else by confrontational attitudes at appropriate times and in vulnerable places.

The implication, that Stalin's state was run by men who thought in terms of cynical statecraft as well as ideological objectives, was not in fact offensive to communists themselves—though they could hardly admit it. But it was deeply wounding to the illusions of fellow-traveling intellectuals of the neutralist left, like Claude Bourdet or Jean-Marie Domenach; the ease with which Aron burst the bubbles of their own internationalist fantasies, and his ability to relate the French communists' domestic practices to a broader Soviet strategy deeply offended the sensibilities of such men and contributed mightily to their lifelong enmity toward him.[29]

It is hard to recall, today, the Manichean mood of those early Cold War years. For the *bien pensant* left-wing intelligentsia, anyone who wasn't sympathetic to the French communists and the Soviet Union, who was unwilling to give them the benefit of every doubt, to ascribe to them every good intention, must be a conscious agent of the United States, an active advocate of confrontation and even war. In fact Aron was strikingly moderate, not unlike George Kennan in later years. He held the opinion that the Soviet Union would never deliberately push the world to the brink of war, preferring to attain its objectives by subtle pressure—hence the alternating styles of compromise and confrontation.

For this reason Aron, like postwar British Foreign Secretary Ernest Bevin, saw the construction of the Western Alliance as a political, even a psychological move rather than a military one—designed to reassure Western Europe and in so doing render it less vulnerable to communist pressure at home and abroad. In these circumstances, as Aron famously put it in an article in September 1947, peace might be impossible but war was improbable.[30]

Aron's cool realism in these matters allowed him to see beyond the illusions and switchback hopes and disappointments of the post-Stalin decade, as Western politicians and commentators scrutinized every gesture of Soviet leaders in the search for some evidence of détente or a new approach. In Aron's eyes the inscrutable Mr. Molotov was a useful prophylactic against a return to the interwar illusions of Geneva—the idea that "peace depends on words rather than on the courage of men and the balance of forces." Writing in 1956, after the upheavals in Poland but before the repression of the Hungarian revolution, Aron reminded his readers that "if the Soviets felt truly threatened, they would return to the rigidity of earlier years. . . . Let us not mistake our dreams for near reality." And when Khrushchev did indeed return for a while to the style and methods of Stalinist foreign policy, Aron used the occasion to point out how little influence Western actions really had on Soviet behavior: when it suited the Soviet leadership to end the Korean War, sign the Austrian Peace Treaty, or make up with Tito they just went ahead and did so; but only then and not before.[31]

Aron's insights derived in part from his grasp of the ideological and political nature of communism, but at least as much from his more old-fashioned understanding of interstate relations. In his words, "The division of humanity into sovereign states preceded capitalism and will outlive it." There were limits to what even the great powers could do, but there were equally limits on what could be done to prevent them doing as they wished—hence his mildly skeptical attitude toward the United Nations and other international agencies. This fundamentally tragic vision—the belief that there can be no end to the conflicts among states and the best that could be hoped for was constant vigilance to limit the risks and damage of confrontations—placed Aron at odds with the dominant sensibility of his era: the view, held by many on both sides, that the object of international relations was somehow to put an end to all wars; whether through nuclear stalemate, the negotiation of a definitive "peace settlement," or final victory by one side or the other. Aron was too conscious of the unusual situation and history of Europe to be drawn into such illusory hopes: "Europeans would like to escape from their history, a 'great' history written in letters of blood. But others, by the hundreds of millions, are taking it up for the first time, or coming back to it."[32]

Despite sharing some of de Gaulle's criticism of American foreign and economic policy, and reacting with the wounded sensibilities of a Frenchman to attacks on his country at the United Nations, Aron was reluctant to support the broader Gaullist objectives of nuclear autonomy and "independence." This was partly because he regarded any weakening of the Western Alliance as a gift to the Soviet Union; but his chief objection to Gaullist dreams of nuclear grandeur lay elsewhere. Raymond Aron saw very early on, at least two decades before most professional military strategists, the limits to the diplomatic and military uses of nuclear weaponry. In 1957, ten years before the British retreat from east of Suez, he pointed out that the British military's growing reliance on atomic weapons and its reduced expenditure on the conventional variety would undercut its freedom of military and therefore diplomatic maneuver without doing anything to improve its security. Two years later he made the identical point about the French *force de frappe*—French nuclear weapons only made sense in the hypothetical context of a conflict between NATO and the USSR, whereas for France's real problems in Africa or the Middle East they would be of absolutely no use whatsoever.[33]

Despite his emphasis upon the main conflict—with the USSR—Aron was thus alert to the changes already taking place in the postwar world from the late 1950s. Even in 1954 he had warned against betting the entire military budget and calculations on a single weapon; the wars of the future were likely to be quite different and require a very different sort of arsenal. Moreover, such local wars need not lead to international conflicts on a nuclear scale; on the contrary, since if the nuclear "umbrella" secured anything it was the space for greater and lesser powers to engage in local or partial conflicts without putting "peace" at risk. The logic of power politics remained in force, and with it the need to think militarily in a variety of keys and not just that of nuclear devastation. "One does not increase the risk of total war by accepting the obligations of local wars."[34]

Aron's sense of the limits and realities of international politics contributed to his attitude toward the question of a new "Europe." Unlike Jean Monnet and his acolytes in the French planning ministries, Aron was not at first a wholehearted enthusiast for Continental European political unity. The future of postwar Western Europe, in his view, depended on economic reconstruction and collective defense, neither of which could be achieved except in close association with the United States and Great Britain. He was even initially sympathetic to British desires to keep a healthy distance from European political projects ("the example of French and Italian parliaments hardly inspires unconditional confidence"), though by the 1960s the altered situation led him to chastise the British for their failure to adapt to a changed world: "Don't be half a century behind. Accept that the Old Continent is seeking its future beyond nationalisms."[35]

Although his instincts preserved him from the illusion of a single European economy—Aron always understood that the *economic* community represented a happy arrangement of fortuitously compatible national economic strategies—the same grasp of postwar realities led Aron to the conclusion that the age of independent European nation-states was gone for good: "Without denying the hurdles to be overcome, the idea of a united Europe represents, in our century, the last hope of old nations lacking the immense spaces of Eurasia and America." He thus navigated steadily between the twin dangers of Gaullist national illusion and leftist disdain for a "capitalist" Europe.

But the "ever-closer union" of the founding fathers of the European community held little appeal to Aron, and not just because he was skeptical of their chances of forging a single European economic entity. He also appreciated from an early stage something that has only just now begun to dawn on the political and administrative leadership of the western half of the Continent: that without a European foreign policy and a European army to enforce it, the Continent lacked the fundamental building blocks of any sovereign entity and would remain at the mercy of its separate interests. Until this situation changed, international political and military crises would continue to be addressed not by some present or future "European Assembly" but by the powers directly involved—an observation as pertinent today as when Aron first made it in the context of an early crisis in NATO's leadership in 1959.[36]

Aron's chief interest in the project of Europe was shared with at least some French and other European policymakers: the need to address and resolve the "German question." Writing in *Combat* in February 1947, at a time when intellectuals and politicians in France were still advocating a variety of solutions to the German dilemma, from multiple partition to unified neutrality, Aron argued that the only hope for a secure European future lay in reconstituting a stable German state *within* a West European setting. He would return again and again to this theme: never again would Germany be so *disponible,* so open to an international solution and too weak to oppose it. Now, he wrote in January 1949, is the time to act: "Never have circumstances been so propitious for putting an end to a century-long conflict."

For the same reasons, Aron was a committed advocate of West German rearmament, when the question arose in the early 1950s. Like so much else in Aron's style of reasoning, this conclusion was reached not on principle but as the recognition of a reality, albeit unwelcome: "It is unfortunate that circumstances oblige us to arm Germany. It would be even more unfortunate if those arms were to come from the 'pacifists' in the Kremlin."[37]

The overwhelming strategic goal was first to invent a democratic German state, then to tie it and its citizenry to the Western Alliance, and then to give it the means to play its role in the defense of that alliance. This outcome was by no means guaranteed, or even likely, in the immediate postwar years, and was fought at each stage in France by an unholy alliance of communists, pacifists, nationalists, and Gaullists. Aron himself recognized the irony and unpopularity of a remilitarized German state a mere decade after the defeat of Hitler—just as he warned as early as 1956, in an essay coauthored with Daniel Lerner, about the risks of talking pompously of "European unity" as though the other half of Europe (and Germany) simply didn't exist. But in neither case did he make the mistake of confusing his desires (or emotions) with harsh reality.

Throughout Raymond Aron's writings, whether philosophical, "social-scientific," or political, there is one constant: realism. The task of the commentator is to address the world as it is and to offer credible answers to the problems it poses. As he wrote of Max Weber, "He was prepared at any moment to answer the question which disconcerts all our amateur politicians: 'What would you do if you were a Cabinet minister?'" Intellectuals who confined themselves to describing—or admonishing—the world stood condemned: "If one has nothing to say about politics except to explain what other people are doing, it would be better not to write about it at all." This distinctive understanding of the duties of the intellectual set Aron quite apart from his fellow writers, for whom the idea of the public intellectual was inseparable from irresponsible grandstanding.

Even when he agreed with their goals, Aron preferred not to put his name to collective intellectual utterances. He refused to join the Committee of Anti-Fascist Intellectuals in the 1930s because of what he regarded as their pacifist illusions. And he took his distance from advocates of neutrality in the following decade, not because he thought that neutrality was in itself an undesirable objective but because to advocate it for France in 1949 was to deny the facts of international political life: "The formula of neutrality, even armed neutrality, is typical of the refusal to face reality, of the desire for escape which characterize a large fraction of the western intelligentsia." Men like Claude Bourdet or Maurice Duverger were irresponsible, unable to transcend in their imagination the difference between writing an article and governing a country.[38]

It was in large measure to combat such illusions, to lay bare the unreality of intellectual political engagement, that Aron resorted to a rigorous logic in his arguments. This could be disconcerting even to his friends. Despite his unambiguous commitment to the Free French (he spent the war years in London writing for their newspaper), Aron took great care in his analyses to present Vichy as preeminently an error of political judgment. The Pétainist mistake had been to suppose that Vichy might benefit from its place in Hitler's Europe—a dangerous and ultimately tragic misjudgment, but one that needed to be understood in the context of the events of 1940. The point was to acknowledge the facts, however uncomfortable or inconvenient: "The analyst doesn't create the history that he interprets."[39]

This awareness of the troubling and confusing quality of reality was shaped in part by Aron's sense of the distance that lay between his own world and that of the great social observers of an earlier time. Auguste Comte, he noted, could arrange the world according to the tidy rules of a universally applicable positivism. Tocqueville could bring to bear upon his social observations a theory of the virtues and defects of democracy in what he understood to be its universal (American) incarnation. Marx could apply the universal panacea of socialism as a future solution and thus prospective explanation for the contradictions of his own world. But a commentator in the mid-twentieth century has no such certainties. The modern world is too complex to be reduced to a formula, a condemnation, or a solution: "Modern society . . . is a democratic society to be observed without transports of enthusiasm or indignation."[40]

Nevertheless, at no point did Aron ever conclude from this observation that the commentator is left with little choice but to accept the verdict of history. Indeed, it was implicit in his critique of Karl Mannheim, his later thoughts about Max Weber, and his polemical engagement with the whole Marxist project that fatalism—whether it consisted of "taking the long view," ascribing to History some transcendental meaning, or assigning to a class or nation a privileged role in the unfolding of that meaning—was an epistemological error that could only bring political disaster. The danger of justifying false realists (or idealists) was ever present in all such forms of historicism.

Nor was Aron a "realist" in the sense people mean when they speak of realpolitik—the practice of making political judgments derived exclusively from a calculation of possibilities and outcomes based on past experience. He had no time for that sort of "theoretical realism," which led in practice to *unrealistic* decisions like that of Chamberlain at Munich. His objection to this style of thinking lay partly in its frequently misguided conclusions, but above all in its rigidity, with the result that what begins as empirical calculation nearly always ends up as rule-bound dogma: "In my opinion pseudo-certainty, based on the relationship between the stakes and the risks, on some rational calculation ascribed to a likely aggressor, is of no more value than the dogmatism of the Maginot line."[41]

What does it mean, then, to speak of Raymond Aron as a "realist"? In properly philosophical terms he most certainly was one. But that was not what he himself meant when he spoke of being a realist. He meant, rather, that he took into account, in his efforts to understand the world, all that he took to be real about it—and only what he took to be real. As he explained in 1938 in the defense of his philosophical dissertation: "My book proposes that we renounce the abstractions of moralism and ideology and look instead for the true content of possible choices, limited as they are by reality itself."

But, and this is the important point, Aron's reality encompassed not only interests and power but also ideas. Like Clausewitz, he took it for granted that *Glaubensache*—beliefs of all kinds—constitute a fact about society. Men have beliefs and are moved by them in various ways, and this is as much a part of reality as the disposition of armaments or the forms of production. "Realism," in Aron's view, was simply unrealistic if it ignored the moral judgments that citizens pass on governments, or the real and imagined moral interests of all actors in a society. It is for this reason that Raymond Aron's realism was so much better at explaining and predicting events in his time than the disabused and "realist" commentaries and prognostications of sovietologists and others who shared his concerns but not his breadth of understanding.

But the same sensitivity to the varieties of human motivation that made Aron's realism so different from the knowing skepticism of some of his colleagues also set him firmly against any inclination to what he contemptuously dismissed as "moralizing." In one of his earliest pieces of writing, the January 1934 article arguing against conscientious objection that first brought him to the attention of Elie Halévy among others, Aron spelled out the distinction that would inform his political analyses throughout his life: "The minister who condemns war and prepares for it cannot be accused of hypocrisy. It is simply a question of the distinction between personal ethics and real politics." The point is repeated in a long-unpublished manuscript from the later 1930s, where Aron quotes Pareto: "Whoever looks at the facts objectively and who does not deliberately close his eyes to the light, is all the same forced to recognize that it is not by playing the nervous moralists that rulers bring prosperity to their peoples."[42]

This careful extrusion of the moralizing dimension from all his analytical writings has given Aron the reputation of a cold writer, unmoved by feelings (his own or others) and confined in the grip of what François Mauriac once called his "icy clarity." There is no doubt that Aron made a point of being clear and rational above all else—*ce vertige de lucidité* as Alfred Fabre-Luce described it—and saw no virtue in appealing to a reader's or an audience's sentiments or sensibilities. This did not mean that he lacked feelings. Far from it—but the private tragedies of his life (one child died of leukemia when she was six, another was born handicapped) had taught him to isolate his emotions from his reason, the better to preserve the latter. As he described himself when he was admitted to the Institut in 1965, he was a "man without a party, whose opinions offend first one side and then another, who is all the more unbearable because he takes his moderation to excess and *hides his passions under his arguments*."[43]

Such men have always been at a disadvantage in France. "Representatives of the critical spirit in France are discredited through the accusation of coldness. They are presumed to lack imagination, hope, and generosity, as though intelligence can only thrive at the cost of atrophied sensibilities."[44] In Aron's case, the consequences can be seen perhaps most clearly in his contribution to the agonized French debate over Algeria.

Raymond Aron was not against French colonies on principle. He resented the American and British failure to assist the embattled French forces in Vietnam and shared the view, widespread in the political class of his time, that France's identity was intimately bound up with its worldwide possessions and influence; France has a duty, he wrote in *Le Figaro* in October 1955, to try and keep North Africa "in the sphere of modern civilization." But lacking any personal experience of North Africa in general, and Algeria in particular, he felt no particular emotional attachment to the Maghreb and came to see his country's embroilment there as costly and pointless. The rebellion in Algeria made it depressingly clear that France could only retain control of the country by the application of considerable force.

Accordingly, as Aron argued in two trenchant pamphlets published in 1957 and 1958, the time had come to give the Algerians their independence. He based this conclusion on three characteristically Aronian grounds. To improve the condition of the indigenous population of Algeria to a level compatible with equal membership of the French nation, and to provide them with equal political rights and representation, as proposed by liberal-minded defenders of the status quo, would be unsustainably expensive (and therefore unpopular with the taxpaying citizenry). It would also entail a degree of Algerian presence in French political life—projecting ahead the far higher growth rates of the Arab population—that was likely to be unacceptable to the metropolitan French themselves. In short, the French were deluding themselves, not to speak of misleading the Arabs, when they promised equality and equal representation in the future—having steadfastly refused it in the past.

Second, while it was true that the Arab Algerians would be vastly better off if they stayed under French rule, this was not a factor that they could be expected to take into account. "It is a denial of the experience of our century to suppose that men will sacrifice their passions to their interests." While he had no interest in the nationalist case as such, Aron was capable of understanding its power to move millions, and the foolhardiness of opposing it. And he saw no point in debating whether or not there truly *was* an "Algerian nation" with claims to self-government and the like, as though the assertion by some that "Algerianness" was a modern invention would somehow undermine the case for independence. "It hardly matters whether this nationalism is the expression of a real or an imaginary nation. Nationalism is a passion, resolved to create the entity it invokes."

Third, once it was clear that the only mutually acceptable solution to the Algerian imbroglio was a parting of the ways—and to Aron this was obvious by 1957—it made absolutely no sense to wait. "The multiplication of would-be sovereign states, lacking the intellectual, economic, and administrative resources necessary for the exercise of sovereignty, is not inherently desirable. I am not a fanatic for the 'abandonment of sovereignty.' But I am more opposed to colonial wars than to the abandonment of sovereignty, because the former anyway produces the latter—under the worst possible conditions."

Note that Aron is not invoking historical inevitability here, much less a theory of necessary progress. The Algerian war need not have happened. The interests of its participants were not best served by the outcomes they sought. And even if the outcome was in one sense foreordained, if only by French colonial malpractice, that did not make it "right." But the French had failed to hold on to North Africa, and the time had come to recognize this and draw the only possible conclusion. Reasonable men might disagree on this—as Aron wrote in a different context, "Faced with this tragic dilemma men of equal patriotism might make utterly opposed choices." But for just that reason patriotism could not be invoked on either side—though France's practical interest might be, as Aron sought to demonstrate.[45]

Raymond Aron thus came down in favor of Algerian independence, like the overwhelming majority of other French intellectuals. But his arguments were utterly unlike theirs. He did not seek to show the legitimacy of the Arab claim to independence. He was not interested, for these purposes, in the moral debt the French had inherited from their colonial past, which could only be liquidated by the abandonment of colonial power. He never invoked the course of history or the "natural" move to a postcolonial world. And, above all, he did not refer to the emotive issue of French military and police practices in Algeria itself, the use of torture to extract confessions from suspected terrorists and the price that was being paid for these crimes in the soul of the French Republic. The Algerian tragedy, for Aron, lay not in the moral dilemma posed to individuals caught in the "dirty war" but in the absence of a satisfactory third alternative to a continuing conflict or a "catastrophic" independence. "Political action is a response to circumstances, not a theoretical disquisition or the expression of feelings."

Aron was accused at the time of having precisely neglected the "moral" dimension of France's Algerian crisis, of failing to grasp the true heart of the tragedy in his frozen concern with logic. His reply, when this charge was put to him again many years later, is revealing. Why did he not add his voice to those who were speaking out against the use of torture? "But what would I have achieved by proclaiming my opposition to torture? I have never met anyone who is in favor of torture." And, more generally, why did he not invoke moral criteria in his case for Algerian independence? Others were doing that already, and anyone who was open to that sort of argument was probably already convinced. "The important thing was to convince those who were arguing the opposite position."[46]

There can be no doubt that those were Aron's motives, and they are as consistent and as rational as always. But the care Aron took to avoid *any* appearance of passion or feeling at a time of highly emotive public debate raises the suspicion that, in addition to the rewards of influence and respect that came his way as a result of such carefully disengaged reasoning, he took some satisfaction in icy dispassion for its own sake. As he noted admiringly of Clausewitz: "*Sine ire et studio*: he neither approves nor condemns, he merely records." But that is not a stance entirely compatible with political responsibility, and as Aron noted in his memoirs apropos his own support for U.S. policy in Vietnam, one cannot restrict oneself to the role of "the observer of the follies and disasters of mankind." There was thus a self-inflicted discomfort in Aron's ultrarational approach to especially heated debates: he deprived himself of the pleasure of indulging his own human feelings. As he said, again in the context of his study of Clausewitz, "whoever reflects today upon wars and strategy must erect a barrier between his intelligence and his compassion." But Aron forced his readers to admire him, despite themselves, for the sheer power of his reasoning: "Democrats and liberals, if they understand him properly, can at least learn from him conceptual rigor."[47]

Whatever its costs, this conceptual rigor made Aron, for his admirers at least, the "ethical and logical anchor in contemporary French thought" (Serge-Cristophe Kolm). His singular ability to see clearly the developments of his time, and to interpret them accurately, marks him out from his fellow intellectuals. On almost every issue of importance to his former colleagues on the left, Aron understood the stakes sooner, and better. He was remarkably prescient not only about the rise of fascism but also its likely outcome: in 1939 he noted that whereas Mussolini's regime might well give way to a legal or conservative political restoration, the Nazi revolution could not.

By the beginning of the 1960s Aron was correctly predicting that French support for Israel, then quite marked, would be replaced by an inevitable effort at reconciliation with former colonies across the Mediterranean. By 1956 he had already anticipated, thirty years ahead of most other commentators, the problems that the Soviet Union would face in its "colonial" holdings in Central Asia, paying the price for its encouragement of anticolonialism elsewhere; and in 1969 he foresaw the coming explosions in Poland, remarking on the alienation of men and institutions from the regime, at a time when communism's grip on that country seemed unshakable for decades to come.[48]

Even Aron's "reactionary" stance of 1968, in horrified recoil at the disproportionate civic turmoil brought on by the "psychodrama" of the student revolt, was accompanied by his dissent from the conventional, conservative response. He had no patience for those who condemned "consumer society" while poverty still stalked much of the globe; "but those who are obsessed with rates of growth or levels of prosperity are no less irritating." The Gaullist regime was now paying the price for its smug authoritarianism, he concluded: it needed the shock brought on by "a reservoir of violence and mass indignation." Aron combined understanding for French frustration at inefficiency and the abuse of power in educational institutions and the workplace with a skeptical dismissal of the delusionary "revolutionary" mood of the hour. In retrospect, this seems a reasonable and on the whole fair assessment of events, though it won him few friends at the time.[49]

What he perhaps did not fully grasp was the characteristic mood of the "generation of '68," with the result that his dismissal of their self-indulgent imitation of revolutionary style led him to underestimate the longer-term impact on French public life and culture of the events of that year. But here, too, his response seems if not all-comprehending, then at least somehow fitting. There was something embarrassing and occasionally grotesque about the enthusiasm with which many other senior professors grew their hair, renewed their opinions, spiced their language, and strove demagogically to outdo their own students in iconoclastic fervor. What Aron lost in support he gained in respect and dignity; this, too, is a way of being right.

Aron was not, of course, always correct or consistent, even by his own lights. During the 1950s he occasionally struck an inappropriately alarmist note, usually in his journalism. In February 1955 he seems to have been unnecessarily worried that Adenauer might not be able to keep not just the Federal Republic but even his own Christian Democrats free from the temptations of neutralism. His angry dislike for Nasser ("the Egyptian *Führer*") led him at the time of the Suez crisis to make implausible and misleading analogies with Munich and utterly misread American interests and intentions ("Forced to choose, Washington will not opt for Nasser's Egypt against Great

Britain and France"—which is, of course, just what Eisenhower did). He even ventured wild and unsupported predictions of disaster in the event of Nasser's victory: "If pan-Islamism pushes the British out of the Near East and the French out of North Africa, it will not be long before the Americans are chased out of Europe."[50]

As that last remark suggests, such mistakes as Aron made in his assessment of the political situation in the postwar years usually derived from his overwhelming concern with the Soviet Union and the threat it posed. Having been one of the first to grasp, in 1945, the part that the USSR would play after Hitler's defeat, Aron fell occasionally victim to the Soviet Union's own assessment of its prospects. In 1975 he could write that "the superiority of the American republic over the Soviet Union belongs to the past." But he also understood the risk of distortion that he ran in this unswerving attention to the Soviet threat—at the end of the 1960s, in a mildly self-critical passage, he acknowledged how easy it was to forget that the United States, in its fear of global communism, also sustains indefensible regimes. It may be, as André Maurois once remarked and Aron half admitted, that he might have come a lot closer to being the Montesquieu of our times had he taken a little more distance from the course of events.[51]

Whether or not he aspired to emulate Montesquieu (or Tocqueville), there is no doubt that Aron, especially in his later years, was moved by the sense that he had not fulfilled his promise. The clue to this lies in his answer to a journalist who asked him, a few years before his death, which of his own books he liked the best. He passed over all his occasional pieces, his postwar journalism, his polemical essays, and his many forays into sociological theory, political science, and international relations. What he most admired in his own writing, he thought, were three books: the *Introduction à la philosophie de l'histoire*; *Histoire et dialectique de la violence* (his lengthy analysis and response to Sartre's *Critique de la raison dialectique*); and *Penser la guerre: Clausewitz*. Perhaps also his *Essai sur les libertés*.

This is a very revealing list. It shows that even at the end of his career Aron saw himself as what he had been at the outset—a philosopher. And he clearly regretted not having written the great work of philosophy that had been expected of him. Instead, history had intervened. As he wrote to Guéhenno from Cologne in May 1931, "I believe that in another time I would have been tempted to wander among the dilemmas of metaphysics; but like all my generation I feel a sense of instability and anxiety that allow little space for leisurely pursuits." Instead, Aron expended his time and energy on a dozen different fields, none of them fully worthy of his talents. It is not clear whether the book he would have written would have been a sequel to his dissertation or a full-length commentary on Marxism, "the book . . . I have been thinking about for nearly forty years." In either case it would have completed a whole. As for the works he *had* written, "All that forms no unity, it is imperfect and unfinished; but whoever wants to learn everything can pursue to the full none of the subjects he engages."[52]

The two-volume study of Clausewitz, whatever its virtues as a revisionist account of the nineteenth-century German military theorist, is interesting (and perhaps found favor with its author) because it is a revealing account of Aron's own sensibilities. He identified closely with Clausewitz's loneliness and independence of mind: "Of conservative opinions, he was taken for a killjoy, a wet blanket, such was his insistence upon sticking to an opinion if he thought it right." And Clausewitz, too, was consumed at the end with a sense of having not quite met his own demanding standards. "As to my innermost feelings: if I have not recorded a great body of exploits, I am at least free of any burden of guilt" (Pour ce qui est de mes dispositions intérieures, si je ne rapporte pas un riche butin de grands exploits, je suis du moins libre de tout fardeau de culpabilité).[53]

Of all Aron's self-criticisms, the most revealing is the one that may prove most perplexing to posterity: his lifelong complex of inadequacy vis-à-vis Jean-Paul Sartre. It is not that Raymond Aron felt himself in any way Sartre's inferior as a philosopher—indeed, he was one of the few men of his generation who could match Sartre in this field and engage him on his own terms (as Sartre well knew and had acknowledged in earlier, friendlier days). Nor did Aron have much respect for Sartre's forays into political or social argument over the course of the postwar decades, as he showed in his devastating polemical destruction of his old friend's various convoluted efforts to marry "existentialist" reasoning with Marxist analysis.

But that is just the point. Aron spent an inordinate amount of time reading and replying to Sartre's publications, treating them with utter seriousness. He remained, from their break in 1947 until their formal reconciliation shortly before Sartre's death in 1980, the latter's best and most sympathetic reader and critic. Sartre, in contrast, royally ignored Aron's own writings after 1947, distorted their content and meaning on the rare occasions when he did refer to them, and refused any exchange or discussion.

Aron's behavior is readily explained. He admired and thought he found in Sartre just what, by his own account, was lacking in his own work. Sartre was ambitious, a maker of systems, an "original" thinker who could write plays and novels with the same ease that he turned out multivolume tomes of applied epistemology. Aron, in contrast, was driven by fear of error, saying and writing only what he knew to be true and could support with logic and evidence. He lacked—or thought he lacked—the spark of creative, risk-taking originality that would have freed him to write his great book. He was well aware that Sartre's philosophical output was a failure (typically, he did not feel competent to judge his fiction and drama); but it was a *grand* failure.

Aron's writing was, in his eyes, on the whole a success. But it was a *partial* success, and he envied Sartre the *grandeur* of his capacities and his ambitions. This lifelong sense of inadequacy—the full extent of which was not revealed until the publication of his memoirs just before he died, and even then only in a muted key—was, like so much about Aron, to his credit. He was too honest and too self-critical to withhold admiration from a political opponent or deny an earlier intellectual companionship. But far from making him friends, this distinctively *moral* stance, in an intellectual community characterized by personal rivalry and bad faith, simply isolated him further from those to whom he was instinctively drawn.

That Aron was a lonely figure in French intellectual life for most of his adult life, until he became at the very end an object of uncritical adulation and respect, is beyond question. But one should not exaggerate his isolation. According to Branko Lazitch, "It is an understatement to say that he was not welcome in the Parisian intellectual establishment. He was banished from the community." And it is true that his uncompromising anticommunism made Aron unwelcome in *bien pensant* intellectual and academic circles from 1947 until the early 1970s. But there were other worlds and in these he was well received and greatly respected. He was a founding member of the Congress for Cultural Freedom in 1950, a frequent contributor to *Preuves* and other respected periodicals, and a regular and highly regarded participant in scholarly and intellectual gatherings abroad, where he gathered many honors and accolades.[54]

Moreover, Aron probably took some pleasure in provoking the animosity and resentment of his erstwhile companions among the left-leaning French intelligentsia. Like Clausewitz, he had little but scorn for the "higher idiocies of philosophers and public opinion." His haughty dismissal of the demagogic populism of his fellow professors in 1968 catches something of this: "Intellectuals—real ones, great ones, and even the not so great and the not very real—will continue to despise me for not playing the game, for not chasing after popularity by flattering the young and by making concessions to fashionable ideas." If Aron was alone—in December 1967 he described a book he had just written as "this testimony of a solitary man"—the condition was not wholly unpleasing to him.[55]

There were other benefits to intellectual isolation. As François Furet has noted, Aron's avoidance of engagements of all kinds served as a "system of mental protection," allowing him to pick and choose among his affinities and styles of argument without being in thrall to any. He was a political liberal writing in a conservative daily paper; an economic liberal who abhorred Hayekian system building (while admiring the Austrian's nonconformist courage); a critic of the establishment who evinced deep distaste for all forms of disorder and confusion, mental and social alike; an anticommunist who found little to admire or emulate in the American model: "The U.S. economy seems to me a model neither for humanity nor for the West," and so on.

From this uncomfortable but unimpeachable perch atop a variety of fences he denied himself the easy pleasure of submitting to either history or principle. When it came to deciding about first-order political institutions such as forms of suffrage or levels of taxation, Aron found fault with *all* forms of dogmatism and came close to a version of pragmatic reason: "It is not some general principle which decides such matters, but rather the agreed values of the community."[56]

Nonetheless, isolation is isolation, and Aron paid a price. He was regularly vilified by his former friends and their followers for over a quarter of a century. His intellectual and scholarly instincts drew him to seek engagement with a community that refused to listen or respond. It took considerable moral courage—and physical courage too, on various occasions—to stand up against intellectual fashions and political currents and deny himself the pleasures of communion with his natural peers. Like Machiavelli, he had the courage to pursue the logic of his ideas—with some similar consequences in the degree to which they became distorted at the hands of his enemies.

His friend Manès Sperber noted Aron's unusual independence of mind and his ability to stand his ground in the face of "the provocations of the powerful." And it was Sperber, too, who offered a general observation about intellectual independence that applies with special force to Aron: "Every person determines on his own authority the price that he can pay, or refuse to pay, for his life, and in the same way everyone decides what *sacrificium intellectus* he can make for the preservation of the valuable concord with his friends." Aron determined quite early in his life that in his case the intellectual sacrifice would not be paid. In the revealing phrase that he employed in 1950 to describe David Rousset's public stand against Stalin's concentration camps, Aron "came out" against intellectual confusion and compromise, and he stayed out.[57]

There is, however, one dimension of Aron's life and thought where some degree of confusion did indeed reign and where, by his own admission, he made compromises he would later regret. Raymond Aron was a Jew. Like most French Jews of his generation and background (his family came originally from Lorraine), he was thoroughly assimilated; in his own eyes he was a Frenchman of Jewish origin with none of the objective or subjective traits of membership in a distinctive Jewish community. But this did not mean that Aron was unconscious of his Jewishness, or that it played no part in his public actions.

On the contrary: in his efforts to arouse public awareness of the German threat in the 1930s he quite deliberately played down the anti-Semitic aspect of Nazism. In an article published in September 1933 Aron even acknowledged the German Jews' own share of responsibility for their current plight. "To be sure, the Jews were imprudent. They were too visible." Here, as on other occasions, Aron was conscious of his situation, writing as a Jew at a time when anti-Semitism was on the rise in French public life; many years later he would attribute to this his limited involvement in French public affairs before the war: "I was a Jew, I was suspect."[58]

During the war years in London, Aron's equally cautious criticism of the Vichy regime, which never took up the question of its treatment of Jews, is striking to present-day sensibilities. Some of this can be attributed to his generation, for whom the crimes of Vichy were always in the first instance political rather than moral. But there is no doubt that Aron experienced 1940, as he later wrote, "both as Frenchman and as Jew" (though at the time it was probably his sensibilities as a Frenchman that suffered the greater injury). In exile, however, he took the "emotional precaution" of thinking as little as possible about what Frenchmen were doing to Jews, and his writings in the Free French press revealed no interest in the subject (though in this he was no different from his fellow Gaullists and other resisters). Even after the war he showed only occasional interest in the subject of Jews, addressing B'nai B'rith in 1951 in the first person plural, "we Jews," but writing very rarely about Israel and never about the Shoah.[59]

This "repression," as Aron later came to see it, was characteristic of assimilated Jews everywhere in the aftermath of Auschwitz. But for Aron, as for many French Jews, everything changed on November 27, 1967. On that day President de Gaulle held a press conference on the subject of the Middle East, designed in part to recover France's audience and friends in the Arab states, alienated by what they saw as France's military contribution to Israeli success in the Six Day War earlier that year. In the course of a prepared statement de Gaulle described the Jews as "an elite people, self-assured and domineering" (*sûr de lui et dominateur*). From that moment on, and until the end of his life, Aron grappled unhappily with his Jewishness, unwilling to suppress it in the face of prejudice, unable to assume it fully. This private struggle was largely masked from public view, partly because Aron always kept his private troubles to himself, partly because it was overlaid with more visible public disputes—over the events of May 1968, over the Common Program of the Left in the 1973 elections, and so forth. But its salience in Aron's own thinking is beyond question.

Aron's anger at de Gaulle's language has been described by one biographer as a compensation for the frustration—and perhaps guilt—of his London years, his long silence about Vichy. Perhaps. But there can be little doubt that, in Aron's own words, "a burst of Jewishness exploded within my French consciousness." And it began to invade Aron's political thinking, retroactively as it were. He became ever more preoccupied with the war years: "In a way, the events of the war have burrowed ever deeper inside me. They mean more for me now [1981] than in 1945 or '46. It is a paradox, but there it is." He started to use Jewish examples in his theoretical writing: in a 1969 article he illustrated the concept of negative freedom by reference to the right to attend or not attend temple. He contemplated calling his planned memoirs "Souvenirs d'un Français juif." And he began to reflect critically on his earlier intolerance of Jews who claimed to be fully Jewish while rejecting both religion and Zionism.[60]

On Israel itself he had always shown a degree of ambivalence, even before de Gaulle's speech. In 1955 he confessed to a natural sympathy for the Israeli case: "My feelings are not neutral and I will willingly defend them." But, utterly in character, he pointed out that he could for just that reason understand the Arab position as well. "I see no reason why an Arab would not be irresistibly drawn to the opposite position." The following year, after his first visit to Israel, Aron expressed warm admiration for the Israeli army and its "fighting pioneers." He declared himself convinced that a self-confident Israel would grow and thrive.[61]

But curiously, in the aftermath of 1967, Aron's analytical grip on the whole complex of issues entailed in his Jewish identity grew less firm and not only, as he admitted after the Six Day War, because his judgment of Israel's military prospects in that war had been clouded by his fears for its future. Thus the essays in the 1968 collection *De Gaulle, Israel et les juifs* are uncharacteristically loose and inconclusive, as though the author had not been able to bring his arguments to a sharp resolution. In the course of the 1970s the issue of his relation to Israel as a French Jew comes up in unlikely places—in the conclusion to his study of Clausewitz, where he wanders uncertainly across the terrain of Israeli-Palestinian claims, or earlier in that same book where Clausewitz's own odyssey, from Jena to Waterloo, is implausibly compared to that of the Jews of the ship *Exodus*, driven from port to port "in search of a soil where they might exercise the rights of men by becoming once again citizens." In various essays and lectures he engages the problem of Jewish identity—is it ethnic, religious, historical, cultural, national? The reader is surprised and disappointed to discover that Raymond Aron has nothing more interesting or clear-headed to say on these vexed topics than any other commentator.

Finally, in 1983, Aron gave an interview to the French Jewish journal *L'Arche*, in which at one point he was asked why he, a nonpracticing, assimilated French Jew, felt unable to break his links with Judaism and Israel, particularly in view of his criticisms of Israeli politics in recent years. His answer may stand as a marker, a guide to the outer limits of Aronian rationalism: "In the final analysis I don't know. I know I don't wish to make that break. Maybe out of loyalty to my roots and to my forefathers. Maybe from what I would call the fear of tearing those roots from their soil. *But that is all abstract: it is merely the justification for an existential choice. I cannot say more.*"[62]

Raymond Aron wrote and acted against the grain of the France of his time in so many ways that it takes an effort of the imagination to see in him the man he truly was: a patriot for France and an utterly French thinker. His patriotism is palpable—he once described his two passions in politics as France and freedom. It is clear that in important ways the two were for him but one. On more than one occasion in the 1950s his feelings as a Frenchman were audibly hurt by international criticism of his country—in one angry commentary on Third World attacks at the United Nations he wrote that "we have had enough of being lectured by governments who do not apply and have no intention of applying the ideas they got from us and in whose name they condemn us."[63] This wounded national sentiment occasionally colored his judgments, as we have seen at the time of Suez.

It was Aron's identification with France and her interests that brought him close to General de Gaulle, though he was never a Gaullist (Jean-Louis Crémieux-Brilhac describes him as the "only nonpassionate anti-Gaullist in wartime London"). In the immediate postwar years he supported the general, recognizing in him a man who had, in Aron's words, all the qualities and all the defects of Machiavelli's Prince, and he offered his guarded support again when de Gaulle returned as a result of the Algerian crisis of 1958. During the 1950s he even shared de Gaulle's own views on the hypocrisy of American policy toward the Third World. "The Americans don't have a bad conscience when oil companies pay feudal rulers millions of dollars to support sordid regimes; but they would feel bad if their influence or their money helped the North Africans (French and Moslem) to build together a community shaped by the spirit of Western civilization."[64]

But their relationship was always a difficult one. Aron regarded the Gaullist approach to foreign policy, nuclear arms, and the Western Alliance as cavalier, contradictory, and at times irresponsible. His reading of de Gaulle's belligerence, which did nothing to enhance France's security but everything to isolate her from her friends, is interesting: the general, he thought, didn't take half of what he himself said very seriously, deriving instead some pleasure from the confusion that he sowed. He watched from an Olympian height while his followers and his critics dredged his rhetoric and his writings for clues to his deepest convictions, while they were in practice nothing more than the "temporary instruments of his acts." Aron found such behavior irresponsible, the worst possible combination of autocracy and self-indulgence and boding no good for the country.

De Gaulle, who wrote regularly to Aron to commend him on his publications, was no less caustic in return. His response to the publication of *Le grand débat*, Aron's 1963 essay on the problems of the Western Alliance, is typically Gaullist but perceptive nonetheless: "I have read *Le grand débat*, as I often read you, here and there, on the same subject. It seems to me that if you return to it incessantly and with such verve it may be because the line you have adopted does not fully satisfy even you. In the end everything: 'Europe,' 'Atlantic community,' 'Nato,' 'armaments,' etc., comes down to one single dispute: should France be France, yes or no? It was already the question in the days of the Resistance. You know how I chose, and I know that theologians can never be at rest."[65]

Aron remained a firm critic of Gaullist international illusions long after the general's departure. In April 1981 he reminded readers of *L'Express* that the French attitude toward the Soviet Union, born of fantasies about playing a role between and independent of the "two hegemonies," was the work of de Gaulle. It was he who must take responsibility for bequeathing to his successors the illusion that France had some special place in the hearts and policies of Soviet leaders. The issue here was not so much France's impact on international affairs—which Aron rightly took to be negligible—but rather the widespread French failure to look clear-sightedly at the true condition and capacities of their country.

Indeed, from his very first postwar article, in *Les Temps Modernes* in October 1945 and titled "The Disillusions of Freedom," through his daily journalism of the 1950s and 1960s and on to his final years, Aron insisted that the first duty of the French was to understand what had befallen their country and what had now to be done. France, he explained, was a second-order country—on the world scale in 1949 it was what Belgium had been in Europe in earlier decades.

What it needed above all was to set aside the self-serving myths—about France's wartime role, about its postwar prospects—and address practical and glaring deficiencies: in its governing apparatus, its economic infrastructure, its political culture. It was absurd to the point of tragedy, he wrote in 1947, that "in year three of the atomic age" the country's political debates were still focused on a nineteenth-century squabble over the place of religion in education. The anachronistic flavor of French political language was a theme that would preoccupy him for the next three decades.[66]

It was Aron's close attention to the practical problems of his country—and his frustration at the failure of intellectuals and politicians alike to see them and take them seriously—that contributed to the acerbic tone of his engagements with his contemporaries. It was their ignorance and *irresponsibility* that he found so annoying, and in such contrast (in the case of intellectuals) with the claims they made on their own behalf. More than anything else, they were utterly provincial—and their lack of interest in the reality of France, their preference for engaging with universal problems and foreign utopias, paradoxically confirmed this.

French thinkers, Aron observed in 1955, subscribe enthusiastically to the great ideas of yesterday—Sartre especially being "always one turning point behind." The loyalty of French writers, thinkers, and professors to their ideas was only matched by their utter indifference to reality. Outsiders were right to be suspicious of French intellectual life. The self-regarding isolation of French thinkers was such that they never considered anything important or essential unless the debate in question was being conducted on *their* terms and regarding matters of interest to *them*.

Yet this critique conceals a paradox. There is a distinctively *French* tone to Aron's condemnation of his fellow Frenchmen, and it is not without an elitist edge. Aron knew that he was not only better informed and more engaged with the real world than most French intellectuals, but also more talented and clever. He writes on a number of occasions of *nos agrégés-théologiens* (much as Camus writes of the same people as *nos juges-pénitents*), and he had an abiding scorn for the superficiality of many intellectuals, notably those of the structuralist and poststructuralist era. "Our Parisian philosophers prefer a rough sketch to a finished work, they appreciate mere drafts if they are sufficiently obscurantist. . . . Only the hidden is truly scientific, burbles the tribe of Parisian philosophizers—none of whom has ever practiced any science at all."

In France, Aron concluded, a certain "general culture" is prized largely because it allows one to disquisition agreeably on things about which one knows nothing. Despite his own criticism of the sclerotic effect of the French system of selection and examination, Aron, who was one of the most brilliant products of that very system, could not help but be suspicious of the compromised objectives of mass higher education. In 1968 he drew the typically Aronian conclusion that if the "university is to prepare people for nothing, then let it be reserved for a minority. Open to the mass, it will have to do more than train people to read Virgil, *with the help of a dictionary, moreover.*[67]

In view of Raymond Aron's broad appeal to the non-French scholarly world, and the ease and familiarity with which he moved in Anglo-American and German intellectual circles, it is worth emphasizing that his polemical relationship with his fellow French intellectuals, as well as his properly scholarly writings, reveal him to be a distinctively *French* thinker. His close familiarity with the German philosophical tradition that so dominated recent French thought did not disarm his very French skepticism. "The German language is exceptionally supple in philosophy, as a result of which we tend to think German philosophers more profound than they really are." Nor would he have situated himself in the British or American traditions. Logical positivism he dismissed as "just as provincial, perhaps more provincial, than [the philosophy of] Saint Germain des Prés and the French intelligentsia of the left."

Aron was decidedly not an empiricist, for all his concern with facts, and he was instinctively averse to the skeptical minimalism of modern English-language analytical philosophy. As he argued in 1938, "History is always made and studied in relation to a philosophy, without which we would be faced with an incoherent plurality," a position from which he never moved very far. Thirty years later the same epistemological a priori led him to conclude that "it is mere wordplay and an abuse of false analogies to present all human aspirations in the language of rights and liberties."[68]

It is worth pausing to reflect on that last remark. A third of a century later a new generation of French political thinkers is only now beginning to grapple with modern American liberal political philosophy and to recognize its limits, the reduction of so much of human aspiration and experience to a laudable but constricting debate about rights. When Aron made his comment in 1965 he was acknowledging the central failing of modern French political thought, its persistent failure to engage the issue of rights as an ethical and political problem, while warning against the mirage of an easy, all-encompassing imported solution. Aron was assuredly a liberal, but in a distinctively French, eighteenth-century sense; in certain important ways the British liberal tradition and its contemporary descendants remained quite alien to him.

This inheritance from an earlier, lost tradition of French political reasoning is above all what distinguishes Aron and establishes his claim on the attention of posterity. The radical romanticism of Sartre and his followers was paradoxically conservative. Posing no threat to the habits of mind of its audience, and showing no concern to investigate the space between changing everything and doing nothing, it was in its essence conventional. It was thus *irresponsible* in just the way that Sartre himself had once warned against, whereas Aron took utterly seriously the original meaning of "engagement," to which he added a distinctive concern with coherence and consistency.

French intellectuals, he once observed, seek neither to understand the world nor to change it, but to *denounce* it. In so doing they not only abdicate responsibility for their own circumstances but misunderstand the nature of the human condition. Ours "is never a struggle between good and evil but between the preferable and the detestable." This assertion, which has become a commonplace among a new generation of French writers but risks being quickly forgotten, was both courageous and truly countercultural in the time and place that Aron made it. Like the Owl of Minerva, Aron brought wisdom to the French intellectual community in its twilight years; but the belated appreciation of his work and his long isolation have obscured the heroic scale of his contribution to French public life. Aron was no moralist. But his whole career constituted a bet on Reason against History, and to the extent that he has won he will in time be recognized as the greatest intellectual dissenter of his age and the man who laid the foundations for a fresh departure in French public debate.

NOTES

1. François Furet, "Raymond Aron 1905–1983: Histoire et politique," *Commentaire*, Winter 1985, 52.
2. Raymond Aron, *Mémoires: 50 ans de réflexion politique* (Paris: Julliard, 1983), 31.
3. Raymond Aron, *Introduction à la philosophie de l'histoire: Essai sur les limites de l'objectivité historique* (1938; Paris: Gallimard, 1986), 70.
4. Aron, *Introduction*, 91.
5. Aron, "A propos de la théorie politique," *Revue Française de Science Politique* 12 (1962): i; reprinted in *Etudes Politiques* (Paris: Gallimard, 1972). See p. 168.
6. Aron, *Introduction*, 420–21.
7. See "Un philosophe libéral dans l'histoire" (1973) in Aron, *Essais sur la condition juive contemporaine* (Paris: Editions de Fallois, 1989), 222.
8. See Aron, "Max Weber et la politique de puissance" (1964), in *Machiavel et les tyrannies modernes* (Paris: Editions de Fallois, 1993), 226.
9. Aron claimed never to have come across the name Tocqueville during his studies, neither at the Ecole Normale nor the Sorbonne! See Aron, *Le spectateur engagé* (Paris: Julliard, 1981), 7.
10. See Aron, *German Sociology* (New York: Free Press, 1964), 51; first published in France in 1936 as *La sociologie allemande contemporaine*. Commenting elsewhere on the airy reflections by André Malraux and others about postindustrial society, the end of a civilization, and so on, Aron remarked, "These vast bird's-eye perspectives terrify me. I plead ignorance." See Aron, *La révolution introuvable* (Paris: Fayard, 1968), 46.

11. See Aron, *Penser la guerre: Clausewitz* (Paris: Gallimard, 1976), 1:98. See also Aron, "Réveil du nationalisme?" *Le Figaro,* February 24, 1964.

12. Aron, *Les etapes de la pensée sociologique* (Paris: Gallimard, 1967), 229. Note, though, that Aron hastened to add that in the 1930s it was *Marx*'s account of the human condition that rang most true.

13. Aron, *Etapes de la pensée sociologique*, 18.

14. Aron, *D'une sainte famille à l'autre: Essais sur les marxismes imaginaires* (Paris: Gallimard, 1969), 20; *L'opium des intellectuels* (1955). In English, *The Opium of the Intellectuals,* trans. Terence Kilmartin (Lanham, Md.: University Press of America, 1985), 133, 137.

15. See Aron, "Macht, power, puissance: Prose démocratique ou poésie démoniaque?" (1964), in *Etudes politiques*, 179.

16. Aron, *Révolution introuvable*, 132.

17. Aron in *Esprit*, February 1933, 735–43. See also Marie-Christine Granjon, "L'Allemagne de Raymond Aron et de Jean-Paul Sartre," in H.-M. Bock, R. Mayer-Kalkus, and M. Trebitsch, eds., *Entre Locarno et Vichy: Les relations culturelles franco-allemandes dans les années 1930* (Paris: CNRS, 1993), 468–77; and Nicole Racine, "*La Revue Europe* et l'Allemagne, 1929–1936," in Bock et al., *Entre Locarno et Vichy,* 631–58.

18. See, e.g., Aron, *Spectateur engagé*, 88.

19. "La Cité déchirée: L'Etat et les communistes," *Le Figaro*, April 11, 1948.

20. See Aron, *Révolution introuvable*, 13, 35.

21. Aron, *Les désillusions du progrès* (Paris: Calmann-Lévy, 1969), xviii–xix. See also *D'une sainte-famille à l'autre*, 43; and "Le Socialisme et la guerre" (1939) in *Machiavel et les tyrannies modernes*, 309–31.

22. See Aron, "Messianisme et sagesse," *Liberté de l'esprit*, December 1949, 159–62.

23. See "Fidélité des apostats" (1950), in Aron, *Polémiques* (Paris: Gallimard, 1955), 81; "Les deux Allemagnes," *Le Figaro*, August 25, 1948.

24. "Remarques sur la pensée politique d'Alain," *Revue de Métaphysique et Morale*, April-June 1952; reprinted in *Commentaire* 28–29 (1985). See p. 411.

25. See Aron, *Opium*, 55; and Aron, *Clausewitz,* 2:218.

26. Aron, "Réflexions sur les problèmes économiques français," in *Revue de Métaphysique et Morale*, November 1937, 793–822; quote from p. 794.

27. See, e.g., Aron, "Marxisme et contre-Marxisme," *Le Figaro*, October 5, 1959; also Aron, *German Sociology*, 127.

28. Aron, "La société industrielle et les dialogues politiques de l'Occident," in *Colloques de Rheinfelden* (Paris: Calmann-Lévy, 1960), 13; also "1788 ou le malade imaginaire?" *Le Figaro*, October 19, 1954.

29. See Aron, "La fin des illusions," *Le Figaro*, July 5, 1947; and Aron, "Les alternances de la paix belliqueuse," *Le Figaro*, February 26, 1948.

30. Aron, "Stupide résignation," *Le Figaro*, September 21–22, 1947.

31. Aron, "Conférence sans surprise," *Le Figaro*, July 27, 1955; "Après Poznan détente sans reniement," *Le Figaro*, July 3, 1956; "Reprise de la guerre froide," *Le Figaro*, June 28, 1958.

32. *D'une sainte famille à l'autre*, 13; *Clausewitz,* 2:283. A little later Aron ruefully observes that "what honorable professors lack is a sense of history and of the tragic." *Clausewitz,* 2:285.

33. Aron, "Après Eden, Lord Salisbury: La crise du Parti Conservateur," *Le Figaro*, April 4, 1957; "L'Accession au club atomique," *Le Figaro*, August 14, 1959.

34. "Neutralité ou engagement," presentation to Congress for Cultural Freedom in Berlin, July 1950; reprinted in *Polémiques*, 199–217.

35. "L'echec des négotiations Franco-Britanniques sur l'Assemblée Européenne," *Le Figaro,* January 26, 1949; "Lettre à un ami anglais," *Le Figaro*, April 7, 1960.

36. "Peut-on gouverner sans les communistes?" *Le Figaro*, June 29–30, 1947; "Force de frappe européenne?" *Le Figaro*, December 10, 1959. See also "Universalité de l'idée de nation et contestation" (1976) in *Essais sur la condition juive contemporaine*, 231–51.

37. "Quelques faits et quelques mots," *Le Figaro*, December 27, 1954.

38. *German Sociology*, 86; see also *Commentaire* 28–29 (1985): 394, 402. Note too the observation in Aron's memoirs: "For a half century I have restricted my own criticisms by posing this question: What would I do in their place?" *Mémoires*, 632.

39. For an example of the bemusement of his wartime colleagues at Aron's cool dispassion, see Daniel Cordier's remarks in *Commentaire* 28–29 (1985): 24–27; also *Clausewitz*, 1:53.

40. *Etapes*, 296.

41. *Clausewitz*, 2:179.

42. See Aron, "De l'objection de conscience" (January 1934); reprinted in *Commentaire* 28–29 (1985); Elie Halévy, *Correspondance, 1891–1937* (Paris: Editions de Fallois, 1996), 775; Aron, "La comparaison de Machiavel et Pareto," in *Machiavel et les tyrannies modernes*, 101.

43. Quoted in Nicolas Baverez, *Raymond Aron* (Paris: Flammarion, 1993), 338. The italics are mine.

44. See the introduction by Bernard de Fallois to Emmanuel Berl, *Essais* (Paris: Julliard, 1985), 13.

45. See "L'unité française en péril," *Le Figaro,* October 15, 1955. The reference is to June 1940. For Aron's views on Algeria, see *La tragédie algérienne* (Paris: Plon, 1957) and especially *L'Algérie et la république* (Paris: Plon, 1958).

46. *Spectateur engagé*, 193, 210.

47. See *Clausewitz*, 2:12, 267–68.

48. See "Machiavélisme et tyrannies," in *Machiavel et les tyrannies modernes*, 139; "1955, année de la clarification," *Le Figaro*, January 7–8, 1956; "Les juifs et l'état d'Israel," *Figaro littéraire*, February 24, 1962; reprinted in *Essais sur la condition juive contemporaine*; Aron, *Les désillusions du progrès* (Paris: Calmann-Lévy, 1969), 178.

49. See *Désillusions du progrès*, 340; and *Révolution introuvable*, 106. Aron had anticipated the coming demand for *autogestion* (self-management) in the preface to his *La lutte de classes: Nouvelles leçons sur les sociétés industrielles* (Paris: Gallimard, 1964).

50. See "L'Europe en péril: Les responsabilités de la France," *Le Figaro*, February 3, 1955; "L'unité atlantique: Enjeu de la crise de Suez," *Le Figaro*, August 8, 1956; "La démonstration nécessaire," *Le Figaro*, September 13, 1956; "La force n'est qu'un moyen," *Le Figaro*, November 2, 1956.

51. See *Clausewitz*, 2:284; *Les désillusions du progrès*, 304.

52. See *Spectateur engagé*, 10–11, 300. On his lifelong engagement with Marx, Aron had this to say: "Like the friends of my youth I never separated philosophy from

politics, nor thought from commitment; but I devoted rather more time than them to the study of economic and social mechanisms. In this sense I believe I was more faithful to Marx than they were."

53. Quoted by Aron in *Clausewitz*, 1:44; see also p. 71.

54. Branko Lazitch, in *Commentaire* 28–29 (1985): 48.

55. See *Révolution introuvable*, 135; and *Essais sur la condition juive contemporaine*, 42.

56. *Essai sur les libertés* (Paris: Calmann-Lévy, 1965), 128.

57. See Manès Sperber, *Until My Eyes Are Closed with Shards* (New York: Holmes & Meier, 1994), 137, 234.

58. See Aron, "La révolution nationale en Allemagne," in *Europe*, September 15, 1933; *Spectateur engagé*, 49.

59. See *Clausewitz*, 2:227 (where Aron's own divided identity gets a footnote); *Spectateur engagé*, 85, 101; *Essais sur la condition juive contemporaine*, 29.

60. See Baverez, *Raymond Aron*, 185; Aron, *Mémoires*, 500; *Spectateur engagé*, 106; "Liberté, libérale ou libertaire?" (1969), reprinted in *Etudes politiques*, 235–74, quotation from p. 237; "De Gaulle, Israel et les juifs" (1968), reprinted in *Essais sur la condition juive contemporaine*, 35–183; quotation from p. 171.

61. See, e.g., "Millénarisme ou sagesse?" in *Polémiques*, 63, n.1, and "Visite en Israel," *Le Figaro*, June 12, 1956.

62. "Un interrogateur permanent," *L'Arche*, September-October 1983; reprinted in *Eassais sur la condition juive contemporaine*, 267–80. Quotation from p. 272 (my italics).

63. "Le scandale de l'O.N.U.," *Le Figaro*, October 4, 1955.

64. "L'unité française en péril," *Le Figaro*, October 15, 1955. See also Jean-Louis Crémieux-Brilhac, *La France libre* (Paris: Gallimard, 1996), 192, 389.

65. Charles de Gaulle, *Lettres, notes et carnets, janvier 1961–décembre 1963* (Paris: Plon, 1986); letter to Raymond Aron, December 9, 1963, 400.

66. See *Les Temps Modernes* 1, no. 1 (1945); "Stupide résignation," *Le Figaro*, September 21–22, 1947.

67. *Révolution introuvable*, 77 (emphasis added); see also p. 122; *D'Une sainte famille à l'autre*, 172–75.

68. See *Spectateur engagé*, 38; *Opium of the Intellectuals*, xiv; *Introduction à la philosophie critique de l'histoire*, 452 and appendixes; *Etudes sur la liberté*, 224.

10

Gray Is Beautiful

Adam Michnik

I

People from Central Europe like to tell jokes. For years, jokes offered them asylum. In the world of jokes, they not only felt free and sovereign within captivity and Soviet domination, but they also laughed.

So: two people, with the experience that comes with age, were playing tennis. The tennis ball ended up in the bushes. Looking for the ball, one of the players saw a frog. The frog spoke to him with a human voice: "I'm a beautiful princess, turned into a frog by a mischievous wizard. If you kiss me, I will become a princess once again. I will marry you, you will be a prince, and we will live happily ever after."

The player put the frog in his pocket, found the ball, and continued the game. After a while the frog again spoke to him, this time from his pocket: "Sir, did you forget about me? I am this beautiful princess, turned into a frog. If you kiss me, I will become a princess again. We will get married and live happily ever after!"

And then she heard his answer: "Dear lady frog, I will be completely honest with you. I have reached the age at which I would rather have a talking frog than a new wife."

This frog is Central Europe, knocking at the gates of NATO and the European Union. NATO and the European Union have not yet made up their minds to kiss. They don't yet know whether they prefer to have a talking frog or a new wife.

II

Let us skip the controversies about defining the borders of Central Europe. Let's remind ourselves, however, of a statement by Hungarian writer Gyorgy

Konrad: "It is we, who live in Central Europe, who began the two great world wars." Put differently, this multinational mosaic, conquered by German, Austro-Hungarian, Russian, and Ottoman empires, was and still is a source of conflict and destabilization. Today, years after the collapse of the Berlin Wall, the nations of Central Europe are facing new opportunities and new challenges. How will things turn out for them?

More than ten years ago, through the works of its artists, philosophers, and writers, Central Europe came to be thought of as a realm of spiritual freedom, diversity, and tolerance. Milan Kundera was creating this myth against the fact of Soviet domination: in the place of the Anglo-Saxon formula "the countries of the Soviet bloc" an image appeared of Central Europe as a home of equal nations with abundant, colorful culture, nurtured by a diversity of languages, religions, traditions, and personalities.

It was not an absurd idea, and it was not a false image. Kundera—as well as Havel, Konrad, and others—was fully justified in rereading and in presenting to the world the cultural heritage of this region of borderlands—where nations, religions, and cultures rub up against one another. They were fully justified in presenting it as the realization of a multicultural ideal of society—a miniature Europe of nations—founded on the principle of maximum diversity in minimum space. These writers also had a wise idea concerning spiritual-political strategy: these nations, strikingly weak and powerless in confronting the imperial appetites of their neighbors, are transforming this powerlessness into power. Here we have a land of small nations, conquered, subjected, and enslaved for generations, transforming itself into the fertile soil that gave birth to Robert Musil and Franz Kafka, Thomas Masaryk and Karel Capek, Mickiewicz and Conrad, Singer and Einstein, Krleza and Tatarka, Milosz and Seifert, Canetti and Levinas, Ionesco and Lukács.

The trump card of these small nations was their nonimperial character, which made them natural allies of freedom and tolerance. Decades and centuries of existence in an environment of oppression and repression produced a specific culture, characterized by honor and self-irony, the stubbornness to stand by values, and the courage to believe in romantic ideals. Here national and civic consciousness developed as a result of human bonds—and not by the order of state institutions; here it was easier to devise the idea of civil society, precisely because the sovereign national state remained largely in the realm of dreams. The great cultural diversity of this region was to be—and frequently was—the best weapon of self-defense against the claims of ethnic or ideological powers. "The Eastern European," wrote Barbara Torunczyk in 1987, "already has his own kingdom. It emerges in the place where he lives. It is a realm of the spirit but firmly rooted in reality. Today the East European of the post-Yalta generation can do without a cult of the West. . . . He gives new names to Europe and does it from right here at home."

What remains of this vision years after the fall of communism?

III

Communism was like a freezer. Within it a diverse world of tensions and values, emotions and conflicts, was covered with a thick layer of ice. The defrosting process was a gradual one—first we saw beautiful flowers, and only later the rot. First came the grandiloquence of the peaceful fall of the Berlin Wall and the Velvet Revolution in Czechoslovakia; later a wave of xenophobic rage that took over Germany in 1992–1993, and the breakup of Czechoslovakia. First was the memorable "Autumn of the Nations" in 1989. Freedom returned to Central Europe, and Central Europe returned to history. It returned as a messenger of not only freedom and tolerance but also hatred and intolerance, both ethnic and religious. Conflicts—difficult to understand for people who perceive this territory simply as the Soviet bloc—came to life once more. But these conflicts were understood all too well by the inhabitants of those lands. They were understood because this world of many nations and cultures had experienced the deep ambiguity of the right of nations to sovereign existence: the right of one nation usually endangered the right of another nation, and this would bring about ethnic cleansing. Grillparzer, a great Austrian writer of the nineteenth century, warned prophetically against the road that leads "from humanism, through nationality, to bestiality."

IV

I suppose, for the American public, these meanderings of Central European democratic thought may appear a bit exotic. This thought was put to a double test: the test of captivity and the test of freedom. Hence, some statements will appear unclear and others, perfectly banal. However, it seems to me that this thought was born out of a common inspiration: a passionate dream about freedom and democratic order.

Democracy is not identical with freedom. Democracy is freedom written into the rule of law. Freedom in itself, without the limits imposed on it by law and tradition, is a road to anarchy and chaos—where the right of the strongest rules. For my generation, the road to freedom began in 1968. In that year tens of thousands of students filled the streets to demonstrate and protest against the establishment. Was there any common denominator in the rebellions of students in Berkeley, Paris, and West Berlin and those on the streets of Warsaw and Prague? At first glance these were completely different phenomena: the students of Berkeley and Paris rejected the order of bourgeois democracy. The students of Prague and Warsaw were fighting for the freedom that bourgeois democracy guaranteed. Moreover, the students of Berkeley and Paris were fascinated by the communist project and by the revolutionary rhetoric of Mao Tse-tung—of which the students of Warsaw and Prague had had enough.

Nevertheless, there were some common threads: the antiauthoritarian spirit, a sense of emancipation, and the conviction that "to be a realist means to demand the impossible." And finally the need for rebellion, rooted in the conviction that "as long as the world is as it is, it is not worth it to die quietly in your own bed." "The world as it is" meant an unjust world.

So there we are! At the root of rebellion in 1968 was a need for justice: a need to have access to freedom and to bread, to truth and to power. There was something wonderfully uplifting in this rebellion, which transformed not just the collective consciousness of one generation. But there was also something frightening in it: the vandalized universities, destroyed libraries, barbarian slogans that substituted for intellectual reflection, and finally violence, terrorism, and political killings. All of this also belongs to the heritage of 1968.

At that time we defined ourselves as socialists and people of the left. Why today does this formula cause in me an internal protest? Why do I myself not want to subscribe to any of the great ideologies? Here, I believe, lies the source of many arguments with my American friends. But possibly, this is more an argument about language than about ideas. I once asked Jürgen Habermas: "What do we have left of the idealistic faith in the freedom-oriented socialism of the 1960s?" His answer was: "Radical democracy." Since this formula is close to me, I will try to decipher it in my own way.

V

The system of parliamentary democracy and market economy has had fierce adversaries since its inception. Let's give them the symbolic names of "conservative" and "socialist." For the conservative, the democratic order was a negation of tradition—the defeat of the Christian spirit by a rapacious nihilism; the total victory of relativism over the world of tested and absolute values. For the socialist, it was a system that generated, disguised, and perpetuated inequality and injustice. The conservative saw in man a wild being that cannot be domesticated by calls to reason. Only strong institutions can achieve this. The socialist, on the other hand, saw in man a good being, forced by inhuman social conditions into animal behavior. Both conservative and socialist rejected the order of a freedom based on the free play of political and economic forces, on the specific domination of property and money.

The conservative held that this order liberates in man an animal rapaciousness, while the socialist was of the opinion that this order virtually requires an animal aggression. This is how the two great utopias were established: one retrospective, and the other prospective, a utopia of conservative, hierarchical harmony, and a utopia of egalitarian, socialist harmony. One can debate the relations of both these utopias with the two totalitarianisms of the twentieth century. One can argue whether bolshevism was preying on the socialist idea, or whether the socialist idea provided bolshevism with its intellectual and political arguments. One can also try to explore whether fascism used the antiliberal arguments of conservatives and the conservative dream of returning to a world of preindustrial values, or whether the conservatives saw in fascism a way to defend themselves against demo-liberal destruction. But there is no doubt that such connections existed, even though we can find conservatives among the antifascist opposition, and we can find socialists among the most consistent adversaries of bolshevism. The crowning for both antiliberal utopias became the totalitarian systems. I lived in one of them for forty years, but I learned to distrust both.

VI

Why did we rebel against communism? Why did we prefer to become a small, repressed minority rather than join the majority living and pursuing careers in the world of totalitarian dictatorship?

We rejected communism for several different reasons: it was a lie, and we were searching for the truth; communism meant conformity, and we desired authenticity; communism was enslavement, fear, and censorship, and we desired freedom; it was an ongoing attack on tradition and national identity that we held to be ours; it was social inequality and injustice, and we believed in equality and justice; communism was a grotesquely deficient economy, and we sought rationality, efficiency, and affluence; communism meant the suppression of religion, and we held freedom of conscience to be a fundamental human right. So we rejected communism for reasons equally dear to a conservative, a socialist, and a liberal. In this way, a peculiar coalition of ideas emerged, which Leszek Kolakowski noted in his well-known essay, "How to Be a Conservative-Liberal Socialist?" This coalition collapsed along with communism. But before it collapsed, the coalition had marked public debate with a specific tone of moral absolutism.

The moral absolutism of the anticommunist opposition required us to believe that communism is inherently evil, the evil empire, the devil of our times, and that resistance to communism and communists is something naturally good, noble, and beautiful. The democratic opposition demonized communists and sanctified itself. I know what I am writing about because this moral absolutism was to a certain degree also my experience. I don't regret this experience, nor do I think I need to be ashamed of it. Standing up to the world of totalitarian dictatorship was a risk, even a sacrifice, not only to one's own safety but also to that of one's friends and family. One had to believe that "human life is a serious game," as a church historian of the communist period wrote. Each day one had to make a choice that could have costly consequences. Those decisions were not the result of academic debates, but were moral acts that frequently carried a cost of imprisonment or ruined careers. For active dissidents, this situation created a climate favorable for harsh and demanding valuations. One professed humanistic values but lived within heroic values, with their fundamental principle of loyalty to one's own identity and loyalty to one's friends from the democratic opposition; loyalty to values that were betrayed and mocked; loyalty to the nation, to the church, and to tradition. "The weak side," wrote Bogdan Cywinski, "was always under siege." The most outstanding witnesses of resistance in those years—Solzhenitsyn, Havel, Herbert—defended absolute values. Herbert wrote: "let your sister Scorn not leave you for the informers executioners cowards—they will win."[1]

And in the end it was we who won. But woe to those moral absolutists who emerge victorious in political struggles—even if only for a while.

VII

Moral absolutism is a great strength for individuals and groups struggling against dictatorship. But it is a weakness for individuals and groups active in a world where democratic procedures are being built on the rubble of totalitarian dictatorships. There is no more room there for the utopias of a just, harmonious, and perfect world or for moral absolutism. Both of these come down to either anachronism or hypocrisy; both threaten the democratic order. A democratic world is a chronically imperfect one. It's a world of freedom (sinful, corrupt, and fragile) that came after the collapse of the world of totalitarian necessity (also, luckily, imperfect).

This world not only forced the collapse of the coalition of antitotalitarian ideas but also revealed their contradictory character. Egalitarianism found itself in conflict with the principles of liberal economy; conservatism challenged the spirit of liberal tolerance. Dilemmas appeared that the socialist, the conservative, and the liberal resolved in different ways. Let's mention some of them: the ways of dealing with the communist past; the shape of the market; the fundamental principles of the state; the place of the church and religious values in the new reality.

For the socialist, the central issue will be giving a human face to a rapacious market economy, defending the poorest sectors in society, maintaining the secular character of the state, and tolerating people of different faiths and nationalities.

The conservative would bring back the continuity of national symbols, fight for a Christian reshaping of the constitution and institutions, warn against the dangers coming from liberalism and relativism, and demand harsh treatment for people of the old regime.

The liberal would look to the economy first—economic growth, clear rules of the market, stable system of taxation, privatization, exchangeable currency. He would be a careful defender of the idea of a tolerant state—with regard to the church, national minorities, neighboring countries, and the past. The point is, that each of them will be formulating his ideas in a new context: the context of a new, populist, and still unnamed ideology.

There is a bit of fascism in it, and a bit of communism; a bit of egalitarianism, and a bit of clericalism. These slogans will be accompanied by a radical criticism of the ideology of the Enlightenment, and by the harsh language of moral absolutism. At the same time, a nostalgia will appear, surprising for all—the socialist, the liberal, and the conservative. A nostalgia for the security of the "good old communist days," when, as they said, "the state pretended to pay the people, and the people pretended to work."

One who wishes to understand the dilemmas of the new postcommunist democracies must understand this context. Dealing with the communist past has divided the participants of the debate into spokesmen for justice and spokesmen for reconciliation. The first demanded the methodical punishment of the guilty parties. The second proposed a process of national reconciliation in the name of future challenges. Both attitudes at times took on a grotesque form: the first went so far as to demand discrimination against the members of the communist apparatus; the second behaved as if they had forgotten that the past dictatorship ever existed. The formula for which I was a spokesman, "Amnesty yes; amnesia no," turned out to be too difficult for the people of the democratic opposition.

The dispute over the shape of the market economy took on the form of a social conflict in which the arguments of the socialist and the conservative came together in a criticism of the policies of liberal transformation. Unemployment, social contrasts, and the frustration of employees slowed down the pace of reform. The dispute over the shape of the state—should it be national or civil—turned out to be fundamental, especially in multinational countries that had just regained independence after their long enslavement.

Conservative partisans of national principle emphasized the need to reconstruct the ethnic fabric destroyed through the years of official denationalization; the partisans of the civil principle were defending the fundamental tenets of democracy against an invasion of intolerant chauvinism. And finally, the church, after years of repression, reasserted its claim to a place in the public debate. In communities where the national identity was frequently accompanied by a religious identity, there is a natural temptation to endow those new states with a religious identity. The church called for a constitution and criminal code that would be in accordance with the moral norms of religion. The debate around the penalization of abortion was a classic illustration of the argument about the axiological foundation of the state. Does the admissibility of abortion imply approval of the murder of unborn children? Does the criminalization of abortion constitute an attack on the fundamental right of a woman to decide about her own maternity? Each of those arguments was accompanied by extreme emotional tensions: there was a constant appeal to moral arguments, and the language of war propaganda was used. Two opposing worlds of values confronted each other: the pragmatic, often saturated with corruption and the cynicism of people of the old regime, versus the chronic patriotism of people of the world of conservative values, which in the recent past had resisted communism. The heroism that resisted repression showed its second face: intolerant, fanatical, and resistant to new, modernizing ideas. This is a natural turn of events in the world of postcommunist democracies.

VIII

None of these disputes is fatal for democracy, which after all is a permanent debate. Fatal indeed would be an intensification of conflict in which all sides, while absolutizing their positions, become incapable of compromise. Then it would be easy to undermine the procedures of the democratic state. Radical movements—under black or red banners—gladly use the procedures and institutions of democracy in order to obliterate it. In the meantime, democracy is neither black nor red. Democracy is not infallible because in its debates all are equal. This is why it lends itself to manipulation and may be helpless against corruption. This is why it frequently chooses banality over excellence, shrewdness over nobility, empty promise over true competence. Democracy is a continuous articulation of particular interests, a diligent search for compromise among them, a marketplace of passions, emotions, hatreds, and hopes; it is eternal imperfection, a mixture of sinfulness, saintliness, and monkey business. This is why those who seek a moral state and a perfectly just society do not like democracy. But only democracy—having the capacity to question itself—also has the capacity to correct its own mistakes. Dictatorships, whether red or black, destroy the human capacity for creation; they kill the taste for human life and eventually life itself. Only gray democracy, with its human rights and institutions of civil society, can replace weapons with arguments. Parliamentarianism became an alternative to civil wars, even though a conservative would argue with a liberal or a social democrat about whether that was the result of common sense or the wisdom that comes from misfortune.

IX

The subject of democracy is people, not ideas. And this is why, in the framework of democratic institutions, citizens can meet and collaborate independently of their faith, nationality, or ideology. Today the classic ideological positions—liberalism, conservatism, socialism—do not dominate public debate about taxes, health reform, or insurance. Yet in each of those debates, there is a need for the presence of a socialist care for the poorest, a conservative defense of tradition, and a liberal reflection on efficiency and growth. Each of those values is needed in democratic politics. Taken together, they give color and diversity to our life and equip us with the capacity to choose. It is thanks to their mutual contradictions that we can afford inconsistency, experimentation, changes of opinion, and changes of government. In opposition to so-called corrupt demo-liberalism, the fanaticism of ideological inquisitors offers again and again new projects for a "promised land." Fundamentalists of different varieties condemn the moral relativism of democracy, as though it were the state that should be the guardian or moral virtue. We, however, the defenders of gray democracy, do not grant the state this right. We want human virtues to be guarded by the human conscience. That is why we say, "gray is beautiful."

And all of this has been told to you by a frog from Central Europe.

—Translated by Elzbieta Matynia

NOTE

1. Zbigniew Herbert, "The Envoy of Mr. Cogito," in *Mr. Cogito* (New York: Ecco, 1993), 61. Translated from the Polish by John Carpenter and Bogdana Carpenter.

II

PRACTICE

11

The Professional Scholar as Public Intellectual: Reflections Prompted by Karl Mannheim, Robert K. Merton, and C. Wright Mills

Ira Katznelson

"It is my aim in this book to define the meaning of the social sciences for the cultural tasks of our time," C. Wright Mills wrote in *The Sociological Imagination*, an iconoclastic manifesto published not long before his untimely death. Advocating social science with a public purpose, Mills declared the goal of his craft to be acts of translation and empowerment. The social scientist is responsible for showing nonspecialist citizens how their private troubles link to public issues, and, in this way, "to make clear the elements of contemporary uneasiness and indifference." Arguing against trends ascendant in the late 1950s—transhistorical, general histories (in the mode of Oswald Spengler and Arnold Toynbee), Grand Theory's arid formalism (Talcott Parsons provided his target), and fact-grubbing empirical studies devoted more to method than substance (here, breaking a taboo, he named his Columbia colleague Paul Lazarsfeld)—Mills recommended an engaged style of inquiry devoted to asking three questions: "What is the structure of this particular society as a whole?" "Where does this society stand in human history?" "What varieties of men and women now prevail in this society and in this period?"[1]

Mills's stinging critique of business as usual in the academy still rings true. The social sciences continue to be divided between scholarship so abstract and "general that its practitioners cannot logically get down to observation . . . in their historical and structural contexts" and an empiricism so nitty-gritty that "there is a pronounced tendency to confuse whatever is to be studied with the set of methods suggested for its study." These ways of working, he argued, lack engagement with public, political affairs and project an uncritical, often fawning relationship between scholars and those with power.

Mills prodded his colleagues to do better, "to define the meaning of the social sciences for the cultural tasks of our time" by seizing the chance to deploy their well-crafted scholarship to public purpose and by securing "the social scientist's foremost political and intellectual tasks—for here the two coincide—to make clear the elements of contemporary uneasiness and indifference." He suggested they do so by returning to the questions he believed to have been at the heart of the late nineteenth- and early twentieth-century classics of social science pivoting on issues of structure, history, and identity.[2]

This call for an engaged social science was grounded attractively in commitments to intellectual craftsmanship, Enlightenment values of freedom and reason, and a pragmatist orientation to democracy. Mills urged scholars to find a personal voice rather than write in aseptic, impersonal, mannered prose and to direct that voice at an audience composed not just of professionals and students but of interested people who "have a right to know"[3] in order to combat commercialization, bureaucratic manipulation, and the deterioration of reason. To fight back, he counseled, social scientists should "remain independent" and direct their writing "*at* kings as well as *to* 'publics.'"[4]

I still recall the *frisson* I experienced when, as an undergraduate, I first read *The Sociological Imagination*. By way of its sharp critiques, advocacy of historically grounded analysis between abstracted empiricism and high theory, and normative brief for truth and reason to combat obscurantism, it seemed to show how serious scholars devoted to intellectual craftsmanship and to a tradition of social theory associated with figures as diverse as Comte, Marx, Durkheim, Weber, Veblen, Mannheim, and Schumpeter could also function as public intellectuals. Such a "public role has two goals," Mills wrote: "to turn personal troubles and concerns into social issues and problems open to reason . . . [and] to combat all those forces which are destroying genuine publics and creating a mass society."[5]

This powerful intervention, balancing realism and utopianism, positioned Mills as a particular kind of scholar who is also a particular kind of intellectual, an example of what Pierre Bourdieu called "bidirectional beings" who overcome "the opposition between pure culture and engagement." They belong "to an intellectually autonomous field, one independent of religious, political, economic or other powers, and they must respect that field's particular laws"; but if autonomous they also are engaged, for they "deploy their specific expertise and authority in their particular intellectual domain in a political activity outside it." Combining detachment with engagement and universal scientific and ethical legitimation with local interventions, scholars as intellectuals share commitments to autonomy, scholarly authority, and to the institutional requisites for rational thinking, but not as exclusive values. Their public aspirations also enmesh them in the wider culture's institutions, values, and practices, where the judgments of nonscholars about what is important usually count the most.[6]

More recently, Bourdieu distinguished *Le Fast Talker*—media and sound bite–oriented thinkers who debase the role of public intellectual—from research-oriented scholars who respect learned standards and conventions and direct their writing mainly to other professional academics, thus largely abjuring a public role. As intended, this contrast between thin and thick, ephemeral and serious, slick and sober, scored points and sparked a hot debate in France about the level of public discourse. This stark antinomy signified the difficulties inherent in working inside a bidirectional field of tension where work is neither exclusively professional, wholly enveloped within academic disciplines, nor merely ephemeral, as in an op-ed column. Like Mills, Bourdieu strongly prefers this in-between space to be filled by serious professional scholars who seek to function as public intellectuals. Otherwise, he cautions, the academy's organized disciplines risk solipsistic enclosure and public culture faces the jeopardy of debasement.

I remain keenly attracted to this double-sided possibility, but unlike the undergraduate reader of Mills I am rather more inclined to see problems and pitfalls as well as opportunities. Hence I should like to do a bit more than issue yet another call for scholars to become embattled on behalf of matters of public significance.

I am still drawn to *The Sociological Imagination* as a spunky critique of what social scientists do and as a set of suggestions for what we might try to accomplish in the public realm. But there were too many silences and too much substitution of injunction for argument in Mills's text, I now realize. By bearing in mind the changing institutional milieu of public intellectuals and by reconsidering Karl Mannheim's once influential sociology of knowledge, itself an important influence on Mills, especially as it was reworked by Robert Merton, I want to provide missing warrants and connective tissue for Mills's position. In turning to Mannheim, I am interested not only in how the social location and lived experience of intellectuals shapes their ideas, questions for which he is best known, but also in his provocative discussion of the choices public scholars face and in his suggestions about how these selections can affect the character and fate of liberal democracy.

UNRESOLVED PERPLEXITIES

There was a time, say in the late nineteenth century, when a text like *The Sociological Imagination* would have seemed superfluous. In the half century spanning 1870 to 1920, the period when the professional study of history and society came to be organized by disciplines and university departments, such leading figures as William James, Wilhelm Dilthey, T. H. Green, John Dewey, and Max Weber made multiple connections "between knowledge, responsibility, and reform" on the assumption that there was no contradiction between speaking to audiences in the civic and university spheres.[7] Indeed, they thought these to be double-sided aspects of a single public arena inhabited and governed by a cohort of educated elites responsible for the liberal professions and for the fate of the broadly liberal politics to which they were committed. They were able to make these connections because of their epistemological commitments to contextualism, the contingency of truth and knowledge, and intersubjective verification. In part, too, it was their concern with the social question and their conviction that systematic inquiry entwined with lived experience could combine to direct thought and action in ways that might usefully address deep inequality without generating violent upheaval that made this seemingly effortless boundary crossing possible.

A century ago, moreover, intellectuals in the West who wrote to affect public life barely had to face dilemmas attendant on living within scholarly disciplines and the civic realm simultaneously or with the challenges of a broadly, if not deeply, educated mass public and its cultural institutions. The organized disciplines then were young, just fledgling, really, not terribly specialized, technical, or fragmented. Liberal democracy of the mass kind, even in the United States, was in its infancy. In political circumstances characterized by a first phase of entry for enormous numbers of new political participants and by the expansion in numbers and composition of the political class, these scholar-intellectuals functioned as public moralists who sought to assert the centrality of reason based on systematic inquiry and entwined with normative purpose, rather than passion, as the basis for public discussion and decision. They were far more impressed with the common claims to rationality, professionalism, and science grounding both their scholarly and public activities, distinguishing them from the contributions of more traditional and, as they saw it, less systematic modes of thought, than with the tensions characterizing the relationship linking their roles as methodical creators of knowledge and as active participants in political argument.

Decades later, we cannot escape these issues or these tensions. Our social science disciplines have changed beyond recognition. Increasingly separated from their lineages of political, social, and economic thought, confidently technical, and developed by distinctive scholarly subgroups, the social sciences mainly advance self-referentially, inside specialized conversations.[8] Today, social scientists who are public intellectuals tend to be critics of their own disciplines who rarely practice their given craft in "mainstream" fashion. On the left, for example, Robert Heilbroner is an erudite historian of economic thought who frequently ventures into the public realm; he does not write technical economics.[9] On the right, the late Allan Bloom helped alter the public conversation about American higher education, but his best-selling *Closing of the American Mind*[10] stood apart from his recondite scholarship on Plato, Rousseau, or love and friendship; as a political scientist, moreover, he wrote at the fringes of the discipline, uneasy with most of the moves it had made in the past half century. Of course there are more representative scholars currently at work who try to straddle the divide between their professional craft and public discourse—the sociologists William Julius Wilson and Theda Skocpol quickly come to mind as leading examples[11]—but these figures straddle the divide in the relatively "easy case" of public policy analysis.

It now takes a high degree of self-consciousness and resistance to sustain the role of the scholar as public intellectual in the intellectual space between the rarefied ivory tower and the seductions of mass culture. Some years ago, Russell Jacoby deliberately raised hackles in the academy by arguing that university life as such militated against this role; and further, that the disappearance of nonacademic intellectuals, the result of both their incorporation into university life and the demands made by their disciplines, has impoverished our political culture. For Jacoby, there is a missing generation of public intellectuals because the veterans of the New Left have allowed themselves to be absorbed into the country's campuses, captured by its journals and monographs. If they continue to be radicals, he argues, they are rebels only in academe. By contrast, their impact on the public sphere is small to nil.[12] Where Bourdieu prefers the venue and pace of the university and the research center as loci for grounding a public role for scholars, Jacoby excoriates these sites as sources of political banality and irrelevance.

In spite of these differences in emphasis and argument, both Bourdieu's and Jacoby's critical prose invites attention to the contradictions and choices scholars face when they seek to perform the role of public intellectual responsibly. Bourdieu is right to observe that the seductions of "fast talk" militate against this purpose and Jacoby surely is correct to think that the pressures of university careers strain against it as well. What is required, however, is fewer laments for our condition and more purposeful considerations of how it is possible to sustain the dualism of a university career and a public voice, against odds, without lapsing into media glibness or scholarly hypercircumscription.

My main preoccupations, however, are concerned less with the conditions these critics have fastened on than with their silences. I take for granted that we live in a media age and that the vast majority of writers and intellectuals of any kind must earn their keep these days inside the hallowed halls of academe. Further, I would assert, with Bourdieu, that especially under current conditions the role of public intellectual is unsustainable unless its practitioners earn their authority inside their distinctive epistemic communities. This claim implies they must master, or at least deal with, a necessary division of labor since disciplinary success is a condition of being heard in a particular way in the public realm; that is, to be heard in a manner more consequential than mere "fast talkers" can hope to obtain. Scholarly reputations, however ill understood outside the halls of academe, nonetheless are essential requisites for public influence, at least of a certain kind, and such reputations are not won by writing and speaking exclusively in a public voice, at least, for better or worse, not today. When William Julius Wilson writes on race relations in contemporary America he carries far more weight than, say, Dinesh D'Souza, quite apart from the respective merits of their views, because Wilson has earned esteem inside his field of sociology by dint of his research and conceptual thinking.[13] Similarly, John Hope Franklin was invited to chair President Clinton's national conversation on race not mainly by reason of his articulateness or photogenic appearance, but because, as a considerable historian, he bears a high standard of accomplishment and prestige.

Taking the requirement of living in two worlds for granted, I primarily want to bring into focus a series of issues that are both "internalist," that is, inside decisions about audience, intent, subject matter, standards, and language, and "externalist," in the sense of questions that focus on the historical and situational determinations of the style and content of thought. Both are linked as aspects of the vexing problem of translation Wright Mills sought to highlight. When serious scholars intervene in ongoing civil conversations in order to change them, they do so by rendering their scholarship intelligible and by situating their achievements in altered civic and political contexts. I wish to explore the challenges and choices they make in committing these acts of translation because there is altogether too little self-consciousness about their implications and terms both among practitioners and their critics and because the tension between the autonomy of ideas and their social causes and utility intensifies when scholars become public intellectuals, exacerbating always present issues of independence, relativism, objectivity, and authoritative means of judgment and evaluation.

These are questions *The Sociological Imagination* raises but sidesteps; surprisingly so, one might think, since Karl Mannheim's attempt to grapple with them in *Ideologie und Utopie*[14] constituted the bridge Mills crossed from the study of philosophy at the University of Texas to sociology at the University of Wisconsin in the late 1930s and early 1940s. His first published article on "Language, Logic, and Culture," devoted to the "problems of a sociology of knowledge," opened with a consideration of this text.[15]

Though unfortunate, this avoidance is understandable. For the issues Mannheim raised, which are central to the role of the scholar as a public intellectual, represent questions without adequate solutions. They demarcate tensions that cannot be resolved. Yet precisely because no crisp resolutions are available under the heterogeneous and conflict-ridden conditions of modernity, the discovery of a viable public role for intellectuals must depend on a high degree of reflexive self-consciousness about the questions Mannheim placed front and center but Mills elided. If we are doomed to live inconclusively with particular conundrums, better that we understand them.

Despite its flaws and vexing qualities, *Ideologie und Utopie* remains unsurpassed as a handmaiden for this task. Setting out to write this chapter, I discovered a letter the sociologist Daniel Bell addressed to me in 1991. "In one's older years," he wrote, "one returns to the unresolved perplexities of one's youth. And I have done so here. The issue is the relation of ideology to the sociology of knowledge, a problem introduced by Karl Mannheim (in English) in 1936, but marred by a weak epistemology and a muddled set of thoughts on the relation of the social location of groups to particular idea systems." The problem on which I focus is the same as Bell's, but I find more sustenance from Mannheim's text, especially from some of its neglected elements. I also think its most glaring epistemological and substantive flaws can be remedied, much as Robert Merton thought they could when he published an appreciative and tough-minded consideration in 1941 as a ground-clearing exercise for his own work on the sociology of knowledge.

MANNHEIM AS GUIDE

Written urgently inside late Weimar Germany, Mannheim's excursion into *Wissenssoziologie* was composed at the tail end of the period when the stark division between the academic and the public had not yet appeared. Quite apart from its suggestive merits as social theory and social science—his sharp, but not antiscience, critique of the surface orientations of behaviorism alone is worth the price of admission—*Ideologie* focuses intensively on what then was the dominant intellectual mode, not very distant from what Gramsci labeled the role of the organic intellectual attached to particular groups and social movements. Above all, Mannheim sought to discover "a new type of objectivity," one obtained "not through the exclusion of evaluations but through the critical awareness and control of them."[16] Attending to how Mannheim addressed this challenge yields, I believe, a particularly sharp set of formulations and questions about issues of objectivity and political debate central to the relationship joining scholarly and public intellectuality.

If the situation of public intellectuals in the United States today differs radically in institutional and other ways from that of comparable figures in Germany some eighty years ago, what Mannheim described as "the contemporary predicament of thought," understood as "the continuous elaboration of concepts concerning things and situations has collapsed in the face of a multiplicity of fundamentally divergent definitions," has not changed. Unlike static societies where thought tends to be uniform, scholastic, and tethered to dogmatized truth, he argued, the new "free" intelligentsia in modern Western countries is confronted with "the irreconcilability of the conflicting conceptions of the world."[17]

These, he thought, at least in good measure, are not simply the products of individual thought but are shaped considerably by collective social locations. In *marxisant* fashion, Mannheim vested social being as determining social consciousness; but unlike Marx, he declined to privilege any particular social position, nor did he consider determination of ideas by reality to be simple, linear, or strictly confining.[18] What Mannheim failed to do, Merton pointed out, was "specify the *type* or *mode* of relations between social structure and knowledge, with the result "that the failure to specify these types virtually precludes the possibility of formulating problems for empirical investigation." Mannheim's work, Merton correctly noted, contained quite a variety of propositions concerning the relationship between thought and social situation. These formulations include claims of direct causation; the assumption that interests shape and constrain ideas; the contention that particular social positions direct foci of attention to particular subjects and not others; and the idea that some structures are prerequisites to specific kinds of thought.[19]

But if we treat these overlapping formulations more sympathetically as competing hypotheses and cast them in probabilistic terms, then, as Merton also observed (and as Mills had argued in his early published papers), Mannheim's perspectivalism can become a powerful instrument of inquiry with an elective affinity to the pragmatism of Peirce and James, mediated by Dewey and Mead. Conduct is a test of ideas that are transformed in the crucible of experience which then, in turn, reshape experience. Further, when Mannheim's more mechanical formulations are refashioned to reflect a causal sense that treats determination as the exertion of pressures, his assertions do not differ very much from the perspectivalism of Max Weber, who had argued that "values are relevant to the formulation of the scientific problem and choice of materials but are not relevant to the validity of the results."[20] Read this way, Mannheim's kitbag of assertions, hypotheses, and concerns about situated knowledge is still unequaled. For all their resemblance, they certainly are more than orthodox Marxist reductions that consider nothing to be signified unless it is real. Equally, they differ from recent antiessentialist tendencies in literary criticism and cultural studies that treat nothing as real unless it is signified.

The imbrication of life situations and thought is accompanied in Mannheim's account of the public intellectual by a deep, but not always self-aware, interconnection between politics, which uses ideas to elevate itself above a mere struggle for power, and systematic thinking, which, however much it tries, cannot entirely escape some degree of political coloration. In such difficult, inherently complex, modern circumstances, knowledge, he argued, tilts in one of two directions. The first is ideology, referring in his usage to thinking so intensively bound up with the interests of ruling groups that "they simply are no longer able to see certain facts which would undermine their sense of domination," thus obscuring "the real condition of society both to itself and to other." In this way, ideologies are forces for stability. The second is utopian thinking, "which reflects the opposite discovery of the political struggle, namely that certain oppressed groups are intellectually so strongly interested in the destruction and transformation of a given condition of society they unwittingly see only those elements in the situation which tend to negate it."[21]

Mannheim did not quite discount ideologies or utopias as meaningful knowledge. To the contrary, they reveal truths, since both are grounded in key features of social reality.[22] Writing not simply as a social scientist but as an engaged actor fearful for the fate of Weimar's liberal political order, he sought to turn the partial and the positional features of knowledge to some advantage, for he thought these to be inevitable aspects of the irreducible plurality of modernity, by harnessing the multiplicity of views and attaching them to systematic, social-scientific, norms of rationality. This connection, he believed, is made possible by the relatively free-floating, transclass, position of systematic, knowledge-producing intellectuals who thus are in a special position to contribute new terms to the negotiation between knowledge and politics. His keen hope was that a realistic and appreciative understanding of the inevitability of multiple perspectives by scholarly intellectuals combined with their assertions on behalf of systematic understanding made possible by their special social and institutional positioning would allow and induce them to make vital, engaged, contributions, as scholars and as public intellectuals, to the quality and character of liberal politics, respecting plurality without lapsing into irrationality.

Highlighting this insufficiently attended feature of *Ideologie und Utopie*, David Kettler, Volker Meja, and Nico Stehr observe, "Mannheim speaks of sociology of knowledge as an 'organon for a science of politics,' a way of bringing historically adequate political knowledge into being by virtue of this sociology's dynamic effects on a critically deadlocked ideological field." He thought that intellectuals, by revealing the partial, perspectival qualities of conflicting political positions, might both respect and tame them; even, in a formulation that anticipates John Rawls's recent notion of an overlapping consensus,[23] by bringing individuals and groups who hold radically different values and positions to a common understanding of the degree of interest they share in the rules of the game and in combating sheer irrationality.

The vocation of the intellectual, especially the scholarly intellectual who not only produces but also studies and understands knowledge, is particularly valuable, for it advances an open, rational politics respectful of plurality.[24] Public intellectuals thus have a vital role to play, Mannheim counseled, especially in circumstances of "upheaval," where "intellectual conflict can go so far that antagonists will seek to annihilate not merely the specific beliefs and attitudes of one another, but also the intellectual foundations on which these beliefs and attitudes rest."[25]

The enemy of the good, he reminds us, is not ideology or utopia, for these are certain forms of modern knowledge, but totalistic versions of each. So it is here, in Mannheim's view, that political and scholarly intention should meld to give purpose to the public intellectual who, by applying a sociologically oriented history of ideas, can transform and limit the knowledge claims of differently situated social actors: "For as soon as all parties are able to analyse the ideas of their opponents in ideological terms, all elements of meaning are qualitatively changed and the word ideology acquires a totally new meaning." In this way, "the simple theory of ideology develops into the sociology of knowledge. What was once the intellectual armament of a party is transformed into a method of research."[26]

The consequences of this shift, he urged, are profound both for politics, which thus loses its most dangerous, totalizing, features, and for scholarship, which must come to terms with relational knowledge and the disenchantment that must come with the recognition that there is no single, unitary truth to be found. Truth and objectivity do not disappear as norms or goals, but they now are processual in character; it is to this rule-governed process that intellectuals, even when they are also engaged as political actors, must hold. What makes this double-sided participation possible is "one of the most impressive facts of modern life." For, in arguably Mannheim's most famous and controversial formulation, "unlike preceding cultures, intellectual activity is not carried on exclusively by a socially rigidly determined class, such as a priesthood, but rather by a social stratum which is to a large degree unattached to any social class and which is recruited from an increasingly inclusive area of social life."[27]

It follows from this analysis, he argued, that intellectuals have two choices: to affiliate with parties, groups, and classes, thus elevating conflicts of interest into conflicts of ideas, or to become aware of their distinctive position outside other positions and pursue "the mission implicit in it"[28]—one that protects plurality while advancing a dynamic reconciliation of perspectives, or at least secures the conditions required to make a continuing engagement of perspectives possible—based on a degree of self-consciousness uniquely available to the stratum of knowledge producers.

Mannheim's sociology of intellectuals and the production of knowledge, focusing on cognition and the social processes that bear on knowledge, thus constitutes a research program seeking to understand the complex ties between environments, experience, and ideas. It also defines a search for standards of validity both inside and outside particular perspectives and standpoints, and it identifies a sociologically realistic, broadly liberal, political project oriented both to sustain and to constrain ideologies and utopias.[29]

This complex, suggestive exercise is better read as a persistent set of challenges than as a set of solutions. For classical Marxism, class relations and locations strongly determine the production of ideas. For Mannheim, this degree of determination was loosened considerably by the twentieth century's far greater heterogeneity in bases of interest and identity, thus raising two key issues as questions rather than as fixed answers: which affiliations among this variety of locations shape ideas in particular settings and circumstances, and the degree to which ideas are determined by situations rather than by their intrinsic worth.

Merton's important contribution was to insist these are open empirical questions about "the connectives of thought and society" and the relationship between knowledge, its production, and the segments and networks of society within which they are produced and to which they are oriented.[30] My point is related but distinctive. When scholars take on the role of public intellectual, the value of their effort depends in no small measure on purposeful attention to these issues. Indeed, this is precisely what distinguishes the scholar who adopts the bidirectional strategy Bourdieu identified from other idea-based participants in the public realm. For it is here, as Mills, following Mannheim, understood, that our advantage lies and our most important contributions can be situated, geared, as he put it in *The Sociological Imagination*'s concluding paragraph, "to make reason democratically relevant to human affairs in a free society, and so realize the classic values that underlie the promise of our studies."[31]

NOTES

1. C. Wright Mills, *The Sociological Imagination* (New York: Oxford University Press, 1959), 8, 13, 6–7.

2. Mills, *Sociological Imagination*, 33, 51, 18.

3. Mills, *Sociological Imagination*, 221.

4. Mills, *Sociological Imagination*, 181. Mills, of course, identified politically with the left (a year after he issued *The Sociological Imagination* he penned his famous "Letter to the New Left," widely credited with jump-starting the student movement of the 1960s); but the form of his call, combining jeremiad with advocacy, is a familiar one crossing many boundaries. For all the differences in politics, knowledge, style, and temperament with Mills and his book, think also of Allan Bloom's *The Closing of the American Mind*. Like *The Sociological Imagination*, it combines a tough-minded, take-no-prisoners diagnosis with a radical, against-the-current program, in his case counseling that we find refuge from the degradation of the modern university and American culture in the verities of the ancients. C. Wright Mills, "Letter to the New Left," *New Left Review*, September-October 1960; reprinted as "On the New Left," *Studies on the Left* 2, no. 1 (1961); Allan Bloom, *The Closing of the American Mind* (New York: Simon & Schuster, 1987).

5. Mills, *Sociological Imagination*, 186.

6. Pierre Bourdieu, "The Corporation of the Universal: The Role of Intellectuals in the Modern World," *Telos*, Fall 1989, 99.

7. James T. Kloppenberg, *Uncertain Victory: Social Democracy and Progressivism in European and American Thought, 1870–1920* (New York: Oxford University Press, 1986), 159.

8. A useful overview is provided in Thomas Bender and Carl E. Schorske, eds., *American Academic Culture in Transformation: Fifty Years, Four Disciplines* (Princeton: Princeton University Press, 1998).

9. One of many examples is Robert Heilbroner, *The Nature and Logic of Capitalism* (New York: Norton, 1985).

10. Bloom, *Closing*.

11. William Julius Wilson, *When Work Disappears: The World of the New Urban Poor* (New York: Knopf, 1996); Theda Skocpol, *Boomerang* (New York: Norton, 1996). For a discussion of Wilson's policy analyses and public stance, see Ira Katznelson, "Du Bois for the 1990s," *Boston Review*, February–March 1997.

12. Russell Jacoby, *The Last Intellectuals: American Culture in the Age of Academe* (New York: Basic Books, 1987).

13. Compare Dinesh D'Souza, *The End of Racism: Principles for a Multiracial Society* (New York: Free Press, 1995) and William Julius Wilson, *The Declining Significance of Race* (Chicago: University of Chicago Press, 1978).

14. Karl Mannheim, *Ideologie und Utopie* (Bonn: F. Cohen, 1929).

15. For discussions, see Irving Louis Horowitz, *C. Wright Mills: An American Utopian* (New York: Free Press, 1983), chap. 7; and John Eldridge, *C. Wright Mills* (London: Tavistock, 1983), 14–25.

16. Karl Mannheim, *Ideology and Utopia: An Introduction to the Sociology of Knowledge*, trans. Edward Shils and Louis Worth (London: Routledge & Kegan Paul, 1936). This translation of *Ideolgie und Utopie* also incorporates "Wissenssoziologie," in Alfred Vierkandt, ed., *Handwörterbuch* (Stuttgart: F. Enke, 1931), 5.

17. Mannheim, *Ideology*, 5, 7.

18. Mannheim discussed his relationship to Marxist thought in a lecture delivered in Amsterdam in October 1933, "The Sociology of Intellectuals," *Theory, Culture, and Society*, August 10, 1993. This publication is accompanied by a useful introduction by Dick Pels, "Missionary Sociology between Left and Right: A Critical Introduction to Mannheim." I am indebted to the discussion in David Kettler, Volker Meja, and Nico Stehr, "Rationalizing the Irrational: Karl Mannheim and the Besetting Sin of German Intellectuals," *American Journal of Sociology*, May 1990, 1457, which stresses Mannheim's intellectual relationship with his mentor, Georg Lukács, as well as their differences. "Thanks to his close reading of Lukács' early Marxist writings," they note, "Mannheim is fully persuaded that the infinitely privileged class consciousness of the revolutionary class is the central concept of Marxism, and he is fully aware that his approach is built on a rejection of that concept."

19. Robert K. Merton, "Karl Mannheim and the Sociology of Knowledge," *Journal of Liberal Religion*, Winter 1941, 135–38.

20. Merton, "Mannheim," 144.

21. Mannheim, *Ideology*, 36.

22. For a discussion, see David Kettler, Volker Meja, and Nico Stehr, *Karl Mannheim* (London: Tavistock, 1984), 64; also see David Kettler and Volker Meja, *Karl Mannheim and the Crisis of Liberalism: The Secret of These New Times* (New Brunswick, N.J.: Transaction, 1995).

23. John Rawls, *Political Liberalism* (New York: Columbia University Press, 1993).

24. Kettler, Meja, and Stehr, "Rationalizing the Irrational," 1458. Mannheim was not alone in seeking to advance this project. There is a suggestive consideration of the relationship between Mannheim's thought and that of other Weimar social democrats like Franz Neumann, Adolph Lowe, and Emil Lederer in David Kettler and Volker Meja, "The Reconstitution of Political Life: The Contemporary Relevance of Karl Mannheim's Political Project," *Polity*, Summer 1988. After Nazism's triumph and his own exile, Mannheim abandoned this position as inadequate, instead juxtaposing planning to irrationality. A useful discussion contrasting Mannheim's German phase, culminating in *Ideologie und Utopie* focusing on cognition, knowledge, and the processes bearing on them, with his English exile phase focusing on planning, see Kurt Wolff, "Karl Mannheim: An Intellectual Itinerary," *Society*, March–April 1984.

25. Mannheim, *Ideology*, 57.

26. Mannheim, *Ideology*, 68–69.

27. Mannheim, *Ideology*, 139.

28. Mannheim, *Ideology*, 142.

29. For a still useful discussion, see Hans Speier, "The Social Determination of Ideas," *Social Research* 5 (1938).

30. Robert K. Merton, "The Sociology of Knowledge," in Merton, *Social Theory, and Social Structure* (Glencoe, Ill.: Free Press, 1949).

31. Mills, *Imagination*, 194.

12

Public Philosophy and International Feminism

Martha C. Nussbaum

> Do you want to know what philosophy offers humanity? Practical guidance. One man is on the verge of death. Another is rubbed down by poverty. . . . These are ill treated by men, those by the gods. Why, then, do you write me these frivolities? There is no time for playing around: you have been retained as lawyer for unhappy humanity. You have promised to bring help to the shipwrecked, the imprisoned, the sick, the poor, to those whose heads are under the poised axe.
>
> —Seneca, *Moral Epistles*

> In your joint family, I am known as the second daughter-in-law. All these years I have known myself as no more than that. Today, after fifteen years, as I stand alone by the sea, I know that I have another identity, which is my relationship with the universe and its creator. That gives me the courage to write this letter as myself, not as the second daughter-in-law of your family. . . .
>
> I am not one to die easily. That is what I want to say in this letter.
>
> —Rabindranath Tagore, "Letter from a Wife" (1914)

TWO WOMEN TRYING TO FLOURISH

Ahmedabad, in Gujerat, is the textile mill city where Mahatma Gandhi organized labor in accordance with his principles of nonviolent resistance. Tourists visit it for its textile museum and its Gandhi ashram. But today it attracts attention, too, as the home of another resistance movement: the Self-Employed Women's Association (SEWA), with more than fifty thousand members, which for more than twenty years has been helping female workers in the informal sector to improve their living conditions through credit, education, and a labor union. (In India 92.7 percent of the labor force works in the informal sector, and 60 percent of these informal sector workers are women.) On one side of the polluted river that bisects the city is the shabby old building where SEWA was first established, now used as offices for staff. On the other side are the education offices and the SEWA bank, newly housed in a marble office building. All the customers and all the employees are women. Women like to say, "This bank is like our mother's place" because, says SEWA's founder Ela Bhatt, a woman's mother takes her seriously, keeps her secrets, and helps her solve her problems.[1]

Vasanti sits on the floor in the meeting room of the old office building, where SEWA members meet to consult with staff. A tiny dark woman in her early thirties, she wears an attractive electric blue sari, and her long hair is wound neatly into a bun on the top of her head. Soft and round, she seems more comfortable sitting than walking. Her teeth are uneven and discolored, but otherwise she looks in reasonable health. Martha Chen (who has organized the meeting) tells me later she is a Rajput, that is, of good caste; I've never figured out how one would know that. She has come with her older (and lower-caste) friend Kokila, maker of clay pots and a janitor at the local conference hall, a tall fiery community organizer who helps the police identify cases of domestic violence. Vasanti speaks quietly, looking down often as she speaks, but there is animation in her eyes.

Vasanti's husband was a gambler and an alcoholic. He used the household money to get drunk, and when he ran out of that money he got a vasectomy in order to take the cash incentive payment offered by local government. So Vasanti has no children to help her. Eventually, as her husband became more abusive, she could live with him no longer and returned to her own family. Her father, who used to make Singer sewing machine parts, has died, but her brothers run an auto parts business in what used to be his shop. Using a machine that used to be her father's, and living in the shop itself, she earned a small income making eyeholes for the hooks on sari tops. Her brothers got her a lawyer to take her husband to court for maintenance—quite an unusual step in her economic class—but the case has dragged on for years with no conclusion in sight. Meanwhile, her brothers also gave her a loan to get the machine that rolls the edges of the sari; but she didn't like being dependent on them, since they are married and have children and may not want to support her much longer. With the help of SEWA, therefore, she got a bank loan of her own to pay back the brothers, and by now she has paid back almost all of the SEWA loan. She now earns five hundred rupees a month, a decent living.[2] She has two savings accounts and is eager to get more involved in the SEWA union. Usually, she says, women lack unity, and rich women take advantage of poor women. In SEWA, by contrast, she has found a sense of community. She clearly finds pleasure in the company of Kokila, a woman of very different social class and temperament.

By now, Vasanti is animated; she is looking us straight in the eye, and her voice is strong and clear. Women in India have a lot of pain, she says. And I,

I have had quite a lot of sorrow in my life. But from the pain, our strength is born. Now that we are doing better ourselves, we want to do some good for other women, to feel that we are good human beings.

Jayamma stands outside her hut in the oven-like heat of a late March day in Trivandrum.[3] The first thing you notice about her is the straightness of her back and the muscular strength of her movements. Her teeth are falling out, her eyesight seems clouded, and her hair is thin—but she could be a captain of the regiment, ordering her troops into battle. It doesn't surprise me that her history speaks of fierce quarrels with her children and her neighbors. Her jaw juts out as she chews tobacco. An Ezhava—a lower but not "scheduled" caste—Jayamma loses out two ways, lacking good social standing but ineligible for the affirmative action programs established by government for the lowest castes. She still lives in a squatter's colony on some government land on the outskirts of Trivandrum. Although I am told that I am seeing the worst poverty in all Trivandrum, given Kerala's generally high living standard it seems remarkably good compared to poor areas in Bombay and in rural areas. The huts in the squat are clean and cool, solidly walled, some with mud, some with brick, decorated with photos and children's artwork; some of them command a stunning view of a lake covered with water hyacinth. Many have toilets, as the result of a local government program; both water and electricity reach the settlement reliably. Although the settlers were originally squatters, by now they have some property rights in the land. The bus stops right outside on a well-maintained road; there is a hospital not far away; and there's a cheerful primary school in the squat itself. Older children all seem to be enrolled in school: clean and proud in their school uniforms, looking healthy and well nourished, they escort visitors around the settlement.

For approximately forty-five years, until her recent retirement, Jayamma went every day to the brick kiln and spent eight hours a day carrying bricks on her head, five hundred to seven hundred bricks per day. (She never earned more than five rupees a day, and employment depends on weather.) Jayamma balanced a plank on her head, stacked twenty bricks at a time on the plank, and then walked rapidly, balancing the bricks by the strength of her neck, to the kiln, where she then had to unload the bricks without twisting her neck, handing them two by two to the man who loads the kiln. Men in the brick industry typically do this sort of heavy labor for a while and then graduate to the skilled (but less arduous) tasks of brick molding and kiln loading, which they can continue into middle and advanced ages. Those jobs pay up to twice as much, though they are less dangerous and lighter. Women are never considered for these promotions and are never permitted to learn the skills involved. Like most small businesses in India, the brick kiln is defined as a cottage industry and thus its workers are not protected by any union. All workers are badly paid, but women suffer special disabilities. Jayamma felt she had a bad deal, but she didn't see any way of changing it.

Thus in her middle sixties, unable to perform the physically taxing job of brick carrying, Jayamma has no employment to fall back on. She is unwilling to become a domestic servant because in her community such work is considered shameful and degrading. Jayamma adds a political explanation: "As a servant, your alliance is with a class that is your enemy." A widow, she is unable to collect a widows' pension from the government: the village office told her that she was ineligible because she has able-bodied sons, although in fact her sons refuse to support her. Despite all these reversals (and others), Jayamma is tough, defiant, and healthy. She doesn't seem interested in talking, but she shows her visitors around and makes sure that they are offered lime juice and water.

What is a philosopher doing in the slums of Trivandrum? And is there any reason to think that philosophy has anything to contribute, as such, to the amelioration of lives such as those of Vasanti and Jayamma? I shall argue that philosophy does indeed have something to contribute to the guidance of public life, in ways highly relevant to shaping policies that influence these women's lives. Focusing on the role of philosophy in articulating and debating norms of "the quality of life," I shall claim that philosophy provides a badly needed counterweight to simplistic approaches deriving from a certain brand of economic thought. More generally, philosophy has rich resources to offer to any policymaker who wants to think well about distributive justice in connection with women's inequality. But philosophy cannot do its job well unless it is informed by fact and experience: that is why the philosopher, while neither a fieldworker nor a politician, should try to get close to the reality she describes.

I shall discuss these issues by narrating, first, the history of the quality of life project in which I was involved through the World Institute for Development Economics Research (WIDER) of the United Nations University. I shall then describe my subsequent work on women and quality of life, particularly in connection with the trip to India during which I met Vasanti and Jayamma. Finally, I shall reflect about the contribution philosophy can make to an international feminism, thinking about both the need practice has for theory and the need theory has for practice.

THE WIDER PROJECT

In 1985 a new institute for development economics was founded under the auspices of the United Nations, after consultation with a wide range of specialists, prominently including Albert Hirschman, Paul Streeten, and Amartya Sen. The goal of the institute was to make development economics more interdisciplinary, enriching it with insights drawn from disciplines such as sociology, political theory, and anthropology. Sen, who had opposed the formation of the new institute, was therefore put on its board, so that he could ask skeptical questions and try to ensure that the institute's programs were not (as he had feared) replications of work that was already being done elsewhere. The acronym WIDER, chosen before the name itself (World Institute for Development Economics Research), designated both the group's commitment to interdisciplinarity and its preoccupation with issues of undernutrition and poverty (therefore with making human beings "wider" in a very literal sense). A number of countries put in bids to be the location of the new institute, but the proposal by the Finnish government, which promised a small endowment and the use of excellent downtown Helsinki office space, was judged the best.[4] For its director, the new institute chose Lal Jayawardena, a Sri Lankan economist and politician. Jayawardena's wife, Kumari Jayawardena, a leading writer on international feminism,[5] played a valuable role in shaping the institute, although her political work in Sri Lanka did not permit her to spend long stretches of time there. For this reason and because of Sen's long-standing commitment to feminism, the institute from the first put problems of sex equality at the center of its program.

The institute undertook many different types of projects, discussing approaches to macroeconomics, the balance of trade, poverty and nutrition, technology and development, and many other topics.[6] Its general orientation was left of center, at least in U.S. terms; its leading economists tended to be neoclassical rather than Marxian, but neoclassical economists who were critical of some prevailing conceptions and models in the field, and who did not believe that free markets could solve all problems of social justice. Although the institute did have some year-round resident scholars,[7] on the whole it functioned by putting scholars who worked elsewhere under year-round contract as "research advisers." A research adviser was responsible for organizing a project under the supervision of the director and the board; he or she was expected to spend one month a year at WIDER, but much of the work usually took place elsewhere. Typically he or she organized conferences and research projects involving the participation of many other scholars. In the very first year of the institute's operations, Sen resigned from the board in order to become a research adviser, directing the institute's programs on poverty and nutrition, the program that produced the monumental work *Hunger and Public Action*, coauthored by Sen and Jean Drèze, along with three edited volumes of articles on the same topic.[8] In addition, Drèze and Sen worked more intensively on India, producing the book *India: Economic Development and Social Opportunity*,[9] accompanied by a volume of regional studies,[10] all commissioned by the WIDER project and published in the WIDER book series.

I first came to WIDER in the summer of 1986 to participate in a conference on value and technology, for which I had coauthored a paper with Sen. The value-technology project was codirected by Stephen Marglin, a well-known left-wing economist,[11] and his wife Frédérique, an anthropologist who studies women in India.[12] Throughout much of my time at WIDER, the Marglins were Sen's and my major intellectual adversaries. They took the very plausible view that development is a normative concept, and that we should not proceed with "economic development" without asking normative questions. Plausibly again, they argued that opulence was not the only relevant aspect of people's quality of life, and that we should ask about the impact of economic growth on the other constituents. Growth, they rightly insisted, does not always mean "development" in the sense of things getting better. However, from that plausible starting point they leapt rather rapidly to the implausible conclusion that no traditional practice ought to be changed, and that economic growth and agricultural modernization should be discouraged on the grounds that they disrupt traditions. From what struck Sen and me as a vantage point of secure distance from the real sufferings of people, they romanticized such traditional practices as menstruation taboos, child temple prostitution, traditional gendered divisions of labor, and even the absence of smallpox vaccine—which, in an extraordinary moment, Frédérique Marglin blamed for having eradicated the cult of Sittala Devi, the goddess to whom one prays in order to avert the disease![13]

From the first, Sen objected vehemently to the depiction of this reactionary traditionalism as "Indian culture." Sen comes from the liberal and critical Bengali intelligentsia, which introduced educational reforms for women in the early nineteenth century, in advance of most Western nations. His mother was a student and friend of Rabindranath Tagore, the cosmopolitan humanist thinker, and he grew up in Santiniketan, where Tagore founded his school and the university called Vishva-Bharati or "All the World" University. Far from being a "westernized" Indian, he is deeply learned in Indian texts and history. Impatient with the tendency of Americans to romanticize India as the mystical "other," he has throughout his career stressed the variety of Indian traditions, and especially the presence from an early date of rationalist and critical schools of thought.[14] We discovered that there was a good fit between some things Sen wanted to say about internal debate in India and some things I was thinking about Aristotle's notion of critical refinement of the *endoxa* (reliable beliefs). We therefore decided that Sen's presentation at the Marglins' conference would be a coauthored paper, and we wrote "Internal Criticism and Indian Rationalist Traditions."[15]

This was a methodological paper, focused on the importance of hearing voices of critique when a tradition is described. But Sen and I had already discovered another convergence in our philosophical interests, between his "capabilities approach" and my interest in Aristotle's ideas of human functioning and capability as a basis for political distribution. (Indeed, Sen's capabilities approach, though not directly inspired by a reading of Aristotle, clearly owes a good deal to Marx's reading of Aristotle, which focused on the importance of making "truly human functioning," rather than the distribution of commodities in and of itself, the central political goal.[16]) The capabilities approach has above all been used as a measure of the quality of life in a nation; we have also used it to articulate a view of the proper goal of politics.[17]

The approach claims that when we ask how people are doing in a nation or region, it is not enough to look at their satisfactions; for satisfactions can be easily deformed by adaptation to a bad state of affairs, or by habits of luxury.[18] Nor is it enough to look at the presence or absence of resources, even when their distribution is taken into account. Individuals differ in their needs for different kinds of resources and also in their ability to convert resources into valued functionings. For example, people who encounter cultural obstacles to literacy, or working outside the home, will need larger amounts of resources in order to become literate, or capable of working, than people who do not encounter such obstacles. For these reasons, any approach that really wants to know how people are doing needs to look at what they are actually able to do and to be. The approach looks not at actual functioning, since individuals in a liberal society may choose not to avail themselves of opportunities to function, but at the opportunities or "capabilities" they have. These, however, are understood not in a merely formal manner but as involving a set of material preconditions that must be met before one would be willing to say that the person is genuinely capable of going to school or taking a job. Our central claim has been that these capabilities of persons are the measure of quality of life, and that a central goal of politics should be to provide all citizens with at least a basic level of these capabilities.[19]

The capabilities approach advances some universal cross-cultural norms that should guide public policy. I have from the beginning been concerned to advance and defend an explicit list of such norms, basing my argument on a notion of "truly human functioning" that has roots in Aristotle and the early Marx.[20] Sen has not committed himself either to such a definite list or to the Aristotelian mode of justification I articulate, but he does commit himself to universal norms of several sorts, in areas such as bodily well-being, education, and the political liberties. From the first, therefore, Sen and I have been concerned to answer objections from the side of cultural relativism. We do so in part by stressing the fact that the approach is designed to leave a great deal of room for plural specification of the major capabilities; in part by stressing that the goal is capability, not actual functioning (leaving individuals free to choose which functions they will perform). (I now interpret the list of central capabilities in the spirit of a Rawlsian "political liberalism," as a core of basic goods about which citizens can agree, though they differ about their more comprehensive conceptions of the good.[21]) But throughout our work, Sen and I have also stressed that our universalism derives support from a complex understanding of cultures as sites of resistance and internal critique. Our paper for the Marglins' conference was our first statement of this methodological point; it thus complemented the substantive work on capabilities that was already in progress.

The Marglins' conference combined postmodernist jargon and reactionary politics in an extraordinary way. Western medicine was attacked on the grounds that it presupposed a "binary opposition" between life and death.[22] Traditional antifemale taboos were defended on the grounds that they ensured an "embedded way of life," the same values (of sex hierarchy) prevailing in both the home and the workplace.[23] We heard that all criticism of tradition is tyrannical, on the grounds that Derrida and Foucault have shown that there is "no privileged place to stand." At one point Eric Hobsbawm (an onlooker) was asked to leave the room, after he had pointed out that the defense of tradition is often constructed by reactionary political forces for their own benefit.[24]

I sat there thinking how terrible it was that this marvelous opportunity to inject good normative ethical argument into the development and policy arena should be thrown away on such intellectually slipshod work. If there was a need to debate about relativism and universalism, fine, but it should be done well, at a high level of philosophical sophistication. Again, if we were going to question reigning economic models of development, fine again, but let it be done with good philosophy rather than trendy sloganeering. I drew up a proposal for a project bringing philosophy together with economics, focusing on the articulation of the concept of the "quality of life." The proposal was accepted, and I became a research adviser at WIDER. From 1987 to 1993 I was under year-round contract; I spent a month there every summer. At first, Sen helped organize our conferences; later, as Sen was increasingly involved with the hunger project, the director approved the addition of Jonathan Glover to the team, and Glover served as research adviser from 1989 to 1993.

In some ways it was a long leap from working on Aristotle to working on development and the quality of life. One thing I quickly realized was how inadequate my own prior education had been in preparing me to function in an international setting. Everyone I met from Sri Lanka and India knew a lot about Aristotle, but I knew virtually nothing about Buddhism, Hinduism, or Islam. I had, and have, a lot of learning to do.[25] In another way, however, my training had prepared me to make a contribution, since Aristotle's ethical and political thought, as I continue to believe, offers rich resources for contemporary political thought, particularly when we try to define norms of life quality. It also soon seemed clear to me that philosophical arguments about relativism and universalism, and about utilitarianism and the critique of utilitarianism, had a valuable contribution to make to the further development and defense of the capabilities approach. Over the years, Sen has continued to focus on the political economy aspects of the approach and on the normative critique of utilitarianism, while I have focused more on the critique of relativism, on issues of justification and basic philosophical motivation (the notion of "truly human functioning"), and on the articulation of the substantive content of the list of capabilities. Although we continue to differ on some important issues, we agree in allying the approach rather closely with liberalism of a Rawlsian type, and in insisting that it offers a friendly amendment to liberalism, rather than a wholesale replacement.[26] (I have recently allied the approach with political rather than comprehensive liberalism; Sen has not made his view on this question clear.) We agree in stressing the central role of the political liberties among the human capabilities.[27]

Our first conference, then, addressed the general issue of "the quality of life." Its aim was to provide a solid basis for new policies of quality of life measurement and for innovation in other areas of development planning. When policymakers and development professionals compared countries in those days, they used to use GNP per capita as a handy measure of quality of life. This crude measure, of course, doesn't even ask about the distribution of wealth and income, far less about elements of people's lives that are important but not perfectly correlated with GNP, even when distribution has been weighed in infant mortality, life expectancy, educational opportunities, the quality of race and gender relations, the presence or absence of political and religious liberty. Even the slightly less crude move of polling people about their satisfactions does not do well enough, since people's satisfaction reports are frequently shaped by lack of information, lack of opportunity, intimidation, and sheer habit. The aim of the first phase of the quality of life project was to confront development economists coming out of the narrow economic-utilitarian tradition with the wealth of subtle argument on these questions that philosophy had long been producing. We planned to have debate both about the adequacy of utilitarianism as a normative framework for public choice, and also about the ideas of cultural relativism and universalism that had been discussed so unclearly at the Marglins' conference. We also planned to focus on two specific issues, health and sex equality, issues that seemed likely to provide valuable tests of the merits of the different approaches.[28]

Why did we think philosophy would help us make progress on these issues? The simplistic aspects of a Marglin-type approach to culture have been criticized from within anthropology and sociology themselves, where scholars now increasingly stress the fact that cultures are not homogeneous but complex, not tranquil but suffused with conflict.[29] The assumptions of development economics have been criticized from within economics (for example, by feminist economists working on bargaining models of the family),[30] and also by scholars in political science and sociology. To some extent, then, the shortcomings we found in both groups of opponents might have been addressed simply by bringing in different social scientists. We did use such thinkers in our project.[31] But we gave philosophers a central role from the beginning. One immediate reason for this decision was that the Marglins themselves, like other postmodernist relativists, had used appeals to philosophical authority to underwrite their claims. Without going over any arguments, they proceeded as if the very name of Derrida or Foucault could show that these issues had been settled. In gaining a hearing for our universalist proposal, therefore, we needed to show the real dimensions and complexity of the philosophical debate and provide philosophical backing for universalism. But there were two deeper reasons for introducing philosophy into the world of development economics.

The first is that, on foundational issues such as relativism and universalism, or the pros and cons of utilitarianism, philosophers generally produce more rigorous and elaborate arguments than are typically found in the social sciences. There is, of course, no orthodoxy among philosophers on such questions, but debates are typically refined and developed in such a way that real progress is made: the issues are clearly demarcated, many untenable contenders are ruled out, and so forth, until we understand the competing proposals and the arguments that support them with considerable clarity. This happens far less, I believe, in other related fields. There is no shortage of discussion of cultural relativism in the social sciences, for example; but it is usually not as systematic, rigorous, or wide-ranging as the debate in philosophy, which typically draws together considerations from the philosophy of science, the philosophy of language, and the philosophy of mind, using considerations from these areas to illuminate the complex issues of culture. In general, philosophy in our culture has high standards of rigor and refinement in argument; debates on related issues in other professions often seem sloppy by comparison, or lacking in a set of distinctions that have already enabled philosophers to make progress.

Nor is this simply an accident of professional evolution. Philosophers in the Western tradition are the heirs of Socrates. They have a commitment to the critical scrutiny of arguments that makes them good at refining distinctions, detecting fallacies, and doing the kind of work that all thinkers about society—and indeed, at some level all citizens—should be doing, but often don't do.[32] It's not obvious that other disciplines really believe that "the unexamined life is not worth living for a human being," or that rhetoric is inferior to the humble search for correct accounts. Philosophy, while certainly not without its own pockets of dogmatism and blindness, tries hard to live in the spirit of the Socratic ideal, and does so not too badly.[33]

The second reason for making philosophy central to a project on international development can also be traced to the example of Socrates. Philosophers ask the "What is it?" question. Every academic profession has its core concepts, and all make at least some attempt to define them. But philosophy, from its start, has been that irritating gadfly that keeps asking questions about the core concepts—both its own and (irritatingly, but valuably) those of other disciplines and people. Sometimes this function has been understood in too narrow a way: as if, for example, moral philosophy should only engage in "conceptual analysis" and not in the construction and refinement of theories; or as if conceptual analysis of the most relevant sort did not require attention to empirical facts. But if we have a sufficiently subtle and inclusive understanding of the "What is it?" question, it seems right to think that its pursuit is one of the central tasks of our discipline.

Thus many other disciplines, especially economics, concern themselves with the ideas of utilitarianism; but it falls to philosophy, above all, to ask what this theory is, how it is related to other ethical theories, and how to define each of the core concepts on which it relies. Other disciplines concern themselves with ideas of human flourishing, of "the good life," but it is the special job of philosophy to ask what exactly that obscure notion might be, and how we might adjudicate the debate among different rival specifications of it. Other disciplines (for example, law and public policy) use notions of freedom and responsibility, and have some working definitions of these notions; but it falls to philosophy to think through the "What is it?" question here too, debating the merits of various different ways of conceiving of these obscure and difficult notions, until by now a highly refined set of alternatives has been worked out, of which legal and political academics are usually only dimly aware. Economists and political scientists are all the time talking about preference, choice, and desire. But it is the special job of philosophy to provide a perspicuous investigation of these foundational concepts, distinguishing desire from intention, emotion, impulse, and other psychological items, asking questions about the relationship of each of these to belief and learning, and so forth. By pursuing these inquiries, philosophy has, again, evolved a highly refined account of the alternatives in this area, and its accounts show that many aspects of at least some parts of economics rest on a foundation that is not just crude, but also highly unreliable.[34] Again, thinkers in a variety of fields have shown sympathy with the capabilities approach; but it falls to philosophy to investigate more precisely the all-important distinction between capability and functioning,[35] and related distinctions between different types of human capabilities.[36] Finally, philosophy characteristically, and far more than other fields, turns its own "What is it?" question on its own methods and inquiries, asking, for example, what justification is in political theory, or what judgments, intuitions, or emotions a political argument might reasonably rely on. These questions are rarely asked with comparable pertinacity and subtlety in other disciplines concerned with social life.

These conceptual inquiries are sometimes viewed as examples of obsessive intellectual fussiness; they have, however, important practical consequences, which need to be taken into account in practical political programs. This can be shown in many areas. But to stick to the capabilities approach, the distinction between capabilities and functioning is of the greatest practical importance: a policy that aims at a single desired mode of functioning will often be quite different from one that tries to promote opportunities for citizens to choose that function or not to choose it. Thus a policy aimed at urging all women to seek employment outside the home will be very different from a policy that aims at giving all women the choice to work outside the home or not to do so. Both policies will need to protect women from discrimination in employment and from intimidation and harassment in the employment process. But the latter, unlike the former, will also need to attend to the social meaning of domestic labor, promoting a sense that a traditional domestic life is worthwhile and consistent with human dignity; it will also need to make such choices economically feasible for women, and not unduly risky, by attending to the economic value of domestic labor when calculating settlement after divorce. Similarly, it seems very important to distinguish the different types of human capabilities: a policy that aims simply at putting people in the internal state to function well will often be very different from a policy that aims both at creating the internal prerequisites of functioning and at shaping the surrounding material and social environment so that it is favorable for the exercise of choice in the relevant area. If this distinction is not clearly made, the merits of different policy choices will probably not be clearly debated. Thus a policy aimed at promoting only the internal capability for freedom of expression would only need to educate people; it would not need to construct circumstances in which they can actually speak freely without penalty. A policy aimed at women's internal capability for employment outside the home would need to focus only on education and skills training; a policy aimed at the combined capability would need to focus, as well, on nondiscrimination in hiring, on sexual harassment, and on protecting women from threat and intimidation from members of their own family. The "What is it?" question, in short, is profoundly practical. In its absence, public life will be governed by "what is usually said in a jumbled fashion," as Aristotle so nicely put this point.[37]

Aristotle used this Socratic idea of philosophy to argue that philosophy is an important part of the equipment of every person who aims to take an active role in public life. And for the two reasons I have given here, I believe, with him, that philosophy is an essential part of the training of any citizen who will need to deliberate with other citizens, vote, serve on a jury, or just think clearly, in areas involving debates and concepts such as the ones I have mentioned. I have therefore argued elsewhere that two semesters of philosophy should be part of the undergraduate liberal arts education of every college or university undergraduate.[38] But even those who are not persuaded by that educational proposal should acknowledge, I believe, that philosophers are badly needed in academic deliberations about public policy, as critical scrutinizers of arguments and as obsessive pursuers of the foundational concepts and questions. For here if anywhere, it is important to seek rigor and conceptual clarity. To perform their role successfully, however, philosophers will have to overcome two obstacles, one created by the resistance of economics to foundational criticism, the other by philosophy's own professional habits.

Our first conference assembled a distinguished group of philosophers, all of whom did interesting work.[39] But in two related ways the conference, which was supposed to provide policymakers and development workers with a new conceptual basis for their efforts, seemed to me a failure. Both involved the reluctance of specialists to go beyond the models and vocabularies they standardly use in writing for fellow specialists. First, we more or less entirely failed to get leading economists to take the philosophical critique of their foundations seriously. The philosophers in our group were deliberately chosen for diversity of views; they included utilitarians, Kantians, and neo-Aristotelians. We wanted, indeed, to highlight arguments that could be made for and against the capabilities approach. But even the utilitarian philosophers had many conceptual and foundational criticisms to make of economic welfarism; in many respects the type of utilitarianism defended by the philosophers who wished to defend it was far closer to neo-Aristotelianism and Kantianism, as a result of debates that have unfolded over the decades, than it was to the simpler form of utilitarianism dominant in neoclassical economics. There was unanimous agreement among the philosophers that the foundations of economics need thorough rethinking. Those criticisms, however, had little effect. With the exception of John Roemer, who has long since been a quasi-philosopher, nobody seemed to understand that what we were saying had implications for the ways in which models should henceforth be built. The general reaction was, "You have a very interesting profession there," or (still worse), "Sen is now doing philosophy, not economics." As Roemer observed at the conference, economists are highly committed to their models, which involve a great deal of formal sophistication; frequently they are selected for success in the profession in accordance with formal ability. If people just talk ordinary language and don't present them with alternative models, they are not likely to switch over to a new way of thinking about things, especially if it involves jettisoning formal work in which a lot has been invested. The philosophical recalcitrance of economists, and their refusal to admit that their work does make substantive philosophical commitments that need to be scrutinized, continues to be one of the greatest barriers to philosophy's effective participation in public life. Given the public dominance of economics, any profession that cannot get itself taken seriously by it will have tough going. But economics is extremely self-satisfied, and its tendency to repudiate nonformal and foundational work as irrelevant to its concerns poses a major problem.

The philosophers had an analogous problem. The people in our team did good work; and yet they did not altogether fulfill their assignment. Sen and I commissioned the papers (with very generous stipends), asking people to spend time familiarizing themselves with pertinent pieces of the development literature, so that they could relate their abstract discussions to these debates. We also asked them to address an audience of policymakers and nonspecialists. Nonetheless, people have a marked tendency to present the work that they are doing anyway, and philosophers are in the habit of addressing their peers, rather than the general public. I see no reason why the issues of our conference cannot be discussed, at a high degree of sophistication, in a clear and jargon-free language, with concrete factual or narrative examples.[40] But philosophers need to have more practice in this type of writing if they are to do it effectively. The fact that this type of writing is not rewarded by the profession or encouraged in graduate programs poses an obstacle to philosophy's public influence.

We had already decided that the next conference would focus on women's quality of life. Women's issues, as I said, had been at the center of our concern from the beginning, both for their own sake, as especially urgent issues of justice, and for the very clear challenge they posed both to cultural relativism and to normative utilitarianism. Women are especially likely to be the losers if we defer uncritically to local traditions, or, rather, to the voices of powerful men that have usually been permitted to define what a "tradition" is; they also frequently have preferences that are distorted by absence of information, intimidation, and long schooling in self-abnegation. Looking at what a normative theory can say about these problems offers us a good way of assessing that theory.

Reflecting on our previous difficulties, I made several decisions. First, persuading the economists could wait, and we would just get on with our work; henceforth, we included only Roemer and Sen on the economic side of our project. Second, we needed a field study so that the philosophers would have something very concrete around which to orient their work. We therefore commissioned Martha Chen to do a field study of women's right to work in India and Bangladesh.[41] We asked her to focus on women's right to work because we felt that this would provide a fertile starting point for discussion of many related human capabilities, such as nutrition and health, bodily integrity, political participation, dignity and self-respect. Third, instead of presenting a menu of different philosophical options, as the first conference had done, we would now try to produce a more coherent philosophical account, focusing on the issue of relativism and universalism. Finally, we would try to integrate into the project philosophers from developing countries who also had some contact with fieldwork and the women's movements in their own countries.[42]

The 1990 conference from which *Women, Culture, and Development* grew was, I believe, our most successful conference. Our aim was to articulate and defend a form of universalism based on the capabilities approach, answering objections from the side of relativism. At the same time, we aimed to develop a more complex conception of cultural tradition and intracultural debate than is frequently used in such discussions (a return to the theme of Sen's and my original coauthored paper).

As tends to happen, people defended a universal approach to human functioning in their own characteristic ways, and the contributions were thus heterogeneous in terminology and philosophical orientation.[43] Nonetheless, we converged on many important matters, and it was intellectually fruitful to see how similar arguments against traditionalism and relativism could be made from a variety of distinct philosophical starting points. Especially valuable was Chen's fine field study (accompanied by a film), which provided a solid starting point for our more abstract ruminations. Chen's detailed account of two representative women, secluded widow Metha Bai and women's employment activist Saleha Begum, caught the imaginations of the participants and provided a valuable focal point for discussion of a wide range of human capabilities. Our feminist writers, whether philosophers or not, wrote better for a general public audience, on the whole, than had the writers of the previous volume—perhaps because feminist theory has always kept its feet squarely planted in the empirical reality of women's lives. Because of our focus on the field study, the papers did not suffer from the remote nonpractical abstractness that often characterized the papers in the earlier volume.

We held one more conference, in 1992. Glover was its primary organizer, and it focused on new reproductive technologies and their relation to women's equality. Its aim was to examine a wide range of new reproductive techniques in the context of women's capabilities and functioning, asking what line an approach such as ours should take about the roles of law and public policy in the area of reproductive choice. For this conference we assembled an unusually broad and internationally diverse group of participants, but the philosophical level of the contributions was uneven, and we are still supplementing this material and getting it revised for publication.

We had two further plans. One involved questioning the anthropocentrism of the capabilities approach and trying to figure out what the approach ought to say about the status of other species and the world of nature. The second involved asking about the relationship of the capabilities approach to various concrete areas of public and civic life. We had planned an ambitious conference—which, among other things, would have brought various religious thinkers to WIDER to talk about the relationship of our universal account of human capabilities to the understandings of the major religious traditions. This is a topic that had been notably absent in our project.[44]

These plans never materialized because of the abrupt curtailment of research activities at WIDER. It is painful to describe these events, since they show so clearly the pitfalls of trying to do good intellectual work within the UN bureaucracy, which ought to support such work. But the United Nations University, the UN wing under which WIDER had been located, is a rather low-level enterprise, run by an agency that does not care a lot (or cares negatively) about good intellectual work. When Jayawardena completed his two terms as director, UN rules did not permit him to serve again; at this point, the UNU hierarchy intervened to ensure that WIDER's future would not involve high-profile research projects such as our own and others that had made WIDER a name in the professions. The difficult sequence of events, during the administration of an acting director handpicked by the bureaucratic agency, included firing almost all the year-round researchers, refusing to accept new proposals by research advisers, and a series of false accusations against Jayawardena that caused most of us to want nothing further to do with the future of WIDER.[45] There is now a new director, but he has decided that the future of WIDER will involve standard noninterdisciplinary development projects, which appear to be intellectually unambitious.

Those of us most committed to the work at WIDER now carry it on under other auspices.[46] Sen and his coauthor Jean Drèze have spent the past few years completing the ambitious WIDER project on India that has generated the book *India: Economic Development and Social Opportunity*, as well as a companion volume of regional field studies. Although much of his current research lies in social choice theory, his other primary area of expertise, Sen regularly writes on development issues, such as women's hunger, global population, and India's rationalist traditions.[47]

A particularly important practical project growing out of the WIDER work can be found in the *Human Development Reports* issued annually since 1991 by the United Nations Development Program in New York, using a theoretical approach designed by Sen, Sudhir Anand, and other economists sympathetic to the capabilities approach, most of whom worked at WIDER. It is one thing to grouse about the use of GNP to measure quality of life; it is another to propose an alternative measure. Such a measure, since it will have to use existing data from the 173 countries on the list, needs to be somewhat cruder than would be ideal. (My own normative proposal, including, as it does, such hard-to-measure items as emotional capacities and the preservation of human dignity, is not a good basis for a measure that the UNDP can go out and use right now.) But even if the measure is not ideal, just getting richer comparisons out there in quantitative form is one big step forward.

The *Human Development Reports* proceed in two ways. First, they simply present large amounts of data in easily digestible form—not only overall data about matters such as health care, education, wages, employment opportunities, life expectancy, infant and maternal mortality, political participation, and so forth, but also data organized to bring out inequalities that might be of special interest for governments and NGOs: inequalities between rural and urban, poor and rich, male and female. The description of male-female gaps has been an especially prominent part of the reports since their inception; simply describing these gaps is progress because it draws attention to them and presents them as a problem to be overcome. Even in small ways, the reports have always emphasized the question of gender: for example, in the little boxes that highlight a specific issue not covered in the overall data, the reports have discussed items such as gender inequality in Japan and legal progress on violence against women in Turkey. The 1995 report was centrally focused on gender issues.

The second feature of the reports is their use of a variety of aggregative measures to rank nations. Since 1991, the reports have ranked countries in accordance with the Human Development Index, a measure that includes three components: longevity (measured by life expectancy at birth), knowledge (measured by adult literacy and mean years of schooling), and income (using the Atkinson formulation for the utility of income, which assumes diminishing returns as income rises). These three components are aggregated by a complex weighting process described in the 1991 report. The report lists countries in the order of their HDI rank, thus attempting to provide governments with incentives to compete for better rankings along these parameters.

Third, from the beginning the report included other devices of aggregation. The HDI was adjusted, for example, for gender disparity and income distribution, producing the Gender-Disparity Adjusted HDI and the Income-Distribution Adjusted HDI. More recently, these indices have been supplemented with related measures in the areas of gender and poverty: the Gender-Related Development Index (GDI) and the Gender Empowerment Measure (GEM), the former being a version of the old gender-adjusted HDI, the latter being a complex measure concentrating on economic, political, and professional participation. Finally, in 1996, the CPM, or Capability Poverty Measure, was added: it focuses on the percentage of children under age five who are underweight, the percentage of births unattended by trained health personnel, and the percentage of women over age fifteen who are illiterate. (These are meant to be ways of capturing nutritional health, reproductive health, and educational capability; these choices are defended as fundamental items in the capabilities approach.)

The reports are, of course, imperfect. Compilers have to rely on data from the countries, which are highly flawed. Even when the numbers are accurate, moreover, they are hard to interpret: years of schooling, even if accurately stated, doesn't convey a clear idea of educational attainment or capability. Some important capabilities are simply omitted from the data: above all, one notices the absence of the various political rights and liberties. This is not because Sen and the other compilers consider them of secondary importance; indeed, Sen has defended a version of the Rawlsian priority of liberty.[48] The omission reflects, instead, the fact that these liberties are extremely difficult to measure on the basis of information supplied by the nations in question. Partha Dasgupta has used a measure of political liberty to rank a number of countries.[49] But using this proposal would involve the UNDP in independent information gathering, something the index has not had the resources to do. Other gaps are in areas that resist numerical formulation, such as dignity and self-respect. One might also object to the selection of central components of the HDI from among the many types of data presented. Thus, education is included in the HDI, but employment opportunities are not, although many feminists consider employment to be at least as important in women's well-being. (The GEM does attempt to include employment-related capabilities.) Property rights, another issue of central importance to feminists in developing countries, are not described at all in the reports. Finally, scholars will differ about the weighting mechanism proposed in constructing the HDI. (These issues have opened up a burgeoning field of academic work.) But despite these imperfections, the HDR continues to provide an important contribution of theory to practice.

INDIAN WOMEN AND FEMINIST INTERNATIONALISM

After the breakup of WIDER, I continued working on women's quality of life, using my own research funds. Because I felt that I needed to see and learn more about how poor women were really thinking about their lives, I went to India in the spring of 1997 for a field trip, visiting various women's development projects, especially those connected with credit and employment. I had decided to focus on a single country that I could get to know in some depth, instead of (as often happens) culling examples from dozens of countries without appreciating their social context. I chose India because I had spent time there before, because I have contacts there, because it is a democracy where one can hear what people really think, and because I love the country. Martha (Marty) Chen was my invaluable guide, translator, and coordinator. During my previous visit to India in 1988 I had spent my time primarily in Delhi, Calcutta, and Santiniketan[50] and had learned a lot about the

Bengali renaissance from spending time with Amita Sen both in Santiniketan itself and on many other occasions in Britain and the United States. But I had never pursued my own intellectual projects in the field, and I felt I needed to do this before writing any further.

The project in connection with which I took the trip is a series of lectures developing my version of the capabilities approach as a basis for an international feminism. I defend a substantive account of the central capabilities as a basis for a political-liberal consensus about some core aspects of basic social justice. I argue that people should have these capabilities, whatever else they also have and pursue. In the process, I develop a framework for justifying the list of capabilities in connection with an Aristotelian/Marxian idea of truly human functioning. I also relate my substantive-good approach to various informed-desire and procedural approaches. Finally, I address several topics that the WIDER project on women did not address, particularly religion and distributive justice within the family. The capabilities approach is of course not restricted to women, but I focus on these problems because of their urgency and centrality. Moreover, the general merit of the approach becomes especially evident when we see that it gives us better ways to handle these problems than do other prominent approaches to thinking about the quality of life.

I told everyone I met that I was a feminist political theorist writing on "the quality of life" and developing a universal cross-cultural account of that issue with a particular focus on women. I said that I wanted my account to be not remote from reality but responsive to what people were really thinking about their lives. I asked lots of questions about how people saw their lives: what were the central constituents of life quality that one might focus on for purposes of formal and informal social planning. I shall focus here on just three portions of the trip that are exemplary of ways in which it influenced the development of my ideas.[51]

Toward the beginning of my trip, I joined Marty in Ahmedabad, Gujerat, where she had been working for some months gathering data for a project on the lives of widows in rural India. With her I spent time at SEWA, which organizes female laborers in the informal sector to demand better conditions and extends credit to women through a credit union—now, as I have mentioned, an all-woman bank. SEWA also has programs in education and child care. I met with SEWA's current director, its heads of child care and education, various officers of the SEWA women's bank, and a variety of women who participate in SEWA projects, among them Vasanti. One of the highlights of my trip was a meeting with SEWA's founder, Ela Bhatt, one of the world's most influential women's activists, who now organizes informal sector workers worldwide. A woman of electric intelligence and deeply moving simplicity, she organized SEWA around Gandhian principles of self-rule. Just as for Gandhi, India could only achieve self-rule and dignity if it first established economic independence from Britain, so, Bhatt argues, women need to focus on economic independence from men, if they are to achieve the appropriate level of autonomy and dignity. As I shall later describe, Bhatt's observations about the importance of credit, property rights, and self-sufficiency have been especially influential in leading me to revise some of my views.[52]

Jayamma's life has obviously been a tough one, but it has been improved by government action. My ideas about the scope and potential for government action promoting human capabilities were strongly influenced by the time I spent in Trivandrum, the major city of the province of Kerala, at the southern tip of India. Kerala has frequently been studied for its contrasts to other regions. Although it is a relatively poor province, it does extremely well on literacy and health care, and the position of women is markedly better than in many other regions. Female literacy, 39 percent in India as a whole, is 86 percent in Kerala, and close to 100 percent among adolescents. The female-male ratio, 92/100 in India generally, is 104/100, a figure comparable to those of Europe and North America.[53] Among the factors that make Kerala different are its traditions of matrilineal inheritance, plural female marriages, and matrilocal residence, which date from the eleventh century; the complex influence of Christian missionaries, who influenced this region far more than the rest of India; and the presence of a communist regional government (which has done poorly on economic growth, but very well in health and education). In Kerala, our primary hosts were Iqbal Gulati, chief economic adviser to the government, and Leela Gulati, a leading researcher in the Center for Development Studies, author of an important book on female poverty.[54]

With Leela Gulati (who is fluent in Malayalam, a Dravidian language that Marty does not speak), we visited Jayamma and her family in the squat that Leela has studied for more than twenty years, talking to various family members and neighbors and gathering an enthusiastic following of little girls, who trouped behind us everywhere in their crisp school uniforms. We went to the primary school in the squatter settlement, where we found quite an upbeat situation; indeed, among the places we visited in the 100 degree heat, the squat, with its lake covered with water hyacinth,[55] was far from the least pleasant. Kerala gives a feminist thinker a great deal to reflect about; in particular one observes the impact of government programs promoting both literacy and property rights on the lives of poor women and girls.

In Andhra Pradesh, a chaotic and ill-governed province, I saw another side of the issue of government action, observing the way in which a national government project focused on consciousness raising could enhance women's sense of their rights as citizens and inspire efforts to extract better material and educational services from local government. Here I was also dramatically exposed to the power of women's collectives in raising women's self-esteem and coordinating efforts for change. As I shall later describe, this experience had philosophical relevance, altering some aspects of my thinking.

My host, Yedla Padmavathi, is the Andhra Pradesh director of a national government program, the Mahila Samakhya (Women's Collectives) Project.

Andhra Pradesh is an especially corrupt and anarchic state; the city of Hyderabad is booming economically, but rural areas frequently lack essential services, such as water, buses, electricity, and schools. The point of the project (given that the national government has little money to improve services on its own) is to enhance women's awareness of their rights and to encourage them to mobilize to demand basic services from the local government. The program is therefore quite unpopular with the local government; Padma told me in matter-of-fact tones that she fully expected assassination attempts —a common style of politics in Andhra Pradesh. With Padma and two coworkers I was driven three hours from Hyderabad to the small city of Mahabubnagar, where we spent some time at the local project field station. As usual, I asked questions about life quality: what are you working for, what do you think is important, and so forth. Padma wanted me to visit an extremely poor area that had been in the project only a short time, so I would see how the program grapples with extreme poverty. We made our way in a jeep for another hour and a half into the desert to a village that lacked electricity, bus service, and a reliable water supply. Here was the worst poverty that I observed and yet, as before, women's attitudes seemed astonishingly hopeful. We sat and talked about hopes, aims, the program, life conditions. The women sang me a traditional song whose lyrics used to be "Women, why are you crying?" and then the woman would tell all the bad things in a woman's lot. Now the lyrics have been rewritten: "Women, why are you crying? Your tears should become your thoughts." They then asked me to sing an American feminist song. Thinking rapidly, I came up with "We Shall Overcome." They smiled, for they already knew that song. By the second verse, they were singing along in Telugu.

As Strether says in *The Ambassadors*, "There's all the indescribable: what one gets only on the spot." How Vasanti's eyes look up and look down; the muscles of Jayamma's neck; the electrifying simplicity of Ela Bhatt; how each poor woman does her daily accounting; how the air around her smells and tastes: these things have a bearing on a theory of gender justice. The feminist dictum that we must "start from women's experience" does not seem to me altogether correct. We won't learn much from what we see if we do not bring to our fieldwork such theories of justice and human good as we have managed to work out until then. One thing good theory tells us is the extent to which deprivation, ignorance, and intimidation corrupt experience itself, making it a very incomplete guide to what ought to be done. Nonetheless, it is also plain that most philosophers know little about the lives of impoverished women, especially in developing countries, and can't even imagine those lives without seeing and learning a lot more than philosophers typically do. Even the debate between cultural relativism and universalism has an empirical component. Our answers will properly be influenced by answers to empirical questions such as, How much internal debate and plurality do traditional cultures contain? What common needs and strivings do we find when we look at the lives of people in many parts of the world? And what do women say about their lives, when they are in a setting characterized by freedom from fear and freedom from hierarchical authority? The fact that we look for those answers rather than the answers they give when they are in fear or cowed by authority shows that we are proceeding with a prima facie theory as we work; nonetheless, these provisional fixed points might themselves be called into question as a result of what we discover.

We would, then, need experience even if we already knew the right questions to ask. But experience is often required to get the right questions onto the table. Theories of justice have avoided the thorny question of the distribution of resources and opportunities within the family;[56] some have treated the family as a private sphere of love and care into which the state should not meddle. Sex-specific issues such as domestic violence and marital rape have not always been on the table—although John Stuart Mill is a distinguished exception to this claim. We should insist that theories of justice come to grips with the problems women face in the family and in the larger society, and we should make recommendations for their solution. Philosophers need Vasanti and Jayamma, then, to goad them to ask some central questions that have not always been asked.

Feminist philosophy, of course, has tackled such women's issues. And yet it has frequently stopped well short of the international women's movement itself, by focusing on the problems of middle-class women in America rather than on the urgent needs and interests of poor women in the developing world. A more international focus will not require feminist philosophy to turn away from its traditional themes, such as employment discrimination, domestic violence, sexual harassment, and the reform of rape law; these are all as central to women in developing countries as to Western women. But feminism will have to add new topics to its agenda if it is to approach the developing world in a productive way; among these topics are hunger and nutrition, literacy, land rights, the right to seek employment outside the home, child marriage, and child labor. These topics raise philosophical questions. To deal with them well, we need to think about how care and love of various forms play a role in women's lives; about the various forms of affective ties that form the structure of societies of various types; about the relationship between property and self-respect. Thinking about these practical issues also shapes what we say about these more abstract topics. To approach these issues well, feminist philosophers need to learn a lot more than most Americans know about the variety of religious and cultural traditions, as well as the political, legal, and economic structures of nations in which large numbers of poor women dwell. (For example, in my experience almost all philosophers and legal thinkers are astounded to discover that India does not have a uniform code of civil law, and that the various religious systems of personal law manage things in the domain of property and inheritance, as well as marriage, divorce, custody, and maintenance. But if they don't know this, they can hardly begin to conceive of the problems women in India face or to frame the interesting philosophical issues of sex equality and religious free exercise in a relevant manner.) In short, even feminist philosophers, whose theories have been unusually responsive to and shaped by practice, need to look at Vasanti and Jayamma and consider the challenge their lives pose to thought.

In my own case, several major changes were brought about by my confrontation with these lives. The first was that I now stress far more than I had done previously the importance of property rights, access to credit, and opportunities to seek employment outside the home, as capabilities valuable in themselves and strongly linked to others, such as the ability to preserve one's bodily integrity, the ability to think and plan for oneself. Perhaps because I have been teaching in Chicago, where one hears so much about property rights every day, often in a manner that shows little compassion for the poor, I had tended to underrate the importance of property rights in poor women's lives. Everywhere I went, however, I heard women saying that having equal land rights (as women do not currently have under the Hindu legal code) and having access to credit are crucial determinants of their life quality; Bhatt powerfully linked this issue with the Gandhian conception of self-sufficiency in an anticolonial struggle. Indeed, I learned to value the concept of self-sufficiency itself more than I had previously. In defending liberal individualism against feminist objections, I had insisted, somewhat defensively, that an interest in promoting the dignity and opportunities of *each person* did not entail valuing self-sufficiency as a normative goal.[57] I now understand the value this norm can have, when one is accustomed to a life in which one's survival itself depends on the goodwill of others. Access to employment had been important in my approach since Chen's field study for our project; but seeing the importance of employment opportunities in lives on the edge of starvation made their importance far more vivid.

A second important change was a greater emphasis on the Kantian ideas of dignity and nonhumiliation, which had been implicit in the notion of practical reason I developed in the capabilities account but which I had insufficiently stressed. My Aristotelian starting point was helpful for the way in which it fostered attention to a variety of meaningful forms of affiliation and friendship, especially forms based on equality. The importance of friendship was amply confirmed by my experiences in women's collectives, where it is hard to convey the delight of women who join with other women in groups based on equality, rather than families based on hierarchy and fear. However, one would be missing something of great importance if one did not add that a crucial constituent of these friendships is a shared interest in dignity and in avoiding situations of humiliation.[58] Thinking about this is essential to thinking well about how women can be integrated into a previously all-male workplace, as well as about the political capabilities.

Finally, to return to friendship, my experience in India showed me the great political importance of groups of affiliation among women, as sources of self-respect, friendship, and delight. Relatively few Western women, even women who derive great support from consciousness-raising groups and the women's movement, have lives in which the primary affective tie is to a group of women as such. Such ties, a common reality in developing countries, are of long standing in sub-Saharan Africa,[59] more recent but extremely powerful in India. For most of us, by contrast, the hold of traditions concerning the nuclear family is such that our primary affective ties are usually to a far smaller unit focused on the home. For many Western women, an especially deep part of the search for the meaning of life is played by romantic love, whether of a woman or a man; this tie and the search for this tie to some extent pull against women's solidarity with other women in groups. Everywhere I went in India, by contrast, women related to the group as to their primary community and source of emotional sustenance; the Western woman's focus on romance and (in many cases) men is regarded as somewhat strange, and not necessarily conducive to women's functioning. In general, deep affection and trust are more separated from sexuality than they tend to be in our lives. Western women are thought to emphasize the sexual tie more than is good for their social lives.

These are difficult issues for Western feminists to ponder, for they lie very deep in many people's emotions. But I believe we should be more agnostic than liberal theory currently is about what fundamental affective ties the "basic structure of society" should include, and in what form. The debate in liberal theory usually takes the form of asking how far law is involved in the construction of the family, and how far and in what ways it should be involved. But the centrality of something like the heterosexual nuclear family with children (perhaps with suitable extensions to recognize same-sex couples and groups of relatives) is usually taken for granted, and it is this family institution that usually gets special support as part of society's basic structure. I believe this emphasis needs rethinking. Any workable account of quality of life should surely make room for these women's collectives as one valuable specification of general goods of affiliation, and it is not clear to me that the state ought to give priority to the Western-style nuclear family over such groupings in allocating benefits and privileges. By creating the Mahila Samakhya project, the government of India took a different line, I believe wisely.

THEORY AND PRACTICE

But why does practice need theory? What might philosophy offer to lives such as those of Vasanti and Jayamma? The first thing we must say here is that theory is in those lives already, frequently in a bad way. International development economics has a tremendous impact on people's lives because its theories have great influence on development practice and on the formation of public policy. More generally, economics exerts influence the world over, not only as a source of prediction but frequently as a source of normative guidance as well. It is very common for economists to slide over from the explanatory/predictive mode into a normative mode, although nothing in their training or argumentative practice really equips them to justify norms for public policy. Thus when we see wealth maximization proposed as the goal of a good legal system,[60] when we see the maximization of satisfaction used as a goal in the selection of public policy on education or population, when we see GNP per capita used as an index of "the quality of life," economists are playing the role of normative theoretical guide, a role that they typically do not play with great subtlety. Even their predictive work is sometimes marred by conceptual crudeness or questionable motivational assumptions, in ways that can at times affect the models' predictive value.[61] They typically take philosophical positions on a variety of contested issues, though usually without realizing that they are doing so or providing arguments for the position taken.

As I have suggested, economists are not readily receptive to philosophical critique. But this is all the more reason why philosophers need to enter the public arena and make these points themselves to policymakers, legal thinkers, and development workers. We need to get people thinking about the adequacy or inadequacy of utilitarian criteria of well-being; about the commensurability or incommensurability of values; about the relationship between well-being and agency; about the structure of political liberalism and the role of ideas of the good in a liberalism of this type; about the relationship between resources and human functioning; about cultural relativism and its critique; and much more. Policymakers, leaders of NGOs, development workers: all these people, like the students we teach, can join in philosophical debates about these issues if they are presented in a clear and accessible way. In this way, philosophers can try to shape development practice even without converting the economists!

The *Human Development Reports* offer one device through which philosophy is already influencing practice in a good way. The HDR is useful because it offers a concrete set of tools for measurement and ranking. But, even where it performs its function as well as possible, it is crude. It does not offer much in the way of justification, and it does not really delve into philosophical distinctions that are ultimately relevant to practice, such as the distinction between well-being and agency, or even the distinction between functioning and capability. Therefore practice also needs more extensive and analytical discussions. One may hope to reach an audience of not only philosophers and social scientists but also policymakers and development workers, showing them the arguments that lie behind the approach and its substantive content. It is not easy to do this, and frequently one must work on several different levels, presenting material in one way for an audience that would like to know exactly how the approach is related to Rawls's political liberalism, another way for an audience that just wants to see the approach itself in its general outlines. But there is no reason why a philosopher cannot reach a broad audience if enough attention is devoted to writing. In the past, philosophers such as John Stuart Mill and William James were also distinguished writers for a general educated public. These are good examples for our profession to emulate. If we don't, many public debates will go on without philosophical input.

This emphatically does not mean that philosophers should stop doing systematic philosophy and become essayists or politicians. Of course they may do this, in this area and in others. Some philosophers, for example Bertrand Russell, have in effect had two careers, the philosophical work being quite far removed from the public political contribution. But there is a different contribution to political practice that philosophy can only make by remaining itself, that is, concerned with conceptual subtleties and the clear articulation of distinctions, concerned with systematic argument and theory construction. It is precisely because philosophers have thought with such subtlety and rigor about the nature of well-being and the foundations of human action that they are equipped to make the criticisms of the foundations of economics that they cogently make. When Seneca said that the philosopher should be a "lawyer for humanity," he meant that highly abstract ideas about the nature of anger, the social origins of greed, and so on, needed to be brought to bear on the real-world political scene.[62] But these ideas would only enrich the political scene, giving it something it didn't have already, if they were presented with the cogent and patient arguments characteristic of philosophy. Philosophy that moves to the practical "bottom line" too quickly will fail to deliver its characteristic practical benefits. These benefits require systematizing intuitions, sorting for consistency and fit, and articulating clearly the outlines of concepts that are usually employed in a muddy fashion.

Political people often get impatient with philosophers because of their interest in patient argumentation and systematic theory building. They want a quick move to the "bottom line," and if they can't see an immediate relation to the practical, they tend to assume that one cannot be found. Philosophers find this response painful. They do not like to be treated as ivory tower elitists who have nothing useful to offer. They are therefore sorely tempted either to withdraw or to stop doing real philosophy in order to accede to the demand for something immediately useful. Marx's doctoral dissertation (about the Hellenistic philosophers) contains an eloquent warning about this state of affairs:

> When philosophy turns itself as will against the world of appearance, then . . . it has become one aspect of the world which opposes another. Its relationship to the world is that of reflection. Inspired by the urge to realize itself, it enters into tension against the other. The inner self-containment and completeness has been broken. What was inner light has become consuming flame turning outwards. The result is that as the world becomes philosophical, philosophy also becomes worldly, that its realization is also its loss, that what it struggles against on the outside is its own inner deficiency.[63]

In other words, to the extent that the philosopher engages in political action, she risks losing the unworldly qualities of precision, self-containment, and reflectiveness that inform her own characteristic mode of activity.

I agree with Marx to this extent: when we enter politics, we run some risk of losing the characteristic philosophical virtues. (I believe that Cicero and Seneca sometimes, though certainly not always, show such defects.) But there is no reason why this must happen. We need to keep reminding ourselves that philosophers are not especially likely to be good politicians. Cicero, Seneca, Marcus Aurelius, and Karl Marx offer distinguished examples of the combination. The fact that Cicero could write both the *Catilinarians* and the *De Officiis* is a remarkable coincidence, and it is a little surprising that someone so interested in philosophy would be willing to get so immersed in rather shady rhetoric. More often, the professional training of the philosopher makes people ill suited to a world of political action. They get too interested in how things really are and not enough in how they will sound; they would rather make the distinction that can survive scrutiny rather than the one that will bring about a politically valuable result.[64] Philosophers charged with uselessness, then, had better not jettison philosophy and take up political speechmaking unless they think they have a special talent for it, to some extent independent of their philosophical ability. More often, we should conclude that what we do best by training is also the best thing we have to offer to practice: systematic accounts that convey an overall understanding of a domain of human affairs, crafted in such a way that intuitions are brought to bear on a practical problem in a new manner.

The Hellenistic philosophers make a valuable point in this regard. Whether in law or medicine or politics, they say, if you give a lot of prescriptions at an intermediate level of generality, you will not necessarily understand the rationale behind the prescriptions and you will be at a loss to prescribe for a new case of some complexity. You will tend to be rigid, afraid to depart from the rule. If, on the other hand, you seek a deeper and more general understanding of what generates the concrete prescriptions—if you really understand the concepts involved and can connect them in a systematic way—you will be in a far better position to face the new case, especially where the existing prescriptions are ambiguous or incomplete. That, I think, is how we should understand philosophy's potential contribution to law, to medicine, to development policy: it provides the type of foundational and systematic understanding that can guide prescriptions and laws. Philosophy has to be grounded in experience and concerned with practice, or it will rightly be dismissed as irrelevant. Vasanti and Jayamma were not in my mind before I met them, and to that extent my mind was ill prepared for its theoretical task. But the commitment to reality does not entail that philosophy should not also be abstract, theoretical, and concerned with conceptual distinctions. Only by retaining these concerns can it make a distinctive practical contribution.[65]

Kant observed that it is very difficult, looking at the evil in the world, to sustain the hopes for human progress that are probably necessary to sustain us in work that is aimed at practical change. But he also argues that we may adopt some optimistic beliefs as "practical postulates," precisely in order to support our continued engagement with humanity:

> History may well give rise to endless doubts about my hopes, and if these doubts could be proved, they might persuade me to desist from an apparently futile task. But so long as they do not have the force of certainty, I cannot exchange my duty . . . for a rule of expediency which says that I ought not to attempt the impracticable. . . . And however uncertain I may be and may remain as to whether we can hope for anything better for mankind, this uncertainty cannot detract from the maxim I have adopted, or from the necessity of assuming for practical purposes that human progress is possible.
>
> This hope for better times to come, without which an earnest desire to do something useful for the common good would never have inspired the human heart, has always influenced the activities of right-thinking people.[66]

Feminist philosophers have special difficulty taking up Kant's practical postulate, since in all cultures throughout history the inequality of women has been an established fact of life. Despite the impressive progress women have made in the twentieth century, there is still no country in which women do as well as men on the measures proposed by the human development reports. As the lives of Vasanti and Jayamma illustrate, women continue to suffer pervasive discrimination with respect to all the major human capabilities, including life itself. So a feminist philosopher might not unreasonably judge that "history" does indeed "give rise to endless doubts about [her] hopes," and that the task that she attempts is indeed futile.

It seems to me that Kant is right. The large-scale practical task is too important not to be attempted. As long as there is no certainty that it will prove futile, it is morally valuable to entertain the hopeful thoughts about human goodness that will sustain us in our work.[67]

NOTES

1. Bhatt, interview, May 1988, reproduced in Kalima Rose, *Where Women Are Leaders: The SEWA Movement in India* (Delhi: Vistaar, 1992), 172–74.

2. The amount of maintenance allotted to destitute women under India's Criminal Procedure Code was 180 rupees per month in 1986.

3. Unlike Vasanti, Jayamma has already been studied in the development economics literature. See the chapter "Jayamma, the Brick Worker," in Leela Gulati, *Profiles in Female Poverty: A Study of Five Poor Working Women in Kerala* (Delhi: Hindustan, 1981); and Leela Gulati and Mitu Gulati, "Female Labour in the Unorganised Sector: The Brick Worker Revisited," *Economic and Political Weekly,* May 3, 1997, 968–71; also published in Martha Chen, ed., *Widows in India: Social Neglect and Public Action* (Delhi: Sage, 1998).

4. Throughout its existence, the institute operated largely on soft money. Our project was eventually funded primarily by the Swedish Development Agency (SEDA) under the auspices of Karl Tham, now minister for education in Sweden's Social-Democratic government.

5. See Kumari Jayawardena, *Feminism and Nationalism in the Third World* (London: Zed, 1986); and Jayawardena, *The White Woman's Other Burden: Western Women and South Asia during British Rule* (New York: Routledge, 1995).

6. The studies were published in the WIDER Series by the Clarendon Press, Oxford, as well as in a series of WIDER Working Papers.

7. A leading example was the Bangladeshi nutritional economist Siddiq Osmani; see Osmani, ed., *Nutrition and Poverty* (Oxford: Clarendon, 1990). Osmani, "On Some Controversies in the Measurement of Under-Nutrition," pp. 121–61, powerfully criticizes cultural relativism in nutrition science (the argument that "stunting" is a felicitous adaptation to local conditions). Another leading example is Iranian sociologist Valentine Moghadam, who coordinated women's programs; see Moghadam, *Modernizing Women: Gender and Social Change in the Middle East* (Boulder: Lynne Rienner, 1993); Moghadam, "Against Eurocentrism and Nativism," *Socialism and Democracy,* Fall-Winter 1989, 81–104; Moghadam, *Gender, Development, and Policy: Toward Equity and Empowerment*, UNU/WIDER Research-for-Action Series, November 1990.

8. Drèze and Sen, *Hunger and Public Action* (Oxford: Clarendon, 1989); Drèze and Sen, eds., *The Political Economy of Hunger*, 3 vols. (Oxford: Clarendon, 1990). Drèze, Sen, and A. Hussain, eds., *The Political Economy of Hunger: Selected Essays* (Oxford: Clarendon, 1995). The latter is a one-volume selection from the three-volume work.

9. Oxford: Clarendon, 1995.

10. Drèze and Sen, eds., *Indian Development: Selected Regional Perspectives* (New York: Oxford University Press, 1994).

11. See S. A. Marglin, *Growth, Distribution, and Prices* (Cambridge: Harvard University Press, 1984).

12. See Frédérique Apffel-Marglin, *Wives of the God King: The Rituals of the Devadasis of Puri* (Delhi: Oxford University Press, 1985), a work whose nostalgic and aestheticizing attitude to the practice of child temple prostitution prefigures many of the debates we had with the Marglins at WIDER.

13. See "Smallpox in Two Systems of Knowledge," in F. A. Marglin and S. A. Marglin, eds., *Dominating Knowledge: Development, Culture, and Resistance* (Oxford: Clarendon, 1990), 102–44.

14. See Sen, "Human Rights and Asian Values," *New Republic,* July 10–17, 1997; and Sen, "Tagore and His India," *New York Review of Books,* June 26, 1997, 55–63.

15. Published in Michael Krausz, ed., *Relativism: Interpretation and Confrontation* (Notre Dame, Ind.: University of Notre Dame Press, 1989), 299–325.

16. On the Aristotle-Marx relationship, see Nussbaum, "Nature, Function, and Capability: Aristotle on Political Distribution," *Oxford Studies in Ancient Philosophy,* supp. vol. 1 (1988), 145–84; reprinted in G. E. McCarthy, ed., *Marx and Aristotle* (Savage, Md.: Rowman & Littlefield, 1992), 175–212; and "Aristotle on Human Nature and the Foundations of Ethics," in J. E. J. Altham and Ross Harrison, eds., *World, Mind, and Ethics: Essays on the Ethical Philosophy of Bernard Williams* (Cambridge: Cambridge University Press, 1995), 86–131.

17. Central statements of the approach by Sen include "Equality of What?" in S. M. McMurrin, ed., *Tanner Lectures on Human Values*, no. 1 (Salt Lake City: University of Utah Press, 1980); reprinted in Sen, *Choice, Welfare, and Measurement* (Oxford: Basil Blackwell, 1982), 353–69; Sen, *Commodities and Capabilities* (Amsterdam: North-Holland, 1985); many papers in *Resources, Values, and Development* (Oxford: Blackwell, 1984); "Well-Being, Agency, and Freedom: The Dewey Lectures 1984," *Journal of Philosophy* 82 (1985): 169–221; Sen, "Capability and Well-Being," in Nussbaum and Sen, eds., *The Quality of Life* (Oxford: Clarendon, 1993), 30–53.

18. This idea, which is prominent in the ancient philosophers, has been developed by Jon Elster in *Sour Grapes* (Cambridge: Cambridge University Press, 1983), and by Sen in many places, for example, "Gender Inequality and Theories of Justice," in *Women, Culture, and Development*, 259–73.

19. However, Sen has also prominently used the approach as a measure of equality, and I have argued that systematic inequalities reflecting traditional social hierarchies are themselves cases of capability failure.

20. One might also mention Mill's development of an Aristotelian idea of human flourishing in chapter 3 of *On Liberty*. Mill's approach is perfectionist, aimed at functioning as a goal, whereas my approach aims at capability as goal in order to construct a type of political liberalism.

21. "Women and Cultural Universals," in Nussbaum, *Sex and Social Justice* (New York: Oxford University Press, 1998), and *Women and Human Development* (Cambridge: Cambridge University Press, 2000). Sen has not taken a stand on this issue; in "Freedoms and Needs" he appears to endorse a comprehensive rather than a political form of liberalism.

22. See the critique of "binary thinking" as peculiarly Western, in S. A. Marglin, "Toward the Decolonization of the Mind," in Marglin and Marglin, *Dominating Knowledge,* 1–28.

23. See S. A. Marglin, "Losing Touch: The Cultural Conditions of Worker Accommodation and Resistance," in Marglin and Marglin, *Dominating Knowledge,* 217–82.

24. For an account of some of these moments, see Nussbaum, "Human Functioning and Social Justice: In Defense of Aristotelian Essentialism," in *Political Theory* 20 (1992): 202–46; and Nussbaum, "Human Capabilities, Female Human Beings," in M. Nussbaum and J. Glover, eds., *Women, Culture, and Development* (Oxford: Clarendon, 1995), 61—104. Sen's and my paper was refused publication in the Marglins' conference volume, since it did not "fit" with the orientation of the other papers (it certainly didn't), and it was later published elsewhere.

25. This experience led me to focus on the importance of the study of non-Western traditions in undergraduate liberal arts curricula: see Nussbaum, *Cultivating Humanity: A Classical Defense of Reform in Liberal Education* (Cambridge: Harvard University Press, 1997).

26. See Sen, "Freedoms and Needs," *New Republic,* January 10–17, 1994; Nussbaum, "The Good as Discipline, the Good as Freedom," in D. Crocker and T. Linden, eds., *Ethics of Consumption: The Good Life, Justice, and Global Stewardship* (Lanham, Md.: Rowman & Littlefield, 1998), 312–41.

27. For a clear account of our approaches and their differences, see David Crocker, "Functioning and Capability: The Foundations of Sen's and Nussbaum's Development Ethic, Part I," *Political Theory* 20 (1992): 584–612; and "Part II" in *Women, Culture, and Development*, 153–98.

28. Although the 1987 conference group consisted primarily of philosophers and economists, we also included two Scandinavian sociologists who had been using a plural metric of life quality similar to the one we were inclined to support.

29. For just two valuable recent examples of such an approach, see John L. and Jean Comaroff, *Of Revelation and Revolution: The Dialectics of Modernity on a South African Frontier* (Chicago: University of Chicago Press; vol. 1, 1991, vol. 2, 1997); and, showing division and conflict even in a community generally imagined as especially peaceful and homogeneous, Fred Kniss, *Disquiet in the Land: Cultural*

Conflict in American Mennonite Communities (New Brunswick, N.J.: Rutgers University Press, 1997).

30. See A. Sen, "Gender and Cooperative Conflicts," in I. Tinker, ed., *Persistent Inequalities* (New York: Oxford University Press, 1991), 123–49; Partha Dasgupta, *An Inquiry Into Well-Being and Destitution* (Oxford: Clarendon, 1993), chap. 11. For other useful examples of bargaining approaches, see Bina Agarwal, *A Field of One's Own: Gender and Land Rights in South Asia* (Cambridge: Cambridge University Press, 1994); and Agarwal, "'Bargaining' and Gender Relations: Within and Beyond the Household," FCND Discussion Paper, International Food Policy Research Institute, March 1997; Shelly Lundberg and Robert A. Pollak, "Bargaining and Distribution in Marriage," *Journal of Economic Perspectives* 10 (1996): 139–58; L. Chen, E. Huq, and S. D'Souza, "Sex Bias in the Family Allocation of Food and Health Care in Rural Bangladesh," *Population and Development Review* 7 (1981): 55–70.

31. Sociologists Robert Eriksson, Erik Allardt, Nancy Chodorow, and Valentine Moghadam, anthropologist Martha Chen, political theorists Susan Moller Okin and Seyla Benhabib, economists John Roemer, Jean Drèze, Amartya Sen, and (in a related project) Partha Dasgupta all played a role in our first two conferences; the third included, in addition, health policy and medical experts. Other WIDER projects involved still more social scientists from other disciplines.

32. For this reason, I argue in *Cultivating Humanity* that, although in principle the abilities of "Socratic self-examination" that citizens need could be imparted through courses in many different disciplines, in practice this will best be done by courses in philosophy.

33. For my own understanding of the Socratic elenchus and its contribution, see my review essay of Gregory Vlastos's "Socratic Studies," *Journal of Philosophy* 94 (1997): 27–45.

34. See Nussbaum, "Flawed Foundations: The Philosophical Critique of (a Particular Type of) Economics," *University of Chicago Law Review* 64 (1997): 1197–1214.

35. Both Sen and I argue that respect for choice should lead us to make capability, rather than functioning, the political goal; by contrast, perfectionist liberalisms such as those of John Stuart Mill and Joseph Raz (*The Morality of Freedom* [Oxford: Clarendon, 1986]) prefer to construe the goal in terms of functioning.

36. I argue for three distinct types of capabilities that need to figure in the approach: *basic capabilities*, or the innate equipment of human beings that enables them, with sufficient support and care, to attain higher-level capabilities; *internal capabilities*, or states of the person that would, in suitable circumstances, prove sufficient for the exercise of the relevant functioning; and *combined capabilities*, or the internal state combined with suitable external circumstances for the exercise of the function. (For example, a woman who has had some education and training but is threatened with physical violence if she leaves the house to look for work has the internal but not the combined capability to seek employment outside the house.) Politics should aim at the production of combined capabilities. See "The Good as Discipline" for the most recent statement of this position.

37. *Eudemian Ethics* 1216a30–39: "For from what is said truly but not clearly, as we advance we will also get clarity, always moving from what is usually said in a jumbled fashion to a more perspicuous view. There is a difference in every inquiry between arguments that are said in a philosophical way and those that are not. Hence we must not think that it is superfluous for the political person to engage in the sort of reflection that makes perspicuous not only the 'that' but also the 'why': for this is

the contribution of the philosopher in each area." Aristotle connects understanding the "why" closely to the task of giving definitions and accounts.

38. See *Cultivating Humanity*, chap. 1.

39. Nussbaum and Sen, eds., *The Quality of Life* (Oxford: Clarendon, 1993).

40. Dan Brock's "Quality of Life Measures in Health Care and Medical Ethics" is a fine example of such clear writing (and of research specifically responsive to our commission). Charles Taylor's "Explanation and Practical Reason," though not originally commissioned for our volume (since Taylor replaced another participant at a late date), is another extremely lucid and readable paper. It is interesting that both of these authors have spent time in practical politics and therefore know from experience what sort of writing will be effective.

41. Chen is a highly experienced fieldworker and social scientist who has spent over half her life in India and is fluent in three modern Indian languages, as well as Sanskrit. She worked closely with Jean Drèze on a research project involving widows and was therefore well acquainted with our work at WIDER. Because she understands the philosophical concepts and yet has experience in fieldwork that we lack, she has been and continues to be an invaluable intermediary. She is also an eloquent writer with the rare ability to let real women's voices emerge clearly. See Martha Alter Chen, *A Quiet Revolution: Women in Transition in Rural Bangladesh* (Cambridge, Mass.: Schenkman, 1983).

42. This was not easy, since philosophy, unlike economics, is not an international profession; it lacks a common language and a common set of paradigms. Nor are the reigning paradigms especially revealing of indigenous thought: for example, one philosopher from Brazil who was highly recommended to us turned out to be a graduate of UC–Santa Cruz who spoke entirely in the abstract language of French philosophy. We attempted to find people with whom we spoke a sufficiently common philosophical language that we could communicate reasonably well, and who at the same time related their general claims to their own cultural and religious traditions, and who had done practical political work in addition to their philosophical work. In this way, we integrated into the project Roop Rekha Verma, Nkiru Nzegwu, Xiaorong Li, and Margarita Valdés (who had already been a commentator at our previous conference); we were ably assisted by the fine work of Moghadam, who had recently been appointed to reside at WIDER year-round, coordinating women's projects.

43. Hilary and Ruth Anna Putnam began from Dewey, Seyla Benhabib from Habermas, Jonathan Glover from a type of utilitarianism, Onora O'Neill and Roop Rekha Verma from a type of Kantianism, quite a few of us from a type of liberal Aristotelianism already familiar from the prior project.

44. I continue to feel this a major gap, which I am attempting to address in my own current work. See, for example, "Religion and Women's Human Rights," in *Religion and Contemporary Liberalism*, ed. Paul Weithman (Notre Dame, Ind.: University of Notre Dame Press, 1997), 93–137; Saul M. Olyan and Martha C. Nussbaum, eds., *Sexual Orientation and Human Rights in American Religious Discourse* (New York: Oxford University Press, 1998).

45. Further complications involved Finnish politics, since a leading candidate for the presidency of Finland (who eventually won the election) is a close friend of Jayawardena; his political opponents saw blackening WIDER as a way of scoring political points prior to the election.

46. David Crocker does related work at the Center for Philosophy and Public Policy at the University of Maryland. He has focused on the ethics of consumption and

global stewardship; see Crocker and Toby Linden, eds., *Ethics of Consumption: The Good Life, Justice, and Global Stewardship* (Lanham, Md.: Rowman & Littlefield, 1998), which includes several WIDER colleagues as contributors. Glover recently became director of the Institute for Law and Medical Ethics at King's College, London; Valentine Moghadam is director of women's studies at Illinois State University, where she continues her work on women and modernization.

47. See Sen, "More Than 100 Million Women Are Missing," *New York Review of Books* 37 (1990): 61–66; Sen, "Fertility and Coercion," *University of Chicago Law Review* 63 (1996): 1035–61; Sen, "Population: Delusion and Reality," *New York Review of Books,* September 22, 1994; Sen, "Tagore and His India"; Sen, "Human Rights and Asian Values."

48. See Sen, "Freedoms and Needs"; Nussbaum, "The Good as Discipline, the Good as Freedom"; Nussbaum, "Capabilities and Human Rights."

49. Dasgupta, *An Inquiry into Well-Being and Destitution* (Oxford: Clarendon, 1993), 129–31; the proposal is based on an index developed by C. L. Taylor and D. A. Jodice, *World Handbook of Political and Social Indicators* (New Haven: Yale University Press, 1983).

50. Santiniketan is in West Bengal, about three hours by train from Calcutta.

51. The trip also included many meetings with scholars and activists, who were in various ways of great help to me. These included Muslim political theorist Zoya Hasan, who writes about internal diversity within Islamic culture; economist Bina Agarwal, who writes on gender and land rights, developing a bargaining model of the family; feminist lawyer Indira Jaising, who runs the Lawyers Cooperative, a group that takes on sex equality and sexual harassment cases and publishes a journal devoted to issues of sex equality in the law; anthropologist Veena Das, who writes about resistance to the dominant culture from a viewpoint sympathetic to cultural relativism; publisher Ritu Menon, director of the feminist press Kali, who later organized a lecture for me to present my ideas at the end of my trip; Romila Thapar, a distinguished historian of India; Patricia Uberoi, a sociologist who works on the Indian family; Devaki Jain, an activist and scholar affiliated with the government women's association; Renana Jhabvala of the Self-Employed Women's Association; Antara Dev Sen, a journalist with the *Hindustan Times* who reports on women's issues; Abha Bhaiya, director of Jagori, a project that works with domestic violence in the slums. I note that women in India do extremely well in the academy, better than in any other nation I know, in terms of occupying top positions in a variety of fields. On the other hand, philosophy is an underdeveloped and low-prestige field, and none of my feminist contacts was a philosopher.

52. I also visited a very similar program in Bombay, the Annapurna Mahila Mandel. Directed by Prema Purao, a former freedom fighter from Goa, the program organizes women who make a living cooking for male laborers who come to the city without their families. The project sells them wholesale grain, grants credit, and operates a variety of social programs, including one that gives job training to daughters of prostitutes, so that they may have the choice to avoid that occupation.

53. See Drèze and Sen, *India*, 64, 140–78; on p. 142 they note that the sex ratio is influenced by male out-migration, but that even adjusted for this, the ratio is above unity.

54. We were also helped greatly by Sardamoni, an eminent historian of Kerala, who spent a lot of time with us discussing why women's position is different there.

55. This lovely plant, introduced by foreign visitors, has overgrown and snarled up the local waterways. Jayamma's husband, a boatman, had to retire early because it got too hard to propel the boat through the tangles.

56. See Susan Okin, *Justice, Gender, and the Family* (New York: Basic Books, 1989).

57. See "The Feminist Critique of Liberalism," a Lindley Lecture (University Press of Kansas, 1997), in Nussbaum, *Sex and Social Justice*.

58. See, for example, the valuable treatment of these notions in Avishai Margalit, *The Decent Society* (Cambridge, Mass.: Harvard University Press, 1996).

59. See Nkiru Nzegwu, "Recovering Igbo Tradition: A Case for Indigenous Women's Organizations in Development," in *Woman, Culture, and Development*, 444–66.

60. See, for a typical example, Richard Posner, *The Economics of Justice* (Cambridge: Harvard University Press, 1981).

61. For a more extensive treatment, see Nussbaum, "Flawed Foundations."

62. See Nussbaum, "'Lawyer for Humanity': Theory and Practice in Ancient Political Thought," *Nomos* 37 (1995): 181–215.

63. Karl Marx, *Doctoral Dissertation: Difference between the Democritean and Epicurean Philosophy of Nature*, in Karl Marx and Friedrich Engels, *Collected Works* (London: Lawrence & Wishard, 1975), 1:85.

64. See Dan W. Brock on this topic, in *Life and Death* (Cambridge: Cambridge University Press, 1993).

65. See on this point John Rawls, *Political Liberalism*, introduction to the paper edition (New York: Columbia University Press, 1996), p. lxii; see also Nussbaum, "Why Practice Needs Ethical Theory: Particularism, Principle, and Bad Behavior," in *The Path of the Law in the Twentieth Century*, ed. S. Burton (Cambridge: Cambridge University Press, 1998).

66. "On the Common Saying: 'This May Be True in Theory, but It Does Not Apply in Practice,'" in *Kant: Political Writings*, ed. Hans Reiss, trans. H. B. Nisbet, 2d ed. (Cambridge: Cambridge University Press, 1991), 89. I have altered the final word of the translation, substituting "people" for his "men." The German has a substantivized adjective, "the right-thinking ones."

67. I am grateful to John Deigh and Cass Sunstein for comments on an earlier draft of this chapter.

13

Wit Irony Fun Games

Saul Bellow

My topic in this chapter is fun and games. And invariably the fun goes out of comedy as soon as you lay a theorist's hand on it. The subject for obvious reasons defies definition—it is diabolically resistant to formulation. Something like fifty years ago (possibly sixty) I read some books that analyzed wit, humor, laughter and found that they had little to tell me. From the philosopher Bergson I learned that we are moved to laugh when the living creature momentarily resembles an artificial one, or is helplessly subject to the laws of physics. A man slips on a banana peel and when he falls he resembles a bundle of sticks and causes onlookers to laugh. According to Elias Canetti *(Crowds and Power)* we laugh when someone falls because of our dormant cannibalistic tendencies. In showing our teeth to the sprawling accident victim we notify him that we could eat him if we liked but that civilized persons no longer do that sort of thing. Canetti was a gifted writer but a grim one. Even a comic genius like the Victorian Samuel Butler has written that when a mother says to her infant "I could eat you up" she is prompted by an impulse from her primitive nature to ingest what she loves.

Sigmund Freud also wrote a book about the comic sense. He claimed that wit brought relief from the rigors of repression by jokes or slips of the tongue and functioned as a sort of countermadness, a small garden within the mangrove swamp of the irrational unconscious. Wit is seen as the court fool of Id, the King.

As you can gather from the samples I have submitted, highly accredited intellectuals have done comedy the honor of taking it seriously. Freud's *Wit and the Unconscious* contains many excellent jokes, and even some of the interpretations and commentaries are—for Freud—lighthearted.

With this we abandon the quest for definitions and turn instead to our earliest experiences with comedy. When do we begin to respond to it? To this question the most sensible answer is clearly a personal one. My parents were frequently amused by the antics and outcries of their children, or by the unconscious charm, perhaps, of their antics. My eldest brother loved to clown. He was ludicrously overweight, a slovenly eater who dunked bread in his cocoa cup. Frequently scolded, disciplined, slapped by an immigrant father struggling for survival in the New World, the poor greedy brother masked his rage and shot comical looks to the rest of us. He was a huge kid in short pants and a striped jersey pulled over his provoking belly, a misfit, something of a monster. For that very reason, perhaps, he was greatly loved by our mother.

But these kitchen scenes were given a comical spin by the willed idiocy of the stare that went beyond the enraged father to the rest of the kids. This defiant brother, in retrospect, was in his untutored way a humorist and took a sort of angry pleasure in these confrontations over the kitchen table. It was this same brother who brought home books—boys adventure stories by Henty, Street & Smith Nick Carter detective novels. He and I also read the funny papers, of course. There were no comic books in the early twenties, only funnies from the Sunday papers.

In the children's ward of the Royal Victoria Hospital, where some months of my eighth year were spent, there was not much else to read. Raggedy Ann and Little Lord Fauntleroy could not hope to compete with the violent colors and the sensational burlesques—the huge grins, the fat noses and piercing whiskers, the chases, the punches, the kicks, the *Bams* and *Ouches*, and the *Take Thats!* You may not recognize the names of the cartoon heroes and the girls they loved. They were Slim Jim, Mutt and Jeff, Boob McNutt, Happy Hooligan who carried an empty tin can on his head, Maggie and Jiggs—an Irish couple, he with a top hat, she with a rolling pin, Moon Mullins who wore a derby hat and his little brother Kayo who wore a smaller derby, shared Moon's bedroom, and slept in a dresser drawer. Boob McNutt, overcoming Shrimp Smith his enemy, ties him hand and foot and stows him in the overhead baggage rack on the train, saying, "You're the only man in the world that I can lick."

This meant that even I, a puny child and hospital patient, *could* lick someone.

These funnies took me from the family circle and the narrow neighborhood streets; they carried me into the life of the country—of the entire English-speaking continent. There was no reason why I should not be a part of it. My small mind was added to the millions of other minds that constituted "the public." The greens, the yellows, the boisterous reds of the funnies that overflowed the features, the figures, and the frames also acted as the solvent of many limitations. The fun of all these grotesque absurdities made you feel democracy as a sort of joke in which everybody participated.

"This is a nation of jokes," says a character of Ralph Ellison's. He adds toward the end of his narrative, "some of the things [he] said were amusing but true. And perhaps their truth lay precisely in their being seen humorously."

Wit, this seems to say, is like the forked branch of the water witch or dowser; it will lead us to the truth.

Abraham Lincoln, who prefaced the discussion of very grave questions with lively back-home anecdotes or parables, offended the clergy and the newspaper publishers of the eastern seaboard with his unstatesmanlike jokes. The Civil War was no joke, certainly.

But it would not be too far-fetched to ponder whether Lincoln's parables and circuit-riding quips might not have been indispensable preludes to his wide and deep mental contrapuntal constructions. It must have been clear to everyone that the casualties his generals reported made him suffer deeply.

But I must check my tendency to ramble.

The Chicago of the twenties in which I grew up was dominated by machine politicians, lawyers, judges, and officials. The bootleggers' gang wars did not affect the man in the street—civilians looked on from a safe distance. The average reader followed the scandals and murders in the papers and enjoyed Chicago's national and international reputation as a gang city, the home and base of Al Capone. The mayor, Big Bill Thompson, was himself a clown, and the newspapers made the most of the moonshine wars. They reported them as if they were covering a visiting circus.

It was assumed as a matter of course by the man in the street that public life was corrupt, that the courts were venal, the police were on the take, that city and county employees had their hands out, that decent simpletons were Johns or marks—that life was a racket. The muckraking writers of the early years of the century—Lincoln Steffens, Ida Tarbell, Upton Sinclair—were followed, after the Great War, by the debunkers. Historians like W. E. Woodward demythologized our great men, lifted up their togas to show us their feet of clay. They told us that George Washington was pompous, that U. S. Grant was a heavy drinker, that Teddy Roosevelt was an exhibitionist and Woodrow Wilson in Versailles at the peace conference was a long-faced virgin surrounded by whores. This last metaphor came from John Dos Passos's U.S.A. trilogy. Dos Passos, a highly gifted novelist, was not primarily a debunker. He was a populist and the currents of populist skepticism eroded the prestige of the founders of great fortunes, the Rockefellers and Harrimans, the master politicians, the famous revivalists, the top brass everywhere, the Jim Crow South: the sex scandals of sugar daddies and the ladies they kept in love nests (the celebrated possibly Mr. Browning and Peaches, the darling of his life).

I wish I could transmit the flavor of the *Police Gazette*'s pink pages or of twenties tabloids—one can occasionally still taste it in the novels of Sinclair Lewis, especially *Babbit* and *Elmer Gantry*. It occurs, earlier, in the stories of O. Henry: the hicks in their long johns and the grifters and pitchmen who preyed on them. I may be overdoing the skeptical wise guy twenties, but through the daily papers in syndicated columns they were read by hundreds of thousands, perhaps millions, of schoolchildren. William Randolph Hearst himself seemed to have a taste for them, and in Chicago there were two Hearst papers. Everybody followed Odd McIntyre and, in the *Examiner*, a cracked, ingenious humorist named Ted Cook. In his Kookoos column I discovered the haikus of a Japanese poet whose name was T. S. Nakano. Cook's parodies led me at the age of thirteen or fourteen to Eliot, who was himself a humorist, in part, and a satirist.

In the streets, in shops, on the trains, in daily contacts there was an agreeable sociability—banter, an exchange of wisecracks between passengers on the elevated trains of Chicago, or with the lady in the change booth beside the turnstile whose name you were never to know. Wit was the nonideological bond, the scarcely conscious ingredient in the transitory contacts. I see these contacts now as an expression of democratic mutuality—epiphenomena deriving from wit offerings of well-disposed casual strangers and floating in the streets and shops.

Some of the leading intellectuals of the time were gifted comedians, too. That made a substantial difference in the mental life of the country. The chief comedian of the twenties and thirties was H. L. Mencken, editor of the *American Mercury*. His gift for invective was remarkably funny. He referred to the average man as *boobus Americanus*. He detested clergymen and college professors, Babbits; he gave short shrift to men of letters, members of the Congress—the top brass everywhere, prohibitionists, Southern Bourbons—all the vain idols of the crowd. No vulgarian, Mencken wrote first-rate appreciations of Theodore Dreiser and other American and English novelists. He wrote about Nietzsche; he was familiar with Beethoven and Wagner. In politics he was, generally, a right-winger. German by descent, he sympathized with the kaiser. He detested Prohibition, he wrote brilliantly about William Jennings Bryan, the representative of the Bible Belt and of creationism at the Scopes Trial. He wrote on the woman question, on Nietzsche; he was a fine literary critic. Mencken's *American Mercury* showed adolescents of my generation how to reject the false teachings of the booboisie (and, I am afraid, many true ones as well). Most of all, we learned from him how to take an independent critical stand against the Press, the Church, the Schools, and the Party—against Vulgarity. What we got from Mencken was mainly the idea that dissent was possible and that its sharpest weapons were language and wit. The high school children of the twentieth century were not then aware that Mencken and his *American Mercury* continued the work of Thomas Paine—of Voltaire and Diderot and Rousseau in the eighteenth century and that these built on the thought of their seventeenth-century predecessors.

A more recent writer, one of our own contemporaries, has observed that the eighteenth-century rationalists, unable to prove that revelation—as in revealed religion—had not actually taken place, tried to dismiss it with satire. They poked fun at it and hoped, by so doing, to divert our attention from a great defect, a giant hole in their position.

Perhaps this accounts for the prevalence of comedy in the present age—one more consequence of the attempt to win the world for rationality. But as the world changes, we witness strange shifts and metamorphoses in the comic, which is now called on from many unexpected quarters.

"Religion," says Peter Berger of Boston University in a lecture titled "Humor as a Religious Phenomenon," puts in question "the paramount reality" of the empirical world. Humor, according to Professor Berger, "opens up, however briefly, a different world, the world of the comic, which is counterfactual and meta-empirical. That is, of course, why humor flourishes in situations where there is every reason to seek an escape, for example under tyrannical regimes or in wartime. . . . It conjures up islands within an allegedly 'serious' world, magically different and comforting in this difference. Humor allows us to take brief island vacations from our 'serious' concerns. Humor is also dangerous, because there is a temptation to go on vacation permanently. . . . If large numbers did, social order would collapse. That is why society creates enclaves within which the comic is permitted to exist, enclaves both in space and time—within theaters or cabarets, or for the duration of the carnival or the time it takes to tell a joke."

All this is true enough, though truer perhaps in former times than it is now. Ours has been a century for testing, or tampering with, definitions. This tampering, more often than not, amounts to a curious comic reduction in rank. What I have in mind is one description of a Nazi slave-labor camp. It is described by David Rousset, a French novelist, one of a small number of survivors, who tells us that "the camps were the realm of King Ubu." King Ubu is the obese, obscene hero of a play by a sixteen-year-old Alfred Jarry, produced in Paris in 1896. It has been described as an *Alice in Wonderland* written not by a Victorian mathematician but by a gang of vicious dead-end kids. Ramon Guthrie, author of the introduction to Rousset's book, writes that Ubu is "the Pope of unreason, of a grisly unreason devoid of any real merriment. Ubu, with his gross lust to destroy, his retinue of bureaucrats . . . his Debraining machine—'for scooping out brains'—is so complete a personification of Fascism as a whole that even physically . . . he is a composite portrait of Himmler, Goering and Adolf Hitler."

"These concentration camps are the realm of King Ubu," says Rousset. "Buchenwald lives under the sign of a monstrous whimsicality, a tragic buffoonery. In the first gray of dawn, the unreal platforms under the white glare of floodlights, the SS swaggering in high boots, gripping their rubber bludgeons, the barking dogs straining at their supple leashes. The men crouching ready to jump from the freight cars, blinded by blows that catch them off guard, reel back, stumble against each other . . . tottering on their bare feet in the dirty snow, hobbled with fear, their stiff, nightmare gestures like rickety automatons."

There is a discovery here: Death's victims are, or can be, a comic subject, a burlesque, an entertainment, a game. This is not the "comic relief" of the gravedigger in *Hamlet* nor of the gatekeeper in *Macbeth,* but the mammoth playfulness of the German conquerors of Poland and then the rest of Eastern Europe. This was a game played with doomed people. Frequently their humanity and their lives were comically taken away from them. During World War II this was done in Poland, in the Ukraine, in the Balkans. It was even a

French phenomenon. But originally it had a specifically German character. The underlying idea (if it may legitimately be called an idea) is that the Jews are not quite human, and their evil has a biological base. They belong to a subspecies. They are hostile and dangerous, dominate by money and intrigue, cunning and intrigue. Jews must therefore be eliminated. If they are treated as grotesque, we need not suffer when we destroy them.

In many respects this is a "modern" or "European" approach: it has an experimental, pseudoscientific side. It has a tendency (a weakness) for trying out anything and everything that can be imagined. In modern life, everything conceivable may also be feasible. As soon as it is thought it has to be done. Whatever is imaginable demands that we attempt to realize it. To lift it into reality, to give the process a scientific rationale and an administrative character.

Linked with this demand is the modern condition called nihilism. Nihilism is loosely defined as seeing no reason why you should not do what you wish to do. No moral prohibition from the past has the power to prevent its being done, for your actions are meaningless by any standard of meaning. You have rejected all standards. There is only a recollection of former religious or ethical ideals that seem to have no other application or use except to be rejected. But there is one more function and it has significant bearing on the subject: nihilism is a principal source of comedy in contemporary fiction and poetry. We call on our available recollections of art or religion or virtue, or on ideas of, say, love—ideas that prevailed until recently and now summon us to teach them.

A good fictional example of the comical possibilities of these questionable residues of past standards is found in L.-F. Céline's novel *Voyage au bout de la nuit*. Toward the end of the journey, Ferdinand, the narrator (definitely nonheroic), witnesses a strange confrontation between his idol, a man named Robinson, and a young woman who demands that Robinson say "I love you." When Robinson refuses she pulls a gun from her pocketbook and shoots him dead. Robinson, according to one commentator, *believes* in something and this belief (in the truth) sets him above Ferdinand's own nihilism. In this strange turn of belief there is no limit to the ugliness of the human condition, and the odd virtue associated with this condition is "authenticity." The "authentic" man rejects all consolation as false. "Hell is—other people," said Sartre.

Nihilistic authenticity has driven out Rousseau's "sincerity," which today is seen as Romantic foolishness. Brush away the dust and the debris of three centuries and you find the basic truth, according to Hobbes, about the condition of man in the state of nature.

I have spoken about these matters because they force themselves into this discussion. My own attitude toward them is that they are not or should not be the writer's direct concern. Cassius and Brutus are right to ask what poets, "these jigging fools," have to do with the wars—with the way things actually are. The proper sphere of novelists is the sphere of the phenomena.

We do not lay down the law—we speak, or should speak, of the way things are. The less philosophy the better, from the writer's and also the reader's point of view.

But philosophy has infiltrated the arts, and the arts have run over into our private lives. You can see this when you direct your gaze toward the events of the new millennium—a scene of nihilism, unmistakably. People are turning to society in their quest for things to do that are lacking in meaning. They find daily examples or suggestions of this in the newspapers and on TV.

Activities meaningless in themselves are considered to make a statement. They are hip with a radical edge. They seem at times to prefer these activities to be collective and preverbal. The young people participate in night-long "raves" and gather in large crowds and mill about till dawn to electronic "music." This is an aspect of contemporary life that we cannot avoid considering. The rave dancers, I have been told, drift from city to city. They take night jobs in convenience stores and "crash"—in the term we used long ago—in flats rented by the week or month. Although they "hang out" and practice a kind of mutual aid, lasting intimacies are seldom formed.

There are frequent moves between the civilized state and the state of nature. In these, one actor is both Caliban and Prospero. A good example of this may be the example of Larry Flynt, the editor of *Hustler* and the protagonist of the widely shown and much discussed film *The People vs. Larry Flynt.* I quote from the *Wall Street Journal* review of this movie (December 27, 1996). "Who would have thought that Milos Forman and his writers, Scott Alexander and Larry Karazhewski, would make a largely entertaining if manipulative film about a scummy, self-promoting smut-peddler and his punked-out druggy wife? Yet they did. They found a shrewd pretext—the publisher of *Hustler* magazine as a poster boy for the first amendment—and ran with it all the way to the Supreme Court . . . after a would-be assassin's bullet condemns him to pain-racked life in a wheel chair, he swings wildly between popping pills in his fortified bedroom, which resembles a bank-vault with bolsters, and mocking various judges and prosecutors by showing up in court in a combat helmet and a flak jacket, or with an American flag rampant on a field of blue polyester, or in a diaper made from an American flag. (We get to see the real-life Larry Flynt in a cameo as a judge in Cincinnati, and it's pretty chilling: real life has not been kind.)"

But "real life" is nourished in part by this mixed diet of civil liberties and pornography. Pornography, in the argument made in this film before the U.S. Supreme Court is, when everything is said and done, a good thing, insofar as it protects our liberties by the test it poses for the Constitution. Porn is made to look like one of the pillars of the First Amendment. And as for the profitability of obscenity, that confirms somehow its high political importance. It may be bad for kids but it is good for law and order.

What this film brings out is that our democratic ideals of liberty and equality, of free speech and of justice require that we remember that boys will be boys—more particularly good old boys from the heart of the country who are free to commute between their natural and their civil rights. The argument is made, heavily and repeatedly, that sexual repression is a bottomless danger. Nations that stifle the sexual exuberance of lusty young men become fascistic. The Holocaust itself, the film argues, was produced by an unnatural Puritanism as well as by a lack of disrespect for authority. A true American is not intimidated by uniforms or decorous courtrooms and will defy judges in black robes who have the power to shut you up and put you behind grills and prison bars. Not to be intimidated is therefore the plain duty of a good old boy and true American. This is easily and naturally understood by good old boys and good old girls. They understand that the boys need access to girls, and that the girls have much the same need. To interfere with this is to block the channels of freedom. Lastly, the fairy-tale prosperity we enjoy is simply the reward of our sexual sanity or enlightenment. All these assumptions are at the heart of our distinctively American contribution to comedy.

I speak of a distinctively American contribution to comedy. But all over the modern industrial world writers are, and have been for the last two centuries, comedians. You will of course be listing the classics. God forbid that we should fail to give *Anna Karenina* or *Moby Dick* the full measure of respect they deserve. But the odd fact is that by a very wide margin most novels have been written by ironists, satirists, and comedians. Even in *The Brothers Karamazov* the murdered father, a great grotesque, overshadows both the passionate Dmitri and the holy Alyosha. Only Ivan approaches the old man in stature. So that even in this great tragic work comedy is irrepressible. In *Othello, Macbeth,* or *Lear* there are no such comic characters.

Two of the most terrible wars in history were fought in my lifetime. The second ended with the dropping of the atomic bomb. So that the triumph of the comic—or would it be better to refer to it as the prevalence or persistence of comedy or a cover of laughter—is certainly paradoxical. I have often gone round and round this question, inspecting it. And although I am as fertile in explanations as other writers, I have failed to come up with an acceptable explanation. The usual suspects appear but have to be released. The most usual and most detainable is of course democracy. Democracy is the most arrestable—the commonest, vividest, most debased, the most problematic. I am tempted to believe that there is a nucleus of comedy in the middle of democracy, especially mass democracy, and a wild inventiveness is present in the character of modern democratic man. There is also a notable drop in his valuation. By the standards of earlier ages modern democratic man has no stature to speak of. But he understands well enough that he belongs nevertheless to the human family, and it is that family that made the transformation of the earth possible by its discoveries.

"But humanity is never more sphinx-like than when it is expressing itself," wrote Rebecca West in her brilliant study of the novel *(The Court and the Castle)*. I would suggest putting it a little differently: "Or when it is presented by an artist as expressing itself."

T. S. Eliot (hisself) observed that poetry is a kind of higher amusement. By which he means, perhaps, that it is a legacy from a higher past which throws its rich beam on a degraded present. It is for the few. The many never see it.

But I already made my point in mentioning Old Karamazov. The modern writer, when he portrays modern man, quickly learns that modern man has chosen to conceive himself as a compound of comical elements. The boldest comedians are the ones who, like Old Karamazov, have revised all social and traditional fictions in the clear light of first principles as *they* see them.

Since the mid-nineteenth century, novelists and poets, too, are deeply concerned about the survival of art and artists in a commercial civilization and their tendency is to charge the language richly and multiply their allusions. There is a lost-cause or last-stand atmosphere about some of them. A novel like Flaubert's *Sentimental Education* exhibits a perfection of language and a skill in every detail of the execution that underlines the rift between the wealth of artistic means and the poverty of the human material. The "best" writers of Flaubert's century, and of our own (Joyce, Eliot, etc.), tell us that beauty continues to be made but that the obstacles to its making are very great and that the makers—and their small and shrinking public—are surrounded by a deepening nihilistic darkness. Joyce, in a language that only initiates and connoisseurs can read, describes the kitchen in which L. Bloom fries his pork kidney, and the privy where he sits down with his newspaper. He attaches his great art to the small persons kicking around Dublin on their quotidian errands.

We who follow them out to the cemetery, back again for lunch et cetera, enjoy the comic contrast between the richness of the art and the Chaplinesque little man ad-solicitor-father-husband-cuckold-masturbator. And this is what our masterpieces are like. We understand too well for comfort the contrasts between a consciousness swollen with the knowledge accumulated over decades of reading and reflection and the inadequacy of the company we have to keep—knowledge just ain't power. At bottom it is just another form of helplessness. . . .

—When I consider the heavens, the work of Thy fingers
What is man that Thou should'st be mindful of him?

Some writers tell us that their art, the way they write, gives the only ethical standard we are likely to see. But this too is comedy. Another way to put it is that we are invited to join in the pleasure of seeing the modern world as artists of the greatest power and scope see it.

There is something in this. But you can't expect serious persons to refrain from asking for more.

Well, serious people perhaps needn't be as serious as all that. As I see the subject we address, their seriousness has been compromised by a vast transformation of the "reality." To be consistent with my view of it, I have framed the word *reality* in quotation marks. Anyway, these quotes will soon wither away.

My aim is to bring to your attention that this "reality" has undergone a series of tremendous transformations. We have been so busy adapting ourselves, bailing out the flood of overwhelming transformations, that there has been little or no opportunity to understand them.

Let me begin with Ortega y Gasset, the Spanish author of *The Revolt of the Masses* (a charming book), who argued that ordinary workaday mankind doesn't distinguish clearly between nature and human invention, and that it views electricity (I choose this one item for the purpose of illustration) as something that comes on when you push a button. It doesn't see a difference, really, between the sunlight and the ceiling fixtures. To him these are free or nearly free commodities, like our drinking water. An educated person understands that these are two quite different things.

Ortega gives the educated person far too much credit. Of course we know that there are generators in which various fuels are transformed into energy and stored, and so on. But having said that, how far have we gotten? Not very far at all. Our education is more or less a humbug. We have learned how to conceal the vast extent of our ignorance. Suppose we consider the word *metabolism*. What is it? Well, metabolism consists of the breaking down and transformation of matter ingested by the body and its utilization, excretion, and so on. The true fact, however, is that metabolism is a mystery. Up to a point we can describe it but we cannot account for it.

Lecturers used to tell undergraduates in my day that anabolism and catabolism were the breaking down and the building up of tissues, and I suppose the satisfaction this gave us was similar to what was felt by children learning the catechism. The children were put at ease about a deep mystery. It was not then as evident as it is now that we were learning what it was to fake knowledge.

Fake knowledge, as I presently understood, was a comical subject. But it was not the biology lecturer who taught me this. I learned it in a French course from Molière's phony, fast-talking "progressive" doctor who listened to his patient's heart on the right side saying, when the invalid sets him straight, "Nous avons change tout cela."

A degree of progress is revealed when we are able to laugh at our ignorance of certain mysteries. This progress is small but it is important.

I shall carry this a step or two further.

About twenty-five years ago in Milan I was, so to speak, caught laughing in public. I can no longer recall what caused me to laugh, but I remember that I had carried the audience with me—not a very difficult thing to do. As the laughter was dying down a young man stood up and said, "Why do Americans laugh so much—all of them. You never see a U.S. president or even a high-ranking general who is solemn, or even sober looking. They are always grinning, chuckling, smiling, or bursting with laughter."

Today, I can't remember just how I answered. It couldn't have been very hard to do. True, you never saw Hitler smiling in public. And the Duce was not one of your smiling men. Stalin as a rule looked severe. De Gaulle wouldn't have dreamed of grinning for the photographers. Churchill for all his burdens did smile occasionally. F.D.R., undoubtedly, was a fabulous smiler. Truman laughed less often than Roosevelt in his pictures, but he was neither dour nor severe. I believe that in Milan I did speak of these leaders and describe their public faces. I did not fail to add that there was a hint of existentialism about the posture and voice of my questioner; I said that he appeared to be pledged to dreadful freedom or despair and that though the annoying exuberance of the Americans might strike some Europeans as vacuous it may also be a sign of their belief in the success of their political and economic ideas.

Here I may have gone too far. For do we—you and I—understand these ideas? Our understanding of them is obviously partial and certainly faulty. We assume, however, that there are persons who do grasp the underlying principles of America's success. We send our sons and daughters to the university to study them. The results are not always gratifying. The young, almost by instinct, learn to use the most advanced digital equipment—they know software, they know e-mail and are at home on the Internet. But have they (or we) the knowledge that this moment demands?

We use instruments that we do not understand. But how much do we understand of anything? To a very large number of questions, only specialists have the answers. And how much knowledge do we need? For practical purposes, a general idea will do.

What makes such questions comical is the fairy-tale variety of today's technical devices in common use. We are told, for instance, that a recording is digital, and this means that for each note there is a number assigned—but how or why background noises are eliminated by these members is an elusive mystery. High tech takes away our status as educated men and women and sends us back to the masses.

We can't begin to make sense of any of this unless we bear in mind the grand project set for us by the philosophers of the Enlightenment. Civilized man was advised by them that nature was there to be conquered.

And so, in the twentieth century, we fly through the air, we see and hear people on other continents. They speak to us from space ships. To quote Professor Berger again: "Naked Hindu godmen fly in their 747s. . . . Militant mullahs in Iran demonstrate wearing Adidas running shoes. Boris Yeltsin campaigns for the Russian presidency dancing to rock music." His comment is this: "These features of the modern world force an awareness of incongruity on even very humorless people."

Humor, for Professor Berger, I remind you, is "a signal of transcendence." It tells us that the empirical reality, the "paramount reality," is not all there is.

I approach the subject from a somewhat different angle. I ask, How has life been transformed by technology? Has it been perverted? Well, then, how do we come to terms with so many man-made realities? We seem to have fused the mysteries of nature with artificialities beyond our ability to explain or distinguish. The artifacts are familiar to us through daily use but we are not able to account for their existence. Our ignorance—and we are at times aware of it—resembles that of primitive men. Except that the mysteries of primitives are revered. We face ours with secular cockiness. Occasionally we do think, "This was done by mankind. To which *I* belong—same species. Actually, then, *we* have done this."

So we use artifacts that we don't understand. But why should that bother us?

Well, for one thing, we the educated take pride in our rationality and we do everything possible to avoid being identified with the mindless, backward masses. We adopt a rational worldview and describe our condition as secular, et cetera. In daily life we meet and try to deal with a diversity of abstract topics. We think—or believe that we are thinking. We experience the comedy of a life of thought. Thought is forced on us and propels us into a variety of comic conditions. We feel that we have to account for our decisions and our conduct. We judge ourselves and are judged by others on our knowledge and intelligence.

And this describes our mental life—up to a point.

But allow me to go a step or two beyond this point and direct your attention once more to the revolution or revolutions caused by the conquest of nature called for by the thinkers of the Enlightenment. Let us add that this effort to conquer nature is also directed against scarcity. And certainly the Western world has given us reason to feel that this eventuality appears possible. In the United States we are faced with the possibility that technology may be able to provide for all the necessities of hundreds of millions or billions of people. Some thinkers assume that this has happened in North America. The late philosopher A. Kojève has gone so far as to declare that the aims of Lenin's revolution in Russia have been achieved not in Russia but in our own U.S.A. Kojève sees this not as a great triumph but as the beginning of the end. He assumes that history has come to a close with this achievement, and that historical man has ceased to exist. What we are looking at is a condition of animal mindlessness created by this curious liberation from pressing material needs. We are free, in the new circumstances now developing, to live like mere creatures, indulging ourselves in instinctual pleasures and losing all capacity for what we call—or perhaps *used* to call—a higher life.

I have saved this aspect of modern comedy for last. This is the aspect in which we see the economic success of the Western world. It is the future foreseen by Francis Bacon early in the seventeenth century. Writing of man's growing power over nature, Bacon told us that an evolving technology would result in a vast increase in the production of goods together with a reduction of labor. We in the West now live in a society controlled (in a general way) by scientific technology. Technology has had a great, an unparalleled economic success, and it has also extended the human life span. Life expectancy in the industrial West at the beginning of the century was about thirty years of age for men. The figure has more than doubled. It stands today at seventy.

High tech has brought us to an apocalyptic height of development. When I say such things to friends, they remind me that around the world millions of people are still dying every year of hunger. I am quite aware of this, of course, because we all read the same newspapers and magazines and we all see the faces of famine victims on TV.

But I am speaking of the industrial West, and the industrial West is the cynosure of what we like to call the "developing" world. I don't say that what we have done is the best humankind can hope for; I say only that its shining images are everywhere—that it represents a great ineluctable fact: the conquest of hunger is a very real possibility.

But let us return to our own U.S.A. An ocean of manufactured products—things to eat, to wear, to smell, to rub on or to remove, to ride or to fly in; instruments with which one can "surf" and that give access to mountain ranges of data or of commercial opportunities. New worlds open for supply and demand. No need is too special to be met. We are boundlessly busy with shopping and with use. We learn to take new readings or find new perspectives on infinity or on boundaries. All this is bound up with the life of one's country and of the world. A vast joint project that demands our participation. And it signifies that man has shown it is possible to overcome the scarcities imposed by nature and that it is our duty to celebrate this conquest, to acknowledge the instruments and the products. This demands that our days, nights, years—our lives, in short—be devoted to observance. It demands that everybody be included, that all should participate in the recognition that the material foundations of our existence can never again be what they were in our previous history.

Is the conquest complete? No, far from it. But in thought it is already foreseen, and I have all along had thought in mind—a comedy of thought. Thought is thrust upon us and we all seem to be forced into abstraction. But here I remind you—I ask you to remember that I am elaborating on the supposition of the philosopher Kojève, who has said that the revolution Lenin believed he was leading, the proletarian revolution, did not occur in Russia, but in our own U.S.A. It is we who enjoy the abundance of goods expected by the Bolsheviks.

It is thus that history ended and with its end came the destruction of man's picture of himself. Loving the stature that history gave him, he became merely a consuming animal. Our task, our social duty, perhaps, is to consume commodities. They are inexhaustible, in good supply and fairly cheap. The goods are widely available, and we serve society by buying and using its manufactured products. Harsh Darwinian capitalists of the last century used to argue that unproductive and superfluous populations should be written off, but in our time the victory over nature has been so brilliantly complete that welfare is, broadly speaking, good for the economy—better, at any rate, than confrontation and class warfare. In technically advanced countries there is much talk about revolution, but perhaps it's not revolution in the older (French? Russian?) sense of the word but rather the dismantling of historic restraints and the abolition of ancient negative sanctions. Thus the novelist Mark Helprin (*Wall Street Journal,* January 15, 1997) speaks of "a revolution in which individual rights have become group right, in which responsibility has become entitlement, marriage has become divorce, birth has become abortion, homosexuality is a norm, murder is neither a surprise nor necessarily punishable, pornography is piped into almost every home, gambling is legal. . . . The catalogue of this revolution is a record of modern life."

I have appended Helprin's list of charges to Kojève's conclusion that the U.S.A. is leading the West to a new and radically unhistorical condition in which men will no longer be men in the old sense but will please themselves like the anthropoid apes with the products of a fabulous technology.

Kojève has an Aristophanic genius for tremendous absurdities. One does not have to agree with him that we are entering a new time in which the human qualities developed in what we call "history" are once and for all wiped out. We can see for ourselves that the final conquest of scarcity is moving quickly from the horizon toward the center. We don't have to die of plague and famine—and what we feel is the sudden release from the tension of millennia of scarcity and its cares. We seem to be standing on a boundary line and we can almost feel it underfoot. Perhaps the true significance of the discovery of this continent, five centuries ago, is now about to be revealed.

Everything the leaders of thought tell us seeps back and down into the consciousness of the great public. We should not be too surprised one of these days to learn that posthistorical man has identified himself at last. "I am posthistorical man." You can already hear him saying it. With some justification he may say about civilization (or the civilizations) that they are a product of extensive collaborations, and that in certain basic respects "we" (i.e., you and I) created them. All such creations are our common property, the products of man's peculiar genius. Suppose then that all that was highest was done by humankind in Athens and Jerusalem and during the Renaissance and finally in the eighteenth century. The rest is to be left to us, to posthistorical man, to mobs, to mass democracy. And we will fill in the low as our great predecessors did the high. Because we know the low so well. It's all we've got. After all, we belong to the same species, and we should be represented—because it is all one and the same and therefore should have a place in the full picture. We will do for the low what others did for the high. And then the human picture will be complete and fit to be shown. This is what our capitalist democracy has done, and this perhaps lies beneath the fun and games of our times.

Index

About the Contributors

Saul Bellow is University Professor and Professor of English at Boston University. He was awarded the Nobel Prize in Literature in 1976 and received the National Book Award in 1953, 1964, and 1971. His most recent novels are *Dean's December* (1998) and *Ravelstein* (2000).

John Patrick Diggins is Distinguished Professor of History at the Graduate Center of the City University of New York. His books include *Max Weber: Politics and the Spirit of Tragedy* (1996) and *On Hallowed Ground: Abraham Lincoln and the Foundations of American History* (2000).

Pierre Hassner is senior research associate at the Centre d'Etudes et de Recherches Internationales and professor at the Institut d'Etudes Politiques in Paris. He is the author of *Totalitarismes* (with Guy Hermet and Jacques Rupnik) (1984) and *Violence and Peace: From the Atomic Bomb to Ethnic Cleansing* (1997).

Josef Joffe is editor and publisher of *Die Zeit* and associate of the Olin Center for Strategic Studies at Harvard University. His books include *Limited Partnership: Europe, the United States, and the Burdens of Alliance* (1987) and *The Great Powers* (1998).

Tony Judt is Erich Maria Remarque Professor of European Studies and director of the Remarque Institute at New York University. His most recent books are *A Grand Illusion? An Essay on Europe* (1996) and *The Burden of Responsibility: Blum, Camus, Aron, and the French Twentieth Century* (1998).

Ira Katznelson is Ruggles Professor of Political Science at Columbia University. His books include *Marxism and the City* (1992) and *Liberalism's Crooked Circle: Letters to Adam Michnik* (1996).

Christopher Kelly is professor of political science at Boston College. He is the author of *Rousseau's Exemplary Life: The Confessions as Political Philosophy* (1987) and the editor (with Roger D. Masters) of *The Collected Writings of Rousseau* (eight volumes to date).

Arthur M. Melzer is professor of political science at Michigan State University. He is the author of *The Natural Goodness of Man: On the System of Rousseau's Thought* (1990). He is codirector of the Symposium on Science, Reason, and Modern Democracy and an editor of its first five volumes of essays, the most recent of which is *Politics at the Turn of the Century* (2001).

Adam Michnik is editor in chief of the *Gazeta Wyborcza*. His works include *Letters from Prison and Other Essays* (1985) and *Letters from Freedom: Post–Cold War Realities and Perspectives* (1998).

Martha C. Nussbaum is Ernst Freund Distinguished Service Professor of Law and Ethics at the University of Chicago Law School. Her most recent books are *Women and Human Development: The Capabilities Approach* (2000) and *Upheavals of Thought: The Intelligence of Emotions* (2001).

Thomas L. Pangle is University Professor of Political Science at the University of Toronto. His books include *The Learning of Liberty: The Educational Ideas of the American Founders* (with Lorraine Smith Pangle) (1993) and *Justice among Nations: On the Moral Basis of Power and Peace* (with Peter Ahrensdorf) (1999).

Paul A. Rahe is Jay P. Walker Professor of American History at the University of Tulsa. He is the author of *Republics, Ancient and Modern: Classical Republicanism and the American Revolution* (1994).

Jerry Weinberger is professor of political science at Michigan State University. His books include *Science, Faith, and Politics: Francis Bacon and the Utopian Roots of the Modern Age* (1985) and new editions of Bacon's *History of the Reign of King Henry the Seventh* (1996) and *The Advancement of Learning* (2001). He is the director of the LeFrak Forum, codirector of the Symposium on Science, Reason, and Modern Democracy, and an editor of the symposium's first five volumes of essays.

Gordon S. Wood is Alva O. Way University Professor and Professor of History at Brown University. He is the author of *The Creation of the American Republic, 1776–1787* (1969) and *The Radicalism of the American Revolution* (1992).

M. Richard Zinman is University Distinguished Professor of Political Theory in James Madison College at Michigan State University. He is executive director of the Symposium on Science, Reason, and Modern Democracy and an editor of its first five volumes of essays.